The Castells Reader on Cities and Social Theory

THE CASTELLS READER ON

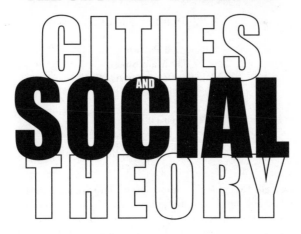

CITIES AND SOCIAL THEORY

Edited by Ida Susser

BLACKWELL *Publishers*

First published 2002

2 4 6 8 10 9 7 5 3 1

Blackwell Publishers Inc.
350 Main Street
Malden, Massachusetts 02148
USA

Blackwell Publishers Ltd
108 Cowley Road
Oxford OX4 1JF
UK

Library of Congress Cataloging-in-Publication Data

The Castells reader on cities and social theory / edited by Ida Susser.
   p.   cm.
Includes bibliographical references and index.
ISBN 0-631-21932-3 (alk. paper) — ISBN 0-631-21933-1 (pb. : alk. paper)
1. Sociology, Urban. 2. Social movements. 3. Cities and towns—Effect
of technological innovations on. I. Susser, Ida.

HT151 .C377 2001
307.76—dc21

00-069790

British Library Cataloguing in Publication Data

A CIP catalogue record for this book is available from the British Library.

Typeset in 10 on 12 pt Baskerville by Ace Filmsetting Ltd, Frome, Somerset
Printed in Great Britain by TJ International, Padstow, Cornwall

This book is printed on acid-free paper.

Contents

Figures

Tables

Acknowledgments

The editor and publishers wish to thank copyright holders for permission to reproduce copyright material. The sources for the readings in this volume are as follows:

Chapters 1 and 2 were first published in French in *La question urbaine* (Paris: Maspero, 1972; rev edn, Paris: La Decouverte, 1980). The material reproduced here is taken from the English translation, *The Urban Question: A Marxist Approach*, trans. Alan Sheridan (London: Edward Arnold, 1977), pp. 1–19 and 73–112.

Chapter 3, "Immigrant Workers and Class Struggles in Advanced Capitalism: The Western European Experience," first appeared in *Politics and Society*, 5 (1) (1975), pp. 33–66 (London: Sage Publications).

Chapter 4 is taken from *City, Class, and Power* (1979), pp. 15–36, and is reproduced by permission of St Martin's Press, New York and Macmillan Press Ltd, London.

Chapter 5 is taken from *The City and the Grassroots* (Berkeley, CA: University of California Press, 1983), pp. 99–170 and 346–362.

Chapters 6 and 7 are reproduced from *The Informational City* (Oxford: Blackwell, 1989), pp. 7–32 and pp. 203–228.

Chapter 8 first appeared in *The Rise of the Network Society*, volume I of the trilogy, *The Information Age: Economy, Society and Culture* (Oxford: Blackwell, 1996, 2nd edn 2000), pp. 407–459.

Chapter 9 was prepared for the Library of Congress Conference "Frontiers of the Mind in the Twenty-first Century," held in Washington, DC, June 14–18, 1999, and is published here for the first time.

The *Conclusion*, "Urban Sociology in the Twenty-first Century," was written by Manuel Castells especially for this volume.

Manuel Castells: Conceptualizing the City in the Information Age

Ida Susser

From his initial publications in the early 1970s, Manuel Castells has rigorously examined the categories of urban research and reframed the thinking of urban sociology. He has developed broad-ranging and challenging analyses of urban structure and spatial dynamics, immigration, the informal economy, and urban culture and social movements within the changing face of world capitalism. In his latest vision of the global economy and the network society, published in the three encyclopedic volumes of *The Information Age*, Castells (1996, 1997, 1998) presents a comprehensive theoretical framework, outlining the development of an informational mode of production, which follows the industrial mode of production, in the shaping of advanced capitalism.

This volume traces Castells's ideas on cities and social theory from their formative period to the present and illustrates changes in his approach over time as he grappled with changing urban and global realities. It is divided into three sections: theories of the city in advanced capitalism; social movements and urban culture; and the city in the Information Age. Castells's extensive urban research also includes works published in Spanish, French, and other languages which have not yet been translated into English and are not included here. The Conclusion was written by Castells specifically for this volume and outlines the most pressing issues that he sees for urban sociology in the twenty-first century.

Castells's work has emerged from his experiences as an empirical researcher, a social theorist, and a political activist. Born in Spain in 1942, Castells grew up in Barcelona under the fascist regime of General Francisco Franco. As an undergraduate, studying law and economics at the University of Barcelona, he became active in the resistance to Franco. At the age of twenty he had to flee Spain, while many of his friends in the Catalan Socialist Party were arrested and tortured. As a political exile in Paris, Castells finished a degree in public law and political economy at the Sorbonne. Staying on in Paris and under the supervision of Alain Touraine, he completed a PhD in sociology at the Ecole des

Hautes Etudes en Sciences Sociales. Interestingly enough, considering his later focus on information processing, his research involved a statistical analysis of the location strategies of high-technology companies in the metropolitan area of Paris.

At this time, just before the momentous events of the spring of 1968, Paris was a vibrant intellectual milieu and an international center of Marxist controversy. Nicos Poulantzas, a good friend of Castells and also in Paris, was analyzing the structure of the state (see Poulantzas, 1968), and Louis Althusser was conducting seminars at the Ecole Normale Superieure which resulted in the publication of *Reading Capital* (Althusser and Balibar, 1970).

Castells finished his dissertation in 1967, and was appointed assistant professor at the newly created campus of the University of Paris at Nanterre. He found himself, as a young faculty member, at the center of the student revolt in Paris. The expulsion of Daniel Cohn Bendit, a social science student, by the Nanterre administration, and the students' rallying to his defence, were the events that launched the student revolution. Cohn Bendit emerged as the student leader, and in May 1968 students took to the streets of Paris and called for French workers to join them. They paralyzed France and almost brought down the government. The student movements of the spring of 1968 – Paris, Columbia, Berlin and beyond – were the source of many of the ideas of social change that would spread throughout Europe and the United States in the next two decades.

As a result of his participation in the Paris uprising, in June 1968, Castells was expelled by the French government. As a political exile once more, he taught in Chile at the Faculty of Social Sciences of UNESCO, where Salvador Allende was soon to lead a democratically elected socialist government. Fernando Cardoso, a friend of Castells from Paris, was also in Chile at the time, formulating key concepts about development and dependence in Latin America (Cardoso and Faletto, 1970). (Twenty-five years later Cardoso was elected president of Brazil.) The following year Castells was appointed assistant professor at the University of Montreal. Both these experiences in exile figure in his later analysis of urban movements.

In 1970, partly through the intervention of his university mentor Alain Touraine, Castells was pardoned by the French government and returned to Paris as associate professor at the Ecole des Hautes Etudes (*de facto* graduate school of the University of Paris) and director of the Methodological Training Program for doctoral students. *The Urban Question* emerged from this turmoil (Castells, 1977). Published first in French in 1972, it reflects the challenging, critical era in which it was conceived. Castells claims that the contemporary focus of governments on "urban" problems is an ideological construct which diverts attention from current political processes. In an explicitly Marxist conceptual framework, Castells argues that cities, as we see and experience them, inscribe in concrete the history of contested power, successes, failures, and compromises within capitalism. He emphasizes the struggle over streets as a mirror of contradictions in society and conceptualizes urban social movements in terms of power struggles over collective consumption. *The Urban Question* develops the theoretical underpinnings for a structural and comparative analysis of the city.

Much of the framework that Castells develops in *The Urban Question* is the basis for sociological analysis of cities in the global economy today. Castells conceptualizes cities as emerging at different conjunctions of the capitalist process. Adopting Althusserian terms, Castells conceives the city in relation to historically specific organizations of the mode of production – in the then industrial states of the United States and France and then in the "dependent" regions such as Latin America, understood in terms used also by Fernando Cardoso. Castells outlines a theory of cities in Latin America based on an analysis of the differing colonial histories of Portugal and Spain and the different positions of the cities in relation to the extraction of raw materials, and the trade and administrative links with the colonial powers. Such analyses provided the groundwork for many later works, which looked at the structure of cities on the periphery in terms of the world system. Castells notes the uneven development between the country and the city, and argues that the massive influx of poor rural migrants to cities of what we might now designate the "South" was a consequence of the disruption of agrarian society through the incursions of capitalist investment. Castells also includes a discussion of cities in the then socialist societies, although he argues that analysis is fragmentary because of the present lack of a systematic framework for understanding socialism. Later, Castells spent much of the 1990s working on a framework to conceptualize the workings of the Soviet Union as well as its collapse (Castells and Kiselyova, 1995).

On the basis of a comparative analysis of historically specific cases of industrial, dependent, and socialist cities (all would be different today, as outlined in later chapters of this volume), Castells proceeds, in *The Urban Question* (see chapter 2), to redefine the concept of the urban. He argues that, as his earlier chapters demonstrate, cities cannot be understood as a phenomenon separate from state and class, and he characterizes much of the then dominant Chicago School of urban sociology as adopting an ideology of the urban which precisely ignores class, inequality, and the state. He also criticizes the ideas of Henri Lefebvre on the urban social movement and urban experience of everday life (Lefebvre, 1996). For Castells, Lefebvre represents a left-wing manifestation of the reification of the urban. Castells insists that cities have to be understood as the historical manifestations of power and production in capitalism. This concerted assault on the ideological connotations of the urban is particularly significant for the reformulation of sociological concepts. The critique mounted by Castells on the reification of the urban is as apt today as it was when it was written, as we read analyses of the problems of "the inner city" or "urban problems." Nevertheless, there is now also an alternative analysis of urban processes much developed from the critical formulations of the 1970s.

Castells critiques the concept of the urban as a self-contained community, even in the radical analyses of urban elites which stressed the existence of an urban ruling group (Hunter, 1953). He argues that, dependent as they were on an image of the isolated urban, such analyses neglected the power of institutional regulation and the state in, for example, the relocation of working-class housing. Castells argues that the idea of "urban crisis" was a cloak for the particular forces of race and class that were manifested in US cities in the 1960s and became an ideological explanation for urban renewal. In a classic of urban critique, he documents the relocation of the poor, the replacement of low-income housing with middle-income residents, and the resulting concentration of the commercial sector. He demonstrates the racism evident in the disproportion of black residents targeted for removal and the damning statistics that show that the private housing market, in fact, provided many more homes without destroying old residences than urban renewal did. He clearly demonstrates that the consequence of urban renewal in industrial cities such as Paris and New York was to remove poor people and industry and replace them with office space. These processes can be understood today as the opening sallies of gentrification and the transformation toward the informational city. While Castells exempts Lewis Mumford, the father of the Marxist analysis of cities, power, and historical process (Mumford, 1961), from the criticisms of reification which he levels at Lefebvre, he notes that Mumford did not integrate an analysis of technological and industrial organization of production in space with his recognition of the city as the manifestation and concentration of power in emergent capitalism.

Castells turns to the Chicago School of urban sociology to commence his analysis of the productive necessities in space: the model of the city organized in concentric circles of manufacturing, worker housing, and a middle-class residential district surrounding the central business district (Burgess, 1925). Discarding the Western-centered and mechanistic aspects of such an analysis, he proceeds to work on the development of a theoretical framework which takes both the social order and the organization of production into account. In the process, Castells developed many of the insights concerning the advantages of the concentration of experts and accessible workers, as well as the significance of the interventions of the state, that have come to inform analyses of advanced capitalist cities.

The Urban Question also draws attention to urban movements in Paris and Montreal, and to land occupation and social movements in Chile. This focus was seminal for much research by sociologists and anthropologists in the 1980s, as land take-overs became a significant form of social protest in Puerto Rico, Brazil, and other areas. Castells concludes with the argument that "New social issues are at the root of new forms of conflict and also of new methods of the collective creation of everyday life. The urban social movements are the most striking expression of this" (Castells, 1977: 376). However, there is no such thing as urban struggle; in fact, "each 'urban struggle' must have its structural content specified, and be considered in terms of the role it plays *vis-à-vis* the various social classes involved. Then and only then will we know what we are talking about" (Castells, 1977: 376). These quotations illustrate both his creative approach to understanding social movements and an attention to class that does not imply that class conflict alone will explain collective action.

During the 1970s, with both Henri Lefebvre and Manuel Castells at the University of Paris, the French School of urban sociology flourished. Castells continued his political involvement in Chile, returning for four months each year from 1970 to 1973 when Allende was brutally deposed by the bloody military coup spearheaded by General Pinochet. From 1977 to 1979, during the first two years of Spanish democracy, Castells was also involved in the Spanish Citizen Movement in Barcelona and Madrid.

In the 1970s the influx of guest workers and the exploitation of immigrant labor in Europe was emerging as a controversial political issue, and Castells, while working with immigrant groups in Paris and throughout Europe, also developed an early theoretical formulation concerning the significance of the new immigrant labor in Western Europe. In his article on this topic, "Immigrant Workers and Class Struggle in Advanced Capitalism" (chapter 3), Castells slices through economic explanations of the new immigration, providing statistical data that contradict the theory that migrants are hired in periods of low unemployment and shows that both immigrant labor and unemployment increased at the same time. He documents the way in which the state both defines foreign workers and regulates their availability, counter-intuitively, but still in response to economic cycles. He argues that because immigrant workers will accept lower wages and work longer hours, they will be hired in periods when unemployment is high and the state in crisis. Under these conditions corporate interests need workers who are cheaper but, in addition, the state does not have to provide for immigrant families in the same way as citizens. Castells describes the way in which citizenship, class, and gender fragment "foreign" workers from resident populations of Europe. The issue of citizenship, currently under much discussion in the sociological and anthropological literature of the global economy, is considered here both with respect to its fragmentation of working-class interests as well as the way in which citizen status can be used to exclude immigrants and, especially, their families from the provisions of the welfare state. This may be one of the central points, raised by Castells in the 1970s, that needs to be re-examined in discussions of the global movement of capital today and is as relevant to an understanding of the movements of populations in the Pacific Rim or southern Africa as it still is in Western Europe.

In a small book of collected essays, also published while he was in Paris, Castells (1978) explains his focus on the environment and issues of collective consumption as they illuminate social movements. In one essay, written in 1971, he describes the early "hippy," romanticized days of the US environmental movement, which was to become a key social movement in his analysis of the Information Age. In another essay (chapter 4) Castells develops a framework for the understanding of social movements, influenced by Alain Touraine, which incorporates issues of class interest but begins to explore collective movements that depend upon a broader base. The key concept here concerns the focus on "collective consumption." Castells notes that there are certain issues, such as environmental pollution, traffic congestion, and housing, which, although they have unequal effects according to class, impact on the "quality of life" for all groups in a society. He sees these issues of collective consumption as crucial to the emergence of effective social movements to precipitate progressive social change. This controversial position, which emphasizes broad-based social movements rather than focusing on the labor movements and class-based initiatives basic to most Marxist analyses, presaged the evolution of Castells's theoretical approach in his next major work.

In 1979 Castells accepted a professorship in urban sociology at the Department of City and Regional Planning at the University of California, Berkeley. During his first few years at Berkeley, Castells published *The City and the Grassroots* (1983), an analysis of social movements clearly deriving from his own experiences of the previous decade in working with squatter movements, citizens organizations, and community issues in France, Chile, Spain, and later San Francisco. For this book Castells received the C. Wright Mills Award in recognition of his contribution to social theory, although Castells was criticized by some reviewers for breaking with his earlier Marxist framework in the analysis of social movements. While Castells's works of the previous decade talk of class conflict in the structuring of space, *The City and the Grassroots* describes social movements that can sometimes follow class lines, as in the Glasgow rent strike organized by working-class women, but at other times can effectively build across class lines, as in the gay coalitions of San Francisco politics (see chapter 5).

The City and the Grassroots documents a series of case studies of collective action some of which demonstrate the power of identity or life-style based movements. As in his earlier discussions of the environment, Castells's work was pioneering in his efforts to understand minority organizations, movements of sexual orientation, and women's community mobilization in a broader framework of collective action. Basing himself on systematic ethnography, Castells is singularly remarkable in his ability to absorb, describe, and then analyze crucial emerging elements of each period. A review of his work of the 1970s and 1980s makes evident the way in which he captured and analyzed new trends that later became central organizing foci of the period.

In *The City and the Grassroots* Castells distinguishes between a political system which "is dependent upon the state, and is part of the state" and social movements which "exist, develop, and relate to civil society, and are not necessarily limited to, or bound by, the rules of the game and the institutionalization of dominant values and norms" (Castells, 1983: 294). Concerned primarily with social change, Castells argues: "Without social movements, no challenge will emerge from civil society able to shake the institutions of the state through which norms are enforced, values preached and property preserved" (1983: 294). In his insistence on the importance of civil society and the political contradictions of citizenship as well as class in the structuring of social movements, Castells confronts issues in the 1980s which are currently being debated twenty years later in analyses of the global economy.

The City and the Grassroots marks Castells's shift from Marxist analyses to a less economically based and more cultural approach. Castells rejects what he regards as the deterministic aspect of the Marxist view of class struggle, as in fact do many Marxists, such as social historians E. P. Thompson and Raymond Williams. When he talks of "the glorious ruins of the Marxist tradition" (1983: 301), Castells seems to be mainly rejecting the doctrine of state monopoly capitalism popularized by the French Communist Party. He argues that he sees no place in a Marxist analysis for social movements as independent agents separate from class. He argues that social movements based on collective consumption cross class lines and have contributed to major shifts in the goals and values of societies. In other words, although members of different classes may experience pollution or health and illness differently, they share a common interest in furthering environmental regulations or medical research. This emphasis on collective consumption is perhaps one of the fundamental arguments that Castells raises in relation to possibilities for progressive social change. It provides an opening for the analysis of culture within the framework of materialist concepts of consumption. Each of the extensive case studies in *The City and the Grassroots* stands by itself as an exemplary analysis of social movements within a particular historical situation. Castells identifies the significance of gay identity and Latino organizations in the changing real estate and politics of San Francisco. The squatter movements of Latin America are explored within the changing context of dependency, social classes, and real-estate interests.

In Castells's chapters on the Citizen Movement in Madrid we see the transformation of urban centers in Madrid, Barcelona, and other cities of Spain in the 1970s and 1980s as a direct result of collective action which crossed class lines and could be understood more in terms of Castells's theories of struggles based on collective consumption than the mobilization of working-class people alone. Based on a review of historical processes in urban development, a factor analysis of Madrid's spatial structure, systematic research, including the mapping and describing of twenty-three neighborhood organizations in Madrid, and a detailed description of the events and political struggles of three neighborhoods, this analysis constitutes a fascinating case study of the relationship between political parties, underground resistance, and neighborhood mobilization in the Spanish struggle against Franco's fascist dictatorship. Castells notes that the political struggles addressed a wide variety of issues and, while they were most common in working-class areas, there were also middle-class neighborhood organizations formed as middle-class people became disillusioned with their suburban havens. Castells does, in fact, document the resulting transformation of Spanish cities in the structure and availability of public housing, the preservation of central city areas, the improvement of city services and the preservation of public space. Re-reading this work, nearly twenty years after the events, knowing of the rise and fall of the Spanish Socialist Party and the changes in city governments, the freshness of the analysis and the importance of the struggles in structuring public life comes through with greater intensity, almost as the historical record of a period of optimism and urban transformation for collective goals.

In its empirical approach and exhaustive but sharply analytical case studies, *The City and the Grassroots* vindicates Castells's efforts to free himself from theoretical constraints. He addresses issues of social class, history, and culture but in each case is more concerned to document urban struggles in their full historical context than to find underlying class explanations as the roots of a diverse group of effective and important social movements.

In 1983, the Socialist Party won the elections in Spain and, from 1984, Castells divided his time between Spain and the US. He held university appointments both at the University of Madrid and the University of California, Berkeley, and he conducted research on regional industrial development, information technology and policy in Spain. Thus, by the mid-1980s, Castells was already conducting research on the social and spatial dimensions of information technology and economic restructuring in California, New York, Spain, Hong Kong and Singapore, and developing a theoretical framework for the implications of this technology for social democracy and political representation.

In 1989, Castells and Portes demonstrated the fallacy of the widely accepted economic and sociological expectation that as industry became rationalized the informal economy would disappear. They argued, instead, that the informal economy was a structural feature of all advanced economies, the boundaries of which were adjusted with political and economic shifts. Defining the informal economy, not as an activity *per se*, but as any income-generating activities that are not regulated in a context in which they are legally required to be, they showed that this unregulated sector was in fact growing rather than disappearing in the centers of capitalist restructuring such as New York City, as well as in newly industrializing cities such as São Paulo. They attributed this newly expanding informal economy, not to any particular influx of immigrant labor, but to the decrease in vertical integration of industry and the spreading patterns of subcontracting and horizontal production networks.

In an effort to develop comparative urban analyses, Castells also studied the phenomenal growth of the city states of Singapore and Hong Kong. Overturning the assumptions of the many Western economists calling for reductions in state spending on social services, Castells demonstrated empirically that it was in fact the strong financial support for public services, including decent affordable shelter for as many as 80 percent of the population, that reinforced the social stability crucial to the growth of these highly successful new economies (Castells et al., 1990).

Pursuing his comparative analysis of the restructuring of advanced capitalist cities and information technology, Castells participated in a lively interdisciplinary seminar with social scientists Ira Katznelson, Saskia Sassen, John Mollenkopf, Roger Waldinger, Edward Soja, Susan and Norman Fainstein, myself and others, which explored the ongoing restructuring of New York City. Castells's vision, outlined in Castells and Mollenkopf (1991), involved a dynamic analysis of the emerging inequalities of the restructured city, based on a shift of information management, finance and service industries accompanied by a burgeoning informal sector, which was, in this instance, predominantly composed of immigrant labor. This work is incorporated in brief form in a case study of New York City (chapter 7) in which Castells links the development of the information society with the emergence of what he labels the "dual city," where he describes the increase in the polarization of rich and poor, combined with an increase in immigration, local sweatshops, an informal economy, and the reduction of social service provision.

In 1989, in *The Informational City*, building on his analysis of the "dual city" as well as comparative research on the social and spatial implications of informational technology, Castells presented a detailed analysis of the relationship between advanced capitalism, the new flexible organization of the global economy, and the potential for the automation of information, which presaged the basic themes of *The Information Age* (1996, 1997, 1998). *The Informational City* builds on Castells's analysis of the crisis of US capitalism to outline the ways in which corporations in the US and other industrial states in the world economy restructured production to address inflation and the falling rates of profit with which they were confronted in the 1970s. Castells argues that the restructuring of capitalism involved, first, the concentration of knowledge as the source of profit and, secondly, the export of production to increase profitability by hiring factory workers in poorer, non-unionized circumstances, mostly involving women workers. Such restructuring required a flexible organization of manufacturing and greatly increased subcontracting so that, as a consequence, horizontal, loosely connected networks directed by elite experts at the center replaced the vertical integration of the industrial era. Such networks are clearly facilitated by the communications revolution which Castells traces to its military roots.

In *The Informational City*, as in his later trilogy, Castells carefully separates the development of information technology from the need for capitalist restructuring but notes that, once the information-processing technology was implemented, this, in turn, transformed the organization of work and power by facilitating the internationalization of all economic processes. The new information production was centered near certain concentrations of experts, such as universities, and led to particular spatial arrangements of high-technology corporations which Castells and Peter Hall (1994) later labeled "technopoles." In linking the development of the Internet with the military, Castells also notes a shift in state intervention from the funding of the welfare state to greater emphasis on political domination and capital accumulation as has later been documented in discussions of the "revanchist city" (Smith, 1996).

While the discussion of the increasing flexibility of capitalism has been noted by other analysts (Harvey, 1989), Castells integrated this with an understanding of the phenomenal impact of the technological revolution in communications. Castells points out that information-processing had been operating at a speed and efficiency little improved since the pre-industrial era. He argues that, as approximately 40 percent of the workforce in industrial societies came to be devoted to information-processing, the lack of automation in this area raised the cost of production. Castells concludes that "When the institutional context of the 1970s and 1980s forced corporations and governments into fully-fledged restructuring, the timely discoveries in information technology of the preceding three decades were at last put to work" (Castells, 1989: 137). Such shifts had far-reaching implications for the organization of work, but changes were not all in one direction. While, initially, office work became more routinized as banks of word processors were employed; later, the interactive nature of the new telecommunications networks allowed the elite knowledge experts to access their own information systems immediately. Castells demonstrates that, in the long run, high technology does not create unemployment or the overall displacement of low-skilled jobs. However, he documents historical trends which increasingly polarize the workforce into highly paid networked experts and low-paid service workers excluded from the global communications networks, and suggests that the restructuring of the workforce increases income inequality in many situations.

In 1993, Castells returned permanently to the United States and devoted himself to the task of writing the three volumes of *The Information Age: The Rise of the Network Society* (1996), *The Power of Identity* (1997), and *End of Millennium* (1998). In a far-reaching and dynamic analysis of the new Information Age, Castells demonstrates the consequences of the newly valuable production of knowledge for the increasing polarization of global information elites in relation to the poor and those disconnected from the global networks.

In the first volume, Castells (1996) outlines the structures of global networks and characterizes the new communications processes as the "space of flows" (see chapter 8). Castells contrasts the impact of the Information Age in different European nations with respect to differing labor histories and industrial regulation. He demonstrates the impact of information technologies and the restructuring of global capitalism in the speeding up of time and the contraction of space as well as in the creation of the virtual space of the Internet.

In the second volume, Castells (1997) analyzes the emergence of social movements in the Information Age and argues that such movements, far from being class-based any longer, emerge in relation to individual isolation in a networked society. He describes religious fundamentalists in Japan, militia movements in the US and elsewhere, and, once again, the international environmental movement as representative of new forms of collective action. However, only the environmental movement and the women's movement are viewed in the positive social and progressive terms of the earlier social movements described by Castells in *The City and the Grassroots*. In this volume, Castells also focuses on the impact on the household of the global hiring of women and, as he argues, "The end of patriarchy." Castells points out that, while women are now employed in many parts of the world, and the feminist movement has mobilized women to significant political effect, the shift to women workers has not led to a new equal relationship between men and women but rather contributed to the isolation and alienation experienced by individuals in the new informational economy, accompanied by the decline of the welfare state and the overall neglect of children and the collective responsibilities of household and family.

In the third volume, Castells (1998) discusses the erosion of the Soviet state as it failed to come to terms with the informational economy. He then documents the increasing gap between the members of the information elite at the center of advanced capitalism and what he terms the "fourth world," not so much a territorial category as the populations switched off from the information society as well as the poor excluded in the center of the global economies, such as US inner cities. He focuses also on the growth of the economies of the Pacific Rim with their innovation in the new high-technology industries, and finally draws into his theoretical framework the powerful emergence of the global criminal economy.

Castells's work has precipitated extensive debate on the importance he assigns to innovations in information technology and the current global economic transformations as well as the qualitative changes he perceives in the capitalist world system. Some contemporary analysts have suggested that the stress on the global informational networks transforming capitalism is less important than the strategies of corporations to lower wages, benefits, and working conditions and undermine working-class organization through the threat that they can easily relocate elsewhere (Harvey, 1989). Such questions are critical in elucidating controversies concerning the increase of poverty and inequality worldwide and the regulation of transnational corporate investment (Susser, 1996a, b). Nevertheless, in Castells's vision, globalization is not everywhere the same but must be understood precisely in relation to an historical, processual analysis of labor in relation to the state and the regulation of the variable incursions, inclusions, or exclusions of the global networks. Cities in this formulation both reflect and recast their place as nodes in the space of network flows.

Overall, Manuel Castells has confronted and analyzed some of the most momentous transformations of the twentieth century and his conceptual clarity provides essential guideposts – and debating points – for research on the cities of the third millennium.

REFERENCES

Althusser, L. and Balibar, E. (1970) *Reading Capital.* London: New Left Books.

Burgess, E. (1925) "The growth of the city," in R. Park, E. Burgess, and R. McKenzie (eds), *The City.* Chicago: University of Chicago Press.

Cardoso, F. and Faletto, E. (1970) *Desarollo y dependencia en America Latina.* Mexico City: Siglo XX1.

Castells, M. (1977) *The Urban Question.* London: Edward Arnold.

Castells, M. (1978) *City, Class and Power,* London: St Martin's Press.

Castells, M. (1980) *The Economic Crisis and American Society.* Oxford: Blackwell/Princeton, NJ: Princeton University Press.

Castells, M. (1983) *The City and the Grassroots.* Berkeley, CA: University of California Press.

Castells, M. (1989) *The Informational City.* Oxford: Blackwell.

Castells, M. (1996) *The Rise of the Network Society.* Oxford: Blackwell.

Castells, M. (1997) *The Power of Identity.* Oxford: Blackwell.

Castells, M. (1998) *End of Millennium.* Oxford: Blackwell.

Castells, M. and Hall, P. (1994) *Technopoles of the World: the Making of 21st Century Industrial Complexes.* London: Routledge.

Castells, M. and Kiselyova, E. (1995) *The Collapse of the Soviet Union: The View from the Information Society.* Berkeley, CA: University of California International Studies Book Series.

Castells, M. and Mollenkopf, J. (1991) "Conclusion: is New York a dual city?," in J. Mollenkpf and M. Castells (eds), *The Dual City: Restructuring New York,* pp. 399–419. New York: Russell Sage.

Castells, M. and Portes, A. (1989) "World underneath: the origins, dynamics, and effects of the informal economy," in A. Portes, M. Castells, and L. Benton (eds), *The Informal Economy: Studies in Advanced and Less Developed Countries,* pp. 11–37. Baltimore, MD: The Johns Hopkins University Press.

Castells, M., Goh, L., and Kwok, R. Y-W. (1990) *The Shek Kip Mei Syndrome: Economic Development and Public Housing in Hong Kong and Singapore.* London: Pion.

Harvey D. (1989) *The Condition of Postmodernity.* Oxford: Blackwell.

Hunter, F. (1953) *Community Power Structure.* Chapel Hill, NJ: University of North Carolina Press.

Lefebvre, H. (1996) *Writings on Cities/Henri Lefebvre,* selected, trans. and intro. by Eleonore Kofman and Elizabeth Lebas. Oxford: Blackwell.

Mumford, L. (1961) *The City in History.* New York: Harcourt Brace.

Poulantzas, N. (1968) *Political Power and Social Classes,* English trans., 1978. London: New Left Books.

Smith, N. (1996) *The New Urban Frontier: Gentrification and the Revanchist City.* London: Routledge.

Susser, I. (1996a) "The construction of poverty and homelessness in US cities," *Annual Reviews of Anthropology,* 25: 411–35.

Susser, I. (1996b) "The shaping of conflict in the space of flows," *Critique of Anthropology,* 16 (1): 39–49.

PART
ONE

A Theoretical Approach to the City in Advanced Capitalism

ONE

Urbanization

(1972)

EPISTEMOLOGICAL INTRODUCTION

This book [*The Urban Question*] was born out of astonishment.

At a time when the waves of the anti-imperialist struggle are sweeping across the world, when movements of revolt are bursting out at the very heart of advanced capitalism, when the revival of working-class action is creating a new political situation in Europe, "urban problems" are becoming an essential element in the policies of governments, in the concerns of the mass media and, consequently, in the everyday life of a large section of the population.

At first sight, the ideological character of such a profound shift of interest – expressing in the terms of an imbalance between technology and environment certain consequences of the existing social contradictions – leaves little doubt as to the need to emerge, theoretically and politically, from this labyrinth of mirrors. But, although it is easy enough to agree as to the broad outlines of such a situation (unless politico-ideological interests are working in the opposite direction), this does not solve the difficulties encountered in social practice. On the contrary, all the problems begin at this point, that is to say, at the point where an attempt is made to *supersede* (and not to *ignore*) the ideology that underlies the "urban question."

For, although it is true that "urbanistic thinking" in its different versions, of which the ideology of the environment seems to be the most advanced, is above all the prerogative of the technocracy and of the ruling strata in general, its effects are to be felt in the working-class movement and, still more, in the currents of cultural and political revolt that are developing in the industrial capitalist societies. Thus, in addition to the hold the various state organs have over the problems associated with the environment, we are witnessing increasing political intervention in the urban neighbourhoods, in public amenities, transport, etc. and, at the same time, the charging of the spheres of "consumption" and "everyday life" with political action and ideological confrontation. Now, very often, this shift of objectives and practices takes place without any change in the thematic register – that is to say, while remaining within the "urban" problematic. It follows that an elucidation of the "urban question" is becoming urgent, not only as a means of demystifying the ideology of the dominant classes, but as a tool of reflection for the political tendencies which, confronted by new social problems, oscillate between the dogmatism of general formulations and the apprehension of these questions in the (inverted) terms of the dominant ideology.

Indeed, it is not simply a question of exposing this ideology, for it is the symptom of a certain intensely experienced, but still inadequately identified, problematic; and if it proves to be socially effective, it is because it is offered as the interpretation of phenomena that have acquired an ever greater importance in advanced capitalism and because Marxist theory, which only poses the problems raised by social and political practice, has not yet proved capable of analysing them in a sufficiently specific way.

In fact, the two aspects of the problem are one. For, once the contours of the ideological discourse on "the urban" have been established, the supersession of this discourse cannot proceed simply by means of a denunciation; it requires a theoretical analysis of the questions of the social practice it connotes. Or, in other words, an ideological misunderstanding/recognition can be superseded, and therefore interpreted, only by a theoretical analysis; this is the only way of avoiding the twin dangers encountered by any theoretical practice:

1   A right-wing (but apparently left-wing) deviation, which consists in recognizing these new problems, but doing so in the terms of the urbanistic ideology, moving away from a Marxist analysis and giving them a theoretical – and political – priority over economic determination and the class struggle.
2   A left-wing deviation, which denies the emergence of new forms of social contradiction in the capitalist societies, confining all discussion of the urban to a purely ideological sphere, while exhausting itself in intellectual acrobatics to reduce the increasing diversity of the forms of class opposition to a direct opposition between capital and labour.

Such an undertaking requires the use of certain theoretical tools in order to transform, through a process of labour, a raw material, both theoretical and ideological, and to obtain a product (which always remains provisional), in which the theoretico-ideological field is modified in the direction of a development of its theoretical elements. The process becomes more complicated in so far as, for us, there is production of knowledge, in the strict sense of the term, only in connection with the analysis of a concrete situation. This means that the product of research is, at least, twofold: there is the effect of specific knowledge of the situation studied, and there is the knowledge of this situation, obtained with the help of more theoretical tools, linked with the general context of historical materialism. The fact that they make a given situation intelligible is demonstrated by the material realization (or experimentation) of the theoretical laws advanced; in becoming more specific, these laws develop, at the same time, the theoretical field of Marxism and, by the same token, increase its efficacy in social practice.

If this seems to be the general schema of theoretical work, its application to the "urban question" comes up against certain particular difficulties. Indeed, "the raw material" of this work, which is made up of three elements (ideological representations, knowledge already acquired, the specificity of the concrete situations studied), is characterized by the almost total predominance of the ideological elements, a very great difficulty in the precise empirical mapping of "urban problems" (precisely because it is a question of an ideological delimitation) and the virtual non-existence of elements of already acquired knowledge in this field, in so far as Marxism has approached it only marginally (Engels on housing) or in a historicist perspective (Marx in *The German Ideology*), or has seen in it no more than a mere transcription of political relations. The "social sciences" for their part, owing to their close links with the explicative ideologies of social evolution, are particularly poor in analyses of the question and of the strategic role played by these ideologies in the mechanisms of social integration.

This situation explains the slow and difficult work that has to be undertaken in matching the general concepts of historical materialism with situations and processes very different from those that were the basis for the production of these concepts. However, we are trying to extend their scope without any change of perspective, for the production of new concepts must take place in the development of fundamental theses, without which there can be no deployment of a theoretical structure, but merely a juxtaposition of "intermediary hypotheses." There is nothing dogmatic about this method of work, in so far as attachment to a particular perspective does not derive from some sort of fidelity to principles, but from the "nature of things" (that is to say, from the objective laws of human history).

Having said this, the paucity of properly theoretical work on the problems connoted by urban ideology obliges us to take as fundamental raw material, on the one hand, the mass of "research" accumulated by "urban sociology" and, on the other hand, a whole series of situations and processes identified as "urban" in social practice.

As far as urban sociology is concerned, it, in fact, constitutes the "scientific foundation" (not the social source) of a great number of ideological discourses that merely enlarge, combine and adapt theses and data accumulated by researchers. Furthermore, even though this field is heavily dominated by ideology, there appear here and there analyses, descriptions, observations of concrete situations that can help us to track down in a specific way themes dealt with in this tradition, and questions perceived as urban in the spontaneous sociology of subjects.

This sociology, like all "specific" sociologies, is, above all, quantitatively and qualitatively, Anglo-Saxon and, more precisely, American. This is the reason, and the only one, why the American and British references in this work are so important. This is reinforced by the fact that, very often "French," "Italian," "Latin American," even "Polish" or "Soviet" sociologies are little more than bad copies of the empirical research and "theoretical" themes of American sociology.

On the other hand, I have tried to diversify, as far as my own limitations allowed me, the historical situations that serve as a concrete mapping for the emergence of this problematic, in order to circumscribe more completely the various types of urban ideology and to locate the different regions of the underlying social structure.

It goes without saying that I do not claim to have arrived at a reformulation of the ideological problematic from which I set out and, still less, therefore, to have carried out true concrete analyses leading to knowledge. This book [*The Urban Question*] merely communicates certain experiences of work in this direction, with the aim of producing a dynamic of research rather than establishing a demonstration, which is in any case unrealizable at the present theoretical conjuncture. The point at which I have arrived is quite simply the belief that any new theoretical position that is not anchored in concrete analyses is redundant. In trying to escape formalism and theoreticism, I have tried to systematize my experiences, so that they may be superseded in the only way in which they can be: in theoretical *and* political practice.

Such an attempt has come up against very serious problems of communication. How is one to express a theoretical *intention* on the basis of material that is above all ideological and which bears on inadequately identified social processes? I have tried to limit the difficulties in two ways: on the one hand, by systematically envisaging the possible effect on research practice of taking these analyses and propositions as a starting point, rather than by aiming at the coherence and correctness of the text itself; on the other hand, by using as the means of expressing a theoretical content, sketches of concrete analyses that are not in fact concrete analyses. Thus this is indeed, then, a properly theoretical work, that is to say, one bearing on the production of tools of knowledge, and not on the production of knowledge relative to concrete situations. But the way of expressing the mediations necessary in order to arrive at the theoretical experiences proposed has consisted in examining this or that historical situation while trying to transform our understanding of it with the help of advanced theoretical instruments or, too, in showing the contradiction between the observations at one's disposal and the ideological discourses that were juxtaposed with them.

This procedure has the advantage of making the problematic concrete, but it involves two serious drawbacks that I would like to point out:

1   It might be thought that the present book is a collection of concrete researches, whereas, apart from a few exceptions, it offers only the beginnings of a theoretical transformation of empirical raw material, the necessary minimum to indicate the direction the work might take; indeed, how could we claim to analyse so rapidly so great a number of theoretical problems and historical situations? The only possible point of the effort expended is to reveal, through a diversity of themes and situations, the emergence of the same problematic throughout its articulations.
2   One might also see here the concrete illustration of a theoretical system, complete and offered as a model, whereas the production of knowledge does not proceed from the establishment of a system, but through the creation of a series of theoretical tools that are never validated by their coherence, but by their fruitfulness in the analysis of concrete situations.

This, then, is the difficulty inherent in this project: on the one hand, it aims at deducing theoretical tools of observation from concrete situations (situations that I have observed myself, or that have been dealt with by sociological ideology), and, on the other hand, it is only one moment in a process that must, at another conjuncture, reverse the approach, setting out from these theoretical tools to know situations.

The importance accorded to the tactical problems of theoretical work (essential, if one wishes to struggle at one and the same time against both formalism and empiricism, while avoiding the voluntarist project of establishing "the foundation of science") is directly reflected in the organization of the work. The first part recognizes the historical terrain, in order to give a relatively precise content to the theme approached. I then try to establish the contours of ideological discourse on "the urban," which is supposed to be a delimitation of a field of "theoretical knowledge" and social practice. In trying to break open this ideological envelope and to reinterpret the concrete questions it contains, the analyses of the structure of urban space offer a first theoretical formulation of the question as a whole, but they show, at the same time, the impossibility of a theory that is not centred on the articulation of the "urban question" with political processes, that is to say, relative to the state apparatus and the class struggle. This book opens, therefore, with a discussion, theoretical and historical, of "urban politics." An illustration of the interaction between urban structure and urban politics is shown through the study of the process of the urban crisis in the US.

Such a conclusion makes it necessary to introduce a remark whose concrete consequences are enormous: there is no purely theoretical possibility of resolving (or superseding) the contradictions that are at the base of the urban question; this supersession can come only from social practice, that is to say, from political practice. But, in order for such practice to be correct and not blind, it is necessary to make explicit theoretically the questions thus approached, developing and specifying the perspectives of historical materialism. The social conditions for the emergence of such a reformulation are extremely complex, but, in any case, one may be sure that they require a point of departure that is historically bound up with the working-class movement and its practice. This excludes all the "avant-gardist" claims of any "individual theory"; but it does not deny the usefulness of certain work of reflection, documentation and inquiry, in as much as such work forms part of a theoretico-practical approach to the urban question, so urgent today in political practice.

THE HISTORICAL PROCESS OF URBANIZATION

Every form of matter has a history or, rather, it is its history. This proposition does not solve the problem of the knowledge of a given reality; on the contrary, it poses that problem. For, to read this history, to discover the laws of its structuring and transformation, one must break down, by theoretical analysis, what is given in a practical synthesis. However, it is useful to fix the historical contours of a phenomenon before undertaking an investigation of it. Or, in other words, it seems more prudent to undertake this search on the basis of a false theoretical innocence, taking a look, in order to discover the conceptual problems that arise whenever one tries – in vain – to apprehend the "concrete." It is in this sense that a study of the history of the process of urbanization would seem to be the best approach to the urban question, for it brings us to the heart of the problematic of the development of societies, and shows us, at the same time, an ideologically determined conceptual imprecision.

But, although it is clear that the process of the formation of cities is the basis of the urban networks and conditions the social organization of space, one remains too often at the level of an over-all presentation, without any specification of a rate of demographic increase, linking in the same ideological discourse the evolution of the spatial forms of a society and the diffusion of a cultural model on the basis of a political domination.

Analyses of the process of urbanization are situated, generally speaking, in an evolutionist theoretical perspective, according to which each social formation is produced, without break, by a duplication of the elements of the preceding social formation. The forms of spatial settlement are therefore one of the most visible expressions of these modifications (Lampard, 1955: 90–

104; Wooley, 1957; Handlin and Burchard, 1963). This evolution of spatial forms has even been used to classify the stages of universal history (Mumford, 1956, 1961). In fact, rather than establishing the criteria of periodization, it is absolutely necessary to study the production of spatial forms on the basis of the underlying social structure.

To explain the social process that underlies the organization of space is not simply a matter of situating the urban phenomenon in its context. A sociological problematic of urbanization must regard it as a process of organization and development and, consequently, set out from the relation between productive forces, social classes and cultural forms (including space). Such a research project cannot proceed solely in the abstract; it must, with the help of its conceptual tools, explain particular historical situations, in sufficient number to reveal the lines of force of the phenomenon studied, the organization of space.

However, the ideologico-theoretical confusion existing in this field forces us to make an initial mapping of our object, both in conceptual terms and in terms of historical reality. This work is in no sense academic and is presented, on the contrary, as a technically indispensable operation if we are to avoid evolutionist connotations and approach, in all clarity, a particular field of our experience.

[. . .]

THE URBAN PHENOMENON

In the jungle of subtle definitions that sociologists have provided us with, it is possible to distinguish very clearly two extremely distinct senses of the term *urbanization* (Eldridge, 1956; Popenoe, 1963).

1 The spatial concentration of a population on the basis of certain limits of dimension and density (Bogue and Hauser, 1963; Davis, 1965).
2 The diffusion of the system of values, attitudes and behaviour called "urban culture" (Friedmann, 1953; Bergel, 1955; Anderson, 1959: 68; Sirjamaki, 1961; Boskoff, 1962; Gist and Fava, 1964).

For a discussion of the problematic of "urban culture," the reader is referred to Part II [of *The Urban Question*; see chapter 2 of this volume] (see Wirth, 1938). But the essence of my conclusion is the following: we are concerned here with the cultural system characteristic of capitalist industrial society.

Furthermore, and following the same line of thought, one assimilates urbanization and industrialization, making an equivalence of the two processes at the level of the choice of the indicators used (Meadows, 1967), in order to construct the corresponding dichotomies, rural/urban and agricultural/industrial employment (Sorokin and Zimmerman, 1929).

In fact, the culturalist tendency in the analysis of urbanization presupposes the correspondence between a certain technical type of production (essentially defined by industrial activity), a system of values ("modernism") and a specific form of spatial organization, the city, whose distinctive features are a certain size and a certain density.

That this correspondence is not obvious may be seen in a simple analytical account of the great pre-industrial urban centres such as that carried out by Sjoberg (1960). Some authors (e.g. Reissman, 1964) remain consistent by refusing to use the term "city" to designate those forms of settlement, thus making explicit the confusion of the "urban" problematic and a given sociocultural organization.

This link between spatial form and cultural content may possibly serve as a hypothesis (which I shall examine in detail in the following pages), but it cannot constitute an element in the definition of urbanization, for the theoretical response would be already contained in the terms in which the problem was posed.

If one is to keep to this distinction, leaving until later the establishment of the theoretical and empirical relations between the two forms, spatial and cultural, one may take, to begin with, the definition of H. T. Eldridge (1956: 338), who characterizes urbanization as a process of population concentration at two levels: (1) the proliferation of points of concentration; (2) the increase in size of each of these points.

Urban would then designate a particular form of the occupation of space by a population, namely, the urban centre resulting from a high concentration and relatively high density, with, as its predictable correlate, greater functional and social differentiation. Granted, but when one wishes to use this "theoretical" definition directly in a concrete analysis, the difficulties begin. On the basis of which levels of dimension and density can a spatial unit be regarded as urban? What, in practice, are the theoretical and empirical foundations of each of the criteria?

Pierre George (George and Randet, 1964: 7–20) has exposed clearly enough the insurmountable contradictions of statistical empiricism in the delimitation of the concept of the urban. Indeed, if the number of inhabitants, corrected by the structure of the active population and administrative divisions, seems to be the most common criterion, the thresholds used vary enormously, the indicators of the different activities are dependent on the individual type of society and, lastly, the same quantities take on an entirely different meaning according to the productive and social structures that determine the organization of space (Beaujeu-Garnier and Chabot, 1963: 35). Thus the United States Census (1961) takes the threshold of 2,500 inhabitants as the criterion of an urban district, but also adds the urban areas strongly linked to a regional metropolitan centre. On the other hand, the European Conference of Statistics at Prague takes 10,000 inhabitants as its criterion, correcting it by the distribution of the active population in the different sectors.

In fact, the most flexible formula consists in classifying the spatial units of each country according to several dimensions and several levels and in establishing between them theoretically significant empirical relations. More concretely, one might distinguish the quantitative importance of the urban areas (10,000 inhabitants, 20,000, 100,000, 1,000,000 etc.), their functional hierarchy (nature of activities, situation in the chain of interdependences), their administrative importance, then, combining several of these characteristics, one might arrive at different types of spatial occupation.

The rural/urban dichotomy then loses all meaning, for one might equally well distinguish between urban and metropolitan, and, above all, cease to think in terms of a continuous movement from one pole to the other and establish a system of relations between the different historically given spatial forms (Ledrut, 1967).

What emerges from these observations is that it is not by seeking academic definitions or criteria of administrative practice that one will achieve a valid delimitation of one's concepts; on the contrary, it is the rapid analysis of a number of historically established relations between space and society that will enable us to give an objective basis to our study.

Archaeological research has shown that the first settled urban areas with a high density of population (Mesopotamia, about 3500 BC; Egypt, 3000 BC; China and India, 3000–2500 BC) (Mumford, 1961; McAdams, 1966; Lampard, 1965) appeared at the end of the Neolithic Age, where the state of technology and the social and natural conditions of labour enabled cultivators to produce more than they needed to subsist. From that time onwards, a system of division and distribution of the product developed, as the expression and deployment of a technical capacity and of a level of social organization. The cities were the residential form adopted by those members of society whose direct presence at the places of agricultural production was not necessary. That is to say, these cities could exist only on the basis of the surplus produced by working the land. They were religious, administrative and political centres, the spatial expression of a social complexity determined by the process of appropriation and reinvestment of the product of labour. It is thus, then, a new social system but one that is not separate from the rural one, nor posterior to it, for they are both closely linked at the heart of the same process of production of social forms, even if, from the point of view of these forms themselves, we are presented with two different situations (Sjoberg, 1960: 27–31; Braidwood and Willey, 1962).

Let us take, for example, V. Gordon Childe's (1960) synthesis of the criteria which, according to existing empirical knowledge, characterized the first urban areas: the existence of non-productive specialists working full time (priests, functionaries, "service workers"); a population of sufficient size and density; a specific art; the use of writing and arithmetical figures; scientific work; a system of taxation that concentrates the surplus of production; a state apparatus; public architecture; external trade; the existence of social classes.

These observations, based on abundant documentation, are of manifest interest, despite a classificatory procedure reminiscent of that of Borges's celebrated Chinese encyclopedia. But reading these data in terms of theory, it becomes clear enough that the city is the geographical locus in which is established the politico-administrative superstructure of a society that has reached that point of technical and social development (natural and cultural) at which there is a differentiation of the product in the simple and the extended reproduction of labour power, culminating in a system of distribution and exchange, which presupposes the existence of: (1) a system of social classes; (2) a political system permitting both the functioning of the social ensemble and the domination of one class; (3) an institutional system of investment, in particular with regard to culture and technology; (4) a system of external exchange (Mumford, 1956).

Even this cursory analysis shows the "urban phenomenon" articulated with the structure of a society. The same approach may be taken up (and lead to a different result in terms of content) in relation to the various historical forms of spatial organization. Although it is not possible in a few sentences to sum up the human history of space, we can, for analytical purposes, make a few remarks on the possible reading of certain significant urban types.

Thus the imperial cities of the earliest historical times, in particular Rome, combined the characteristics mentioned above with commercial and administrative functions deriving from the concentration, in the same urban area, of a power exercised, by conquest, over a vast territory. Similarly, the Roman penetration of other civilizations took the form of urban colonization – a support both for the administrative functions and for mercantile exploitation. The city is not, therefore, a locus of production, but of administration and domination, bound up with the social primacy of the political–administrative apparatus (Mumford, 1961).

It is logical, therefore, that the fall of the Roman Empire in the West brought with it the almost total disappearance of the socio-spatial forms of the city for, the central politico-administrative functions having been replaced by the local domination of the feudal lords, there was no other social reason for maintaining the cities other than the divisions of the ecclesiastical administration or the colonization and defence of the frontier regions (for example, in Catalonia or East Prussia) (Pirenne, 1927).

The medieval city revived as a consequence of a new social dynamic within the preceding social structure. More concretely, it was created by the union of a pre-existing fortress, around which a nucleus of living quarters and services had been organized, and a market, especially after the opening up of the new commercial routes by the Crusades. On this foundation were organized the politico-administrative institutions proper to the city, which gave it an internal coherence and greater autonomy. It is this political specificity of the city that makes it a world in itself and defines its frontiers as a social system. The best analysis of this phenomenon is that of Max Weber (1905). The ideology of belonging to the city, which lasted into advanced industrial society, finds its historical foundation in this kind of situation.

Although this politico-administrative autonomy was common to most of the cities that developed in the early Middle Ages, the concrete social and spatial forms of these cities were strictly dependent on the conjuncture of the new social relations that had appeared as a result of transformations in the system of distribution of the product. In opposition to the feudal power, a mercantile class had formed which, breaking up the vertical system of distribution of the product, established horizontal links by acting as an intermediary, superseded the subsistence economy and accumulated sufficient autonomy to be capable of investing in manufactures (see the extraordinary account in Pizzorno, 1962).

Since the medieval city represents the emancipation of the mercantile bourgeoisie in its struggle to free itself from feudalism and the central power, its evolution will vary greatly according to the links forged between the bourgeoisie and the nobility. Thus, where these links were close, relations between the city and the surrounding territory, dependent on the feudal lords, was organized in a complementary way. Conversely, the conflict of these classes led to urban isolation.

From a different standpoint, the contiguity or geographical separation between the two classes affected the culture of the cities, especially in the spheres of consumption and investment: the integration of the nobility into the bourgeoisie enabled the former to organize the urban system of values according to the aristocratic model, whereas, when the bourgeoisie was left to itself, exposed to the hostility of the surrounding territory, the community of citizens created new values, in particular those relating to thrift and investment; socially isolated and cut off from supplies from the near-by countryside, their survival depended on their financial and manufacturing capacity.

One might also analyse the evolution of the urban system of each country in terms of the triangular relations between bourgeoisie, nobility and monarchy. For example, the underdevelopment of the Spanish commercial cities compared with the Italian or German cities during the sixteenth and seventeenth centuries can be explained by their role as "transmission belt" between the crown and the American trade, contrasting with the role played by the Italian and German cities, which were highly autonomous in relation to the emperor and princes, with whom they formed only temporary alliances.

The development of industrial capitalism, contrary to an all too widespread naïve view, did not bring about a strengthening of the city, but its virtual disappearance as an institutional and relatively autonomous social system, organized around specific objectives. In fact, the constitution of commodities

Table 1.1   Situation and projections of the urban phenomenon in the world (1920–1960 and 1960–1980) in millions (estimation)

Geographical regions and occupation of space	1920 (est.)	1940 (est.)	1960 (est.)	1980 (proj.)	Absolute growth 1920–60	Absolute growth 1960–80
World total						
Total population	1860	2298	2994	4269	1134	1275
Rural and small towns	1607	1871	2242	2909	635	667
Urban	253	427	752	1360	499	608
(Large towns)	(96)	(175)	(351)	(725)	(255)	(374)
Europe (without USSR)						
Total population	324	379	425	479	101	54
Rural and small towns	220	239	251	244	31	7
Urban	104	140	174	235	70	61
(Large towns)	(44)	(61)	(73)	(99)	(29)	(26)
North America						
Total population	116	144	198	262	82	64
Rural and small towns	72	80	86	101	14	15
Urban	44	64	112	161	68	49
(Large towns)	(22)	(30)	(72)	(111)	(50)	(39)
East Asia						
Total population	553	636	794	1038	241	244
Rural and small towns	514	554	634	742	120	108
Urban	39	82	160	296	121	136
(Large towns)	(15)	(34)	(86)	(155)	(71)	(69)
South Asia						
Total population	470	610	858	1366	388	508
Rural and small towns	443	560	742	1079	299	337
Urban	27	50	116	287	89	171
(Large towns)	(5)	(13)	(42)	(149)	(37)	(107)
Soviet Union						
Total population	155	195	214	278	59	64
Rural and small towns	139	148	136	150	3	14
Urban	16	47	78	128	62	50
(Large towns)	(2)	(14)	(27)	(56)	(25)	(29)

			Latin America			
Total population	*90*	*130*	*213*	*374*	*123*	*161*
Rural and small towns	77	105	145	222	68	77
Urban	13	25	68	152	55	84
(Large towns)	(5)	(12)	(35)	(100)	(30)	(65)
			Africa			
Total population	*143*	*192*	*276*	*449*	*133*	*173*
Rural and small towns	136	178	240	360	104	120
Urban	7	14	36	89	29	54
(Large towns)	(1)	(3)	(11)	(47)	(10)	(36)
			Oceania			
Total population	*9*	*12*	*16*	*23*	*7*	*7*
Rural and small towns	6	7	8	11	2	3
Urban	3	5	8	11	5	3
(Large towns)	(2)	(2)	(5)	(8)	(3)	(3)

Source: Population Division, United Nations Bureau of Social Affairs

as a basic cog of the economic system, the technical and social division of labour, the diversification of economic and social interests over a larger space, the homogenization of the institutional system, brought about an explosion of the conjunction of a spatial form, the city, with a sphere of social domination by a specific class, the bourgeoisie. Urban diffusion is precisely balanced by the loss of the city's ecological and cultural particularism. The process of urbanization and the autonomy of the "urban" cultural model are thus revealed as paradoxically contradictory processes (Lefebvre, 1968, 1970a, b).

The urbanization bound up with the first industrial revolution, and accompanying the development of the capitalist mode of production, is a process of organizing space based on two sets of fundamental facts (Labasse, 1966).

1 The *prior* decomposition of the agrarian social structures and the emigration of the population towards the already existing urban areas, providing the labour force essential to industrialization.
2. The passage from a domestic economy to a small-scale manufacturing economy, then to a large-scale manufacturing economy, which meant, at the same time, a concentration of manpower, the creation of a market and the constitution of an industrial mileu.

The towns attracted industry because of these two essential factors (manpower and market) and industry, in its turn, developed new kinds of employment and gave rise to the need for services.

But the reverse process is also important: where functional elements were present, in particular raw materials and means of transport, industry colonized and gave rise to urbanization.

In both cases, the dominant element was industry, which entirely organized the urban landscape. Yet this domination was not a technological fact; it was the expression of the capitalistic logic that lay at the base of industrialization. "Urban disorder" was not in fact disorder at all; it represented the spatial organization created by the market, and derived from the absence of social control of the industrial activity. Technological rationality and the primacy of profit led, on the one hand, to the effacement of any essential difference between the towns and to fusion of cultural types in the overall characteristics of capitalist industrial civilization and, on the other hand, to the development of functional specialization and the social division of labour in space, with a hierarchy between the different urban areas and a process of cumulative growth deriving from the play of external economies (see George, 1950).

Lastly, the present problematic of urbanization revolves around three fundamental facts and one burning question:

1   The acceleration of the rhythm of urbanization throughout the world (see table 1.1).
2   The concentration of this urban growth in the so-called "under-developed" regions, without the corresponding economic growth that had accompanied the first urbanization in the industrialized capitalist countries (see table 1.2).
3   The appearance of new urban forms and, in particular, the great metropolises (see table 1.3).
4   The relation between the urban phenomenon and new forms of social articulation springing from the capitalist mode of production and tending to supersede it.

These problems are clearly posed, though no clearly defined research methods are indicated, in Greer et al. (1968). My research is an attempt to pose these problems theoretically, on the basis of certain definitions that can now be proposed and on the basis of the few historical remarks that I have just made.

1   The term *urbanization* refers both to the constitution of specific spatial forms of human societies characterized by the significant concentration of activities and populations in a limited space and to the existence and diffusion of a particular cultural system, the urban culture. This confusion is ideological and is intended: (a) to establish a correspondence between ecological forms and a cultural content; (b) to suggest an ideology of the production of social values on the basis of a "natural"

Table 1.2 Evolution of urbanization according to levels of development (in millions)

Occupation of space	1920 (est.)	1940 (est.)	1960 (est.)	1980 (proj.)	Absolute growth	
					1920–60	1960–80
World total						
Total population	*1860*	*2298*	*2994*	*4269*	*1134*	*1275*
Rural and small towns	1607	1871	2242	2909	635	667
Urban	253	427	752	1360	499	608
(Large towns)	(96)	(175)	(351)	(725)	(255)	(374)
Developed regions						
Total population	*672*	*821*	*977*	*1189*	*305*	*212*
Rural and small towns	487	530	544	566	57	22
Urban	185	291	433	623	248	190
(Large towns)	(80)	(134)	(212)	(327)	(132)	(115)
Underdeveloped regions						
Total population	*1188*	*1476*	*2017*	*3080*	*829*	*1063*
Rural and small towns	1120	1341	1698	2343	578	645
Urban	68	135	319	737	251	418
(Large towns)	(16)	(41)	(139)	(398)	(123)	(259)
Underdeveloped regions as percentage of whole world						
Total population	*64*	*64*	*67*	*72*	*73*	*83*
Rural and small towns	70	72	76	81	91	97
Urban	27	32	42	54	50	69
(Large towns)	(16)	(24)	(40)	(55)	(48)	(69)

Source: Population Division, United Nations Bureau of Social Affairs

phenomenon of social densification and heterogeneity (see chapter 2 [of *The Urban Question*]).

2   The notion of *urban* (as opposed to *rural*) belongs to the ideological dichotomy of traditional society/modern society and refers to a certain social and functional heterogeneity, without being able to define it in any other way than by its relative distance from modern society. However, the distinction between town and country poses the problem of the differentiation of the spatial forms of social organization. But this differentiation may be reduced neither to a dichotomy nor to a continuous evolution, as natural evolutionism, incapable of understanding

Table 1.3 Growth of large urban areas in the world, 1920–1960 (general estimates of population, in thousands)

City	1920	1930	1940	1950	1960
World total	30 294	48 660	66 364	84 923	141 156
Europe (total)	*16 051*	*18 337*	*18 675*	*18 016*	*18 605*
London	7 236	8 127	8 275	8 366	8 190
Paris	4 965	5 885	6 050	6 300	7 140
Berlin	3 850	4 325	4 350	3 350	3 275
North America (total)	*10 075*	*13 300*	*17 300*	*26 950*	*33 875*
New York	7 125	9 350	10 600	12 350	14 150
Los Angeles	(750)[a]	(1 800)[a]	2 500	4 025	6 525
Chicago	2 950	3 950	4 200	4 950	6 000
Philadelphia	(2 025)[a]	(2 350)[a]	(2 475)[a]	2 950	3 650
Detroit	(1 100)[a]	(1 825)[a]	(2 050)[a]	2 675	3 550
East Asia (total)	*4 168*	*11 773*	*15 789*	*16 487*	*40 806*
Tokyo	4 168	6 064	8 558	8 182	13 534
Shanghai	(2 000)[a]	3 100	3 750	5 250	8 500
Osaka	(1 889)[a]	2 609	3 481	3 055	5 158
Peking	(1 000)[a]	(1 350)[a]	(1 750)[a]	(2 100)[a]	5 000
Tientsin	(800)[a]	(1 000)[a]	(1 500)[a]	(1 900)[a]	3 500
Hong Kong	(550)[a]	(700)[a]	(1 500)[a]	(1 925)[a]	2 614
Shenyang	– [b]	(700)[a]	(1 150)[a]	(1 700)[a]	2 500
South Asia (total)	*–*	*–*	*3 400*	*7 220*	*12 700*
Calcutta	(1 820)[a]	(2 055)[a]	3 400	4 490	5 810
Bombay	(1 275)[a]	(1 300)[a]	(1 660)[a]	2 730	4 040
Djakarta	– [b]	(525)[a]	(1 000)[a]	(1 750)[a]	2 850
Soviet Union (total)	*–*	*2 500*	*7 700*	*4 250*	*9 550*
Moscow	(1 120)[a]	2 500	4 350	4 250	6 150
Leningrad	(740)[a]	(2 000)[a]	3 350	(2 250)[a]	3 400
Latin America (total)	*–*	*2 750*	*3 500*	*12 000*	*22 300*
Buenos Aires	(2 275)[a]	2 750	3 500	5 150	6 775
Mexico City	(835)[a]	(1 435)[a]	(2 175)[a]	3 800	6 450
Rio de Janeiro	(1 325)[a]	(1 675)[a]	(2 150)[a]	3 050	4 700
São Paulo	(600)[a]	(900)[a]	(1 425)[a]	(2 450)[a]	4 375
Africa (total)	*–*	*–*	*–*	*–*	*3 320*
Cairo	(875)[a]	(1 150)[a]	(1 525)[a]	(2 350)[a]	3 320

[a] Towns below 2 500 000 are not included in the totals.
[b] Smaller than 500 000.
Source: Population Division, United Nations Bureau of Social Affairs

these spatial forms as products of a structure and of social processes, supposes. Indeed, the impossibility of finding an empirical criterion for the definition of the urban is merely the expression of theoretical imprecision. This imprecision is ideologically necessary in order to connote, through a material organization, the myth of modernity.

3 Consequently, in anticipation of a properly theoretical discussion of this problem, I shall discuss the theme of the *social production of spatial forms* rather than speak of urbanization. Within this problematic, the ideological notion of urbanization refers to a process by which a significantly large proportion of the population of a society is concentrated on a certain space, in which are constituted urban areas that are functionally and socially independent from an internal point of view and are in a relation of hierarchized articulation (urban network).

4 The analysis of urbanization is closely liked with the problematic of *development*, which is also a term that we ought to define. The notion of development creates the same confusion by referring both to a level (technological, economic) and to a process (qualitative transformation of social structures, permitting an increase of the potential of the productive forces). This confusion corresponds to an ideological function, namely, the function that presents structural transformations as simply an accumulative movement of the technological and material resources of a society. From this point of view, therefore, there would seem to exist different levels and a slow but inevitable evolution that organizes the passage, when there is an excess of resources, to the higher level.

5 The problem evoked by the notion of development is that of the transformation of the social structure on which a society is based in such a way as to free a capacity for gradual accumulation (the investment/consumption ratio).

6 If the notion of development is situated in relation to the articulation of the structures of a given social formation, it cannot be analysed without reference to the articulation of a set of social formations (on the so-called "international" scale). For this, we need a second concept: that of dependence, characterizing asymmetrical relations between social formations of such a kind that the structural organization of one of them has no logic outside its position in the general system.

7 These points enable us to substitute for the ideological problematic (which connotes the relation between national technological evolution and the evolution towards the culture of modern societies) the following theoretical questions: *what is the process of social production of the spatial forms of a society* and, conversely, *what are the relations between the space constituted and the structural transformations of a society, within an intersocietal ensemble characterized by relations of dependence?*

REFERENCES

Anderson, N. (1959) "Urbanism and urbanization," *American Journal of Sociology*, 65: 68.

Beaujeu-Garnier, J. and Chabot, C. (1963) *Traité de géographie urbaine*. Paris: A. Colin (trans. as *Urban Geography*, London: Longman, 1967).

Bergel, E. (1955) *Urban Sociology*. New York: McGraw-Hill.

Bogue, D. J. and Hauser, P. M. (1963) "Population distribution, urbanism and internal migration," World Population Conference (roneo).

Boskoff, A. (1962) *The Sociology of Urban Regions*. New York: Appleton Century Crofts.

Braidwood, R. J. and Willey G. R. (eds) (1962) *Courses towards Urban Life: Archeological Considerations of Some Cultural Alternates*. Chicago: Aldine.

Childe V. G. (1960) "The urban revolution," *Town Planning Review*, April.

Davis, K. (1965) "The urbanization of urban population," *Scientific American*, September (Cities).

Eldridge, H. T. M. (1956) "The process of urbanization," in J. Spengler and O. D. Duncan (eds), *Demographic Analysis*. Glencoe, IL: The Free Press.

Friedmann, G. (1953) *Villes et campagnes*. Paris: A. Colin.

George, P. (1950) *La ville*. Paris: PUF.

George, P. and Randet, P. (1964) *La région parisienne*. Paris: PUF (W. J. Bastié).

Gist, N. P. and Fava, S. F. (1964) *Urban Society*. New York: Thomas Crowell.

Greer, Scott, McElrath, Dennis L., Minar, David W., and Orleans, Peter (eds) (1968) *The New Urbanization*. New York: St Martin's Press.

Handlin, O. and Burchard, J. (eds) (1963) *The Historian and the City*. Cambridge, MA: MIT Press.

Labasse, J. (1966) *L'Organisation de l'espace*. Paris: Hermann.

Lampard, E. (1955) "The history of cities in the economically advanced areas," *Economic Development and Cultural Change*, 3: 90–104.

Lampard, E. (1965) "Historical aspects of urbanization," in P. Hauser and L. F. Schnore (eds), *The Study of Urbanization*. New York: John Wiley.

Ledrut, R. (1967) *Sociologie urbaine*. Paris: PUF.

Lefebvre, H. (1968) *Le droit à la ville*. Paris: Anthropos.

Lefebvre, H. (1970a) *Du rural et de l'urbain*. Paris: Anthropos.

Lefebvre, H. (1970b) *La révolution urbaine*. Paris: Gallimard.

McAdams, Robert C. (1966) *The Evolution of Urban Society*. Chicago: Aldine.

Meadows, P. (1967) "The city, technology and history," *Social Forces*, 36: 141–7.

Mumford, Lewis (1956) *Man's Role in Changing the Face of the Earth*. Chicago, IL: University of Chicago Press.

Mumford, Lewis (1961) *The City in History*. New York: Harcourt Brace.

Pirenne, H. (1927) *Les villes de moyen-Age*. Brussels.

Pizzorno, A. (1962) "Développement économique et urbanisation," *Actes du ve congrès mondiale de sociologie*.

Popenoe, D. (1963) "On the meaning of urban in urban studies," *Urban Affairs Quarterly*, 6, reprinted in P. Meadows and E. H. Mizruchi (eds), *Urbanism, Urbanization and Change*. Reading, MA: Addison-Wesley, 1969.

Reissman, L. (1964) *The Urban Process*. Glencoe, IL: The Free Press.

Sirjamaki, J. (1961) *The Sociology of Cities*. New York: Random House.

Sjoberg, G. (1960) *The Pre-industrial City: Past and Present.* Glencoe, IL: The Free Press.

Sorokin, P. A. and Zimmerman, C. C. (1929) *Principles of Rural–Urban Sociology.* New York: H. Holt.

Weber, Max (1905) *The City* (1966). Glencoe, IL: The Free Press.

Wirth, L. (1938) "Urbanism as a way of life," *American Journal of Sociology*, July.

Wooley, L. (1957) "The urbanization of society," *Journal of World History*, 4.

CHAPTER TWO

The Urban Ideology

(1972)

Is the city a source of creation or decline?

Is the urban lifestyle an expression of civilization? Is the environmental context a determining factor in social relations? One might well deduce as much from the most common formulations about urban questions: high-rise housing estates alienate, the city centre animates, the green spaces relax, the large city is the domain of anonymity, the neighbourhood gives identity, slums produce crime, the new towns create social peace, etc.

If there has been an accelerated development of the urban thematic, this is due, very largely, to its imprecision, which makes it possible to group together under this heading a whole mass of questions felt, but not understood, whose identification (as "urban") makes them less disturbing: one can dismiss them as the natural misdeeds of the environment.

In the parlance of the technocrats, the "city" takes the place of explanation, through evidence, of the cultural transformations that one fails to (or cannot) grasp and control. The transition from a "rural culture" to an "urban culture," with all its implications of "modernity" and resistance to change, establishes the (ideological) framework of the problems of adaptation to new social forms. Society being conceived as a unity, and this society evolving through the transformation of the values on which it is based, nothing remained but to find a quasi-natural cause (technology plus city) for this evolution, in order to establish oneself in the pure administration of a classless society (or one naturally and necessarily divided into classes, which amounts to the same thing) and at grips with the discontinuities and obstructions imposed upon it by its own internal rhythm of development.

The urban ideology is that specific ideology that sees the modes and forms of social organization as characteristic of a phase of the evolution of society, closely linked to the technico-natural conditions of human existence and, ultimately, to its environment. It is this ideology that, in the final analysis, has very largely made possible a "science of the urban," understood as theoretical space defined by the specificity of its object. Indeed, as soon as one thinks one is in the presence of a specific form of social organization – *urban society* – the study of its characteristics and of its laws becomes a major task for the social sciences and its analysis may even govern a study of particular spheres of reality within this specific form. The history of "urban sociology" shows the close link between the development of this "discipline" and the culturalist perspective that sustains it.

The consequence of this double status of urban ideology is that although, *qua ideology*, one may analyse it and explain it on the basis of the effects it produces, *qua theoretical ideology* (producing effects not only in social relations, but also in theoretical practice), one must learn to recognize it in its different versions, through its most rigorous expressions, those that give it its "legitimacy," while at the same time knowing that these are not its social source. For, like all theoretical ideology, it has a history, which we will trace briefly in order to bring out and discuss its essential themes.

THE MYTH OF URBAN CULTURE

When one speaks of "urban society," what is at issue is never the mere observation of a spatial form. "Urban society" is defined above all by a certain culture, *urban culture*, in the anthropological sense of the term; that is to say, a certain system of values, norms and social relations possessing a historical specificity and its own logic of organization and transformation. This being the case, the qualifying term "urban," stuck to the cultural form thus defined, is not innocent. It is surely a case, as I have indicated above (see Part I [of *The Urban Question*]), of connoting the hypothesis of the production of culture by nature or, to put it another way, of the specific system of social relations (urban culture) by a given ecological context (the city) (Castells, 1969).

Such a construction is directly linked to the evolutionist–functionalist thinking of the German sociological school, from Tönnies to Spengler, by way of Simmel. Indeed, the theoretical model of "urban society" was worked out above all in opposition to "rural society" by analysing the passage of the second to the first in terms used by Tönnies, as the evolution of a *community form* to an *associative form*, characterized above all by a segmentation of roles, a multiplicity of loyalties and a primacy of secondary social relations (through specific associations) over primary social relations (direct personal contacts based on affective affinity) (Mann, 1965).

In extending this reflection, Simmel (whose influence on "American sociology" is growing) managed to propose a veritable ideal type of urban civilization, defined above all in psycho-sociological terms: on the basis of the (somewhat Durkheimian) idea of a crisis of personality – subjected to an excess of psychological stimulation by the extreme complexity of the big cities – Simmel deduced the need for a process of fragmentation of activities, and a strong limitation of the commitment of the individual in his different roles as the only possible defence against a general imbalance resulting from the multiplicity of contradictory impulses. Among the consequences that such a process brings about in the social organization, Simmel indicates the formation of a market economy and the development of the great bureaucratic organizations, instruments adequate to the rationalization and depersonalization demanded by urban complexity. On this basis, the circle closes upon itself and the "metropolitan" human type, centred on its individuality and always free in relation to itself, may be understood (Simmel, 1950).

Now although, in the work of Simmel, there remains an ambiguity between a metropolitan civilization conceived as a possible source of social imbalance and a new type of personality that adapts to it by exacerbating his individual freedom, in the prophecies of Spengler the first aspect becomes overtly dominant and urban culture is linked to the last phase of the cycle of civilizations in which, every link of solidarity having been broken, the whole of society must destroy itself in war. But what is interesting in Spengler is the direct links he establishes, first, between the ecological form and the "spirit" of each stage of civilization and, secondly, between "urban culture" and "western culture," which seems to have been manifested, above all in this part of the world, by virtue of the development of urbanization (Spengler, 1928). We know that Toynbee took these theses as his basis when proposing, quite simply, an assimilation between the terms "urbanization" and "westernization." Spengler's formulation has, no doubt, the advantage of clarity; that is to say, he carries the consequences of the culturist perspective to their logical conclusion, by grounding the historical stages in a "spirit" and linking its dynamics to a sort of natural, undifferentiated evolution. Max Weber's *The City* (1905) which, in fact, formed part of *Wirtschaft und Gesellschaft*, has sometimes been interpreted as one of the first formulations of the thesis of urban culture. In fact, in so far as he strongly specifies the economic and political conditions of this administrative autonomy which, according to him, characterizes the city, I think that it is rather a question of a historical localization of the urban, opposed to the evolutionist thesis of the culturalist current, for which urbanization and modernization are equivalent phenomena.

All these themes were taken up again with a good deal of force by the culturalists of the Chicago School, on the basis of the direct influence undergone by Park, the founder of the school, during his studies in Germany. This was how urban sociology, as a science of the new forms of social life appearing in the great metropolises, came about. For Park, it is a question, above all, of using the city, and particularly the astonishing city that Chicago was in the 1920s, as a *social laboratory*, as a place from which questions would emerge, rather than as a source of explanation of the phenomena observed (Park, 1925).

On the other hand, the propositions of his most brilliant disciple, Louis

Wirth, are really an attempt to define the characteristic features of an urban culture and to explain its process of production on the basis of the content of the particular ecological form constituted by the city. In all probability, it is the most serious theoretical attempt ever made, within sociology, to establish a theoretical object (and, consequently, a domain of research) specific to urban sociology. Its echoes, thirty-three years later, still dominate discussion. This has induced me, for once, to attempt a succinct, but faithful, exposition of his point of view, in order to define the theoretical themes of "urban culture" through the most serious of its thinkers.

For Wirth (1938, 1964), the characteristic fact of modern times is a concentration of the human species in gigantic urban areas from which civilization radiates. Faced with the importance of the phenomenon, it is urgent that we establish a sociological theory of the city which, on the one hand, goes beyond simple geographical criteria and, on the other hand, does not reduce it to the expression of an economic process, for example, industrialization or capitalism. To say "sociology," for Wirth, is equivalent to centring one's attention on human beings and on the characteristics of their relations. Given this, the whole problematic is based on a definition and a question. A sociological definition of the city: "A permanent localization, relatively large and dense, of socially heterogeneous individuals." A question: what are the new forms of social life that are produced by these three essential characteristics of *dimension*, *density* and *heterogeneity* of the human urban areas?

It is these causal relations between urban characteristics and cultural forms that Wirth tries to stress. Firstly, to take the *dimension* of a city: the bigger it is, the wider its spectrum of individual variation and, also, the greater its social differentiation; this determines the loosening of community ties, which are replaced by the mechanisms of formal control and by social competition. On the other hand, the multiplication of interactions produces the segmentation of social relations and gives rise to the "schizoid" character of the urban personality. The distinctive features of such a system of behaviour are therefore: anonymity, superficiality, the transitory character of urban social relations, *anomie*, lack of participation. This situation has consequences for the economic process and for the political system: on the one hand, the fragmentation and utilitarianism of urban relations leads to the functional specialization of activity, the division of labour and the market economy; on the other hand, since direct communication is no longer possible, the interests of individuals are defended only by representation.

Secondly, *density* reinforces internal differentiation, for, paradoxically, the closer one is physically the more distant social contacts are, from the moment when it becomes necessary to commit oneself only partially in each of one's loyalties. There is, therefore, a juxtaposition without mixture of different social milieux, which leads to the relativism and secularization of urban society (an indifference to everything that is not directly linked to the objectives proper to each individual). Lastly, cohabitation without the possibility of real expansion leads to individual savagery (in order to avoid social control) and, consequently to aggressiveness.

The *social heterogeneity* of the urban milieu makes possible the fluidity of the class system and the high rate of social mobility explains why membership of groups is not stable, but linked to the transitory position of each individual: there is, therefore, a predominance of *association* (based on the rational affinity of the interests of each individual) over *community* as defined by membership of a class or possession of a status. This social heterogeneity is also in keeping with the diversification of the market economy and a political life based on mass movements.

Lastly, the diversification of activities and urban milieux causes considerable disorganization of the personality, which explains the growth of crime, suicide, corruption and madness in the great metropolises.

On the basis of the perspectives thus described, the city is given a specific cultural content and becomes the explicative variable of this content. And urban culture is offered as a way of life.

In essence these theses concerning urban culture in the strict sense constitute only variations on Wirth's propositions. However, they have been used as an instrument of an evolutionist interpretation of human history, through the theory developed by Redfield (1941, 1947) of the *folk–urban continuum*, which has had an enormous influence in the sociology of development (see also Miner, 1952; Redfield, 1954).

Indeed, Redfield takes up the rural/urban dichotomy and situates it in a perspective of ecologico-cultural evolution, identifying traditional/modern and folk/urban. With this difference that, setting out from an anthropological tradition, he conceives of urban society in relation to a previous characterization of *folk* society: it is a question of a society "small, isolated, non-literate, and homogeneous, with a strong sense of group solidarity. Such a system is what we mean in saying that the folk society is characterized by a 'culture'." Behaviour is "conventional, custom fixes the rights and duties of individuals and knowledge is not critically examined or objectively and systematically formulated . . . behaviour is personal, not impersonal . . . traditional, spontaneous and uncritical." The kinship system, with its relations and institutions, is derived directly from the categories of experience and the unit of action is the familial group. "The sacred dominates the secular; the economy is much more a factor of status than a market element."

The *urban type* is defined by symmetrical opposition to the set of factors enumerated above. It is centred, therefore, on social disorganization, individualization and secularization. The evolution from one pole to the other occurs almost naturally, through the increase in social heterogeneity and possibilities for interaction, as the society grows; furthermore, the loss of isolation, caused by the contact with another society and/or another culture, considerably accelerates the process. Since this construction is ideal–typical, no society corresponds to it fully, but every society is placed somewhere along this continuum, so that the different features cited are present in various proportions according to the degree of social evolution. This would indicate that these characteristics define the central axis of the problematic of society and that, consequently, the gradual densification of a collectivity, with the social complexity it gives rise to, is, then, the natural motive force of historical evolution, which is expressed materially through the forms of the occupation of space.

It is in this sense that Oscar Lewis's criticisms of Redfield's thesis, showing that the "folk" community, which had served him as his first terrain of observation, was torn by internal conflicts and accorded an important place to mercantile relations, are somewhat ill-founded (despite their verve), for the theory of the *folk–urban continuum* is intended as a means of defining the essential elements of a problematic of social change, rather than of describing a reality (Lewis, 1953: 121–34).

On the other hand, Dewey's fundamental critique (1960) constitutes a more radical attack on this perspective by indicating that, although there are, obviously, differences between town and country, they are only the empirical expression of a series of processes that produce at the same time, a whole series of specific effects at other levels of the social structure. In other words, there is a concomitant variation between the evolution of ecological forms and cultural and social forms, without it being any the more possible to affirm that this co-variation is systematic, let alone that the second are produced by the first. This may be proved by the fact that there may be a diffusion of "urban culture" in the country, without any blurring of the difference of ecological forms between the two. We must, therefore, keep the descriptive character of the "folk–urban continuum" thesis, rather than treat it as a general theory of the evolution of societies.

This critique of Dewey's is one of the few, in the literature, that go to the root of the problem for, in general, the debate on urban culture, as formulated by Wirth and Redfield, has revolved around the purely empirical problem of establishing the historical existence or non-existence of such a system, and around discussion of the anti-urban prejudices of the Chicago School, but without going beyond the problematic of the culturalist terrain in which it had been defined. Thus, authors such as Scott Greer (1962) and Dhooge (1961) indicate the importance of the new forms of social solidarity in modern societies and in the great metropolises by exposing the romantic prejudices of the Chicago School, who were incapable of conceiving the functioning of a society other than in the form of community integration which, of course, had to be restricted to primitive and relatively undifferentiated societies. In re-opening the debate, other sociologists have tried to revive Wirth's theses, either on a theoretical plane, as Anderson (1962) has done, or by "verifying" them empirically for the umpteenth time, as Guterman (1969) has tried to do, to mention one of the most recent examples.

More serious are the objections raised in relation to possible causal connections between the spatial forms of the city and the characteristic social content of "urban culture." At a very empirical level, Reiss showed, long ago, the statistical independence (in the American cities) of "urban culture" in relation to the size and density of the population (Duncan and Reiss, 1956). Again, in an extensive inquiry, Duncan found no correlation between the size of the population, on the one hand, and, on the other, income, age-groups, mobility, schooling, family size, membership of ethnic groups, active population – all the factors that ought to specify an "urban" content (Duncan and Reiss, 1956). Again, Sjoberg's great historical inquiry (1965) into the pre-industrial cities shows how completely different in social and cultural content are these "cities" and the "cities" of the early period of capitalist industrialization or of the present metropolitan regions. Ledrut has described in detail and shown in its specificity the different historical types of urban forms, with extremely different social and cultural contents, which are not located on a continuum, for they are spatial and social expressions qualitatively different from one another (Ledrut, 1968: ch. 1).

Must we, then, with Max Weber (1905) or Leonard Reissman (1964) reserve the term *city* for certain definite types of spatial organization, above all in cultural terms (the cities of the Renaissance or "modern," that is to say, advanced capitalist, cities)? Perhaps, but then one slips into a purely cultural definition of the urban, outside any spatial specificity. Now, it is this fusion–confusion between the connotation of a certain ecological form and the assignment of a specific cultural content that is at the root of the whole problematic of urban culture. One had only to examine the characteristics proposed by Wirth to understand that what is called "urban culture" certainly corresponds to a certain historical reality: the mode of social organization linked to capitalist industrialization, in particular in its competitive phase. It is not to be defined, therefore, solely in opposition to *rural* but by a specific content proper to it, above all at a time when generalized urbanization and the interpenetration of town and country make their empirical distinction difficult.

A detailed analysis of each of the features that characterize it would show without difficulty the causal link, at successive levels, between the structural matrix characteristic of the capitalist mode of production and the effect produced on this or that sphere of behaviour. For example, the celebrated "fragmentation of roles," which is the foundation of "urban" social complexity, is directly determined by the status of the "free worker," which Marx showed to be necessary to assuring maximum profitability in the use of labour force. The predominance of "secondary" relations over "primary" and the accelerated individualization of relations also express this economic and political need of the new mode of production to constitute as "free and equal citizens" the respective supports of the means of production and of the labour force (Poulantzas, 1968: 299ff). And so on, though we cannot develop here a complete system of determination of cultural forms in our societies, the purpose of my remarks being simply to treat this social content other than by an analysis in terms of *urban*. However, a major objection might be raised against this interpretation of urban culture. Since the Soviet, non-capitalist, cities present similar features to those of the capitalist societies, are we not confronted by a type of behaviour bound up with the urban ecological form? The question may be answered on two levels: in fact, if we understand by capitalism the legal private ownership of the means of production, this character is not enough to ground the specificity of a cultural system. But, in fact, I am using the term "capitalism" in the sense used by Marx in *Capital*: the particular matrix of the various systems at the basis of a society (economic, political, ideological). However, even in this vulgar definition of capitalism, the resemblance of the cultural types seems to be due, not to the existence of the same ecological form, but to the social and technological complexity that underlies the heterogeneity and concentration of the populations. It would seem to be a question rather of an "industrial culture." The technological fact of industrialization would thus appear to be the major element determining the evolution of the social forms. In this case, we would be coming close to the theses about "industrial societies."

But, on the other hand, if we hold to a scientific definition of capitalism, we can affirm that in historically given societies where studies have been made of the transformation of social relations, the articulation of the dominant mode of production called capitalism may account for the appearance of such a system of relations and of a new ecological form.

The observation of similar behaviour patterns in societies in which one may presume that the capitalist mode of production is not dominant, does not invalidate the previous discovery, for we must reject the crude capitalism/socialism dichotomy as a theoretical instrument. At the same time, this raises a question and calls for research that should have as its objective: (1) to determine whether in fact the real and not only the formal content of these behaviour patterns is the same; (2) to see what is the concrete articulation of the different modes of production in Soviet society, for, indisputably, the capitalist mode of production is present there, even if it is no longer dominant; (3) to establish the contours of the new post-capitalist mode of production, for, although the scientific theory of the capitalist mode of production has been partially elaborated (in *Capital*), there is no equivalent for the socialist mode of production; (4) to elaborate a theory of the links between the concrete articulation of the various modes of production in Soviet society and the systems of behaviour (see Part I [of *The Urban Question*]).

It is obvious that, in such a situation, the problematic of urban culture would no longer be relevant. However, in the absence of any such research, we can say, intuitively: that there are similar technological determinants, which may lead to similarities of behaviour; that this is reinforced by the active presence of capitalist structural elements; that formal similarities in behaviour have meaning only when related to the social structure to which they belong. For to reason otherwise would lead us to the logical conclusion that all societies are one because everyone eats or sleeps more or less regularly.

This being the case, why not accept the term "urban culture" for the system of behaviour bound up with capitalist society? Because, as I have indicated, such an appellation suggests that these cultural forms have been produced by the particular ecological form known as the city. Now, one has only to reflect for a moment to realize the absurdity of a theory of social change based on the growing complexification of human collectivities simply as a result of demographic growth. In effect, there has never been, there can never be, in the evolution of societies, a phenomenon apprehensible solely in some such physical terms as, for example, "size." Any development in the dimensions and differentiation of a social group is itself the product and the expression of a social structure and of its laws of transformation.

Consequently, the mere description of the process does not inform us as to the technico-social complex (for example, the productive forces and the relations of production) at work in the transformation. There is, therefore, a simultaneous and concomitant production of social forms in their different dimensions and, in particular, in their spatial and cultural dimensions. One may pose the problem of their interaction, but one cannot set out from the proposition that one of the forms produces the other. The theses on urban culture were developed in an empiricist perspective, according to which the context of social production was taken to be its source.

Another problem, our problem, is to discover the place and laws of articulation of this "context," that is to say, of the spatial forms, in the social structure as a whole. But, in order to deal with this question, we must first break up the globality of this urban society understood as a true culmination of history in modernity. For, if it is true that, in order to identify them, new phenomena have been named according to their place of origin, the fact remains that "urban culture," as it is presented, is neither a concept nor a theory. It is, strictly speaking, a myth, since it recounts, ideologically, the history of the human species. Consequently, the writings on "urban society" which are based directly on this myth, provide the key-words of an ideology of modernity, assimilated, in an ethnocentric way, to the social forms of liberal capitalism.

In a "vulgarized" form, if one may put it in this way, these writings have had and still have an enormous influence on the ideology of development and on the "spontaneous sociology" of the technocrats. On the other hand, it is in the terms of a passage from "traditional" society to "modern" society (Lerner,

1958) that one transposes the problematic of the "folk–urban continuum" into an analysis of the relations internal to the imperialist system (see Part I, chapter 3, section II [of *The Urban Question*]).

On the other hand, "urban culture" is behind a whole series of discourses that take the place of an analysis of social evolution in the thinking of the western ruling elites and which, therefore, are largely communicated through the mass media and form part of the everyday ideological atmosphere. Thus, for example, the Commissariat Général au Plan (1970), in a series of studies on cities published as preparation for the sixth French Plan, devoted a small volume to "urban society" that constitutes a veritable anthology of this problematic.

Setting out from the affirmation that "every city is the locus of a culture," the document tries to enunciate the conditions for realizing ideal models, conceptions of city-society, while taking into account the "constraints of the economy." This is highly characteristic of a certain technocratic humanism: the city (which is simply society) is made up of the free initiatives of individuals and groups, which are limited but not determined, by the problem of means. And urbanism then becomes the rationality of the possible, trying to link the means at one's disposal and the great objectives one sets oneself.

For the urban phenomenon is "the expression of the system of values current in the culture proper to a place and a time," which explains that "the more a society is conscious of the objectives it pursues . . . the more its cities are typed." Lastly, on the basis of such a social organization, one finds the ecological factors that have long been advanced by the classics of urban culturalism: "The basis of urban society lies in the grouping of a collectivity of a certain size and density, which implies a more or less rigorous division of activities and functions and makes necessary exchanges between the subgroups endowed with a status that is proper to them: to be differentiated is to be linked" (1970: 21). Here we find a whole theory of the production of social, spatial and cultural forms, simply on the basis of an organic phenomenon of growth – as if it were a question of a sort of upwards, linear movement of matter towards spirit.

Now, although it is clear that there are cultural specificities in the different social milieux, it is just as obvious that the cleavage no longer passes through the town/country distinction, and the explanation of each mode of life requires that one should articulate it in a social structure taken as a whole, instead of keeping to the purely empirical correlation between a cultural content and its spatial seat. For our object is quite simply the analysis of the process of the social production of the systems of representation and communication or, to put it another way, of the ideological superstructure.

If these theses on "urban society" are so widespread, this is precisely because they permit one the short cut of studying the emergence of ideological forms on the basis of social contradictions and class division. Society is thus unified and develops in an organic way, producing universal types, formerly opposed by way of being unsynchronized but never, within any given social structure, opposed by way of contradiction. This, of course, in no way prevents one from commiserating with the alienation of this "unified Man," at grips with the natural and technological constraints that impede the full development of his creativity. The city – regarded both as the complex expression of its social organization and as the milieu determined by fairly rigid technological constraints – thus becomes, in turn, a focus of creation and the locus of oppression by the technico-natural forces brought into being. The social efficacy of this ideology derives from the fact that it describes the everyday problems experienced by people, while offering an interpretation of them in terms of natural evolution, from which the division into antagonistic classes is absent. This has a certain concrete force and gives the reassuring impression of an integrated society, united in facing up to its "common problems."

From Urban Society to Urban Revolution

Long before me, bourgeois historians had described the historical development of this class struggle and bourgeois economists had expressed its economic anatomy. What I did that was new was: 1. to show that the existence of classes is bound up only with stages of historical development determined by production; 2. that the class struggle leads necessarily to the dictatorship of the proletariat; 3. that this dictatorship itself constitutes only a transition towards the abolition of all classes and a classless society.
Karl Marx, letter to Weidemeyer (1852)

The urban ideology has deep social roots. It is not confined to academic tradition or to the milieux of official urbanism. It is, above all, in people's heads. It even penetrates to the thoughts of those who set out from a critical reflection on the social forms of urbanization. And it is there that it does the most damage, for it abandons the integrating, communal, conformist tone, and becomes a discourse on contradictions – on urban contradictions. Now, this shift leaves intact the theoretical problems that have just been raised, while adding new, much more serious, *political* problems. Such flexibility of tone shows very well the ideological character of the theme of urban society, which may be "left-wing" or "right-wing" according to preference, without in any way changing the positive or negative feeling one invests in it, while recognizing urban society as a specific historical type with well-defined characteristics and even as the culmination of human evolution.

The most striking expression of this "left-wing" version of the ideological thesis on urban society is no doubt the urbanistic thinking of one of the greatest theoreticians of contemporary Marxism, Henri Lefebvre. Such intellectual power applied to the urban problematic ought to produce decisive results in this sphere, not only in terms of influence, but also by opening up new approaches, detecting new problems, proposing new hypotheses. However, in the end, the problematic engulfs the thinker and, having set out from a *Marxist analysis of the urban phenomenon*, he comes closer and closer, through a rather curious intellectual evolution, to an *urbanistic theorization of the Marxist problematic*. Thus, for example, after defining the emerging society as urban, he declares that the revolution too, the new revolution, is logically *urban*.

In what sense? Let me try to explain in detail, for we are confronted here by a complex body of thought, full of subtleties and theoretico-political modulations that are impossible to grasp as a coherent whole. Nevertheless, if one looks attentively, beyond its open, asystemic character, there is a nucleus of propositions around which the central axes of the analysis are ordered. Let me sum up briefly and as faithfully as possible what this nucleus is, so that we may discuss in concrete terms its principal implications for a study of urbanization and, indirectly, for Marxism.

Despite the diversity and extent of Lefebvre's thinking (which is no doubt the profoundest intellectual effort that has been made towards understanding the urban problems *of the present day*), we have, in 1971, four texts to help us to grasp it: a collection of his writings on the problem, which includes the most important texts up to 1969, *Du rural et de l'urbain* (which I shall refer to as *DRU*) (Lefebvre, 1970a); a short polemical work, *Le droit à la ville* (*DV*) (1968); and, above all, the first general discussion of the question in *La révolution urbaine* (*RU*) (1970b); lastly, a short piece, "La ville et l'urbain" (*VU*) (1971), which sums up very clearly the principal theses. (I shall continue to specify my textual references even if this seems over-scrupulous.)

Lefebvre's urbanistic exposition is "constructed on a hypothesis, according to which the crisis of urban reality is the most important, more central than any other" (*VU*, p. 3).

This crisis, which has always existed in a latent stage, has been masked, impeded, one might say, by other urgent problems, especially during the period of industrialization: on the one hand, by the "housing question" and, on the other, by industrial organization and overall planning. But, ultimately, this thematic must increasingly gain recognition, because "the development of society is conceivable only in urban life, through the realization of urban society" (*DV*, p. 158).

But what is this "urban society"? The term designates "the tendency, the orientation, the potentiality, rather than an accomplished fact"; it stems both from the complete urbanization of society and from the development of industrialization (one might also call it "post-industrial society") (*RU*, pp. 8, 9).

This is a central point of the analysis: urban society (whose social content defines urbanization as a process rather than the reverse) is produced by a historical process that Lefebvre conceives as a model of dialectical sequence.

In effect, human history is defined by the overlapping succession of three eras, fields or continents: the *agrarian*, the *industrial*, the *urban*. The political city of the first phase gives place to the mercantile city, which is itself swept away by the movement of industrialization, which negates the city; but, at the end of the process, generalized urbanization, created by industry, reconstitutes the city at a higher level: thus the urban supersedes the city that contains it in seed form, but without being able to bring it to flower; on the other hand, the reign of the urban enables it to become both cause and instrument (*RU*, p. 25).

In this evolution, there are two critical phases; the first is the subordination of agriculture to industry; the second, which we see today, is the subordination of industry to urbanization; it is this conjuncture that gives meaning to the expression "urban revolution," conceived as "the ensemble of transformations undergone by contemporary society, in order to pass from the period in which questions of growth and industrialization predominate, to the period in which the urban problematic will decisively triumph, in which the search for solutions and modalities proper to *urban society* will become of prime importance" (*RU*, p. 13).

But what is significant is that these fields, or stages, in human history (what Marxists called modes of production) are not defined by (spatial) forms or techniques (agriculture, industry); they are, above all, "modes of thought, action, life" (*RU*, p. 47). Thus the evolution becomes more clear if one associates each era with its properly social content:

> Need   – Rural
> Work   – Industrial
> Pleasure – Urban (*RU*, p. 47)

The urban, the new era of mankind (*RU*, p. 52), seems to represent, then, deliverance from the determinisms and constraints of earlier stages (*RU*, p. 43). It is nothing less than the culmination of history, a post-history. In the Marxist tradition, one would call this "communism." A veritable *episteme* of a final period (our own period, it seems, forms the hinge between the two ages), the urban is realized and expressed above all by a new humanism, a concrete humanism, defined in the type of *urban man* "for whom and by whom the city and his own everyday life in the city becomes work, appropriation, use-value" (*DV*, p. 163 – see, for the development of the whole problematic in terms of historical transformation, *RU*, pp. 13, 25, 43, 47, 52, 58, 62, 80, 99, 100, etc.).

It is clear that this analysis refers to a historical type of society, urban society, defined by a precise cultural content ("a mode of life, action"), as was the case for the thesis on urban culture or on urban–modern society, even if the content differs. In fact, the essential, in each case, is the identification of a form, the urban, with a content (for some, competitive capitalist society; for others "modern technocratic" society; for Lefebvre, the reign of freedom and the new humanism).

At an initial level of criticism, one might challenge Lefebvre's libertarian and abstract conceptions of the reign of post-historical or communist society, in which one perceives no concrete process of constructing new social relations through the revolutionary transformation of different economic, political, ideological agencies by means of the class struggle and, therefore, of the dictatorship of the proletariat. But this debate would merely, for the most part, reproduce the theoretical argument that has been advanced, for over a century, by Marxists against anarchists, a debate in which the history of the working-class movement has decided much more than a rigorous demonstration would have done. Having no pretension to adding anything new of great importance to a polemic that has largely been superseded by practical politics (spontaneism always destroying itself by its theoretical inability to direct the real processes), I have nothing to say to the resumption of millenarist utopias in Lefebvre's thinking. He is perfectly free, if he so wishes to call "urban" the utopian society in which there would no longer be any repression of the free impulses of desire (*RU*, p. 235), and also to call urban the still inadequately identified cultural transformations that are emerging in the imperialist metropolis.

But the whole problem is here: the term "urban" (as in "urban culture") is not an innocent one; it suggests the hypothesis of a production of social content (the urban) by a trans-historical form (the city) and, beyond this, it expresses a whole general conception of the production of social relations, that is to say, in fact, a theory of social change, a *theory of revolution*. For "the urban" is not only a libertarian utopia; it has a relatively precise content in Lefebvre's thinking: it is a question of centrality or, rather, of simultaneity, of concentration (*RU*, pp. 159, 164, 174; *VU*, p. 5). In urban space, what is characteristic is that "something is always happening" (*RU*, p. 174); it is the place in which the ephemeral dominates, beyond repression. But this "urban," which is therefore nothing more than emancipated creative spontaneity, is produced, not by space or by time, but by a form which, being neither object nor subject, is defined above all by the dialectic of centrality, or of its negation (segregation, dispersal, periphery – *RU*, p. 164).

What we have here is something very close to Wirth's thesis concerning the way social relations are produced. It is density, the warmth of concentration that, by increasing action and communication, encourage at one and the same time a free flowering, the unexpected, pleasure, sociability and desire. In order to be able to justify this mechanism of sociability (which is connected directly to organicism), Lefebvre must advance a mechanistic hypothesis that is quite unjustifiable: the hypothesis according to which "social relations are revealed in the negation of distance" (*RU*, p. 159). And that is what the essence of the urban is in the last resort. For the city creates nothing, but, by centralizing creations, it enables them to flower. However, Lefebvre is aware of the excessively crude character of the thesis according to which mere spatial concentration makes possible the flowering of new relations, as if there were no social and institutional organization outside the arrangement of space. This is why he adds the condition: *providing this concentration is free of all repression*; this is what he calls *the right to the city*. But the introduction of this corrective destroys any causal relation between the form (the city) and human creation (the urban), for if it is possible to have repressive cities and freedoms without place (u-topias), this means that the social determinations of this inactivity, the production of the conditions of emergence of spontaneity, pass elsewhere than through forms – through a political practice, for example. What meaning, then, can the formulation of the problem of freedom in terms of the urban have!

One might add many remarks on the theoretical and historical error of the supposed determination of content by form (a structuralist hypothesis if ever there was one), by observing, to begin with, that it is a question, at most, of a correlation that still requires to be theorized, by linking it to an analysis of the social structure as a whole. And this correlation may even prove to be empirically false. Thus, when Lefebvre speaks of generalized urbanization, including Cuba and China, he is quite simply ignorant of the statistical and historical data of the processes he describes, particularly in the case of China, where urban growth has been limited to the natural growth of the towns (without peasant immigration) and where, on the contrary, one is witnessing a permanent and massive shift towards the countryside, reinforced by the constitution of the people's communes, as forms that integrate town and country. Although the absence of information about the Chinese, Cuban, Vietnamese experiences does not warrant overly affirmative conclusions, we know enough to reject once and for all the notion of the generalization of the urban as the only form, characteristic both of capitalism and socialism. Since, for Lefebvre, the urban is a "productive force," one is directed towards a transcending of the theory of the modes of production, which is reduced to the ranks of "Marxist dogmatism" (*RU*, p. 220), and to its replacement by a dialectic of forms, as explanation of the historical process.

Thus, for example, the class struggle still appears to be regarded as the motive force of history. But what class struggle? It would seem that, for Lefebvre, the urban struggle (understood both as relating to a space and as expressing a project of freedom) has played a determining role in social contradictions, even in the working-class struggle. Thus, for example, the Commune becomes a "revolutionary urban practice," in which the "workers, chased from the centre to the periphery, once again took the road back to this centre occupied by the bourgeoisie." And Lefebvre wonders "how and why the Commune has not been conceived as an *urban revolution*, but as revolution carried out by the industrial proletariat and directed at industrialization, which does not correspond to the historical truth" (*RU*, pp. 148, 149). The opposition between forms without precise structural content (industry, the urban) makes it possible to maintain, by playing on words, that a proletarian revolution must be aimed at industrialization, whereas an urban revolution is centred on the city. The fact that, for Lefebvre, the state must also be a form (always repressive, regardless of its class content) permits this confusion for, political power being the central issue in any revolutionary process, suppressing it condemns one to an interminable opposition of every possible form of the class struggle (industrial, urban, agrarian, cultural), and renders an analysis of the social contradictions on which it is grounded unnecessary.

Such a perspective, if carried to its logical conclusion, even leads to politically dangerous consequences that seem to me to be alien to Lefebvre's thinking, although fairly close to what he actually says. Thus, for example, when the analysis of the process of urbanization enables him to declare that "the vision or conception of the class struggle on a world scale seems today to be superseded. The revolutionary capacity of the peasants is not increasing; it seems even to be on the decline, although unevenly" (*RU*, p. 152), and the blindness of the working-class movement is contrasted with the clear-sightedness, on this theme, of science fiction (*RU*, p. 152). Or again, when he proposes to replace by urban praxis an industrial praxis which is now over. This is an elegant way of speaking of the end of the proletariat (*RU*, p. 184) and leads to the attempt actually to ground a new political strategy not on the basis of the structures of domination, but on the alienation of everyday life.

It is even suggested that the working class no longer has political weight, because it has nothing to offer in terms of urbanism (*RU*, p. 245). However, it remains an essential agent, but one whose actions are given meaning from the outside. A return to Leninism? Not at all! What might illuminate the options of the working class is well known: it is philosophy and art (*DV*, p. 163). At the intersection of these two, then, urbanistic thought plays a strategic role and may be regarded as a veritable avant-garde, capable of orientating the revolution towards new social conditions (the urban revolution) (*RU*, p. 215).

Although such statements rise towards metaphilosophical regions, far from the modest scope of the researcher, or even, quite simply, of people at grips with "urban problems," one might, still, wonder what they teach us that is new or original about the urban question in the strict use of the term – about space and/or what is institutionally called the urban. And it is here that one becomes fully aware of the profoundly ideological character of Lefebvre's theses, that is to say, of their social rather than theoretical implication.

Indeed, space, in the last resort, occupies a relatively modest and subordinate place in the whole analysis. The city, according to a famous and on the whole correct formula, projects on the terrain a whole society, with its superstructures, its economic base and its social relations (*DRU*, p. 147). But when it comes to specifying these relations or showing the articulation between the social and spatial problematics, the second is perceived rather as a mere occasion of deploying the first. For space is "the result of a history that must be conceived as the work of social *agents* or *actors*, collective *subjects*, operating by successive thrusts ... From their interactions, their strategies, their successes and defeats, result the qualities and 'properties' of urban space" (*RU*, p. 171). If this thesis means that society creates space, everything still remains to be explained in terms of a mode of specific determination. But it goes much further: it indicates that space, like the whole of society, is the ever-original work of that freedom of creation that is the attribute of Man, and the spontaneous expression of his desire. It is only by accepting this absolute of Lefebvrian humanism (a matter of philosophy or religion) that the analysis might be pursued in this direction: it would always be dependent on its metaphysical foundation.

This spontaneism of social action and the dependence of space upon it becomes still more clear if one refers to the synchronic analysis that Lefebvre has made of urban space (*RU*, p. 129). His keystone is the distinction between three levels: the global or state level; the mixed level or level of "urban organization"; the private level or the "habitat level." Now, what characterizes urbanization in the second critical phase of history is that the global level depends on the mixed level and that the mixed level tends to depend on the "inhabiting." This means, in concrete terms, that it is the inhabiting, *everyday life*, that produces space. Now, such independence of the everyday implies that one refuses to conceive it as the pure expression of general social determinations. It is the expression of human initiative, and this initiative (that is to say, the projects of subjects) is therefore the productive source of space and of urban organization. Thus one arrives at the following paradox: whereas one makes urban practice the centre of social transformations, space and urban structure are pure transparent expressions of the intervention of social actors. Another proof of the use of the term urban to express above all a cultural content (the free work). But one also arrives, at the same time, at this much more serious conclusion, that the whole perspective has no specific answer to give to the theoretical problems posed by the social determination of space and urban organization.

This being the case, "urban practice," understood as a practice of transformation of everyday life, comes up against a number of "obstacles" in terms of institutionalized class domination. Thus Lefebvre is led to pose the problem of urbanism as one of ideological coherence and as the repressive-regulatory intervention of the state apparatus. This is the critical side of Lefebvre's thinking, always accurate, brilliant, knowing how to detect new sources of contradictions. A large part of the social resonance of Lefebvre's urbanistic work derives from the political role played by an implacable critique of the system of official urbanism – a critique that one can only approve and pursue in the direction that Lefebvre has had the courage to open up.

But even this critique is experienced as the problematic of alienation, as opposition on the part of urban spontaneity to the order of urbanism, as a struggle of the everyday against the state, independent of (or above) the class content and specific conjuncture of social relations. That "everydayness," that is to say, social life, governed above all by the rhythms of the ideological, may be the expression of new forms of contradiction in social practice, there can be no doubt. But that it should be the source, rather than the expression, of complex class relations determined, in the last resort, by economic relations, is a reversal of the materialist problematic and sets out from "men" rather than from their social and technological relations of production and domination.

Nevertheless, Lefebvre has seen, on the one hand, the emergence of new contradictions in the cultural and ideological sphere and, on the other hand, he has linked the urban question to the process of the extended reproduction of labour power. In doing so, he has opened up what is perhaps a crucial direction in the study of "the urban." But he has closed it immediately afterwards by falling into the trap that he himself denounced, that is to say, by treating in terms of the urban (and therefore attaching them to a theory of social forms) the social processes that are connoted ideologically by urbanistic thinking. Now, in order to supersede this ideological treatment of the problem, it was necessary:

1 To treat space and the urban separately, that is to say, to treat the process of collective assumption at its different levels.
2 To proceed to the analysis of the social determination of these processes, in particular explaining the new forms of intervention of the state apparatuses in this domain.
3 To study the organization of space as a chapter of social morphology as Lefebvre proposes, while establishing the specificity of such a form, but without treating it as a new motive force of history.
4 Lastly, and above all, to explain the social bases of the ideological link between the problematic of space and that of the reproduction of labour power ("everydayness," to use Lefebvre's term).

Now, in elaborating a new theory of social utopia (or, to put it another way, of the end of history), Lefebvre has found in the urban form a "material" support (a *place*) to which to attach the process of production of new social relations (the urban) through the interaction of creative capacities. Thus his analyses and perspectives, which have opened up new paths in this domain, are lost in the flood of a metaphilosophy of history, which takes the place of theoretical discourse and tries to convey the political spontaneism and the cultural revolt that are being manifested in the imperialist metropolises. This new urban ideology may thus serve noble causes (it is not always completely certain that spontaneism is one of them) while masking fundamental phenomena that theoretical practice still finds difficult to grasp.

The theoretical path opened up and closed by Lefebvre has been taken up in an extremely relevant way by the *Utopie* group, led by Hubert Tonka, which defines the urban problematic as "the problematic of the mode of reproduction of the mode of production" (Utopie, 1970). But, quite unlike Lefebvre, these researchers do not make the "urban," conceived as "everydayness," the axis of social development, nor the cultural culmination of history. On the contrary, centring their analysis on capitalist society, they set out from a study of production and of the realization of surplus value in order to understand the extension of its logic to the world of consumption, an extension itself derived from the development of the productive forces and of the class struggle.

Rather than replace the "industrial" problematic by the "urban" problematic, they take the reverse direction, making the problems of the city entirely dependent on the forms and rhythms of class relations and, more particularly, on the political struggle. "The so-called problems of the city are simply the most refined expression of class antagonisms and of class domination, which, historically, produced the development of civilizations." "Urbanization," as a policy of state power, is taken in the sense of "civility," that is to say, as having the essential aim of resolving class contradictions. However, such an analysis seems to me, on the one hand, utterly to conceal a certain specificity of articulation between space and society and, on the other hand, to underestimate the interventions bearing on other spheres than political class relations, for example, attempts of a reform–integration kind, or the regulation of the economic, etc. It is true, however, that in the final analysis, all social intervention remains marked by its class content, although one must specify its mediations.

The few analyses made by *Utopie* have not been followed up in concrete research, given the essentially critical and political–cultural perspective that the group gives itself – in which it deserves all the support and encouragement of those who, in one way or another, are against the established "urban order." However, they reflect the essential problems to be treated, even if they do not embark on the long road of theoretical mediations to be traversed. But if a fruitful perspective is to be opened up, it will be done by placing oneself in opposition to the culturalist and spontaneist theses; that is to say, by approaching the analysis of new aspects of the capitalist mode of production through the development of new and adequate theoretical tools, which specify, without contradicting them, the fundamental elements of historical materialism.

The urban ideology would thus be superseded and the theme of urban culture, in its different versions, would be regarded as a myth rather than as a specific social process. However, if "the city" or "the urban" cannot be a social source of systems of values considered as a whole, would not certain types of organization of space or certain "urban units" have a specific effect on social practices? Would there be "urban sub-cultures"? And what would be their relation to the social structure?

THE URBAN SUB-CULTURES

The relation between a certain type of habitat and specific modes of behaviour is a classic theme of urban sociology. It is precisely at this level that the "constructors" try to find a use for sociological reflection in their search for formulas that make it possible to express architectural volume or urbanistic space in terms of sociability. The manipulation of social life through the arrangement of the environment is a dream sufficiently linked to the utopists and technocrats to give rise to an ever growing mass of research, aimed at verifying a correlation, empirically observed in another context.

But this relation between context and life-style also occurs spontaneously in the representations of individuals and groups. Everyday reactions are full of associations, derived from a particular experience, according to which one quarter corresponds to a working-class mode of life, another is "bourgeois," X new town is "soulless," while the small town Z has kept its charm. Beyond social images aroused by the urban zones – the analysis of which forms part, strictly speaking, of the ideological representations in relation to the living context (see Part III [of *The Urban Question*]) – we are presented with the following practical and theoretical question: is there a relation, and which relation, between the ecological context and the cultural system?

Now, the analysis of urban sub-cultures has usually come up against a confused amalgam of several research objectives. Cultural monographs of a residential community, usually trying to "test" the emergence of a system of "urban values" have alternated with attempts to link certain behaviour patterns and attitudes to a given ecological context.

That is why a discussion of the whole of the problematic requires a prior distinction between the various questions that are entangled here, the answers to which, theoretical and empirical, are very different. Fortunately, there is available in this field an extraordinary analysis which, after reviewing most of the important contributions made by American and British specialists up to 1968, clears the ground by uncovering a few fundamental theoretical distinctions (Keller, 1968: see also Popenoe, 1963). Keller indicates, quite rightly, that it is a question of two series of non-equivalent questions:

1   The existence of a system of specific behaviour patterns in relation to local social life, in particular, in relation to neighbours. This system of

neighbouring involves at least two distinct dimensions: activities relative to neighbouring (mutual aid, mutual loaning, visits, advice, etc.)
and social relations in the strict sense (namely, the ratio between relations of friendship, of family, of neighbourhood, participation in association and centres of interest, etc.). All these behaviour patterns express
the cultural definition of the role neighbour; this role varies in intensity
and intimacy, according to the dimensions and cultural norms
interiorized by the different social groups.

2   The existence of a particular ecological unit (quarter, neighbourhood,
etc.) with sufficiently well-defined frontiers to produce a socially significant demarcation. In fact, the very problem of the existence of such
urban units within urban areas brings us back immediately to the
criteria for dividing up space (economic, geographical, functional, in
terms of perception or the "feeling of belonging," etc.).

To these two questions must be added the strictly sociological problem of the
relation between each type of ecological unit, defined according to certain
criteria, and each mode of cultural behaviour. The relation, from the theoretical point of view, may be regarded in both senses, for the determination of
behaviour by a context may be reversed through the influence that social
practices may have on the constitution of space. The problematic of the urban
social *milieux* thus poses, at least, these four series of questions, which I shall try
to deal with by referring to the major tendencies, not always mutually consistent, that have emerged in research. After this *ordered* theoretical reading, a
provisional meaning may be attributed to the mass of empirical results in such
a way as to synthesize (or to reprise) the formulation of the problem.

1   *Is there an "urban" behaviour pattern characterizing social life in the residual
    units?*

This is, in fact, a resumption of the theme of urban culture at the specific level
of the residential unit. Thus, if the city as a whole may be summed up by a
single cultural feature, there would be a type of "urban" behaviour characterized by superficiality of contacts and the importance of secondary relations:
this is what Guterman, in a recent study, tried to deduce from the negative
correlation he finds between the size of the urban area and the degree of
intimacy and friendship observed in social relations (Guterman, 1969). However, the matter is more subtle, for the translation from urban culture to
residential unit is not done directly by reproducing, at the lowest level, the
general urban type. It is a case of new formulas of social relations adapted to
the residential milieux of the great urban areas. For, from the moment one
could observe that the "city" was not the equivalent of "social integration," it
was patently necessary to discover the new forms through which the system of
social relations is developed in the situation of generalized urbanization.

The cultural typology suggested by functionalist sociology is thus placed on two axes: on the one hand, the opposition between "local" and "cosmopolitan" expresses the general trend towards a segmentation of roles, and of domination in secondary relations (Dobriner, 1958); on the other hand, the "local" pole is divided between a type of "modern" behaviour and "traditional" behaviour, the second being constituted by the turning in of a residential community upon itself, a strong internal consensus and a strong line of cleavage in relation to the outside, whereas the first is characterized by an open sociability, but one limited in its commitment, since it co-exists with a multiplicity of relations outside the residential community.

It is probably the research of Willmott and Young (1960a, b) of the Institute of Community Studies in London that has best isolated the two types of cultural behaviour by analysing successively an old working-class quarter in East London and a new, middle-class suburb. In the latter, life is centred primarily on the home, with the woman who remains in the house and the man who, outside work, spends most of his time in domestic activities: gardening, doing odd jobs, helping with household tasks. But the home is not everything; a new form of sociability is developing through local organizations, brief visits to neighbours, going to the pub and social gatherings, according to a well-defined rhythm. On the other hand, in the old working-class district, sociability does not need to be institutionalized; the networks of mutual aid are entirely open and the extended family, the central pivot of intimate relations, establishes communication between the elements of different generations.

The two modes of behaviour have been shown to correspond, on the one hand, to the new suburban housing and to the districts of the old town centre; on the other hand to the way of life of the middle class and that of the working class. But, in any case, they are offered as a sequence, as a progressive passage from one to the other. Especially as the suburban residential community is not opposed to the preponderance of secondary relations and group membership at the level of society as a whole; on the contrary, they reinforce each other. Thus, for example, the classic research of M. Axelrod on Detroit shows both the persistence of primary relations of sociability and the concomitant variation of participation in social relations and organized associations (Axelrod, 1956).

This type of behaviour, in so far as its "discovery" is bound up with studies of the new residential milieux of the American suburbs has made possible the emergence of new theses concerning the advent of a cultural form that seems to some extent to have superseded the urban type. The suburban way of life, of which so much has been said (Fava, 1956), is characterized by a veritable system of values, in particular, by the overwhelming importance of family values (in the sense of the nuclear family), a certain intensity of neighbourhood relations (usually polite, but distant), the constant search for an affirmation of social status and profoundly conformist behaviour. Thus, after dubbing the distinctive features of behaviour bound up with the competitive phase of capitalism "urban culture," we are now asked to call "suburban culture" the norms of the "consumer society," individualized and turned in upon its stratified comfort, bound up with the monopolistic phase and the standardization of social life.

Now, the first point to establish seems to be the supposed generality of this new mode of social life that extends the urban, by a process of renewal, outside the context of the city. Whereas, just as the cities presented historically a diversity of cultural contents, the "suburbs" and the residential units display an astonishing variety of modes of behaviour depending on their social structure. Thus, for example, to take only a minimum of studies that might serve as landmarks, Greer and Orleans (1962), in their inquiry into St Louis revealed a very high degree of simultaneous local and political participation and established important differences of attitude between the residential units, showing that they depended on the differential structure of the possibilities they offered.

In a particularly brilliant study of a working-class suburb in California, Bennet M. Berger (1960) sets out to demolish the myth of "suburban culture." His principal empirical discoveries are the following: weak residential mobility, given the economic constraints to which the inhabitants are subjected; a persistence of interest in national politics; on the other hand, weak participation in associations; great poverty of informal social relations; the dominant role of television, a turning in upon the home, little going out, etc. Such a picture, in contradiction with the model of active local participation, leads him to conclude that the mode of life proposed as suburban is, in fact, the model of behaviour of the middle class and that the suburbs do not have a social specificity, only an ecological one. Wendell Bell (1969), through a review of the literature, also shows the diversity of cultural relations in terms of the social characteristics of the residential milieux.

Things become more obvious if one leaves the American cultural context where the myth was forged. Ferrarotti's (1970) important study of the *borgate* of Rome presents a completely different panorama of life in the suburbs. Thus, in *Borgata Alessandrina*, despite the rural origin of the inhabitants, there are practically no social relations on the local plane and, by savagely opposing any threat of promiscuity, the family becomes the sole point of support, completely cut off from the surrounding milieu. The terms are reversed, on the other hand, in the system of relations observed by Gutkind (1966) in the outskirts of Kampala (Uganda): while integrated into urban life, a strong local community exists where everyday life is concerned, and networks of families, friends and neighbours profoundly interpenetrate one another.

In France, observations tend, despite various divergences, to confirm the thesis of the non-existence of a "suburban" model of behaviour beside an "urban" model centred on the *quartier* as such. Thus, although the interesting inquiry by Gabrielle Sautter (1963) into a new district at Pontoise (in the Paris region) depicts a local lower-middle class sociability very close to that of the American "suburb," Retel (1965) concludes his inquiry into social relations in the Paris suburbs by declaring that "urban social life, after passing through a phase of territorial structuring, will find a new lease of life in a strictly socio-logical structuring of urban groups among themselves," given the poverty of social relations of a local kind. Ledrut (1968: 37), in his research into the *grands ensembles* (high-rise housing estates) of Toulouse finds a "fairly good social climate," frequent visits between neighbours and easy, though superfi-cial, relations. Furthermore, he shows that such a situation does not come about by chance: it stems from the non-isolation and social heterogeneity of the milieu for, according to his hypothesis, "the isolation of a residential collectivity, of high density, and feeble differentiation, is the determining con-dition of the most intense social pressure and the sharpest tensions." Now, such a perspective goes beyond a mere observation of the existence or non-existence of a model of behaviour defined by the residential milieu, and is orientated towards the search for differential conditions of relation between these two terms.

Similarly, when Chombart de Lauwe (1965: 67) approaches the cultural problematic of the *quartier*, also proposed by some researchers as specific communities of life, he links it to the urban ensemble, considering the *quartier* as an "elementary unit" of this ensemble, with economic and geographical limits and particular urban and social functions. This means that the "culture of the *quartier*," together with "suburban culture" sometimes offered as par-ticular cultural models, expresses a certain conception of the space/culture relation and that there is no possible urban problematic without previous examination of the ecological foundations of such behaviour.

2 Are there specific urban units?

Although it is obvious that there is a fractional differentiation of urban space linked to the social division of labour, it is much less clear that there are residential units ecologically marked off in such a way that they make it possible to break up an urban area into sub-ensembles possessing real specificity. Now, the existence of such ecological units seems a prior condition of the question as to whether certain spaces determine a certain form of behaviour. Indeed, how could one pose the problem, if there were no real differentiation of residential space?

The tradition of urban ecology tried to define the conditions of existence, within the city, of "natural areas" which, in the classic definition of Paul Hatt (1946: 423–7), were made up of two elements: (1) a spatial unit, limited by natural frontiers within which one finds a homogeneous population with a system of specific values; (2) a spatial unit inhabited by a population structured by internal symbolic relations. There is, therefore, a *link* between ecological frontiers and social characteristics at the very level of the definition of the urban unit.

Such a link between the spatial context and social practice is at the root of the historical typology drawn up by Ledrut in order to differentiate the various forms of territorial collectivity (Ledrut, 1967; see also Frankenberg, 1966). Drawing up a sort of continuum in terms of the increasing complexity of society, Ledrut distinguishes between:

The village, fairly homogeneous, with weak internal differentiation, in which the essential spatial relations involve circulation around centres of activity.

The neighbourhood, defined above all on the basis of residence and of the networks of mutual help and personal contacts that are created in it.

The small town (bourg), a grouping of residences with which an activity is associated and which constitutes, in the strict sense of the term, a community, that is to say, "the spatial, concrete extension that represents the living sphere of the life of each individual," in which one finds, for example, common collective amenities and in which space is on a pedestrian scale.

The quarter, which has a double delimitation: it is provided with public amenities, accessible to the pedestrian; but, in addition, it is constituted around a sub-culture and represents a significant break in the social structure, being capable of reaching even a certain institutionalization in terms of local autonomy.

Lastly, *the city* is posited as a gathering at a higher level of individuals or groups, whereas the *megalopolis* presupposes a spreading of the primary units, foreshadowing, perhaps, a restructuring of local life on other bases.

Now, what is disturbing, even in a categorization as elaborated as that of Ledrut, is the constant repetition of this link between a certain space and a certain culture that seems to be given through an empirically mappable type of territorial collectivity. Now Ledrut himself, after defining the conditions of emergence of these quarters (1968: 148) observes that they are practically non-existent in the Toulouse urban area (1968: 275) and concludes, in another work, that social life is polarized around two extremes, the city and one's residence, with scarcely any possibility of survival for "intermediary groups" in modern society (Ledrut, 1967).

Similarly, the pioneering inquiry of Ruth Glass (1948), which tries to begin by delimiting the ecological frontiers of the neighbourhood units, establishes thirty-six economico-sociographical neighbourhood units for the town studied, but these units prove (with five exceptions) not to coincide with the social use of space. We may, in effect, divide an urban space into as many units as we wish, with the help of a whole battery of criteria. But each division bears an implicit proposition and, consequently, the social specificity of such sub-ensembles is not itself given. In the case of the Glass inquiry, it is very interesting to observe the specificity of the five sectors in which ecological and social specificities do overlap: they are the poor, isolated and socially very homogeneous zones. Since then, Suzanne Keller (1968) has tried to demonstrate the interesting hypothesis that since what reinforces the residential community seems to be precisely its weak capacity for general social initiative, there would seem to be an inverse correlation between local sociability, forming part of a system of generalized interaction, and the existence of a strong cultural specificity bound up with an ecological zone. Similarly, the feeling of attachment to the quarter seems to reflect a general attitude in relation to living conditions, rather than to the characteristics of the surrounding context.

If one then considers whether the polemic is borne out by the properly ecological specificity of the new suburban housing estates, one obtains similar results. Thus, for example, Walter T. Martin's (1958) study of the ecology of the suburbs in the United States distinguishes between the characteristics proper to these residential zones and those that are derived from them. Now, all those belonging to the first group are ecological truisms: location outside the city centre, the importance of commuting, smaller size and less density; but, still more, the derived factors (the predominance of young couples with children, the "middle-class" level, a certain social homogeneity) derive rather from selective migration, which is fundamental to the constitution of these zones. They are, then, "displaced segments" of the social structure, rather than local collectivities structuring themselves in relation to a certain use of space.

Identical discoveries are to be found in the abundant literature on the American suburbs, especially in the classic studies by Dobriner (1958) and Taueber and Taueber (1964).

In France, Paul Clerc's (1967) inquiry into the *grands ensembles* has resulted in showing (astonishingly in view of the social image one generally has of them) a fairly minimal difference between the socio-economic composition of the *grands ensembles* and the urban areas adjacent to them (except for the proportion of "employers," which is very low in the *grands ensembles*, and that of middle management, which is very high). Should we conclude that the *grands ensembles* have no social significance? This would be over hasty, for the fact of concentrating on a limited space the average profile of an urban area – a profile that extends, in reality, through a wide differentiation – is in itself a significant situation. And, furthermore, as Chamboredon and Lemaire (1970) have shown, it would be necessary to differentiate the upper stratum of the population, which is in a process of renewal – the *grands ensembles* being a step in its social progress – from that which permanently remains there and thus constitutes the social base of the milieu of relation. But this goes beyond the question of the ecological specificity of the *grands ensembles* and draws them into a certain social process that still remains to be defined.

This is why one remains sceptical when Chombart de Lauwe (1965) defines the quarters as elementary units of social life "that reveal themselves to the attentive observer," and which are expressed in "the behaviour of the inhabitants, their turn of phrase." These quarters, which, for Chombart de Lauwe, seem to be structured around both socio-economic amenities and meeting-places (above all cafés), are not ecologically given, urban districts, the basis of the urban area, linked together like the parts of a puzzle, but, as the same author observes (1963: 33), "they really exist only in the sectors in which the standard of living is fairly low"; they are produced, in fact, by a certain situation, and the community spirit of the quarter seems to be the result of a certain combination of social life, work life and situation with regard to the relations of production and consumption, both linked through a certain space, rather in the way that Henri Coing (1966) retraces the image of a Parisian quarter demolished by urban renewal.

Henceforth the empiricist debate concerning the existence or non-existence of quarters in modern society, or the possible emergence of new social links in the suburban housing estates, quite simply has no meaning, put in these terms: one does not discover "quarters" as one sees a river, one constructs them; one maps the processes that culminate in the structuring or de-structuring of the social groups in their "inhabiting" (*habiter*), that is to say, one integrates in the processes the role played by the "spatial context," which amounts therefore to denying space as "context," and incorporating it as an element in a certain social practice.

This is what Henri Lefebvre did when, after analysing the community ideology that is at the base of the "quarter, the natural unit of social life," he proposed to study, not the ossified socio-ecological forms (which are, by definition, inapprehensible), but the tendencies of the urban units, their inertia, their explosion, their reorganization, in a word, the practice of "inhabiting," rather than the ecology of the habitat (Lefebvre, 1967). The ideology of the quarter consists precisely in treating the forms of social life as natural phenomena linked to a context.

Thus, just as "urban" or "suburban" culture refers constantly to a spatial specificity, without naming it, the theme of residential units (quarters, suburbs, etc.) has meaning only through the implicit link that is made between an ecological context and a cultural content. The direct link between social and spatial variables seems, therefore, to be at the centre of the whole problematic of urban sub-cultures.

3   *Is there a production of the social by a specific spatial environment?*
In coming down from the heights of the philosophy of history to social research the theses of urban culture become operational; they try to show the

link between certain modes of behaviour and the ecological context in which, according to the culturalist hypotheses, they are grounded. This type of research has a long history and continues to be a privileged tool of "explanation by co-variation," a veritable safeguard of the good conscience of the "empirical sociologist."

It is all the more interesting to sketch the analysis of this perspective in that, on the one hand, it expresses in all its purity the relation of causality postulated between space and culture and that, on the other hand, it serves as a scientific (because observed) foundation for the most general theoretical constructions.

Thus, for example, the classic research by Faris and Dunham (1939) into the ecology of deviance, in Chicago, tried to verify Wirth's theses as to the unbalancing character of the urban milieu, by showing the gradual diminution in the rate of mental illness as one moved further away from the centre of the urban area. Now, this famous study, taken up and extended later to other spheres by dozens of researchers (for example, by Marshall Clinard (1960) to the analysis of criminal behaviour) was based on statistics relating to the public hospitals – which immediately invalidates the observation for if, in the city centre, the socio-economic level of the population causes it to become concentrated in the public hospitals, in the middle-class suburbs, there is a diversification, with a high proportion of patients in private clinics, thus diminishing the rate of illness for the sector. Furthermore, in relation to "criminal behaviour," research like that of Boggs (1964) has shown the close relationship between the attitude to dominant norms and social categories, at the root of ecological co-variations.

If one turns to the level of housing, the determination of behaviour by the habitat is even more uncertain. Of course, the standard of the housing, the overcrowding that one has to put up with, are socially significant, but, again, it is not a question of a social relation, for according to Chombart de Lauwe's perceptive summing up in the now classic inquiry into the question (1960: 77), "it appears that the critical attitude with regard to housing refers more to the way in which this housing is distributed than to the architectural aspect of it."

Furthermore, the way of inhabiting (and therefore the behaviour that should normally undergo the influence of the habitat most directly) is highly differentiated according to the social groups, in each of the new residential units studied by Chombart and his team. Does this mean that the disposition of the housing has no influence on the way of life? Not at all! The relation between habitat and inhabiting operates via a complex link between the specific social characteristics of the inhabitant and the symbolic and functional content of the housing, which takes us far away from any attempt to explain a subculture in terms of a form of habitat.

This being the case, if ecological determinism, in its most elementary forms, has been generally superseded, urban culturalism has been strengthened by a series of studies proposing a certain spatial environment as explanatory of a specific social ambiance, whether in the production of a "traditional" community in the quarters of the old urban nuclei or of a new way of life (the "suburbanism" of the Americans and British) in the suburban housing estates.

One of the best expressions of this perspective is, for example, the technically impeccable research carried out by Sylvia F. Fava (1958) into the system of neighbour relations in three different contexts (a central quarter of New York, the outskirts of the same city and a local suburb). After observing seven variables that ought to have explained the differences of behaviour (sex, age, civil status, educational level, length of residence, origin, size of community of origin), the inquiry reveals the increasing importance of neighbour relations, according to the classic "middle-class" model, as the spatial context moves out towards the suburbs. Hence one deduces the opposition between two cultural models ("urban" and "suburban").

Obviously, one could cite many other inquiries that lead to quite opposite results: for example, Ross's (1965) study of two residential zones, central and peripheral, of the same city of New York, in which differences of life-style are linked above all to the internal cleavages in each zone, according to social characteristics and age groups.

But the problem is not to come down on one side or other: this diversity of situations certainly corresponds to an ensemble of social processes at work, whose concrete combinations lead to different modes of behaviour. This is what Willmott and Young (1960a, b) tried to grasp in their comparative studies of a London working-class quarter and a middle-class suburb. They concluded by establishing a continuum, moving from a model of community relations to a polite but superficial sociability, with, at one extreme the workers of the working-class quarter and, at the other, the middle-class of the suburb and, between them, the workers of this same suburb.

But this interaction between the two types of determinants is not equivalent to recognizing a specificity of the spatial context as such, for the fact of living in a residential unit in which a social group is in the majority may be expressed sociologically as the existence of a social sub-culture, linked to the dominant group and not to the spatial context, which, if taken as a system of cultural reference, affects the behaviour of the minority group (Bell and Forge, 1957). The influence of the variables of social affiliation, with the related phenomena of condensation, distribution and interaction seem ultimately determinant. Both Ledrut's inquiry, already mentioned, into the Toulouse *grands ensembles* and Whyte's (1958) observations on the residential suburb of Park Forest in the Chicago area, show the essential role of social homogeneity if a certain type of behaviour is to develop, directly linked to the social characteristics of the residents. Once this behaviour occurs, spatial concentration may come into play, reinforcing the established system of relations.

In another context, an interesting study by Ion Dragan (1970) of the new district of Crisana, in the Romanian town of Slatina, reveals the profound differentiation of a system of behaving according to social categories within the same housing estate and, in particular, establishes the link between the importance of neighbour relations and the immediately rural origin of the migrants. This supports yet again the thesis of the cultural specificity of the social groups and contradicts the link between these neighbour relations and the suburban way of life (for they are practised to a far less degree by the "suburbanites" of urban extraction).

This predetermination of behaviour by social groups, themselves a function of the place occupied in the social structure, is found again in analyses of "district life" as many investigations in Europe and the United States show (see, for America, Beshers, 1962; for England, Pahl, 1970; for France, Castells, 1968). Among other examples, one striking illustration of the differentiation of social life within the same urban context is the recording made by C. L. Mayerson (1965) of the everyday life of two boys, living a few yards from one another in the centre of New York, one of whom is Puerto Rican and the other the son of well-off, middle-class parents.

Even when a residential zone is strongly defined from the ecological point of view, as in the case of the "marginal" communities established on the periphery of the Latin American cities (sometimes in the city centre, as in Rio), the social differentiation explodes the cultural norms into so many segments. There too, to take only one example, the CIDU inquiry into the enormous "marginal sector" of Manuel Rodriguez, in Santiago, Chile, shows that "each of the sub-populations – differentiated above all in terms of resources and occupation – reveal different standards of living, a different set of values and various degrees of social participation" (Munizaga and Bourdon, 1970: 31). Furthermore, the working-class strata are those that show greater cohesion and a higher level of mobilization, social and political, contrary to the supposed law that links local participation to a "middle-class" model of behaviour.

This does not mean that the concentration of certain social characteristics in a given space has no effect and that there cannot be any link between a certain ecological site and cultural specificity. The North American slums and ghettos are a concrete manifestation of the importance of the organization of a certain space in reinforcing a system of behaviour (Suttles, 1968). But for such effects to be manifested, there must, first of all, be the social production of a certain cultural autonomy, and this production depends on the place occupied in the relations of production, the institutional system and the system of social stratification. Besides, the way in which the ecology accentuates the cultural effects produced is also radically determined; in the case of the American slums, for example, racial discrimination is twofold; it is manifested, on the one hand, by the distribution of "subjects" in the social structure and, on the other, by the distribution of housing and amenities in space. Their high cultural specificity results, therefore, from this correspondence and from the meaning it assumes in the sphere of social relations, through the conditions of the particular organization of the class struggle in the United States.

Similarly, the classic inquiries that try to demonstrate the link between residential proximity and choice of marriage partner ended by isolating a certain effect of spatial proximity (in so far as it increases the probability of interaction), but within a cultural definition of couples, itself determined by membership of different social milieux (Katz and Hill, 1958). Maurice Imbert's inquiry (1965), which shows how spatial distancing in relation to cultural centres reinforces the social differentiation determined by the socio-professional category, education and family situation, arrives at similar conclusions.

Although spatial forms may accentuate or deflect certain systems of behaviour, through the interaction of the social elements that constitute them, they have no independent effect and, consequently, there is no systematic link between different urban contexts and ways of life. Whenever a link of this order is observed, it is the starting-point for research rather than an explanatory argument. Specific urban milieux must, therefore, be understood as social products, and the space/society link must be established as a problematic, as an object of research rather than as an interpretative axis of the diversity of social life, contrary to an ancient tradition in urban sociology (see the work of the Chicago School, esp. Burgess and Bogue, 1964).

4   *Is there production of specific residential milieux by the values of social groups?*
In so far as research has shown the secondary role played by the ecological context in the determination of cultural systems, a reversal of the terms of the problem has taken place, and a strong intellectual tendency seems to be directed towards considering residential milieux as a specification of the norms and values emitted by the preponderant social group in each context. Thus, once again, there seem to be "urban sub-cultures," but their specificity seems to derive from the fact that each racial group chooses and produces a certain space in accordance with its type of behaviour.

In their conclusion on the celebrated problematic of the new American "suburban culture" Gist and Fava (1964) consider that it does in fact exist and that it expresses a profound reorganization in the system of values of American society, evolving from an individualistic, puritan, Protestant ethic towards a profoundly hedonistic, "social" ethic, based on sociability. The suburbs, inhabited by these new strata of the middle class, the bearers of the values of "consumer society" would seem, therefore, to be the *locus* of expression most suited to a particular life-style.

Wendell Bell (1958) goes further, for he sees the ecological form of the suburbs as directly dependent on the new values of these middle strata. These independent values seem to be of three kinds: the importance of family life, a professional career governed by regular upwards mobility, an interest in consumption. Suburbs, both on the symbolic plane and in terms of instrumentality, offer adequate conditions for the realization of these modes of behaviour. In which case, it is not at all surprising that this new culture should be suburban.

This perspective was developed much more vigorously by Melvin and Carolyn Webber (1967), who analyse the different relations to space implied by the values of the intellectual elite on the one hand and of the working class on the other. In the first case, the openness to the world that may be enjoyed by the elite favours a "cosmopolitan" type of relation to time and space, which determines high residential mobility and a habitat that opens on to a multiplicity of relations. On the other hand, for the working class, the impossibility of predicting the future and the need to define oneself always here and now enforce a certain "localism" and the concentration of the residential community around particularly secure primary links. The different types of residential milieux are, therefore, the direct ecological expression of the particular orientations of each of the groups.

In a very different context, the excellent inquiry by Mario Gaviria and his team into the outlying quarter of Gran San Blas, in Madrid (Gaviria et al., 1968) even manages to show how the structuring and functioning of a new town of 52,000 inhabitants are directly determined by the underlying concept of social relations (in this precise case, the urban paternalism of the Falangist unions). As the research report observes, "the conception of an entirely working-class quarter, socially differentiated in space – it is situated close to the industrial zones – a quarter in which all the streets bear the names of trades and jobs, which is inhabited mainly by workers, in which all the public buildings are constructed according to the plans of the unions and in which there was an architectural competition to erect a monument in honour of 'the producer slain in the war' – such a conception is full of sociological significance." (It must be remembered that the unions in question are the fascist unions, the only ones having legal existence in Spain. The war referred to is, of course, the Spanish Civil War.)

It reflects, in physical terms, a society divided into classes and spatially deliberately differentiated: industrial zones, union housing, working-class population, "monument to the producer." It is a form of urbanistic development that "runs the risk of proving full of surprises" (1968: 104).

Gran San Blas obviously represents an extreme case, in so far as residential space is seldom shaped in so direct a way by an overall social conception. Furthermore, one might say that it expresses a specific social relation: that of the direct domination of inhabiting (working-class inhabiting) by a bureaucratic institution possessed of full powers over the habitat. And even in this case, if the residential space presents a certain social coherence in its configuration, the residential milieu that has been constituted in it does not seem to adjust without difficulty to the social appropriation that was envisaged. This residential milieu results rather from the encounter, not always a harmonious one, between the projected environment (linked to a certain policy with regard to the habitat) and the social practice of the inhabitants.

And, in reality, it is the necessary dislocation between the system of the production of space and the system of the production of values and the link between the two in social practice that makes quite impossible the relevance of hypotheses concerning the constitution of the residential milieux as mere projections of the values of each group. In effect, society is not the pure expression of cultures as such, but a more or less contradictory articulation of interests and therefore of social agents, which never present themselves simply as themselves but always, at the same time, in relation to something else. Nor is residential space a page on which the imprint of social values is laid. It is, on the one hand, historically constituted, and on the other, articulated within the social structure as a whole – and not only with the ideological instance.

Consequently, when there is a precise correspondence between the values of a group and the residential community, as a social and ecological unit, it is a question, once again, of a specific social relation, which is not given in the mere internal characteristics of the group, but expresses a social process that must then be established.

Nor can "urban sub-cultures" be regarded as the production of an ecologico-social context by cultural values specific to a group, fraction or social class. When they exist in their specificity, they represent a certain situation whose significance is always discoverable by analysis.

Furthermore, rather than discovering the existence of demonstrating the non-existence of localized types of social relations, we should lay bare the processes of articulation between the urban units and the system of producing social representations and practices. This seems to be the theoretical space connoted by the problematic of the residential sub-cultures.

Many of the observations and arguments advanced in the course of this chapter may have seemed elementary and no more than common sense. This is all the more reason to cling to them and to recall: (1) that there is no cultural system linked to a given form of spatial organization; (2) that the social history of humanity is not determined by the type of development of the territorial collectivities; (3) that the spatial environment is not the root of a specificity of behaviour and representation.

In fact, a pious silence on such digressions would have underestimated the power and influence of the urban ideology, its power of evoking everyday life, its ability to name the phenomena in terms of the experience of each individual and to replace explanation. Urban sociology was founded on these themes, cultural analyses of development derive their support from them, the discourses of moralists and politicians are inspired by them (using a wide gamut of registers), the theoreticians of the "cultural revolution" of the western petty bourgeoisie patch up the myth in order to give a "material base" to their theses on the mutation of our societies. Lastly, the treatment of the fundamental problem, of the relation between "the urban" and the ideological system, required the foregoing theoretical delimitation of so confused a terrain.

Having identified the theoretical question to which the problematic of the "urban sub-culture" refers, we have scarcely progressed in its treatment, for the study of the articulation of the ideological instance within the specificity of the urban units leaves the essence of the difficulty vague. In effect, although the ideological level, despite all its difficulties, may be relatively recognized and defined in theoretical terms, what exactly is one talking about when one refers to "urban units"? The relation between "ideology" and "urban" (and, therefore, between "ideology" and "space") cannot be studied without a previous analysis in depth of the social content of "the urban," that is to say, without an analysis of urban structure.

REFERENCES

Anderson, N. (1962) "The urban way of life," *International Journal of Comparative Sociology*, 3 (2): 175–288.

Axelrod, M. (1956) "Urban structure and social participation," *American Sociological Review*, February.

Bell, W. (1958) "Social choice, life styles and suburban residence," in W. Dobriner (ed.), *The Suburban Community*. New York: Putnams.

Bell, W. (1969) "Urban neighborhoods and individual behaviour," in P. Meadows and E. H. Mizruchi (eds), *Urbanism, Urbanization and Change*. Reading, MA: Addison-Wesley.

Bell, W. and Forge, T. (1957) "Urban neighborhood types and participation in formal associations," *American Sociological Review*, 2 (1): 25–34.

Berger, B. M. (1960) *Working Class Suburb: Study of Autoworkers in Suburbia*. Berkeley, CA: University of California Press.

Beshers, J. M. (1962) *Urban Social Structure*, Glencoe, IL: The Free Press.

Boggs, S. L. (1964) "Urban crime patterns," *American Sociological Review*, 4: 522–9.

Burgess, E. W. and Bogue, D. J. (eds) (1964) *Contributions to Urban Sociology*. Chicago, IL: University of Chicago Press.

Castells, M. (1968) "Y-a-t-il une sociologie urbaine?", *Sociologie du Travail*, 1.

Castells, M. (1969) "Théorie et ideologie en sociologie urbaine," *Sociologie et Sociétés*, 1, (2): 171–91.

Chamboredon, J. C. and Lemaire, M. (1970) "Proximité spatiale et distance sociale dans les grands ensembles," *Revue Française de Sociologie*, January: 3–73.

Chombart de Lauwe, P. H. (1960) *Famille et habitation*. Paris: CNRS 1.

Chombart de Lauwe, P. H. (1963) *Des hommes et des villes*. Paris: Payot.

Chombart de Lauwe, P. H. (1965) *Paris, essais de sociologie, 1952–1964*. Paris: Les Editions Ouvrières.

Clerc, P. (1967) *Grands ensembles, banlieues nouvelles*. Paris: PUF.

Clinard, M. B. (1960) "A cross-cultural replication of the relations of urbanism to criminal behaviour," *American Sociological Review*, April: 253–7.

Coing, H. (1966) *Rénovation urbaine et changement social*. Paris: Les Editions Ouvrières.

Commissariat Général au Plan (1970) *Les villes: la société urbaine*. Paris: A. Colin.

Dewey, R. (1960) "The rural–urban continuum: real but relatively unimportant," *American Journal of Sociology*, 66, (1): 60–7.

Dhooge, J. (1961) "Tendances actuelles en sociologie urbaine," *Social Compass*, 8 (3): 199–209.

Dobriner, W. H. (1958) "Local and cosmopolitan as contemporary suburban character types," in W. H. Dobriner (ed.), *The Suburban Community*. New York: Putnams.

Dragan, I. (1970) "Rhythme de l'urbanisation et intégration urbaine des migrateurs d'origine rurale," Communication au Congrès mondial de sociologie, Varna.

Duncan, O. D. and Reiss, A. J. (1956) *Social Characteristics of Urban and Rural Communities*. New York: John Wiley.

Faris, R. E. L. and Dunham, H. W. (1939) *Mental Disorders in Urban Areas*. Chicago, IL: University of Chicago Press.

Fava, S. F. (1956) "Suburbanism as a way of life," *American Sociological Review*, 21: 34–7.

Fava, S. F. (1958) "Contrast in neighbouring: New York City and a suburban community," in W. Dobriner (ed.), *The Suburban Community*. New York: Putnams.

Ferrarotti, F. (1970) *Roma da capitale a pereferia*. Rome: Laterza.

Frankenberg, R. (1966) *Communities in Britain*. London: Penguin.

Gaviria, M. et al. (1968) "Gran San Blas," *Revista de Arguitectura*, Madrid.

Gist, N. P. and Fava, S. F. (1964) *Urban Society*. New York: Thomas Crowell.

Glass, Ruth (ed.) (1948) *The Social Background of a Plan: A Study of Middlesbrough*. London: Routledge and Kegan Paul.

Greer, S. (1962) *The Emerging City*. Glencoe, IL: The Free Press.

Greer, S. and Orleans, P. (1962) "The mass society and the parapolitical structure," *American Sociological Review*, 27: 634–46.

Guterman, Stanley S. (1969) "In defense of Wirth's urbanism as a way of life," *American Journal of Sociology*, 74: 492–9.

Gutkind, P. C. W. (1966) "African urban family life and the urban system," *Journal of Asian and African Studies*, 1: 35–42.

Hatt, P. (1946) "The concept of natural area," *American Sociological Review*, 11: 423–7.

Imbert, M. (1965) "Aspects comparés de la vie de loisir à Paris et en banlieue," CEGS.

Katz, D. and Hill, T. (1958) "Residential propinquity and marital selection," *Marriage and Family Living*, 20: 27–35.

Keller, S. (1968) *The Urban Neighbourhood: A Sociological Perspective*. New York: Random House.

Ledrut, R. (1967) *Sociologie urbaine*. Paris: PUF.

Ledrut, R. (1968) *L'espace social de la ville*. Paris: Anthropos.

Lefebvre, H. (1967) "Quartier et vie de quartier," Paris: Cahiers de l'IAURP 7.

Lefebvre, H. (1968) *Le droit à la ville*. Paris: Anthropos.

Lefebvre, H. (1970a) *Du rural et de l'urbain*. Paris: Anthropos.

Lefebvre, H. (1970b) *La révolution urbaine*. Paris: Gallimard.

Lefebvre, H. (1971) "La ville et l'urbain," *Espaces et Sociétés*, 2.

Lerner, D. (1958) *The Passing of Traditional Society: Modernizing the Middle East*. Glencoe, IL: The Free Press.

Lewis, O. (1953) "Tepoztlan restudied: a critique of the folk–urban conceptualization of social changes," *Rural Sociology*, 18: 121–38.

Mann, P. H. (1965) *An Approach to Urban Sociology*. London: Routledge.

Martin, W. T. (1958) "The structuring of social relationships engendered by suburban residence," in W. Dobriner (ed.), *The Suburban Community*. New York: Putnams.

Mayerson, C. L. (1965) *Two Blocks Apart*. New York: Holt, Rinehart and Winston.

Miner, H. (1952) "The folk–urban continuum," *American Sociological Review*, 17: 529–37.

Munizaga, G. and Bourdon, C. (1970) *Sector Manuel Rodriguez: Estudio de un sector habitacional popular en Santiago de Chile*. Santiago de Chile: CIDU.

Pahl, R. E. (1970 *Patterns of Urban Life*. London: Longmans.

Park, R. E. (1925) "The city: suggestions for the investigation of human behaviour in the urban environment," in R. E. Park, E. W. Burgess, and R. D. McKenzie (eds), *The City*. Chicago, IL: University of Chicago Press.

Popenoe, D. (1963) "On the meaning of urban in urban studies," *Urban Affairs Quarterly*, 6, reprinted in P. Meadows and E. H. Mizruchi (eds), *Urbanism, Urbanization and Change*. Reading, MA: Addison-Wesley, 1969.

Poulantzas, N. (1968) *Pouvoir politique et classes sociales de l'état capitaliste*. Paris: Maspero.

Redfield, R. (1941) *The Folk Culture of Yucatan*. Chicago, IL: University of Chicago Press.

Redfield, R. (1947) "The folk society," *American Journal of Sociology*, 3 (4): 293–308.

Redfield, R. (1954) "The cultural role of cities," *Economic Development and Cultural Change*, 4.

Retel, J. O. (1965) "Quelques aspects des relations sociales dans l'agglomeration parisienne," in C. Cornuau, M. Imbert, B. Lamy, P. Rendu, and J. O. Retel (eds), *L'attraction de Paris sur sa banlieue*. Paris: Les Editions Ouvrières.

Reissman, L. (1964) *The Urban Process*. Glencoe, IL: The Free Press.

Ross, H. L. (1965) "Uptown and downtown: a study of middle-class residential areas," *American Sociological Review*, 30 (2).

Sautter, Gabrielle (1963) "Naissance de la vie sociale dans un nouveau quartier (Pontoise)," Paris (roneo).

Simmel, G. (1950) "The metropolis and mental life," in K. Wolff (ed.), *The Sociology of Georg Simmel*. Glencoe, IL: The Free Press.

Sjoberg, C. (1965) "Cities in developing and in industrial societies: a cross-cultural analysis," in P. Hauser and L. F. Schnore (eds), *The Study of Urbanization*. New York: John Wiley, pp. 213–65.

Spengler, O. (1928) *The Decline of the West*, vol. 2. London: Allen and Unwin.

Suttles, G. D. (1968) *The Social Order of the Slum*. Chicago, IL: University of Chicago Press.

Taueber, K. E. and Taueber, A. F. (1964) "White migration and socio-economic differences between cities and suburbs," *American Sociological Review*, 5: 718–29.

Utopie (1970) *Urbaniser la lutte de classes*. Paris.

Webber, M. C. and Webber, C. C. (1967) "Culture, territoriality and the elastic middle," in H. W. Eldredge (ed.), *Taming Megalopolis*. New York: Anchor Books.

Weber, Max (1905) *The City* (1966). Glencoe, IL: The Free Press.

Whyte, W. H. (1958) "Urban sprawl," in the Editors of *Fortune* (ed.), *The Exploding Metropolis*, Garden City, NY: Doubleday, pp. 115–39.

Willmott, P. and Young, M. (1960a) *Family and Kinship in East London*. London: Routledge.

Willmott, P. and Young, M. (1960b) *Family and Class in a London Suburb*. London: Routledge.

Wirth, L. (1938) "Urbanism as a way of life," *American Journal of Sociology*, July.

Wirth, L. (1964) *On Cities and Social Life*. Chicago, IL: University of Chicago Press.

PART TWO
Social Movements and Urban Culture

CHAPTER
THREE

Immigrant Workers and Class Struggles in Advanced Capitalism: The Western European Experience

(1975)

Since the great social upheaval of May 1968 in France, class struggles in Western Europe seem to have re-entered a period of progressive development, both through a strengthening of trade-union and traditional political practices and through the appearance of new issues and the mobilization of new social strata around these issues. Thus the "old mole" was far from dormant and its underground workings led sometimes to explosions of mass rage, and sometimes to the consolidation of new bases of protest and opposition to the system.

Among these new developments, the issue of immigration and the mobilization of migrants are particularly prominent. As the major trump card in capitalist expansion, and as the bogy scapegoat of the bourgeoisie always ready to feed the fires of xenophobia and racism, as a pretext for a reluctantly renewed charity, as a myth in mobilizing the European left and as a source of confusion for trade-unions and left-wing parties, immigrant workers constitute both in the reality of their daily oppression and in their potential for social revolt, one of the most important and least known stakes in the newly emerging class struggles of advanced capitalism.

In view of the complexity of the subject, the mass of fragmentary information and the scarcity of adequate economic and statistical data, any analysis of immigrant workers must start out from carefully defined objectives. The problematic we take as a starting-point conditions all our efforts at interpretation, and provides a framework which organizes our approach to this reality. Our aim here is not to expose the scandal of the material conditions under which these workers live and work, nor to justify their presence in order to increase the tolerance of the indigenous population towards them.

Our point of departure is rather the fact of the growing importance of immigrant workers in the wage-earning working population of every country in Western Europe and the increase in political struggles and protest movements concerning them. For us the question is therefore to know the specific effect produced by immigrant workers on a class structure, and on the politics of the class struggle which result thus determined. In answering such a question we will at the same time be able to describe the class content of the struggles of immigrant workers themselves and thereby start to assess their political practices.

An analysis of class struggles must, of course, both be suggested by the practical expressions of these struggles and be able to account for them. But in order to arrive at such a result in an objective manner, it is necessary to start from the position of the immigrant labour force in the structure of social contradictions and from the role given to it by the historical development of the dominant element in this structure, namely, capital in its advanced monopolistic phase.

We shall start by recalling the fundamental structural tendencies of monopoly capitalism in Western Europe in order to locate the phenomenon of immigration within this specific social and economic logic. We will then draw out the implications for the class structure and for the trade-union and political practices which tend to flow from it. Finally we shall see how these different contradictions are articulated in the concrete history of newly emerging class struggles by referring more specifically to immigrant workers' movements in France. Our analysis remains at a fairly high level of generality and the small amount of statistical data used is illustrative rather than demonstrative in purpose. In fact a rigorous study of this subject within the problematic of the class struggle has yet to be undertaken. Thus the present [chapter] does not claim to be the endpoint of research within this perspective but, rather, a point of departure. It is thus necessary to pose theoretically rigorous and historically concrete questions in order to obtain, by stages, answers which, instead of provoking pity for the lot of immigrant workers, will provide them with elements capable of clarifying their practice.[1]

Uneven Development and the Internationalization of the Labour Force

At first glance, migratory movements may be analysed as simply the result of two laws of the capitalist mode of production: *the submission of the worker* to the organization of the means of production dictated by capital (and, hence, to its spatial concentration in areas regarded as most profitable); and the *uneven development* between sectors and regions, and between countries, in accordance with inter-capitalist competition and the political relationships between the major blocs under bourgeois hegemony historically constituted in the various social formations.

Seen this way, migratory movements have existed throughout capitalist development, and rural exodus and the decline of regions whose productive structure has been weakened in favour of the most advanced capitalist forms are basic features of the social structure which constitutes monopoly capitalism. Furthermore, one can even say that a veritable whirlpool of geographical and occupational mobility is inevitable to the extent that capital can only develop by continually decomposing those sectors which are backward compared to the most profitable forms. This frees an even larger labour force whose members lose their existing jobs and move into new posts created in the most advanced sectors, a movement which is far from automatic and which necessitates increasingly costly retraining.

This uneven development does not, of course, derive from disparities in the distribution of natural resources but from the logic of capital and the division of labour it commands according to the imperatives of the rate of profit. Thus, for example, the French steel industry will close down its iron mines in Lorraine and leave the area to establish itself by the sea (Dunkerque, Fos) where it will use imported iron ore from Mauritania and Brazil.[2] Furthermore, in certain cases a political logic (dependent on the general interest of capital) rather than an immediately economic logic is at the source of uneven regional development. Thus, for example, the dichotomy between the highly developed North of Italy and the poverty-stricken Mezzogiorno derives from the particular forms taken by the political bargain underlying the constitution of the dominant class bloc in Italy as a whole: the banking and industrial bourgeoisie of the North accepts the maintenance of the social status quo in the South in order not to overturn the Southern class structure which permits the domination of the traditional landed oligarchy. In exchange, the latter accepts bourgeois hegemony at the level of the state and guarantees the labour reservoir which has always been at the base of Italian capitalist growth.[3]

This same mechanism operates at the international level where labour concentration is determined by the growth of capital. For a long period before the Second World War, the advanced capitalist countries made sporadic use of labour from their colonies and from the backward European countries (Italy, Spain, Poland, etc.). In 1936 there were proportionately more foreigners in France than in 1972 (2,198,000 compared with a little under 4,000,000) and even at the time of the 1929 crisis 7 per cent of the French population were foreigners.

A brief analysis of the countries importing and exporting labour (see table 3.1) is illuminating on this point: the lower a country's level of development (e.g. as measured by per capita GNP) the higher the level of emigration, and vice versa.

At first sight, then emigration/immigration is simply a product of the un-

Table 3.1 Immigration from Mediterranean countries towards selected European countries

Country of emigration	Population 1971 (millions) (0)	Country of immigration									All countries (10)	(11) = $\frac{10}{0}$ = $\frac{\text{Emigrants in Europe}}{\text{Total population}}$ × 100
		Germany (1) (1971)	France (2) (1971)	Belgium (3) (1971)	Luxembourg (4) (1971)	Netherlands (5) (1971)	Switzerland (6) (1969)	Austria (7) (1971)	Sweden (8) (1971)	United Kingdom (9) (1966)		
Mediterranean Europe												
Spain	33,290	270,000	589,925	51,485	1,700	19,810	97,860	270		34,510	1,065,560	3.2
Greece	8,892	395,000	10,125	14,050		1,905	8,000	550	14,000	8,520	452,150	5.1
Italy	53,667	590,000	588,740	188,430	11,000		531,500	1,510	8,000	96,660	2,015,840	3.7
Portugal	9,630	55,214[a]	694,550	4,280	6,300	1,366	2,000			5,420	769,130	7.9
Turkey	35,232	653,000	18,325	12,250		21,746	9,651	22,415		4,310	741,697	2.1
Yugoslavia	20,527	594,000	65,220	2,930	400	7,454	20,800	131,835	37,000	12,290	871,929	4.2
North Africa												
Algeria	14,012	1,985[a]	754,462	3,740							760,187	5.4
Morocco	15,525	10,921	194,296	24,560		20,582					250,359	1.5
Tunisia	5,137	9,918[a]	106,845	1,640		339					118,742	2.3
Population of Mediterranean origin		2,580,038	3,022,488	303,365	19,400	73,202	669,811	156,580	59,000	161,710	7,045,594	3.6
Total foreign population		3,400,000	3,505,210	716,237	36,500	93,093	971,795	72,205	411,280	178,600	11,086,920	

Total population	195,912	61,281,000	51,004,300[b]	9,690,991	337,500[c]	12,878,000[d]	6,184,000[e]	7,391,000[f]	8,081,000	52,303,720
% foreigners in total population	5.55	6.87	7.39	10.81	0.72	15.71	2.3		5	3.4
Total foreign population (%)	76	86	42	53	78	69	90	14	9	63

Sources: (0) IAM Publications, Série Etudes et Documents, no. 6, April, 1973. *Yearbook of Mediterranean Countries*

(1) Federal Statistical Office, Bonn

[a] Employed foreign workers, end June 1971

(2) Ministry of the Interior, Paris. Total foreign population 31 December 1970, including refugees (99,160), exiles (4,082), seasonal workers and illegal immigrants

[b] *Yearbook of Labor Statistics*, 1970, ILO (provisional statistics 1 January 1971)

(3) National Statistical Institute, Brussels. Total foreign population 31 December 1970 including children, refugees and exiles. The data by nationality is drawn from the Administration for Public Safety, Brussels. Foreign population as of 31 December, 1972, except for children under 12 years

(4) Migrant workers only (*Source:* EEC)

[c] *Yearbook of Labor Statistics*, ILD (1969 population)

(5) Active foreign population (*Source:* Ministry for Social Affairs, the Hague. Data from 15 June, 1971)

[d] Total population in 1969 (*Source:* OECD, *Statistics on Active Population*, Paris 1971)

(6) Foreign population in December 1969 except for seasonal workers and border workers (*Source:* Foreigners Police, Bern)

[e] Total population 31 December 1969 (*Source:* OECD, *Statistics on Active Population*, Paris, 1971)

(7) Migrant workers only. Official statistics in November, 1971 reported in *Diako-nische Information*, Sonderheft 2 Diakonische Werk. F. Austria

[f] Total population in 1970 (*Source:* OECD)

(8) *Source:* The Swedish Institute, Stockholm, *Fact Sheets on Sweden*, December, 1971. Population in October, 1971

(9) Foreign population in England and Wales (statistics on Scotland where available) (*Source:* Survey of birthplaces, 10% sample)

(10) Total emigrants in Europe by country of emigration

(11) Share of emigrants in Europe as a percentage of total population of country of emigration

even development inherent in the capitalist mode of production which affects the labour force. It must be noted, however, that this is not the same as viewing migration simply as the product of a succession of economic conditions, and hence as capable of being absorbed into jobs created by economic growth within each country. On the contrary, uneven development is a structural tendency of the mode of production and the gaps between firms, sectors, trusts, regions or countries tend to increase rather than diminish. For example, in recent years, despite having the highest growth rate in Western Europe, Spain has had a regularly increasing level of emigration, with small movements around this trend caused much more by recessions in the countries receiving immigrants than by any decline in requests to emigrate. Similarly, there are over two million Italian workers in other European countries despite Italy's high growth rate and production level. The reasons for such a permanent emigrant labour force are clear from the point of view of the sending country: decomposition of backward productive structures – especially in agriculture; structural unemployment in certain sectors; and the much higher nominal and real wages available in the advanced capitalist countries.

But though differences in levels of development explain the causes of emigration, immigration into the advanced countries is governed by much more deepseated reasons which cannot be reduced simply to the manpower needs of the economy. If this were the cause, immigration would be a conjunctural phenomenon (and highly sensitive to the least sign of economic recession). While it is true that the employment situation is immediately reflected in increases and decreases in the level of immigration (thus, for example, the economic recession in Germany in 1967 resulted in the departure of a large number of immigrants, as shown in table 3.2), it is also the case that the long-term trend is continued growth in immigrant labour, which in 1972 represented at least 10 per cent of the working population in the advanced capitalist countries of Western Europe (the Common Market countries, Austria, Norway, Sweden and Switzerland). It might be argued that this is due precisely to the continuous economic growth of these countries, but this is completely tautological since immigrant labour is in fact one of the motors of this growth, rather than simply a result.[4]

Two facts seem to be particularly significant in this respect: first, the size of the immigrant labour force in the most productive sectors (especially in industry) and its position in the working population as a whole, make it impossible to regard it as a conjunctural phenomenon, even if one were to assume that it resulted simply from a superabundant supply of labour.

Thus, in 1972 there were 2,354,200 foreign workers in *Germany*, representing 10.8 per cent of all wage-earners. They constituted 25 per cent of workers in the building industry and 80 per cent in certain sectors of public works, but were also strongly represented in the metallurgical industry (11 per cent of all wage-earners). In *France*, according to official statistics, there were 1,800,000 immigrant workers on 1 January 1973 (8 per cent of the working population)

Table 3.2 Departures (returns) of foreign workers from Germany

Year	No.	Percentage of foreign workers
1966–67	500,814	46.3
1967–68	207,859	21.3
1968–69	194,550	15.4
1969–70	277,579	16.3
1970–71	308,417	14.9
1971–72	332,520	14.7

Source: SOPEMI, OECD

– a figure which appears to be an underestimate since it takes little account of clandestine work. In building and public works they represent 27 per cent of all workers (but this often rises to 90 per cent on building sites in the Paris region), in metal industries 17 per cent, and in extractive industry 16 per cent. There are 530,000 immigrant workers in the automobile industry, of whom 200,000 in the Paris region, i.e. 46 per cent of all semi-skilled workers, work on the assembly-line. In *Switzerland*, according to official figures for 1968, there were 817,000 immigrant workers representing 29.8 per cent of the working population, but with a high concentration in the building, machine-tool and hotel industries. Almost 40 per cent of workers in Swiss factories are foreigners, and when one considers solely directly productive work, they already constitute a clear majority. In *Belgium*, the 220,000 foreign workers employed in 1971 represented 7.2 per cent of the working population, and were particularly concentrated in the mining, building and metallurgical industries, and this despite a marked recession in the Walloon region, which led to measures to restrict immigration. In *The Netherlands*, the figure of 125,000 employed persons in 1972 (3.2 per cent of the working population) is lower than elsewhere due primarily to trade-union opposition to immigration. In *Denmark* the same phenomenon is found, foreign workers numbering only 30,000 in 1972. In *Great Britain*, the 1,780,000 immigrant workers in 1971 represented 7.3 per cent of the working population in the building and machine-tool industries, commerce and service industries. Immigrant labour is thus a fundamental element in the economic structure of European capitalism, and not simply an extra source of labour in conditions of rapid growth.

But there is a second fact, which is particularly disturbing: namely, the appearance over the long term (1950–70) of a parallel increase between unemployment and immigration in most of the countries, with the *possible* exception of Germany, where, for the most part, full employment seems to have been effectively achieved. A detailed analysis of changes in the levels of unemployment, immigration and productivity, by country, sector, and type of firm,

Table 3.3 Immigration, unemployment and economic growth in France, 1960–1971

Year	Immigration			Unemployment			Economic growth	
	No. of foreigners (thousands)	% foreigners in total population	Rate of growth of immigrant workers	No. (employees) (thousands)	% of active population	Rate of growth	Gross national product (US$ per capita)	Rate of growth
1960	2,178	4.7	1.0 (1959–60)	239,000	1.2	–	1,340	–
1961	2,306	4.9	1.5	203,000	1.0	0.84	1,450	1.08
1962	2,448	5.2	1.5	230,000	1.2	1.13	1,590	1.09
1963	2,574	5.3	1.1	273,000	1.4	1.18	1,750	1.10
1964	2,721	5.6	1.1	216,000	1.1	0.79	1,920	1.09
1965	2,828	5.8	0.9	269,000	1.3	1.24	2,040	1.02
1966	2,873	5.8	1.0	280,000	1.4	1.04	2,200	1.07
1967	2,941	5.9	0.8	365,000	1.8	1.30	2,350	1.06
1968	2,951	5.9	1.0	428,000	2.1	1.17	2,540	1.08
1969	3,122	6.2	1.3	337,000	1.6	0.78	2,790	1.09
1970	3,338	6.5	1.2	336,000	1.7	1.07	2,910	1.04
1971	3,608	7.0	1.0	456,000	2.1	1.25	–	–

1.0 means continuous stable new immigration; <1 means decreasing new immigration; >1 means increasing new immigration.
Sources: Ministère de l'Intérieur and Office National d'Immigration; and OECD

would be necessary in order to verify this tendency. However, certain indications may be obtained by examining the figures for unemployment and immigration in France (table 3.3) and the interrelation of changes in them [. . .]. A combination of two phenomena is apparent: in the short term, for each year, there is a correspondence between the increase in unemployment and the decline in immigration. But in the long term, *there is a tendency for both phenomena to increase together*. This is all the more significant in that the immigration statistics refer only to official entries (a smaller figure) which most closely follow changes in economic conditions.

In other countries, we find the following trends:

- In Belgium and in The Netherlands, unemployment is *stable* and immigration rises moderately. (So, in fact unemployment and immigration *coexist*) (see tables 3.4 and 3.5).

- In Germany, unemployment is stable at a low level; at the same time, immigration arises at a high rate. So, immigration is not produced by a full-employment situation in the labour market but by *selective full employment* (see table 3.6).

- In Switzerland and Luxembourg a real full-employment labour market exists for native workers, with an increasingly strong percentage of immigrants (29.8 per cent of the labour force in Switzerland and 27.8 per cent in Luxembourg). In these countries we could analyse immigration as a matter of labour supply. But even here this interpretation must be linked to an explanation in terms of the specific characteristics of immigrant labour force.

- In Britain, a stable immigrant labour force coexists with an increasing high rate of unemployment. In fact there is no complementary and opposite evolution of two phenomena as liberal economic theory could expect. The explanation must be in the terms of the structural position of immigrant workers in British industry. The case of Great Britain is extremely revealing in this respect because the permanent settlement of a large proportion of the immigrant labour force has been accompanied by a gradual increase in unemployment (up to 3 per cent in 1972) and by a considerable increase in the level of *emigration* by Britons, especially those with high skill to the United States. Thus there is no manpower shortage, but rather a reclassification of the characteristics required to carry out certain jobs.

We thus want to argue that immigration is not a conjunctural phenomenon linked to the manpower needs of expanding economies but a structural tendency characteristic of the current phase of monopoly capitalism. This structural tendency is supported by the discrepancies and disequilibria resulting from uneven development but it is explained primarily by the internal

Table 3.4 Immigration, unemployment and economic growth in Belgium, 1960–1970

Year	Immigration			Unemployment			Economic growth	
	No. of immigrant workers (thousands)	% of all employees	Rate of growth	No. (thousands)	% of active population (employees)	Rate of growth	Gross national product (US$ per capita)	Rate of growth
1960	–	–	–	–	–	–	1,250	–
1961	154,000	5.7	–	89,000	3.4	–	1,320	1.05
1962	157,000	5.8	1.01	75,000	2.8	0.84	1,410	1.06
1963	166,000	6.0	1.05	62,000	2.3	0.82	1,500	1.06
1964	185,000	6.5	1.11	55,000	2.0	0.88	1,660	1.10
1965	200,000	6.9	1.08	63,000	2.2	1.14	1,800	1.08
1966	203,000	7.0	1.01	67,000	2.4	1.06	1,920	1.06
1967	200,000	6.9	0.98	92,000	3.3	1.37	2,050	1.06
1968	196,000	6.7	0.98	110,000	3.9	1.19	2,160	1.05
1969	201,000	6.7	1.02	88,000	3.0	0.80	2,380	1.10
1970	208,000	6.9	1.03	76,000	2.6	0.86	2,670	1.12

Sources: EEC and OECD

Table 3.5 Immigration, unemployment and economic growth in The Netherlands, 1958–1971

	Immigration			Unemployment			Economic growth	
Year	No. of immigrant workers (thousands)	% of all employees	Rate of growth	No. (thousands)	% of active population (employees)	Rate of growth	Gross national product (US$ per capita)	Rate of growth
1958	29,900	0.9	–	–	–	–	–	–
1959	21,200	0.6	0.70	–	–	–	–	–
1960	24,100	0.7	1.13	50,000	1.2	–	980	–
1961	28,000	0.8	1.16	36,000	0.8	0.72	1,070	1.09
1962	32,000	0.9	1.14	35,000	0.8	0.97	1,140	1.06
1963	38,000	1.1	1.18	35,000	0.8	1.00	1,220	1.07
1964	51,600	1.4	1.35	32,000	0.7	0.91	1,420	1.16
1965	63,100	1.7	1.22	36,000	0.8	1.12	1,560	1.09
1966	76,300	2.0	1.20	46,000	1.0	1.27	1,670	1.07
1967	72,100	1.9	0.94	90,000	2.0	1.95	1,820	1.09
1968	80,300	2.1	1.11	84,000	1.8	0.93	1,990	1.09
1969	60,100	1.5	0.74	66,000	1.4	0.78	2,190	1.10
1970	–	–	–	56,000	1.2	0.84	2,400	1.09
1971	–	–	–	69,000	1.4	1.23	–	–

Sources: EEC and OECD

Table 3.6 Immigration, unemployment and economic growth in Germany, 1958–1972

Year	Immigration			Unemployment			Economic growth	
	No. of immigrant workers (thousands)	% of all employees	Rate of growth	No. (thousands)	% of active population (employees)	Rate of growth	Gross national product (US$ per capita)	Rate of growth
1958	127,000	0.7	–	–	–	–	–	–
1959	167,000	0.8	1.31	–	–	–	–	–
1960	279,000	1.4	1.60	271,000	1.4	–	1,300	–
1961	473,000	2.3	1.60	181,000	0.9	0.6	1,470	1.10
1962	629,000	3.0	1.33	154,000	0.7	0.8	1,580	1.00
1963	773,000	3.6	1.21	186,000	0.9	1.2	1,670	1.06
1964	902,000	4.2	1.16	169,000	0.8	0.9	1,810	1.08
1965	1,119,000	5.1	1.24	147,000	0.7	0.8	1,950	1.07
1966	1,244,000	5.7	1.11	161,000	0.8	1.09	2,050	1.05
1967	1,014,000	4.8	0.81	459,000	2.2	2.8	2,070	1.01
1968	1,019,000	4.8	1.00	323,000	1.5	0.7	2,240	1.08
1969	1,366,000	6.2	1.34	179,000	0.8	0.5	2,520	1.12
1970	1,948,900	9.0	1.42	149,000	0.7	0.8	3,030	1.20
1971	2,240,700	10.3	1.15	185,000	0.8	1.2	–	–
1972	2,354,200	10.8	1.05	–	–	–	–	–

Sources: EEC and OECD

dynamic of advanced capitalist societies. While uneven development explains why people emigrate, it does not explain why capital is ready to provide jobs for migrant workers in the advanced countries occasionally even in conditions of unemployment. Neither does it explain why the dominant classes introduce a social and political element (immigrant labour) whose presence contradicts their ideology and necessitates more complex mechanisms of social control. In other words, the extent of immigration and the strategic role of immigration in the European economy has to be explained, not in terms of the technical demands of production, but by the specific interests of capital in a particular phase of its development.

Crisis of Capitalism, Counter-tendencies of Economic Policy and Structural Role of Immigration

What are the current requirements of capital? And how are they translated into manpower policy, especially as regards immigrant labour?

In order to answer these questions we must introduce some elements of Marxist economic theory concerning the contradictory development of the capitalist mode of production. The basic structural contradiction demonstrated by Marx in Volume 3 of *Capital* concerned the *tendency for the rate of profit to fall*, as a result of the increase in the organic composition of capital made inevitable by competition among capitalists, monopolistic concentration and technical progress. If we consider only living labour, the labour force, as creating value, and hence surplus-value, and profit as deriving from it, given the increase in the organic composition of capital, then the rate of profit must fall since the variable capital used to pay the labour force grows more slowly than total capital (constant capital plus variable capital), and thus the source of value becomes proportionately smaller in relation to the mass of capital engaged in production. At the level of the system as a whole and in the long term, there is a tendency for the rate of profit to fall (even if the quantity of surplus-value increases) and hence for the system to move towards crisis to the extent that capital stops investing as investment ceases to be profitable.

However, even though certain studies suggest the validity of this analysis in past periods,[5] the tendencies identified are no more than *tendencies*, i.e. can be partly counteracted in the historical practice of capital by the more or less deliberate introduction of counter-tendencies through economic policy.[6] One of the main examples of such action is the devalorization or "putting to bed" of part of social capital, for which a lower or even nil rate of profit will be accepted, by placing it in the charge of the state. Moreover, this kind of action is combined with various subsidies and assistance from the state to the major private economic groups, drawing on collective resources, and thus removing a share from wages for purposes of accumulation. It may also be noted that state intervention extends to all fields, following the well-known Keynesian model, acting as regulator in every situation and *attempting* to establish a programme for monopoly capital.

Beyond the measures involving capital itself, the basic counter-tendency introduced into the system is an increase in the rate of surplus-value, i.e. the quantity of surplus-value produced by a given variable capital. This increase is obtained in two complementary ways: by higher *productivity* through technical progress (which increases the excess labour in relation to the labour necessary to reproduce the labour force) and by the *reinforcement of exploitation*, either in intensity, in extensiveness, or by reducing the mass of variable capital necessary for a certain quantity of surplus-value.

Thus the first question to be examined is this: *what is the relationship between the massive use of migrant labour and the counter-tendency to the tendency of the rate of profit to fall, especially with regard to the reinforcement of exploitation?*

There are other basic contradictions in the current phase of capitalism which, while related to the first, have relatively autonomous effects. On the one hand, there is the cyclical character of capitalist expansion with periodic recessions due to over-accumulation. Although the cyclical nature of crises was concealed during a long expansionary period, since 1967 Europe has again become used to the idea of sudden fluctuations in economic activity as a part of the functioning of the system. In order to avoid the disequilibrating effect of these fluctuations, due to the chain reactions they cause in the economy, advanced capitalism has set up a number of anti-cyclical mechanisms, one of the most important of which is precisely immigrant labour.

Finally, the excess of capitals seeking investment opportunities and the creation of a mass of floating capitals in the advanced economies, on the one hand, and the necessity for ever-faster growth inherent in monopoly capital, on the other, are the source of the *structural inflation* characteristic of capitalism today. We advance the hypothesis that immigration has a specific role as a basic deflationary factor in controlling these critical effects of inflation. While statistics and economics give little guidance on this subject, a number of suggestions are possible.

If we can determine the role of immigrant labour in the management of these key problems of advanced capitalism, we shall have simultaneously established its place in the structural contradictions and in the social interests underlying different immigration policies and underlying the protests of the workers themselves.

Immigration and the reinforcement of capitalist exploitation

In order to increase the degree of exploitation and raise the rate of surplus-value, capital makes use of two methods, usually in combination: (1) paying a

Table 3.7 Wages of foreign workers compared to all workers in France, 1968 (Employment Committee, VI Plan)

	Overall	*Foreigners*
Paris Region	1,441	1,190
Rhône-Alpes	1,051	878
Provence–Côte d'Azur	1,070	861
North	966	885
Lorraine	973	921
Languedoc	952	741
Alsace	989	892
France overall	1,095	973

This does not take duration of work into account.

proportionately smaller value for the reproduction of the labour force; (2) increasing the duration and intensity of work. We have stated that in both cases immigrant labour represents a decisive trump card for capital. Let us now examine this in more detail.

As far as the first point is concerned, immigrant labour displays the following characteristics:

- It is the part of the labour force that receives the lowest wages (see table 3.7).
- It is the part whose health conditions are best, contrary to widespread opinion. This is so for two very simple reasons: (1) immigrants are generally young and in the prime of their working life [. . .] and (2) very rigorous health examinations ensure that immigrants who are not in good health are quickly replaced. This means that though the health of immigrants as individuals is more severely affected than that of nationals, as a group immigrants are more healthy since only the young and healthy are retained – and only for as long as they remain in that condition.
- It is the part of the labour force that works in the worst safety and health conditions, thereby permitting considerable savings in the organization of work, reducing still further the costs of reproduction.
- When considered from the point of view of capital as a whole, rather than from that of the individual capitalist, one of the essential effects of immigration is to enable considerable savings to be made in the costs of social reproduction of the labour force as a whole, thereby raising correspondingly the overall average rate of profit. This occurs by means of three main mechanisms:

Table 3.8 Rates of activity by nationality in Germany, September 1969

Nationality	Rate of activity (%)
Italians	68
Yugoslavs	80
Turks	76
Greeks	71
Spaniards	71
Portuguese	79
All foreigners	63

Sources: Wirtschaft und Statistik (no. 5, 1970), p. 246, Ausländische Arbeitnehmer 1969, p. 94

1   By recruiting immigrants primarily from among the young and productive (see tables 3.8–3.10), it is possible to avoid paying the costs of
"rearing" the worker, and the maintenance costs after his/her working
life has ended. According to an OECD estimate these costs amount to
$10,000 per worker, which implies a figure for the free human capital
represented by immigrants in Europe of about $50 million.

2   Given the restrictive measures governing immigration and the conditions in which immigrants live and work, the majority are unmarried
or "forced" bachelors (see tables 3.11 and 3.12), and the costs of reproduction of families are not borne by capital, which thereby saves on the

Table 3.9 Rates of activity by country of birth in Great Britain, 1966

Country of birth	Rate of activity (%)
Irish Republic	66
Commonwealth countries	58
Jamaica	73
Rest of Caribbean	68
India	59
Pakistan	72
Cyprus	54
Foreign countries	57
Poland	65
Germany	46
Italy	66
All immigrants	60

Source: 1966 Census, Great Britain summary tables, economic activity tables, part III

Table 3.10   Rates of activity by nationality and sex in France, 1968

Nationality	Rate of activity (%)		
	Total	Male	Female
Algerians	52.5	70.2	4.8
Moroccans	64.0	78.5	13.1
Tunisians	45.2	66.2	16.5
Italians	42.3	63.5	14.7
Spaniards	40.9	60.4	24.8
Portuguese	63.9	74.6	23.9
Yugoslavs	66.6	77.8	48.2
Poles	35.2	50.7	20.0
All foreigners	47.1	64.8	19.8

Figures are for crude rate of activity, i.e. the number of active persons as a percentage of the total number of people (including children) in each group.
Source: 1968 French Census, *Hommes et migrations etudes* (no. 113, 1969)

Table 3.11   Family immigration to France and Germany

	France[a]				Germany[b]	
	No. of families ––––––– Total population	Couples ––––– Married	Children ––––––– Total population	Children ––––– Couples	Married migrants as % of total	Married migrants accompanied by wife as a percentage of married migrants
All foreigners	68.69	35.21	26.75	1.53	70	51
Spanish	79.38	43.5	30.45	1.40	74	60
Greek					78	78
Italian	81.18	40.32	29.57	1.41	64	54
Portuguese	65.98	32.8	29.74	1.71	78	44
Turks					82	34
Yugoslavs	52.65	40.40	14.31	0.66	76	34
Algerians	54.99	20.74	38.88	3.79		
Moroccans	40.77	16.10	21.45	2.76		
Tunisians	63.05	30.48	31.13	2.45		

Sources: [a] *Hommes et Migrations*, "documents" series, no. 829 of 15 June 1972; 1968 Census, April 1 poll
[b] *Bundesanstalt für Arbeit*, August, 1970: results of a special inquiry on the family situation of migrant workers

Table 3.12   Females as a percentage of immigrants

	Portugal	Spain (assisted immigration)	Greece	Turkey	Finland
1969	42.3	16.2	43.6	20.0	47.6
1970	34.7	15.4	42.8	16.1	44.7
1971	42.0	13.0	45.0	16.1	43.5
1972	41.5	13.7	43.6	21.9	46.8

cost of collective facilities, public housing, schools, hospital beds, welfare benefits, etc. The savings are all the more significant in that outlays on such facilities are not profitable since demand for them has to be subsidized.

3   The conditions of reproduction of the immigrants themselves as well as of the families who succeed in accompanying them are clearly below the average standards of indigenous workers. Their housing conditions are particularly bad.[7] Not only does social capital not bear these costs but also the "sleep merchants" profit from the discrimination, creating a parallel housing market for immigrants which becomes even profitable provided legality is set aside and summary methods are used to maintain order in the hostels, furnished rooms or slums.[8]

This is why, to mention but two examples, 32 per cent of immigrants in Germany live in temporary dwellings according to official statistics, while 98 per cent of shantytown dwellers in France are immigrants (see tables 3.13–3.15).

The effect of immigrant workers on wage levels concerns not only their own wages, but also those of wage-earners as a whole, since the possibility of appealing to the manpower of the dependent capitalist countries acts as a veritable world *reserve army* on the working class of the advanced capitalist countries. One cannot infer from this a conflict between the interests of the working class and those of immigrant workers, for once in the same boat together they can only get out of the vicious circle of their exploitation by joining together in opposition to capital. It remains true, *as a tendency*, that the very possibility of recourse to immigration causes a relative lowering of wages thus contributing to the structural counter-tendency which helps delay the fall in the rate of profit.

Finally, turning to the intensity of their exploitation, on average immigrant workers work much longer hours than nationals, occupy the worst jobs, and are subjected to the fastest speeds (to the extent that they work on assembly lines and are paid by piece-work). The much higher rate of work accidents

Table 3.13 Socio-economic status of foreign employees in Germany by nationality and sex, 1968 (per cent)

Socio-economic status	Nationality							
	Italy	Greece	Spain	Turkey	Portugal	Yugoslavia	Others	All foreign
Men								
Non-manual	–	–	–	–	–	–	35	8
Skilled manual	13	7	15	16	12	55	25	20
Semi-skilled manual	37	53	44	38	43	27	22	36
Unskilled manual	48	37	38	43	43	14	12	34
Women								
Non-manual	–	–	–	–	–	–	50	12
Skilled manual	–	–	–	–	–	–	–	3
Semi-skilled manual	34	37	34	33	35	29	15	30
Unskilled manual	63	60	59	62	60	58	18	53

Percentages do not add up to 100 due to omission of certain minor categories, like apprentices, and because of rounding.
Source: "Repräsentativuntersuchung, Herbst 1968," *Ausländische Arbeitnehmer 1969*, p. 86

Table 3.14 Socio-economic status of foreign and Swiss employees, 1960 (per cent)

Socio-economic status	Foreign employees	Swiss employees
Non-manual	15.0	52.0
Skilled manual	25.0	18.5
Semi-skilled manual	37.0	22.5
Unskilled manual	23.0	7.0

Source: P. Granjeat, *Les migrations de travailleurs en Europe* (Paris, Institut International des Etudes Sociales, 1966), p. 82

Table 3.15 Foreign employees in France by socio-economic status, by nationality, 1967 (per cent)

Socio-economic status	Nationality							
	Spain	Italy	Poland	Portugal	Algeria	Morocco	Tunisia	All
Engineers and managers	0.5	0.8	0.8	0.1	–	0.4	1.1	1.2
Supervisory personnel and technicians	1.5	3.0	2.0	0.2	0.1	0.4	1.3	1.7
Non-manual workers	3.9	3.7	3.8	0.9	1.2	2.9	11.2	3.4
Skilled manual	31.5	41.1	24.5	28.8	11.5	14.9	16.1	25.2
Semi-skilled manual	36.5	35.4	42.3	35.1	38.0	46.0	32.0	36.6
Unskilled manual	26.4	16.0	26.6	34.9	49.2	35.4	38.3	31.9

Source: "Enquête effectuée par le Ministère d'Etat chargé des Affaires Sociales"

among immigrants is indicative both of their work conditions and of the speeds they are obliged to maintain.

All these empirically indisputable factors are however too obvious; acceptance of them is too automatic and even hides a sort of unconscious racist preconception. *Why should immigrant labour accept what, for the indigenous working class, has become unacceptable?* Because they are naturally submissive? Because of their extreme need? Even accepting the notion that the poverty experienced in their own countries makes immigrant workers willing to tolerate any and all conditions on their arrival, the problem is why this acceptance persists and, especially, why it is possible to treat them as individual wage-earners whereas the relationship of the indigenous working class with capital is established collectively, through the labour movement. This is the key to answering the question. Though working conditions, wage levels, and social benefits have improved, and though European workers have bettered their living conditions, this has not come about through the goodwill of capital but through the new socio-political conditions which flow from the balance of power between the classes created by the labour movement. In other words, *the utility of immigrant labour to capital derives primarily from the fact that it can act towards it as though the labour movement did not exist*, thereby moving the class struggle back several decades. A twenty-first-century capital and a nineteenth-century proletariat – such is the dream of monopoly capital in order to overcome its crisis. How does this happen? Not because of any presumed submissiveness of immigrants, whose many struggles in recent years have shown a degree of combativeness, however sporadic and limited. Rather their legal–political status as foreigners and their political–ideological isolation lead to the basic point: *their limited capacity for organization and struggle and very great vulnerability to repression.*[9] Their status as foreigners deprives immigrants of political rights and, also, in practice, of their rights as trade-unionists. Their participation in class struggles, their level of organization under these conditions is thus restricted to a vanguard, which is cut off from the mass of immigrants and is often regarded with suspicion by the indigenous labour movement. It is all the more easily repressed. Moreover, since the permanence of immigrant workers in each country is only relative, and their degree of subjective identification weaker, their interest in participating in current struggles is limited, and generally concentrated in outbursts linked to their concrete living and working conditions.

Moreover, the racism and xenophobia diffused by the dominant ideology accentuate the cleavages derived from national cultural particularities[10] and determine the ideological isolation of immigrants. They are thus separated from their class and placed in a balance of power so unfavourable that often they fluctuate between an acceptance of the conditions of capital and pure individual or collective revolt. This cuts them off still more from the labour movement, in a sort of vicious circle which tends to reproduce the fragmentation and dislocation of the working class in advanced capitalism.

This brings us to the first result of our analysis, which should be underlined. Banal though it may be, some crucial implications for immigrant struggles follow from it: the advantage of immigrant labour for capital stems precisely from the specificity of their inferior position in the class struggle, which derives from the legal–political status of immigrants. From the *point of view of capital* this status can be modified in minor ways, but not transformed, because it is the source of the basic structural role of immigration. Thus the basic contradiction concerning immigrants is one which opposes them not directly to capital, but to the state apparatus of capital and to the political status given to them in its institutions. This has the following consequences:

- The position of immigrants in the class struggle is very specific compared with the rest of the labour movement.
- The contradiction in which they occupy the dominated pole is a basic contradiction of capitalism.
- The contradiction is immediately political in so far as it relates directly to the state apparatus.
- Given a basic, directly political and very specific contradiction, reinforced in the ideological sphere by their cultural particularities and the

xenophobic tones of the dominant ideology, immigrants find themselves in an extremely unfavourable balance of power which tends to
reproduce their separation from the rest of the labour movement.

The circle is not completely closed, as we shall see, since immigrants'
membership in the working class determines an objective basis of interests
common to *workers as a whole*. And from this basis, a unified labour movement
can be constructed on the basis of a working class which, though objectively
fragmented, is not split.

This analysis also sheds light on a common argument about the causes of
immigration which we have deliberately left aside in our discussion so as to be
able to provide the answer once it was known. This is the idea that immigrants are necessary to carry out the arduous jobs rejected by the indigenous
population. In fact, this is only a half-truth. While it is certain that immigrants
do carry out the most arduous, the worst-paid and the least skilled jobs (see
tables 3.13–3.15), it does not follow from this that these jobs though necessary, have been given up by other workers. Such jobs are not given up
because they are "dirty" and "soul-destroying" (since the jobs taken instead
can hardly be said to be "fulfilling") but because they are less well-paid.
Whenever arduous work is relatively well-paid (e.g. miners) nationals, in particular, are found doing it. It remains true, however, that these jobs are badly
paid and are most arduous, but *in relation to what standard?* To the historical
standard of the balance of power established by the labour movement in each
country, to what would be unacceptable to a working class which had the
necessary strength to impose better working conditions and higher wage levels. In brief, then, *immigrant workers do not exist because there are "arduous and badly
paid" jobs to be done, but, rather, arduous and badly paid jobs exist because immigrant
workers are present or can be sent for to do them.*

The building industry, for example, has remained largely small-scale in
character because the employment of immigrants has made small fragmented
capitals profitable without recourse to industrialized building methods. If immigrant labour were to disappear, *depending on the balance of power of the labour
movement*, the building industry would be reconverted and modernized. But
this is no more than a pious wish, because such a situation would considerably
reduce the rate of profit, thus precipitating an economic crisis. This is why
capital cannot do without the "arduous jobs" or the immigrant workers who
do them. This is the "invisible structure" of the determination of capital of
which one sees only the effects, sometimes combined with premature interpretations.

We now need to examine whether the political–ideological specificity of
immigrants in the class struggle is also the basic feature which enables them to
play a crucial role in the anticyclical and anti-inflationary policies of monopoly capital.

Economic fluctuations, inflation, immigration

In spite of the systematic intervention of the state apparatus, in spite of the control mechanisms set up, the capitalist economy still undergoes cyclical fluctuations. They are of a new type in so far as the acceleration of technical progress, on the one hand, and the internationalization of capital, on the other, have introduced distortions into the regularity of the cycles, while magnifying the effects of recessionary periods.

In this perspective immigrant workers are one of the basic elements preventing recessions from turning into crises. Instead of accepting the reality of unemployment, advanced capitalist economies have regulated with immigrant labour, temporarily limiting immigration (as in Belgium in 1971, and Germany in 1972), imposing new restrictive legislation (Switzerland, Britain, France), or simply to expelling – in a more or less disguised fashion – part of the immigrant labour force. Thus, the 1967 recession in Germany resulted in a very large reduction in the number of foreign residents, thereby exporting a considerable fraction of the total unemployment (see table 3.2). There were still 459,000 unemployed in 1967 in Germany, and 353,000 in 1968, who naturally received unemployment benefits. It has been calculated that the expulsion of foreign workers enabled savings of over DM1,000 million in unemployment benefits alone.[11]

This general trend, which has also been observed in France [. . .], is often interpreted in the banal terms of the supply and demand of jobs. Its significance lies precisely in the ease with which one can be rid of this labour, due to its inferior legal–political status. This again reveals the basic role of the status of foreigner from the point of view of the functioning of the capitalist economy.

Something more specific is also involved, which requires closer analysis. The crises of capitalism today are not classical crises caused by overproduction, but crises produced primarily by inflation, which is itself the result of capital surpluses and financial movements linked to the activities of multinational firms, among other things.[12] What characterizes these crises is precisely the *combination of inflation and recession*, or "stagflation," as it has become known. The mechanism is quite simple: inflation results not from the play of supply and demand, but from structural features of the current phase of capitalism, which cannot be discussed in detail here.[13] These mean that a rise in product prices is not counteracted by a fall in demand since prices are determined by the cost of the capital invested, itself subject to inflationary pressures through financial mechanisms. Now and then prices will surge ahead of what demand can bear, thus causing relative overproduction which leads to a recession. This further reduces the level of effective demand, but without bringing about a proportionate fall in prices unless a dangerous fall in the average rate of profit is acceptable. Under these conditions, what are the characteristics of the ideal "worker–consumer" in order to counteract these periodic crises?:

1 He/she must be very productive in the expansionary phase.
2 He/she must be excludable without difficulty in the recessionary phase when there is a danger of overproduction.
3 He/she must consume little, in order to reduce inflationary tensions in expansionary periods and especially to cushion the decline in demand in recessionary periods. This is possible since his disappearance as a wage-earner (and hence of his wage as purchasing power) has little effect on the overall level of effective demand. In this way productive capacity can be reduced with little change in effective demand, thereby avoiding the chain of events which can follow from applying brakes to growth. In this way, fluctuations can be prevented from turning into crises.

The central role of immigrant labour as a regulator for capitalist crises is too often ignored, hidden by interpretations phrased in terms of the economic situation (adjustment of supply and demand) without attention to the determinants of these adjustments or discrepancies. Two conditions must be met in order for immigrant labour to play this role:

1 The status of foreigner which is weak in political and ideological terms, must be maintained.
2 The immigration of families must be limited as much as possible and, at most, be restricted to a narrow and higher section of immigrants whose ideological integration acts as an adequate guarantee.

These then are the reasons for the current orientation of immigration policies in all the European countries towards the so-called "German" solution: immigration limited to "unmarried" workers, rigorously controlled, for a limited period, and with a high rate of turnover, in return for an improvement in material living conditions for the limited time during which their services are provided. The British Immigration Act, the new Swiss measures, and, most of all, the Fontanet-Marcellin circular in France, all point in this direction.

It must be mentioned, in passing, that from the point of view of a purely economic logic of capital, the same aims (raising of the rate of profit by excess exploitation, counter-cyclical control) could be achieved by productive investments in the countries from which immigrants come – provided of course that a similar balance of power could be imposed on the workers there, i.e. through police states. Such an approach can be found in various schemes drawn up by large European, and especially French, business. However, in the short term it is unlikely that a policy of this type will emerge since it ignores two basic features of immigration: its position in the various fractions of capital; and its fragmenting, and hence weakening, effect on the working class. This means, in turn, that such a tendency could only emerge once three conditions are met: the final unification of capital around monopolies; the incorporation of the labour movement so that it ceased to constitute a great danger for capital which would thus no longer need to weaken it; finally, and most important, a strong development of immigrant struggles which threatens the social equilibrium constructed at their expense. This latter development is already taking place in Switzerland, while it appears far off in France; Germany is an intermediate case.

This question, however, is significant in that it enables us to establish the limits of a purely economic analysis based on the logic of capital. We must now turn to an analysis of the relationship of immigrants to existing social classes.

Immigration, Social Classes and Class Fractions

Immigrants are not just foreigners. The vast majority are foreign workers (98 per cent in France), i.e. (1) *workers*, (2) *foreigners*. As soon as either of these two features, which define both their class situation, and their specificity as a class fraction, is forgotten one ceases to be able to understand the significance of immigrants for capital, and, beyond that, for the transformation of society.

The specific class situation of foreign workers has to be related to the class struggle and existing class interests in order to uncover current alliances and contradictions and, hence, to deduce appropriate tactics and strategy, given the specific aims of these classes and fractions.

Thus, although the general interests of advanced capitalism concerning immigration may be those we have indicated, they are varied and specific for each fraction of capital, and, in particular, they diverge according to whether we are dealing with monopoly capital or capital invested in industries or sectors with lower rates of profit or smaller quantities of surplus-value. For big capital, the primary aim is to preserve the basic characteristics of the immigrant labour force, while stabilizing[14] it in its production phase, e.g. by providing minimal material conditions for its reproduction. Hence big capital desires the "regularization" of immigration provided that this does not go too far and cause outbursts of trouble nor interfere with the maintenance of the labour force. Thus, for example, measures concerning housing may be taken (France), the consultation of immigrant representatives by local authorities may be proposed (Belgium), or certain social security measures taken (Germany), always of course in a totally inadequate and fragmented way.[15] Big firms may even agree to job security for a small elite group of immigrants, thus offering a carrot to the "good immigrant" to improve his job. More concretely: for big capital the basic concern is to avoid political and trade-union rights for immigrant workers, and hence to lessen their capacity to engage in struggle. Hence its policy of control and minor modification concerning immigration, sometimes paternalist in the economic sphere, always repressive (dissuasive) in the political sphere.

Conversely, for many small and medium-sized firms (especially in the building, textile and service industries) the immigrant labour force is crucial to their *day-to-day survival* because of the excess exploitation that they can carry out given the lack of rights and of organization of these workers. For these firms, immigrants are a source of the excess profit necessary to compensate for their below average rate of profit. They thus violate bourgeois social legality by hiring *clandestine* immigrants in order to exploit the immigrant illegally, avoid paying social security contributions and impose sub-human working conditions on them. In the case of small and medium firms, then, extreme violation of legal rights is added to the legal and controlled violations, regularized over the long term, demanded by large capital. This is why France, the most backward[16] of the receiving countries, and the one with the highest proportion of small and medium-sized firms, tolerated without complaint up to 1972 a level of clandestine immigration which at that time represented almost 80 per cent of all entries [. . .]. For these firms any improvement in the living conditions of immigrants would be unacceptable, since it would affect their necessary excess profits. This argument applies *a fortiori* to speculative capital which profits from the destitute condition of immigrants in order to create a new source of accumulation ("sleep merchants" and others). The two fractions of capital, however, agree on one basic point: the structural need for the systematic political repression of immigrants, and the complete elimination of their ability to defend themselves. Having obtained satisfaction on this basic point, large capital can afford to fall back on "humanitarian" arguments when immigrant struggles oblige it to retreat, whereas for backward firms the excess exploitation of immigrants is a matter of life and death. These differences must be borne in mind in order to understand the variety of capitalist immigration policies. But this fragmentation of interests of capital presupposes a basic agreement on the maintenance of immigrants in a position of social and political "apartheid."

The *objective* political weakness of immigrant workers is not only an important counter-tendency used by capital to avert the impact of its own contradictions, but it also is a major trump card for the bourgeoisie in its struggle against the working class. The very presence of immigrant workers constitutes a permanent source of fragmentation within the working class, both inside and outside the firm. While immigrant and indigenous workers share the same historic interests and some immediate interests, they diverge on other immediate interests, e.g. working and housing conditions, and, in particular, freedom of association, a basic issue for immigrants but superfluous for indigenous workers.

This fragmentation is a permanent and objective obstacle to the struggle and organization of *all* workers, since it places a substantial fraction of them in an inferior position, making participation in the struggle much more difficult and dangerous for them. This is too often forgotten, impressed as we are by the violence and audacity of certain immigrant struggles. On the rare occasions when such struggles do take place, they do so in spite of the initial disadvantages and considerable risks of repression incurred by the immigrants involved. This explains why only a small minority of immigrants takes part in these struggles and why they only develop at the price of very heavy sacrifices which clearly distinguishes them from the rest of the labour movement. For immigrants, then, every struggle puts their embryonic organization in danger. This fragile stake had been overcome by the labour movement in advanced capitalism. The fragmentation of the working class represented by a permanent fraction of immigrant workers is, thus, a basic factor in maintaining immigration as a unified interest of the dominant classes.

This is all the more true since this split does not rest solely on the inferior political status of immigrants, but also on the racist and xenophobic reactions of the bourgeoisie.[17] The success of Enoch Powell and the National Front in Britain; the very large popular vote for the xenophobic bill known as the "Schwarzenbach initiative" in Switzerland; the wave of racist assassinations (especially in Marseille) in autumn 1973, are symptoms of the ultimate weapon for dividing the working class: racism. These reactions occur even within the working class, not only among the indigenous population against immigrants, but also in the opposite direction.

This objective and subjective split between indigenous and immigrant workers is often reinforced by the corporatism and blindness of trade-unions which, under the pretext of defending the jobs of nationals, fail to understand the real strategy of capitalism in this matter. They collaborate, in fact or in intention, with big capital in its policy of regularizing and controlling (ultimately with police help) immigration. Trade-unions are sometimes afraid to counteract the xenophobic attitudes of part of the labour force (under the influence of the dominant ideology), and end up reinforcing the situation which they themselves denounce, or give lip service to denouncing. However it is obvious that trade-unions cannot be considered as a unit, and that their attitudes will depend partly on their general orientation to the class struggle, and partly on the pressure which immigrants are able to exercise on them. Thus, in France, trade-unions attempt immediately to work towards working-class unity[18] whereas in Switzerland they collaborate with the bourgeoisie. But trade-unions no longer have a free hand in this respect, since they increasingly have to take account of the weight of immigrants among their membership. This is perhaps the key to the whole problem since indigenous trade-unions are often reinforced by the suspicion and anti-unionism of many immigrants (due not to excessive consciousness, but to a lack of consciousness!) in a sort of vicious circle which risks reproducing the fragmentation of the working class with catastrophic consequences for the labour movement in advanced capitalism.

This vicious circle can only be broken by the common discovery by immigrant and indigenous workers of their basic identity of interests, an identity which must not be interpreted solely in terms of a distant historical destiny, but in relation to the present conditions of the class struggle. Immigrants will never succeed in imposing their basic demand (equal rights) without a generalized battle supported by the labour and democratic movement as a whole. Indigenous workers must avoid at all costs a rupture in the working class which could lead to a major defeat which would strengthen, perhaps decisively, the balance of power in favour of the bourgeoisie.

This discovery of a concrete community of class interests can only occur through common struggles against capital. And these common struggles will come about through the participation of immigrants and indigenous workers in each other's specific struggles. In other words, the dynamic of social relations, while determined by the class structure, is organized in terms of the historically specific development of the practices of the struggle. This is the subject to which we shall now turn, with special reference to the particularly rich example of France, before drawing some more general conclusions about the role of immigrants in the class struggle.

Immigrant Workers and Class Struggles: The French Example

The resurgence of social struggles in France since 1968 has had a profound effect on immigrant workers. For some time, though they were publicly defined as a "social problem," there were not, strictly speaking, any specific separate struggles of immigrant workers. Up to 1972 there were two basically different types of action concerning immigrant workers – on the one hand, an ideological exposure of the "scandal" of immigrant conditions, led primarily by the left-wing movement in their usual role as revealers of contradictions rather than as a political force; on the other, a series of working-class protest struggles in factories with high proportions of immigrant workers which indicated the concrete potential for mobilizing of this stratum of workers. It may be noted that the most important struggles ("Grosteel" at Le Bourget; "Penarroya" at Lyon, both in 1972) were protest struggles led by trade-unions, especially the CFDT, even though the style of action was quite innovative (primarily because of the severity of the struggles in the face of the intransigence of the employers, which they finally overcame). The struggles by semi-skilled workers at Renault–Billancourt and at Renault–Flins, where there was a high degree of immigrant participation, allowed a new form of working-class struggle to develop outside trade-union channels, due to a certain degree of Maoist penetration among the immigrants, concurrently with powerful trade-union action. What characterizes this set of struggles, however, is that they are working-class struggles involving immigrants but in no case advancing demands specific to immigrants. To this extent the incorrect initial social base persists and the mass of immigrants remains cut off from the struggle of the labour movement, at the same time as the trade-unions rarely go beyond the level of pious wishes with regard to demands for equal rights for all workers. But with the entry into force on 18 September 1972 of new regulations regarding immigration (the Fontanet-Marcellin circular) things are starting to change. These regulations represent a true offensive by large capital to regularize the field of immigration, giving prime emphasis to the repressive and police features of immigration control. The three main measures in the circular can be summarized as follows:

1   No immigrant worker will be able to work or live in France without passing through the legal channels of the Office National d'Immigration. Illegal immigrants will no longer be able to regularize their position (up till then 80 per cent of immigrants were clandestine).
2   Work and residence permits will be linked and granted for the same period. The length of this period will be determined by the work contract, which means that the right to stay in France of an immigrant worker will depend on the goodwill of his employer.
3   Before the issue of a residence permit, an immigrant worker must have a "decent dwelling." But since the causes of the housing crisis are not being touched, this measure may be regarded as a pious wish. In reality, it has a very great but different significance, since the description "decent" will depend on the judgement of the police. It thus introduces an arbitrary element into the granting of residence.
4   Finally, in order to deal with all aspects of the administration of immigrants together, the dossiers will be brought together into a single file in the care of the local police station which will thus be able to carry out repressive operations at leisure.

This set of measures is justified, according to the circular, by the need to "regularize" immigration. In fact it is a regularization which reflects very closely the interests of big capital. It represents:

(a)   The hegemony of monopoly capital over backward capitalism, in the field of immigration policy.
(b)   A drastic attempt to nip in the bud the rudimentary immigrant workers' movement which was starting to develop out of several working-class struggles.

The circular thus has two features: the capitalist rationalization of immigration, and the political repression of immigrants. Initially, labour unions saw only the first feature and were thus not terribly opposed to it (especially the CGT), since they agreed it was necessary to regularize immigration in order to avoid the worst abuses. But they were not aware of the economic impossibility of such a regularization. At the same time they underestimated the importance of the feature of the circular concerning the establishment of arbitrary employer and police power over immigrants as a whole (except for those entering under special agreements: Algerians, black Africans, EEC nationals).

On the other hand, it quickly became evident to immigrants, from their everyday experience that something basic had changed. The police headquarters and local police stations stepped up their administrative checks, and deportations began. The measures taken were carefully thought out and selective: Arab workers were the first to be hit (mainly Tunisians and Moroccans, unprotected by any special status), whose political–legal isolation is well-known, given the widespread anti-Arab racism among the indigenous population. In the face of this intimidation, immigrant workers mobilized in disorder, to a large extent spontaneously. Two tendencies soon appeared within this movement. One tendency started from the specificity of immigrant workers, organizing themselves into a "Defence Committee for Immigrants Rights to Live and Work" (CDVTI), on the fringe of the trade-union movement, and had as a central plank the demand for a guaranteed legal status which would eliminate the arbitrary powers of police and employers and guarantee the presence of immigrants in the country under satisfactory conditions, even while accepting the inferior status of the immigrant, and the regularization of immigration. The other tendency preached the class unity of all workers and demanded equal rights through a common struggle by workers of all nationalities, organized, for example, into "French–Immigrant Unitary Committees" (CUFI). Both tendencies were instigated by revolutionary groups, although the CUFI also contained trade-union militants. The trade-unions, for their part, demanded the repeal of the circular without, however, launching any major battles on this subject. As deportations increased, semi-spontaneous actions were set off. The demands of the CUFI were too ambitious for an immigrant movement to use from the outset: they could only be imposed through trade-union action within firms and the trade-unions had difficulty because of the unresponsiveness of French workers. On the other hand, the "defence of human rights" line of the CDVTI, which was specific to immigrants, gained the support of many of those who were primarily demanding not to be deported, as well as support from prominent liberal and charitable figures (e.g. the Church played a major role). As a form of struggle they chose the *hunger strike* by those threatened with deportation, the first of which was launched in Valence at Christmas 1972. Following the success of this first strike (the position of those involved was regularized "because of the date") a veritable wave of hunger strikes by clandestine immigrants shook the whole of France. Supported by public opinion and with a very high level of mobilization of extreme left militants, almost all of the hunger strikes brought success to the participants, but (a) the circular was not withdrawn; (b) *in particular*, no mass movement was organized since the strikes mostly involved the persons directly affected; and (c) unity with the labour movement was only at the level of declarations. Parallel to this, the CUFI *gave support* to these initiatives and spent most of their time organizing neighbourhood committees containing immigrants of various nationalities and French political militants. They succeeded in achieving national *co-ordination* between the almost one hundred local committees which sprang up semi-spontaneously throughout France.

As soon as the deportation campaign came to an end so did the hunger strikes, thus showing their highly defensive and individual character. Nothing changed at the general level and these struggles did not lead to the creation of any social force.

Immigrant working-class struggles, however, linking labour demands and demands specific to immigrants appeared during the same period (spring, 1973) within certain factories, led primarily by the left wing of the CFDT and by independent groups of immigrants. A new strike at Renault, the Margoline's strike at Nanterre, the strike of Spanish women workers in the "Claude-St Cyr" clothes firm, are tough, exemplary and victorious battles which are starting to link together working-class and immigrant struggles, through the *simultaneous* support of labour unions and nationally-organized independent immigrant organizations (Association of Moroccans in France, Co-ordination of Spanish Workers in the Paris Region, and later the Arab Workers Movement, etc.).

May 1, 1973 was an "Immigrants 1st May" which saw a procession, including thousands of immigrant workers, both inside and outside the trade-union contingents, linking their specific demands to those of the working-class as a whole. And the trade-unions are again taking up their demands.

This created a new balance of power. The government reacted with both integration and repression. On the one hand, the circular was made more "flexible" (for example, by giving a three-month grace period after the expiry of a contract to enable a new job to be found) and it was suspended for four months in order to regularize the position of clandestine workers (which was not in fact done). But, on the other hand, the main provisions remained unchanged, and deportation orders were served *for political reasons* on the leaders of the new immigrant movement which had developed on the fringes of the trade-union movement. Finally, and most important of all, a racist campaign developed (officially disapproved of by the government) which included mass racist demonstrations in Marseille and a wave of assassinations of

Arabs whose authors were never traced. This activity reached such a pitch that Algeria suspended emigration to France. The trial of strength between the immigrant movement and capital, which requires a certain status for immigrants, has started. It will be long and hard. All the more since the immigrant movement is starting to escape its isolation and gradually to find its place again in the trade-union movement through a reciprocal discovery of common class interests through common struggles.[19]

This said, a basic problem has been posed, without yet having really emerged in the practice of the immigrant worker movement: in so far as the class struggle does not stop at protest struggle but is basically pulled together at the political level, what is the relation between immigrants' struggles and the political struggle between classes?

Immigrant Struggles, Working-class Struggles and Political Struggle between Classes

We know[20] that no class struggle *of any consequence* takes place without raising the question of power and hence seeking the destruction–transformation of the state apparatus, the instrument by which the interests of the dominant classes as a whole are realized. Class struggles are thus concentrated within the political struggle between classes, which has as its objective the capture of power and, then, the transformation of social relationships, by ending the exploitation of man by man.

In the case of immigrant workers' struggles one question immediately arises: which states are involved? Which capture of power is being referred to, that in the sending country, or that in the receiving country? This question is by no means unreal, particularly if we bear in mind the whole series of ultra-internationalist interpretations. These argue from the facts of immigration and the internationalization of capital and advocate an international revolution, that is, they deny the possibility of any revolutionary process which operates at less than a European scale, at the very least. According to this view, one should speak of a single international working class since an international proletariat is not only a goal but a reality already present in the relations of production.

Nothing could be further from the truth.

To speak in this way has meaning only in the context of an exclusively trade-union and economistic strategy. Certainly, it is necessary for trade-unions primarily concerned with obtaining the best possible negotiating conditions to develop an international trade-union federation in opposition to the international grouping of employers. But to do no more than this is to forget that the interests of the working class are realized *politically*, that the political process concerns the state, and that the state has forms and patterns of change specific to each nation created by the bourgeoisie. Each state represents a particular system of interests and alliances, and it oppresses in a specific way a section of workers which is relatively united by history and mode of life. The confrontation of each state requires a separate strategy to develop class alliances and class struggle at the political level. It is obvious that there is a holy alliance of international capital. But the idea of an international struggle is no more than an idea. Today there is no united world proletariat confronting a single opponent. The unity of the proletariat will be built in the struggle, through the convergence of interests uncovered in the practices of the struggle. Given the uneven development of the class struggle in relation to each state, each proletariat must necessarily develop its own strategy. To talk of an international working class "on the Common Market level" is either an ideological position, expressing a desire without helping concretely to bring it about, or else an economistic position which identifies the context of negotiations with the Europe of big capital. In neither case is it a political position connected with the strategy of classes engaged in a struggle for power.

To which revolutionary processes, then, does the class fraction, immigrant workers, belong? In relation to which political struggle are they defined? In our view, immigrant workers as a class fraction are defined within the class struggle of the receiving country. Nevertheless, as a labour movement, they have a two-fold definition since *within each country there is a multinational working class which corresponds to a multinational labour movement* and which is doubly linked: as a multinational entity it is directed *politically* towards the struggle whose goal is the state apparatus in the receiving country; and as a national component of such an entity it is part of the labour movement in the sending country, since, in practice, it continues to retain a close relation with the struggles in the sending country.

Such an analysis raises the problem of whether this multinational labour movement should not have a corresponding multinational political leadership. But such a measure would contradict the class alliances necessary in the revolutionary process in each country, in so far as classes other than the working class are not multinational. This is a real "contradiction within the people." But before it can be resolved politically from the point of view of the proletariat, there must first be unity of the multinational proletariat today fragmented within each country. The frequent preference for welding class alliances at the cost of the unity of the proletariat implies an acceptance from the outset of the submission of working-class interests to those of the intermediate strata. This then is an attempt to explain the strange passivity of the labour movement towards its immigrant fraction. The persistence of this fragmentation may be both a basic reason for the political weakness of the labour movement and the result of a strategy of alliances engendered by the interests of other classes. The link between immigrant workers and the political class struggle is thus both close and problematic.

expressed in new social cleavages related to the accessibility and use of certain collective services, from housing conditions to working hours, passing through the type and level of health, educational and cultural facilities. This appears all the more paradoxical in that in many countries collective services are reputed to be administered by the state, with priority given to the social interest they represent rather than their profitability from invested capital. But our hypothesis is precisely that, apart from the superiority granted by the highest levels of income (including housing and collective services), there is a new source of inequality inherent in the very use of these collective goods which have become a fundamental part of the daily consumption pattern.

These problems are treated as "urban" problems to the extent that residential agglomerations constitute the units of collective consumption and that their management is directly allied to the organisation and management of the various collective holdings. Urban organisation is not, then, a simple arrangement of spatial forms, but rather these forms are the expression of the process of collective treatment of the daily consumption patterns of households.[1] This is why the "crisis of the cities" is profoundly felt, for rather than deterioration of the "framework of life" the deterioration of the quality of life itself is involved not so much of physical surroundings but of the way of living, of the very meaning of life.[2]

This said, to go beyond a description of events and attempt to reach the structural tendencies susceptible to more precise investigation, we must take the questioning in reverse, not starting from expressions of inequality but from the evolution of advanced capitalism and the new position occupied by collective goods and services in this evolution. It is only after this that we will be in a position to explain some of the sources of structural disparity between the "users" of such services.[3]

The Strategic Role of Collective Consumption in Neo-capitalist Economies

The transformation of consumption in advanced capitalism is directly determined by the long-term structural tendencies upon which it is based, i.e. the concentration and centralisation of capital and its constant battle against the tendency toward a lower rate of profit, the socialisation of the productive forces, the development of the class struggle, the growing power of the worker movement which extends its bargaining power to all areas of social life, and finally, and above all, to the massive and decisive intervention of the state into the totality of economic activity.[4]

Indeed, the search for new markets for capital is not achieved simply by the penetration of capital into countries under imperialist domination, but by its penetration in pre-capitalist or semi-capitalist sectors of the economy of "metropolitan" countries, i.e. through dissolving the social and economic relationships which exist there. Such is the case particularly in the sector of the production of means of consumption for the popular classes, a sector until recently differing from country to country, and largely dominated by competitive capital.[5]

On the other hand, the class struggle and the growing bargaining power of the workers and popular movement imposes a certain level of consumption and changes the historical definition of "need," both qualitatively and quantitatively,[6] so much the more so in that it is relatively easier for the dominant classes to cede to popular demands in the domain of consumption than it is at the level of production or in matters concerning political power.

Finally, technological progress produces several important effects in matters of consumption: it raises the capacity for response to the demands for consumption, thus permitting its expansion; at the same time, it necessitates, on the one hand, the convergence of this consumption with the reproduction of a labour power which has been rendered specific and non-interchangeable for specialised positions, and on the other hand for the large mass of the unskilled labour force, the socialisation and interdependence of production determined by technological progress requires the smooth functioning of the conditions of collective reproduction of the labour power (thus, for example, a specialised worker can be replaced easily, but it is important that transport assures manpower mobility so that several million workers can be simultaneously on time at their jobs). In fact, the more important constant capital becomes in its size and in relation to the labour power, the more essential its smooth functioning becomes in rendering cybernetic the most unpredictable element of the productive process, i.e. the workers.[7]

Thus we arrive at the phenomenon called *mass consumption*, i.e. the fundamental importance of household consumption, both for making use of accumulated capital and for the smooth functioning of the productive process, even when the production and distribution of these consumer goods is concentrated and achieved on a grand scale and when the whole sector is subject to the special interests of monopolistic capital. This latter aspect is the basis for the principal contradiction between the increasingly collective and interdependent character of the process of consumption and its domination by the interests of private capital.[8]

Such a contradiction not only conditions consumption, reinforcing the use of certain products (through advertising, styles, etc.) and determining the life styles of people as a function of the greatest profit from capital investment in such-and-such a type of product, but also, and above all, it provokes lacunae in vast areas of consumption which are essential to individuals and to economic activity. Such is the case, for example, in housing, socio-cultural facilities, public transport and so on, i.e. the whole sector which the economists call "collective goods" and which are characterised (in terms of liberal economics) by the fact that they do not meet the price of the market, that they are not governed *directly* by supply and demand. Manifestly, this characteristic does not depend on the type of product (the production of housing is not more or less collective in itself than the production of automobiles) but on the type of capital invested, which is determined in the last instance by the relation between the rate of profit of the company and the average rate of profit in each branch. Thus we will see, for example, certain goods (housing itself) fluctuating from one category of consumption to another as a function of the capital cycle and the supply created by demand.[9]

It is at this point that the intervention of the state becomes necessary in order to take charge of the sectors and services which are less profitable (from the point of view of capital) but necessary for the functioning of economic activity and/or the appeasement of social conflicts.[10] Such is the history, repeated in all countries, of public housing,[11] but such is also the case for other types of consumption which are less explicitly public (for example, sports activities, "art cinema," galleries, etc.)[12]

This intervention of the state is functional and necessary to the monopolies, even though it is often done in opposition to some capitalist interests. In effect, it assures the necessary reproduction of the labour power at a minimum level, it lessens the cost of direct salaries (for example, the effect of rent ceilings to combat high salaries), while at the same time easing demands. Besides, public investment, as we know, is an essential form of "devaluation of social capital,"[13] a major recourse for counteracting the tendency toward a lowering of the profit margin. By investing "at a loss," *the general rate of profit of the private sector* holds steady or increases in spite of the lowering of profit relative to social capital as a whole. In this sense, "social" expenditures of the state not only thus favour big capital, but they are also indispensable to the survival of the system.

This said, the intervention of the state in the production and administration of a collective goods is not permanent or "normalised" in the functioning of the economy. It is always done in articulation with private capital, be it in making a sector profitable and in transferring it afterward to the private sector, or be it in assuring a continuous interlacing whereby the intervention of the state covers the functional or economic "holes," thus making it possible for private capital to take over (thus the public highway infrastructure which makes use of the automobile possible, or urban-renewal operations which permit the actions of private promoters, etc.).

The massive intervention of the state in the organisation of collective consumption has specific and decisive effects on this, for if the state intervenes in the economy on the part of the interests of the monopolies, one cannot forget, on the one hand, that it acts in the interests of the whole of the capitalist system and not only as a servant for a given group, and on the other hand, that it has, *above all, a political* logic and that each intervention, even economic, will be marked by that.[14] This double relative autonomy of the state, at once

in the interests represented and in the accomplished function, has two principal effects on the process of collective consumption and on the urban organisation which flows from it:

1　It maximises the *regulation* function of the state, which will be expressed
　　specifically through the process of *planning*, under the double aspect of
　　a technical rationality and calculations in terms of social interests.
2　It *politicises* the urban question in that as the state is the principal
　　responsible agent, which is to say, on the one hand, that collective
　　consumption will be put directly into politico-ideological competition
　　rather than treated in economic terms, and on the other hand, that the
　　demands called "urban" will be strongly articulated to the question of
　　power.[15]

Besides, the systematic intervention of the state in the domain of collective
consumption takes on decisive importance in the current phase of capitalism
characterised by the *internationalisation of capital*[16] and, at the level of the daily
functioning of the economy, by *structural inflation* which results from the specific intervention of multinational firms. In fact, for floating capital the taking
in charge by the national state of the hidden expenses of production becomes
even more advantageous. Able to play on inter-state competition, dependent
on the goodwill of private investment, multinational firms shift the responsibility for infrastructures on to different local or national authorities. This
mechanism is well known when it concerns recourse to national credit, which
has permitted American enterprises to become implanted in Europe by bor-
rowing from private and *public* European banks. But although this aspect is
little studied, it functions still more clearly with collective goods, all the more
so since multinational firms (because "apatriated") can be less mindful of the
social consequences of neglecting the needs of the population.

Another phenomenon, namely, "growth within inflation,"[17] entails still more
important consequences for collective goods. Inflation, as we know: (a) hits
the least-favoured categories of the population; and (b) encourages the pur-
chase of goods already on the market. In other words, therefore, inflation
makes people more consumption-orientated at the same time as it differentiates them according to their capacity for consumption. In these conditions,
two problems, *among others*, must be resolved:[18]

1　Important bottlenecks in the reproduction of the labour power must be
　　avoided, in particular for goods outside the market or those for which
　　the sale is founded on long-term credit and which are therefore made
　　more valuable by monetary devaluation (housing among others).
2　Guaranteed savings capacity, in order to have available at the proper
　　moment new complementary resources, must be preserved. Thus it is

necessary to assume differential costs of reimbursement of immobilised capital.

In both cases public intervention in collective consumption is essential: it attenuates the effects of inflation for the economy as well as for social relations while at the same time preserving the mechanism of monopolistic accumulation, which is what inflation is. In fact, it is clear that the financing of this intervention is achieved by an increased burden of taxation which has a much greater relative effect on the work-force than on capital. Thus the gains in salary obtained by social struggles are not only obliterated by the rise in prices but counteracted by tax laws. Certainly buying power is increased by the combined effect of technical progress and economic growth, but the negative effects of consumption appear essentially at the level of collective goods which are necessary for private capital and which will be provided by the state and thus by the taxpayers. Then, one has only to blame problems on the negative aspects of urban growth, "ineluctable gangrene of industrial civilisation," and the game is won. One can continue the epic of capitalist accumulation and develop individual buying power, all the while intensifying the contradiction between these grandiose perspectives and the historically dated reality of the *level* and *style* of life of people. To close the circle, necessarily individualised, personalised in daily life, in case of "failure" there will always be a psychiatrist, or a policeman!

Let us, then, try to see the more concrete consequences of such an economic and social evolution of the relationship of social groups to collective consumption, limiting ourselves to a review of some examples, taken to be case studies of a general structural logic.

Class Structure, Urban Structure and Collective Consumption: The Social Determinants of the New Inequality

The processes of collective consumption simultaneously express the growing contradiction between their objective socialisation and their management as a function of the interests of capital, the contradictory exigencies of capital, the confrontation of the different factions of capital, and the confrontation between popular demands and the rationality of the dominant class to which the state necessarily subscribes.[19]

This group of contradictions forms the basis for new expressions of social inequality which derive from the importance of collective consumption in advanced capitalist societies.

(1) Thus in matters of *housing* the primary inequality concerns the income

level which conditions access to the type of housing market, but it does not stop there. It is extended by economic and social considerations at each step in the access to a property, and this from the point of view of housing as a product as much as of housing as a means of social expression, or, if you will, as much from the "quantitative" as from the "qualitative" point of view, aspects which are anyway closely related.[20]

Thus the most common case in the United States, with a tendency to be so in Western Europe, is for access to the bulk of the private housing market to depend essentially on the capacity to have access to credit. This itself is also a function of income level (excluding the highest strata), the *stability* and the *predictability* of income in the long term, or in the last analysis on the possibility of a *career*, i.e. a predictable succession of employment positions.[21] In effect, lifetime indebtedness is the mechanism which permits the majority of American families (but also Germans) to have access to ownership of their suburban homes[22]. But the ability to predict employment is not only a function of occupational qualifications; it also depends on the situation of the business and the position occupied within the enterprise. Thus it is that employment within large organisations and the functionality of the position for the enterprise (and not for the productive process) establishes new cleavages. Still more, it is clear that this stability is a direct function of politico-ideological integration in the productive system and in the social hierarchy: one thus finds oneself before this characteristic of the "new society," and one is allocated a certain type of housing according to the level of social integration.[23] If it is true that there has always been repression against "agitators," what is new is the size of the phenomenon, made massive by the generalisation of recourse to credit as well as the refining of the repressive procedure, which takes place not only via the black list but also via the systematic application of a banker's morality in the routes of access to housing.[24]

But the specificity of these new inequalities in housing is even more clear in housing which is called "social," i.e. public or semi-public housing, and which arises theoretically from a logic of service and not from criteria of profitability, for to consider the "public" and the "private" as two autonomous economic spheres is to forget the dominant structural logic. In fact, the intervention of the state is accomplished within the limits of the resources that can be mobilised, and, besides, is distinguished by a subordination to the interests of the monopolies in two ways: first, "social" investments come only after direct aid to industrial enterprises has been effected; second, the constant tendency is to make the sectors of public subsidisation profitable in order to bring them into line with the criteria of private capital so as to be able to transfer them gradually over to it.[25]

Thus access to public housing is limited by a whole series of criteria of selection (ability to pay rent regularly, aptitude for maintenance, size of family, etc.) which are also calculated on the private market even if they are put quantitatively at a lower level. The sources of inequality based on income, employment and education are thus reinforced once more in public housing.

But added to these economic cleavages are new criteria of selection dependent on the social and institutional organisation of access to public housing. Thus the insertion into the system of social security, though it seems consistent, leaves aside a whole series of situations (youth, the unregistered unemployed, the unrecognised sick and handicapped, etc.) which we lump together too quickly in a "marginal" category, whereas they are in each case the result of a precise mechanism of social production.[26] Particularly revealing in this sense is the criterion of limiting the access of immigrant workers to public housing (in France they cannot have more than 6.75 per cent whereas they comprise 30 per cent of the construction workers); equality in housing is thus skewed and the allocation of public housing leads to new disparities.[27]

In the same way the ability to manoeuvre inside the bureaucratic network of public assistance in order to win one's case is a socially determined cultural acquisition and the ability to "make it" is nothing other than the capacity for adaptation to a certain model of behaviour prescribed by dominant values.[28]

As a whole, these informal criteria for selection come from the very same model which governs competition for public housing; basically it consists of a concept of charity which could well be forgotten and which is addressed to "little people."[29] At the extreme of this logic one finds formulas such as those represented in France by the *cités de transit*, slums run by and, above all, controlled by the outcasts of the poorly housed, and where are collected all those who do not qualify under any criteria of selection (even if most of them are wage-earners) and who are left "in transit" for several years, sometimes as many as ten or fifteen.[30]

Besides, in so far as housing is not simply a means to "satisfy a need," but is a *social relationship*, public housing as a formula for privileged intervention by the state makes the style of life of these classes and income levels directly dependent in an area where they ought to have an escape from the economic and ideological direction of the dominant classes. Thus, for example, in France the delay incurred in the years after the war, the popular demands and the opportunity for a strong public voice instigated the policy of construction of large housing projects from 1954 on. As "emergency" policy it was distinguished by the basic choice to construct the maximum amount of housing as quickly as possible at the lowest possible cost. At the urban level, this resulted in the building on cheap land, and therefore in the badly provided outer suburbs, of poor quality housing estates which were occupied even before basic household amenities were installed.[31] At the same time the image of collective public housing deteriorated because such undertakings were also generally associated with leftist municipalities. In 1973 the policy of making housing competitive, of extension of the market towards the middle class, as well as the renewed efforts toward social integration, through an urban organisation centred on the myth of the suburban petty bourgeoisie, led the government to forbid *by law* the big housing projects as "negators of the individual." Can one do today what was not possible in 1954? Let us say, rather, that the financial concentration of housing has become sufficiently consolidated to undertake the rationalisation and the extension of a new housing market over the long run.[32] Public housing is used in the same way in the United States, simultaneously as a response to urgent need and as a starting-gate to feed publicity for parcelling out suburban sub-divisions.[33]

Because of differential ability to gain access to the market, inequality in housing is thus reinforced by the inequality which results from the differential treatment of each class and social level by economic, institutional and cultural mechanisms of production and administration in public housing. Besides, each of these classes and levels is thus submitted to specific forms of manipulation which accord with the social interests of the dominant class.

(2) A similar analysis can be developed concerning the *system of communications* and the *organisation of transport* in large metropolitan areas. In fact, it is the division of labour which is at the basis of the complexity and importance of intra-urban transport systems, and from which one observes the spatial separation of workplace from residence, urban concentration, and the daily rhythms of the city. We know that such phenomena are directly produced by specific forms of social and technical division of work in a period of monopolistic capital. It is not a matter here of any sort of technological determinism, but a real expression of a social relationship. In fact, technical progress is very often considered to be the basis of the metropolis. Despite all the arguments that we will bring to bear on this point, the role played by technology in the transformation of urban models is indisputable. Influence is exerted at the same time by the introduction of new activities of consumption and production, and by the near elimination of the obstacle of space, due to an enormous development in the means of communication. At the time of the second industrial revolution, the generation of electrical energy and the utilisation of the tramway permitted the increased concentration of manpower around more and more vast units of production. Collective transport assured the integration of different zones and activities of the metropolis, dividing the internal fluctuations according to a tolerable time/space relationship. The automobile has contributed to urban dispersion, with enormous zones of individual residences extended over the whole region, and connected by routes of rapid transit to various functional areas. The daily transport of products of current consumption benefit equally from such mobility; without the daily distribution by truck of agricultural products harvested or stored in the region, no large metropolis would be able to subsist. The concentration of business headquarters in certain regions, and the hierarchical decentralisation of centres of production and distribution are possible because of the transmission of information by telegraph, radio and telex. Finally, the development of

air navigation has been fundamental in reinforcing the interdependence of the various metropolitan regions.

Thus technical progress permits, on the one hand, the evolution of urban configurations towards a regional system of interdependencies, due to intervening changes in the means of communication, and on the other hand it reinforces this evolution directly by the transformations created by fundamental social activities, particularly those concerning production. Industry is more and more liberated from factors of rigid spatial location, such as natural resources or specific markets, whereas it is, on the contrary, more and more dependent on qualified manpower and a technical and industrial milieu which stretches across the chains of functional relationships already established. Thus industry is looking above all for its insertion in the urban system, rather than for location in relation to the functional elements (primary materials, resources, outlets) which determined its placement in the first period.

At the same time the growing importance of administration and information, and the liaison of these two activities in the urban milieu, reverse the relations between industry and city, making the former depend more and more on the complex of relationships created by the latter. Thus technological evolution (in particular the development of nuclear energy and the key role of electronics and chemistry) favours the spatial regrouping of activities, reinforcing internal ties to the "technical milieu" and diminishing dependence on the physical environment. It follows that development starts from extant urban-industrial cores and that activity becomes concentrated in the network of interdependencies thus organised.

Finally, changes in the construction industry have also permitted the concentration of functions, in particular functions of administration and exchange, in a reduced space which is accessible to all parts of the metropolis, thanks to high-rise construction. The "prefab" has been the basis for the mass construction of individual houses and, through that, for the phenomenon of residential diffusion.

Yet the metropolitan region is not a necessary result of simple technical progress. For "technical know-how," far from constituting a simple factor, is only one element in the *ensemble* of productive forces, which themselves are primarily social relationships, and thus also constitute a cultural mode of utilisation of work resources. This liaison between space and technology is thus the most immediate material manifestation of a profound articulation between the *ensemble* of a given social structure and the new urban configuration. Urban dispersion and the formation of metropolitan regions are closely allied to the social model of advanced capitalism, designated ideologically by the term "mass society."

In fact, the monopolistic concentration of capital and the technico-social evolution towards organisation of very large units of production are at the root of the spatial decentralisation of functionally related establishments. The existence of big commercial firms, with standardisation of products and prices, permits the diffusion of residences around shopping centres, easily connected by a system of rapid communications.

On the other hand, the standardisation of a growing mass of the population (salaried workers) as concerns their position in the production hierarchy is accompanied by a diversification of levels and by hierarchisation *within* each category – which, in terms of space, gives rise to a real segregation in terms of status by separating and "labelling" the different residential sectors; hence they become a vast field of symbolic display.

The ideological integration of the working class in the dominant ideology goes along with the separation of the activities of work, residence and leisure, a separation which is at the root of functional metropolitan zoning. The value put on the nuclear family, the importance of the mass media and the dominance of individualist ideology react in the direction of an atomisation of relationships and a segmenting of interests in terms of individual aspirations, which, in spatial terms, is translated into the dispersion of individual residences, be it in the isolation of the suburban home or the solitude of the big housing projects.

Finally, the growing concentration of political power, as well as the formation of a technocracy which assures that the long-run interests of the system gradually eliminate local characteristics, tends, through "urban planning," to deal with the problems of the functioning of the *ensemble* by cutting them up into significant spatial units based on networks of interdependencies of the productive system. But this contributes to the regulation of the rhythm of the urban machine by the real functional unity, which is the metropolitan region.

The metropolitan region as a central form of organisation of the space of advanced capitalism diminishes the importance of physical environment in the determination of the system of functional and social relationships, annuls the distinction between "rural" and "urban," and places in the forefront the "dynamic" society, the historic meeting-place of social relations which form its basis. We could address ourselves, eventually, to a major objection concerning this analysis of the production of the metropolitan region as a certain type of space derived from the logic of capitalism as a particular method of production and capitalism in a specific stage, i.e. monopolistic capitalism. Are there not socialist countries in which analagous urban forms develop? Then how can one deny that these are the product of a certain level of technological-economic development, independent of the principles of social organisation? Well, first of all, one must avoid approaching these problems from a capitalist/socialist dichotomy, which is not a theoretical category but a historic pseudo-globalisation which confuses and combines very diverse social processes. We do not use the term "capitalism" to describe a historical reality which would be immutable and directly determined by profit in all social occurrences. We make reference rather to a particular social matrix, economic, political and ideological, which is determined *in the last analysis* by an organisation of social relationships founded on the separation of the worker from the means of production and on the appropriation of the surplus value by the only holders of the means of production. In posing this as a point of departure for the analysis of the determination of social organisation by capital, we have not said all there is to say on the subject; but we have said something essential because we can start from a specific hypothesis concerning the logic and the contradictions inherent in a certain type of urban organisation. It is this that we have outlined in our analysis of the metropolitan region, it is this which tends to prove the *ensemble* of urban research we have cited throughout the text. If in the "non-capitalist" countries there are similar urban forms, that does not weaken the analyses we have made. Our analyses can only be discussed in relation to themselves, by referring to the methods which have been used to demonstrate that metropolitan configurations are derived from specific laws regarding the conversion of capitalist social relationships. In addition, such an observation allows us to pose a *problem* which could not be resolved except by means of specific research: the problem is that of knowing how there is reproduction of analogous social forms on the basis of different social relationships. The answer would require the following:

1 Determining if the content of these urban structures, their practice, and not only their spatial appearance, are effectively the same.
2 Assuming that one does not confuse a mode of production with a political regime, seeing to what extent there is an articulation of different modes of production in each socialist society, especially at the level of the division of labour, and of course recognising the presence, in varying degrees, of the *capitalist* mode of production.
3 Establishing the theoretical basis for analysis of a society in transition, for we do not yet have the equivalent of Marx's *Capital* for societies in transition.[34]
4 Elaborating a theory of the determination of urban space by different types of articulation of the modes of production in a post-capitalist society in transition,[35] and being thus in a position to explain, for example, why there is strong urbanisation in the Soviet Union and disurbanisation in China, or, again, why the under-urbanisation in Hungary plays a very different role from that in Cuba.[36]

Thus we see that we are facing a very different problem: that of opposing capitalism and socialism in general terms so as to unify them in the common semblance of some historically determined urban models. We proceed otherwise: we start from hypotheses concerning the structural arrangement of the laws of the capitalist mode of production in several phases and stages of development of this mode, and at several levels (economic, political, ideological), and in specific historical periods – which it is also necessary to take account of. Thus it is not a matter of finding a "moral responsibility" for all social inequalities, but of studying the validity and the transformation of the social laws which have been established up to this point by research, by specifying them and modifying them if new observations require this. Thus, for example, the American model of the dominant class and middle class fleeing the city and leading to residential dispersion is in the process of being replaced in large European cities (but also in the United States) by a model of a quasi-village community reserved to the leading elite right in the heart of the big metropolis: living in new modern super-deluxe and self-sufficient buildings, built in the central city (very often in urban-renewal projects), working in the headquarters of established big businesses, and monopolising the leisure activities and cultural opportunities concentrated in the central city. Everything happens as if the delocalisation and internationalisation of capital are accompanied by a quasi-communitarian and strongly localised closing off of the executive milieu for whom spatial mobility then comes to mean, primarily, air travel.[37]

On the other hand, for the mass of wage-earners, the tendency is towards the growing spatial diffusion of activities, to the separation, more and more strongly evident, between residence, work, recreation, shopping, etc., and thus to an increased daily dependence on the means of transportation. Such a dependence sets up new cleavages and gives rise to new contradictions.[38]

The social predominance of the market, reinforced by the inevitable necessity for a collective response to the problem, is found in transportation even more clearly than in housing, in so far as this differentiation is expressed very precisely by the different means of transport: the individual, taken in charge by the market (even though only partially – automobiles need roads); and the collective taken on, in general, by the public sector.[39] But what is specific to this differential treatment of transport is the fact that for a large part of the population there is a combined use of the two types; this produces divergent effects, for on the one hand it generalises the problems flowing from the use of transport, and on the other hand it creates new cleavages according to the combination which can be made of the use of the two means by such-and-such a sector of the population.[40]

Each of these types of transport produces specific problems which come to bear on equally specific social categories.

Thus for *public transport* the main problem is its extreme dependence on the social function which has made it necessary, i.e. the daily travel from home to work at hours and locations which are extremely *concentrated* for the large mass of wage-earners who have no possibility of arranging their time or space. Consequently, in the same way as public housing develops at the minimum level which is historically, socially and economically possible, public transport operates at a minimum level, i.e. predominantly at the times we call "rush hour." Thus spatial mobility is worked out according to the time-tables of the big organisations, even when the urban structure of the large cities makes autonomy of activity in the crowded zones or districts almost impossible.[41]

This dependence on the time-table of collective transportation is reinforced by dependence stemming from the routes of the transportation network, itself also conceived according to the capacity to resolve certain problems of spatial distribution of place of work rather than the attempt to increase intra-urban mobility.[42]

One manifest example is the route of the new *Réseau Express Régional* (RER) in Paris, designed to connect the new business centre of La Défense (in the north-west periphery) to zones of heavy residential density of employees in the near south-east suburb, even when the growing difficulties of traffic in the suburbs require other priority measures (for example, the lengthening of various lines of the Paris metro towards the townships of the nearby suburbs).[43] The concrete result for the nearly ten million inhabitants of the Paris region is to see the budget for public transport disappear in operations that increase mobility for only a special segment of the market of tertiary employment and only as concerns mobility for work.

Thus collective transport becomes a synonym for discomfort, for congestion, for oppression, for compulsory timing, if not, as in the New York subway, of personal insecurity. Then one thinks only of escaping it, of autonomy, of the capacity for individual unrestrained mobility; the "need" is thus created and the market is there, all ready to satisfy the demand of the consumer – it is the reign of the "car for individual freedom." And once the cycle is begun, it is impossible to stop it. Cities explode under the weight of a traffic pattern individualised to the point of being absurd, congestion is a constant menace,[44] and becomes the principal cause of air pollution,[45] massive investments in road-building equipment grow continually without even catching up with the problems created, traffic accidents become accepted as a necessary massacre, resulting in a growing number of physically handicapped people. Technically, socially, the reign of the individual automobile as a privileged means of transport in the big metropolitan areas is one of the greatest "absurdities" of our society. However, economically it is a necessity for the present structure of capitalism, ideologically an essential trump card for the development of the individualism and aggressiveness at the base of the dominant culture; here we have a concrete expression of what is called the contradiction between the forces of production and the relationships of production.

Nevertheless, the big car firms and the oil trusts have nothing to fear: the demand for cars, both in quantity and in quality, has continued to increase over the years, and despite the oil crisis does not seem to be seriously threatened in the long run. It seems clear that in the present state of urban organisation, in the situation predominating in public transport, in the framework of capitalist social relationships, it cannot be otherwise. The automobile, outstanding social absurdity, is at the same time one of the strongest social demands as a mythical means for individual autonomy.

This need for the automobile as a means for mobility, made necessary by urban organisation and by the way common transport is managed, is in turn a new source of inequality: on the one hand, because the level of income thus comes to order the capacity for mobility and individual security, depending on the quality of the vehicle used and the physical and psychological mastery of its operation (also socially conditioned); and on the other hand, because this extreme dependence on the automobile creates new sources of discrimination – all non-drivers are seen as virtually handicapped, even more impaired because intra-urban transportation is based on individual means. Such is the case for the aged, for adolescents, for housewives when the husband has gone to work in the car, for the sick, but also for the great segment of the population not equipped with a car: one forgets (bemused by the American image) that almost one French family in two does not possess an automobile – so many groups stuck in the under-equipped residences, so many immobile people destined to consume little else but television, so many "living dead," and so many future buyers (or thieves) of individual automobiles. Such are the everyday forms of oppression and social disparity in advanced capitalism.[46]

(3) *A new historical model of urbanisation.* Such analyses, even though rough and schematic, could be extended to other domains, for example that of educational facilities,[47] or "socio-cultural" ones.[48] But even more significant is the generation of new social constraints by the very type of urban structure which unifies and organises the whole process of collective consumption.[49]

In fact, the big metropolitan areas characteristic of advanced capitalism represent a type of city qualitatively different from the city of capitalist industrialisation.

First, the different elements of the basic urban system are strictly connected and interdependent. Thus, for example, transportation and the localisation of its activities, equipment and housing, the centre and the symbolic signals, as well as each of the elements cited in relation to the others, form an indissoluble whole in constant interaction. It is not a matter of dealing with such-and-such an element of the collective-consumption process, but with the process as a whole; there is no longer the possibility of organising housing without intervening in transport or vice versa; there are no more "urban problems" but crises and contradictions of the urban system.

Second, the structure and the processes of this urban system are directly governed by the logic of capital expressed in a specific way, i.e. according to the dominant function transmitted to each urban system by capital in the collective-consumption process (thus cities controlled by heavy industry or a centre of tourism will have their own forms of conformity to the logic of the capital which determines their existence). What is important is that monopolistic capital in the present phase is itself caught in a pattern of interdependencies, simultaneously by economic sector and at the world-wide level, and that it responds to a logic of long-term profit. This in turn implies the objective necessity for the smooth functioning of the various units of production and consumption according to a logic not accessible to these units but answerable only to the process as a whole.

Third, the intervention of the state in the domain of collective consumption, and the economic and political importance of the centralised regulation of these processes, determine the taking in charge of the units of collective consumption by the organisation. This is done by regulatory entreaties, more or less formalised, which correspond in general to the apparatus of urban planning. The cities of advanced capitalism are thus not only submitted to a rigid capitalist discipline but are organised according to the very requirements of the state intervening in this domain.

This is the completely new urban model that we propose to call *Monopolville* (Monopoly City).[50]

The consequences for the consuming agents across such collective units are numerous and complex, but they can be summarised in three points:

1   Collective consumption and the routines of daily life which depend on it become extremely rigid, standardised and constrained. This is what we call the imposition of veritable rhythms in the area of consumption, similar to the cadences of assembly-line work in a factory. The personal sensation of tension and rush in life in the big cities is a concrete expression of this.

2   The *ensemble* of these problems appears as a coherent whole dominated by an implacable logic. *Monopolville* is, in this sense, a completely totalitarian universe.

3   The supplier, the organiser, the interlocutor, the agent of central initiatives, appears to be the apparatus of the state. It *globalises* and *politicises* all the problems in making their collective treatment more necessary and visible, but at the same time makes their confrontation by the individual more difficult. The impression of powerlessness on the part of the isolated "citizen" is thus increased. As a totalitarian universe, imposing the daily cadence, ruled by the centralised power of a far-away machine, *Monopolville* exacerbates its internal contradictions to the maximum, destroys all protective mechanisms and causes continuous strain in daily life to such a point that it becomes a fetish, a structure which oppresses by an ineluctable process. Such a process of alienation, in the classical sense of the term, reminds one of the making a fetish of money and the "natural" predominance of capital in the relationship of men to the production process. Still, the contradictions and the inequalities created by this process are of

another order and it is in these that the new sources of social inequality produce specific effects on the class structure of advanced capitalism.

Social Inequality and Class Power: New Contradictions and New Models of Change

We have traced the general lines of the structural evolution of advanced capitalism by showing the new strategic role which has developed from the process of collective consumption. We have shown, through several examples, the new contradictions which are born in the process and in the urban systems which constitute the real unit of operation. But where is the social inequality to which we made reference at the start of this chapter? How can we account for the class differences of the problems raised? The theme of inequality carries in fact an implicit reference to the relative positions of the agents. In this sense, have we really demonstrated that the "workers," the "employees" or the "bourgeoisie" have their own relationship to collective consumption which is different from that of other classes or levels?

Such is the question we must pose in order to relate the analysis of the emergence of new social contradictions to the appearance of new forms of social inequality.

At the first level, the income, educational and occupational level, dependent directly on the position occupied in the relationships of production, strongly prescribe the level and style of collective consumption and their relationship to the urban system. We have seen, in fact, that not only the capacity for access to this consumption by the market offered a greater autonomy, but also, and above all, that the internal cleavages of the "public" sector were calculated on criteria of proximity to the market. From this point of view, one can say that collective consumption prolongs and specifies the social stratification determined by the class system.

But, aside from these effects of reinforcing the class structure, one finds new disparities, emerging from the historical mode of dealing with collective consumption, which do not correspond to the position occupied in class relationships but to the position in the consumption process itself, as well as in specific elements of this process and in the units of the urban system where it operates. Such is, for example, the case in the organisation of urban transport, discrimination against old people, or access to housing for immigrant workers (or for black Americans), or, again, the maladaptation of cultural facilities to the taste of young people following their differential insertion simultaneously into the schools system and the urban structure. Such "inequalities" among social groups are not entirely autonomous of the class system since the logic of the latter determines the organisation of consumption, but the positions defined in the specific structure of inequality do not correspond in a one-to-one fashion to the structure of class relationships. It is in this sense that there is specific production of new effects of social inequality.

Furthermore, at a certain level it can be said that the *ensemble* of social groups are caught in the "problems" (bottlenecks or contradictions) created by collective consumption and, in this light, if there is not equalisation in the result experienced, there is, in fact, a relationship which is not antagonistic between the agents but rather partakes (differentially, surely) of the same difficulties. Let us think, for example, of the problems of urban traffic: here it is a matter of questions which become obsessive for nearly the whole population. Also, if for housing the number of privileged people is larger, the crisis of housing largely transcends the frontiers of the popular classes – that is to say, in "urban problems," social inequality articulates a question of more general scope: structural contradiction between the model of collective consumption and the model of relationships of production which is at the root of the class system, for the collective character, objectively socialised by this process of consumption, makes the crises and difficulties more solidified, less dissociable among the agents. Certainly one can escape from pollution and the noise of urban traffic if one is above a certain income level, but one is no less aware of the difficulties; that is, it is at the level of urban problems that one can see most easily how the logic of capital oppresses not only the working class but all the possibilities for human development.

This objective community of interests, this *partial* inter-class nature of the contradictions at the level of collective consumption, are the objective basis for the ideology of environmentalism, which tries to "naturalise" the urban contradictions, welding the *ensemble* of classes and social agents into a single army of boy scouts unified by the high purpose of the preservation of the species. This also conduces to efforts toward social integration in the form of experiments in "citizen participation" in the administration of daily affairs, thus reconfirming the old Anglo-Saxon tradition of the "community" as an instrument of social cohesion which has stood the test of time in the service of the dominant structural logic.

But, at the same time, the accentuation of contradictions, their globalisation, and their direct connection to political power, form the basis for a *practical* articulation of the more general demands for transformation of the societal model. Thus it is that the growing emergence of what are called *urban social movements* in advanced capitalist societies is a major element of the social dynamic in so far as they permit the progressive formation of an anti-capitalist alliance upon a much broader objective basis than that of the specific interests of the proletariat or than the contingent political alliances.[51]

If the stated contradictions at the level of collective consumption do not correspond exactly with those springing directly from the relationships of production, it is essential to understand the gestation of these contradictions, beginning with the dominant logic of monopolistic capital. Analysis in terms of class is thus depersonalised and one can speak of the domination of capital without referring necessarily to the consuming habits of the bourgeoisie. It is at just that historical moment that capital progressively loses any concrete incarnation, that its logic becomes diffused on the world scale, that its power is increasingly identified with that of world-wide political powers, that the conditions are ripe for a collective realisation of the obstacle represented by the social relationships structurally dominated by production for the qualitative transformation of the societal model, but made necessary nevertheless by the transformation of productive forces and the forward leaps of political and ideological practice.

Some people will speak then of stopping growth and returning to nature. Caught between their awareness of the crisis and their class membership, they will choose the flight into utopia.

Others, by contrast, will find in the appearance of these new contradictions a field of choice in which to incorporate the great majority of the people in the political battle against capitalism, the only real historical practice leading to a qualitative transformation of social relationships of production which are the basis for the expression, old and new, of social inequality.

NOTES

1 For a theoretical and empirical argument along these lines, see *The Urban Question*, especially ch. 3.

2 On the relation between urban organisation and life style, see M. Branklin, *The Limits of the City* (New York: Harper and Row, 1973).

3 The analyses presented here will not be supported by statistical data but by reference to generally known social facts, but we accept from the start a certain *schemation* in this text; such is the price we must pay in sorting out the grand tendencies of social evolution to reach beyond the nuances connected with particular historical situations. We prefer to preserve in the proposed analysis its preemptory character, not trying to support and measure it by figures. Besides, the problems evoked here are too vast and too unknown for one to be, from a scientific point of view, as affirmative as we have been *for the sake of clarity* in our text. The attempt here is above all to present a certain number of *ideas* and *hypotheses* which can only be truly clarified by a series of concrete systematic analyses. It is hoped that these will have been made possible by the presentation of the general perspectives to which we address ourselves here.

4 For these analyses I refer to P. Boccara, *Etudes sur la capitalisme monopoliste d'Etat: sa crise et son issue* (Paris: Editions Sociales, 1973): Jean-Pierre Delilez, *Les monopoles* (Paris: Editions Sociales, 1972); P. Herzog, *Politique économique et planification en régime capitaliste* (Paris: Editions Sociales, 1972); P. A. Baran and P. M. Sweezy, *Monopoly Capital* (New York: Monthly Review Press, 1966).

5 For an analysis of this problem, see A. Granou, *Capitalisme et mode de vie* (Paris: Le Cerf, 1973), and for statistical sources which enable an appreciation of this

transformation, the studies of CREDOC (Public Research Centre on Consumption Problems) on the consumption patterns of the French.

6   See J. Brière, "La dialectique des besoins," *La Nouvelle Critique* (April 1974); and A. Heller, *La teoria dei bisogni in Marx* (Milan: Feltrinelli, 1974).

7   On the transformations of the utilisation of the work-force in relation to the new economic requirements, I refer to the general trends developed by M. Paci, applied by him in his study on Italy, *Mercato del lavoro e classi tactali in Italia* (Bologna: Il Mulino, 1973); see also F. Indovina (ed.), *La sprece celetizia* (Padua: Marsilio, 1972).

8   See the problematic elaborated on this point by M. Freyssenet and F. Imbert, "Mouvement du capital et processus de paupérisation," mimeo (Paris: Centre de Sociologie urbaine, 1973).

9   See J. P. Page, "L'utilisation des produits de la croissance," in Darras, *Le partage des bénéfices* (Paris: Minuit, 1966).

10 See the excellent work of J. O'Connor, *The Fiscal Crisis of the State* (New York: St Martin's Press, 1973), both for its analyses and the statistical and economic sources which are cited as a basis for his thesis.

11 See R. Stefanelli, "L'intervento publico: confronti internazionali," in *Es leve del sistema* (Bari: De Donato, 1971), pp. 263–84.

12 See the different sectors where public intervention becomes necessary in A. K. Campbell (ed.), *The States and the Urban Crisis* (New York: American Assembly, 1970).

13 We have allowed ourselves to use here, without repeating the basic concepts, works which have become classics in Marxist economic theory. For more information, we refer the reader to *Capital*, especially book III, section III, or, closer to us, the work of Bettelheim or the *Traité Marxiste d'économie politique* (Paris: Editions Sociales, 1971).

14 See N. Poulantzas, *Classes sociales et pouvoir politique de l'Etat Capitaliste* (Paris: Maspéro, 1968).

15 See M. Castells, *Luttes urbaines et pouvoir politique* (Paris: Maspéro, 1973).

16 See C. Palloix, *Les firmes multinationales et le procès d'internationalisation* (Paris: Maspéro, 1973).

17 We are familiar with the direct connection between the importance of multinational firms and the structural inflation of advanced capitalism; see C. Levinson, *Capital, Inflation and the Multinationals* (London: Allen and Unwin, 1971).

18 See J. L. Dallemagne, *L'inflation capitaliste* (Paris: Maspéro, 1972).

19 On the relationship of determination between classes and the state, I rely on the precise, subtle and new analyses contained in N. Poulantzas, *Les classes sociales dans le capitalisme aujourd'hui* (Paris: Seuil, 1974).

20 I refer for some basic facts to the following works: M. Young (ed.), *Poverty Report 1974* (London: Temple Smith, 1974) esp. ch. 7, by Peter Willmott, for England; F. Ascher and D. Levy, "Logement et construction," *Economie et politique* (May 1973), and to the "Rapport de la C.N.L. sur la situation du logement en France," Colloque de Grenoble, *La nouvelle critique sur l'urbanisme* (1974) for France; the statistics and sources assembled by Francesco Indovina in *Lo Spreco Edilizio* (Padua: Marsilio, 1972) for Italy.

21 See for France the analysis of C. Topalov, "Politique monopoliste et propriété du

logement," *Economie et politique* (March 1974).

22　For the basic facts, see CIEC, *Le financement du logement en France et à l'étranger* (Paris: PUF, 1966).

23　On this point see the extremely important book of D. Harvey, *Social Justice and the City* (1973) esp. pp. 55–84; for empirical evidence on the Paris region, see M. Freyssenet, T. Regazzola and J. Reter, "Ségrégation spatiale et déplacements sociaux," mimeo (Paris: Centre de Sociologie urbaine, 1973).

24　See D. Combes and E. Latapie, "L'intervention des groupes financiers dans l'immobilier," mimeo (Paris: Centre de Sociologie urbaine, 1973).

25　This point is fundamental and perhaps already proven in the present state of research, at least *for France*. We refer for this to the basic texts that we cannot review here in detail: S. Magri, "Politique du logement et besoins en main d'oeuvre: analyse de la politique de l'Etat en relation avec l'évolution du marché de l'emploi avant la deuxième guerre mondiale," mimeo (Paris: Centre de Sociologie urbaine, 1973); C. Pottier, *La logique du financement public de l'urbanisation* (Paris: Mouton, 1975); E. Préteceille, *La production des grands ensembles* (Paris: Mouton, 1973); C. Topalov, *Les promoteurs immobiliers* (Paris: Mouton, 1973); D. Cornuel, "Politique de logement dans le C.I.L. de Roubaix-Tourcoing," mimeo (Paris: Ministry of Equipment, 1973).

26　See P. Hermand, *L'avenir de la securité sociale* (Paris: Seuil, 1967).

27　G. Pierre Calame, *Les travailleurs étrangers en France* (Paris: Editions Ouvrières, 1972).

28　See, in this sense, the very pertinent observations contained in the study of F. Ferrarotti on Rome: *Vite di baracatti* (Naples: Liguori Editore, 1974).

29　See F. Piven, *Regulating the Poor* (New York: Harper and Row, 1971), for France, see the report by Magri on "Le logement des travailleurs" at the Colloque de CERM in 1973 in *Urbanisme monopoliste, urbanisme démocratique* (Paris: Cahiers du Centre d'Etudes et de Recherches Marxistes, 1974) pp. 143–91.

30　See C. Petonnet, *Ces gens-là* (Paris: Maspéro, (1970); G. Heliot, "Le logement des travailleurs immigrés," *Espaces et sociétés*, no. 2 (1971).

31　See E. Préteceille, *La production des grands resembles* (Paris: Mouton, 1973) for the *ensemble* of sources and references on this theme. Very significant in the social logic of housing in France, we refer to the commented bibliographic synthesis by B. Lamy, "Les nouveaux ensembles d'habitation et leur environnement," mimeo (Paris: Centre de Sociologie urbaine, 1971).

32　I refer for an analysis of the social bases of the transformation of housing policy in France to a text which caught this transformation at its beginnings: J. Bobroff and F. Novatin, "La politique Chalandon: nécessité tactique et stratégie de classe," *Espaces et sociétés*, no. 2 (1971).

33　See the classic work of R. M. Fisher, *Twenty Years of Public Housing* (New York: Harper, 1959), as well as the very interesting inquiry of L. Kiesberg, "Neighborhood setting and the isolation of public housing tenants," in *Urbanism, Urbanization and Change*, ed. P. Meadows and E. Mizruchi (Reading, MA: Addison-Wesley, 1969), pp. 276–91.

34　An extreme case is perhaps the construction of the large housing project of Grande-Borne in Grigny, near Paris, by the "official" architect of the French government, Emile Aillaud. He was commissioned to construct these in the name of decor, petrified forms of his personal fantasies. Under the pretext of artistic creation, he has imposed his personal psychic universe on the life of several thousands of families who violently object.

35 C. Bettelheim has made the greatest efforts in this direction, especially in his book *Calcul économique et formes de propriété* (Paris: Maspéro, 1969).

36 The best analysis we know of this sort of problem is that of I. Sizelenyi and G. Konrad, "The social conflicts of underurbanization," Institute of Sociology, Budapest (unpublished) relative to Hungary; for China, we refer to the article of M. Luccioni, "Processus révolutionnaire et organisation de l'espace en Chine," *Espaces et sociétés*, no. 5 (1971).

37 See in this regard the fairly new viewpoint of the development of the suburbs which appears in the collection of C. M. Haar (ed.), *The End of Innocence: A Suburban Reader* (New York: Scott, Foreman, 1972), taking up again in a forward-looking manner the themes that were introduced ten years before by R. Vernon in *The Myth and Reality of our Urban Problems* (Harvard, MA: MIT Press, 1962).

38 See F. Ferrarotti, *Roma, da capitale a periferia* (Bari: Laterza, 1971); J. Remy, "Utilisation de l'espace – innovation technologique et structure sociale," *Espaces et sociétés*, no. 4 (1971); D. Harvey, *Social Justice and the City*, pp. 96–120.

39 See Jean-Noël Chapouteau, Jean Frébault, and Jacques Pellegrin, *Le marché des transports* (Paris: Seuil, 1970).

40 See for the basic statistics (American) the classic by J. R. Meyr, J. F. Kain and M. Wohl, *The Urban Transportation Problem* (Harvard, MA: Harvard University Press, 1965); and for a theoretical analysis of the question, N. Julien and Jean-Claude Veyssilier, "Transports urbains et contradictions sociales," *Architecture d'aujourd'hui* (Paris), no. 1 (1974).

41 See the documents assembled on this problem by the Italian trade unions: *Una Nuova politica peri transporti. Atti della Conferenza nazionale* (Rome: Edizioni Sensi, 1972).

42 See the very concrete analysis concerning the social determination of the Parisian metro routes in A. Cottereau, "Les origines de la planification urbaine dans la région parisienne," *Sociologie du travail*, no. 4 (1969).

43 See the detailed analysis of the logic employed at the RER in J. Lojkine, *La politique urbaine dans la région parisienne* (Paris: Mouton, 1973).

44 See a good summary of some important research in this field in J. F. Kain, "Urban travel behavior," in *Social Science and the City*, ed. Leo A. Schnore (New York: Praeger, 1968), pp. 162–96ff.

45 See the statistics presented by R. Revelle, "Pollution and cities," in *The Metropolitan Enigma*, ed J. Q. Wilson (Harvard, MA: Harvard University Press, 1968) pp. 96–144.

46 See specific analyses and observations of this kind assembled by M. Bosquet in his *Critique du capitalisme quotidien* (Paris: Editions Galilee, 1973).

47 See M. Segré, "Politique scolaire et aménagement du territoire en France," *Espaces et sociétés*, no. 5 (1972) pp. 105–28.

48 See, for example, J. Ion, *Les équipements socio-culturels et la ville* (Paris: Ministry of Equipment, 1972).

49 See specific analyses and observations of this sort in *Urbanisme monopoliste, urbanisme démocratique*, cited above. This problem is approached from a different perspective

by J. Rémy and L. Voyé in *La ville et l'urbanisation* (Brussels: Editions Duculot, 1974) especially in the first part.

50 For an analysis which is both concrete and theoretical of this type of history of urbanisation, we refer to *Monopolville*, to be published in translation by Macmillan.

51 See the analyses of social movements in *Espaces et sociétés*, nos 6, 7, 9 (1972 and 1973), as well as the following: C. Pickvance, "On the study of urban social movements," in *Urban Sociology: Critical Essays*, ed. C. Pickvance (London: Methuen, 1975); E. Mingione et al., *Citta e conflitto* (Milan: Feltrinelli, 1971); A. Daolia, "Le lette per la casa," in *Lo sprees editzio*, ed. F. Indovina; M. Marcelloni, "Le lotte sociale in Italia," unpublished (1973); G. delba Pergola, "Le lotte urbane," *Archivio di sluch urbani et regionali*, vol. 3 (1973); M. Castells, E. Cherki and D. Mehl, *Sociologie des mouvements sociaux urbains. Enquête sur la région parisienne*, 2 vols (Paris: Ecole des Hautes Etudes en Sciences Sociales: Centre d'Etude des Mouvements Sociaux, 1974); J. Borja, *Estructura urbana y movimientos urbanos* (University of Barcelona, 1974).

FIVE

City and Culture: The San Francisco Experience

(1983)

SAN FRANCISCO: THE SOCIAL BASIS OF URBAN QUALITY

The Background

Beautiful San Francisco is a headquarters city. It is the second largest banking centre in America, and the high-rise shape of its new downtown skyline tells the story. Between 1960 and 1980 the total amount of office space in San Francisco doubled, from 35.6 million to 71 million square feet. Twenty-nine high-rise projects of ten stories or more were built between 1970 and 1979. In 1981, 20 additional buildings totalling 7.7 million square feet of office space were under construction, and the Planning Commission had already approved 16 more buildings that will add another 5.1 million square feet of office space.[1] By contrast, Los Angeles with a population five times that of San Francisco added only 0.5 million square feet of office space in 1980, and had just 1.8 million more in the planning stage. In the three-square-mile financial district of San Francisco there was a concentration, in 1980, of 53 million square feet of office space and 200,000 employees. The ten largest corporations based in San Francisco had, in 1979, 42.4 billion dollars in global sales, 37.6 billion dollars in assets, and 276,000 employees.[2] Among them Standard Oil of California, Utah International, Transamerica, Crown Zellerbach, Southern Pacific, Levi-Strauss, Bechtel Corporation, and the biggest bank in the world, the Bank of America.

The types of jobs available in San Francisco depend on the dominant corporations. Between 1960 and 1970, employment increased by 28.4 per cent in services; by 31.9 per cent in finance, insurance, and real estate; and by 26.4 per cent in government; while decreasing by 15.7 per cent in manufacturing.[3] Numbers of professionals climbed from 36,000 in 1950 to 56,000 in

1970, while operatives went down during the same period from 44,000 to 23,000.[4] Although data from the 1980 Census on the occupational structure were not available at the time of writing (October 1981), it seems very likely that the trend in the employment structure has accelerated the shift away from manufacturing to services and government. According to some estimates by the San Francisco Department of City Planning, between 1970 and 1980 the city lost about 22,000 jobs in construction, manufacturing, transportation, utilities, and wholesale trade, while 65,000 jobs were created in retail trade, finance, insurance real estate and services.

At the same time the city's total population steadily decreased between 1950 (775,357) and 1975 (672,700), and has since stabilized at about the last figure (1980 Census estimate: 678,974).[5] Yet the number of households in the city increased by 18,316 between 1970 and 1980, reflecting a major change in life styles that has had, and will continue to have, a significant effect on the use of housing and urban services in San Francisco.

Thus, not unlike the Gold Rush of 1849 which created a trade centre that became San Francisco,[6] the expansion of multinational capital and California's economic boom of the post-1940s gave new impetus to the city.[7] The entire downtown area had been subjected to development projects. Large sections of the city, particularly the predominantly black Western Addition, adjacent to the CBD, were demolished by urban renewal projects, displacing almost 8,000 families, most of them the poor, elderly, and the minorities.[8] With the Embarcadero Centre nearing completion in 1981 and the construction of the Yerba Buena Centre about to begin (now called George Moscone Centre), the role of the city as a service and financial centre will be further enhanced.[9] In order to transport people to their downtown jobs, a regional mass transport system (BART) was built between 1962 and 1974 at a cost of 1.6 billion dollars.[10] As a result of it and the highway network built during the 1950s, San Francisco established itself as the core of a large metropolitan region, the Bay Area, in which 5,284,822 people live (in 1980).[11] This urban development closely followed the pattern characteristic of the rise of the post-industrial city,[12] with the additional assets of natural beauty and a sound international economic base.[13] But this is only one side of the story: during the time that San Francisco emerged as an international city and a sophisticated urban centre, it also became a residential area in which ethnic minorities accounted for about half of its residents.[14]

Black labourers who came to work in the shipyards during the Second World War located in the Fillmore and Western Addition areas which had been evacuated by the massive deportation of its previous Japanese residents. San Francisco's black population jumped from 4,900 in 1940 to 96,000 in 1970, then decreased to 86,400 (12.7 per cent of the city residents) in 1980. But in the past two decades San Francisco became the point of arrival for an increasing flow of ethnic minorities from all over the world. The city's status as a cosmopolitan centre has not only made it attractive to multinational banks and corporations, but also to the masses of foreign nationals forced out of their country of origin by conditions of misery, hunger, war, or political terror. By 1980, Asians and Pacific Islanders accounted for 21.7 per cent of the total population of San Francisco. Latinos, mainly from Central America, make up at least 12.3 per cent, American Indians and Eskimos represent 0.5 per cent, and other races about 2 per cent. This is a very conservative estimate and, in all likelihood, if we could include Hispanics not recorded by the Census Bureau, and illegal immigrants of all origins, the proportion of ethnic minorities in San Francisco would be about 50 per cent of the city's population.[15] This picture closely resembles the model characteristic of central cities in "post-industrial" America[16] – managers and minorities, skyscrapers and ghettos, "the gold coast and the slum."[17]

And yet these demographic data and land use patterns are misleading in relationship to San Francisco's urban dynamics because, unlike most American central cities, there is no sign of urban decay. On the contrary, there is a steady improvement in the quality and maintenance of the housing. The vacancy rate remains at a low 2 per cent of the housing market, two-thirds of which are rental property. It is one of the most active real estate markets in America, with an ever increasing demand from middle income and low income groups.[18] As one would expect, given such a tight market, there is a process of displacement and gentrification under way. Such a process affects primarily the elderly renters and minorities.[19]

A major cause of the housing shortages in San Francisco is that, while the population has decreased, the number of households has increased regularly, with the average size of the households becoming gradually smaller (2.70 in 1950; 2.44 in 1960; 2.34 in 1970; 2.08 in 1980).[20] Divorce and separation seem to be a major cause for the formation of new households (more than 4,000 per year). An increasing proportion of single adults profoundly changed the social profile of the city.[21] New demands for middle class housing led to the displacement of minority residents from some parts of the city, notably through urban renewal projects like the Western Addition. But in the city as a whole, those moving out have been replaced by those coming in from other countries. San Francisco's airport officials report that between 1977 and 1980 5,000 immigrants arrived from Indo-China and 12,000 from Central America.[22] Thus, in spite of the efforts towards urban renewal and gentrification, the population has maintained a high proportion of minorities whose residence can neither be associated with a dilapidation of the housing stock nor any dramatic crisis in the urban services. On the contrary, housing rehabilitation and remodelling is practised on a large scale, most of it by private individuals. Although renovation generally goes along with gentrification by new middle class dwellers settling in an area, it is also a fact that many minority and working class residents are trying to preserve the neighbourhoods from the threat of compulsory urban renewal. Accordingly, housing maintenance is probably better than in any other large American city,[23] and the abandonment of buildings is unknown.

At the same time, the city has one of the best public health systems in the country, operates a large, efficient municipal transportation system, enjoys large areas of open space, and provides some of the most well-kept public facilities of any large metropolitan area in America. Furthermore, neighbour-hood life and urban culture have not been destroyed by the rapid transforma-tion of the city into a world metropolis. New cultures have revitalized street life and public gatherings, and urban life has become richer.

So San Francisco presents something of an urban enigma. While trans-forming itself into one of the centres of the world's corporate establishment, it nevertheless houses expanding communities boasting alternative cultures, from the 1960s' hippies to the 1970s' gays. While the downtown area becomes more concentrated and more skyscrapers are built, old Victorian houses are renovated and street life is fostered. While the residential neighbourhoods are gentrified its minority population is maintained. While keeping its function as a port of entry for poor immigrants is continued, its ethnic ghettos are hardly examples of urban dilapidation. And although the city is losing population and supporting an expanding CBD, it still maintains a satisfactory level of public services. Last but not least, although it is the homeland of corporate banking, the local government has maintained a liberal political orientation in the midst of America's conservative tide of the late 1970s – a trend that accounts for the municipal policy of some social redistribution through public services.

This is, then, the enigma, the workings of which we will try to unveil. Our study of San Francisco is an inquiry into the social roots of urban vitality. It is an attempt to understand how a city with world-wide economic connec-tions can still be shaped by the social interests of its neighbourhoods to achieve the quality of life millions of visitors have come to appreciate.

It is our hypothesis that the unique urban scene of San Francisco has been produced in the past two decades through the interaction of three major socio-political processes:

1   The rise and fall of the pro-growth coalition in the city government and the contradictory development of urban policies that it has put forward.[24]

2   Minority neighbourhood's protest and mobilization, first against urban renewal and displacement, and then to improve living conditions.[25]

3   The emergence of a new urban middle class as a major social force in the local society, a middle class which has been committed to values of urban life, environmental quality, cultural identity, and decentralized self-management, instead of reproducing the social order supported by

the corporate organizations that tend to be their employers or clients.[26] Although gays cannot be singled out as an exclusively middle class phenomenon (since homosexuality is evenly distributed across the social spectrum), the gay community in San Francisco has played the role of a social vanguard struggling to change the city, culturally, spatially, and politically.

Because of our general interest in the pattern of relationships between urban development and the mobilization of neighbourhoods, this analysis will focus on the second and third elements. Nevertheless, their effect on the urban system would be incomprehensible without referring to the local political background against which they have taken place, and most of this will be established in the context of our case studies. But some general description of the changing pattern of San Francisco's local politics must be introduced as it relates to the evolution of urban policies and the transformation of the city.

The Changing Pattern of San Francisco's Local Politics

Perhaps the most striking local political trend is the importance of the broad and loose coalitions on which city government is based.[27] Californian law requires a non-partisan candidacy for local elections. A candidate, in order to have a reasonable chance of success, must obtain a variety of endorsements. Although these may incorporate political parties and personalities, they must rely on economic, social, ethnic, and cultural institutions of local society. In the case of San Francisco this trend is further amplified by the extreme fragmentation of power, established by the city's charter of 1932. A weak mayor shares power with an 11-member, elected board of supervisors. This power is then fragmented among a variety of commissions that, although approved by the mayor, remain largely autonomous. Furthermore, the whole system is constrained by the iron hand of a powerful, immovable civil service under the leadership of a chief administrative officer who enjoys a *de facto* life tenure. The origins of this complex and somewhat paralysing system are generally attributed to the reformist effort to control the widespread corruption that characterized San Francisco's government for the first 50 years of its life, under local bosses such as Christopher Buckley and Abe Ruef.[28]

Our hypothesis is that this system of checks and balances reflects a compromise between two social blocs that fought for the control of the city until the 1960s. On the one hand, corporate business wanted a technocratic government based on an appointed city manager and a chief administrative officer. On the other hand, labour and the Catholic Church, representing Irish and Italian working class neighbourhoods, demanded institutions that would increase citizen representation, starting with an elected mayor and city council.[29] The general strike of 1934 in San Francisco, its bloody repression, and the Longshoremen Union's final victory dramatically highlighted the unstable political domination of business over labour in the city.[30]

In San Francisco's complicated system of local government, political scientists are apt to see a demonstration of pluralism. Historians, however, are more likely to recognize yet another instance of the social basis of weak government institutions: when a social class is unable to impose its will, alliances within an elected body will surely begin to change. This situation does not preclude class domination. In reality it paralyses the public institutions, while dominant classes still impose their conditions on the economy, on the cultural institutions and on the social patterning of daily life. The real problem with this unstable and fragile political domination is that it prevents local governments taking any major social or economic initiatives. Any undertaking by local government is likely to be stalled because of the mayor's inability to negotiate in a labyrinth of decisions rooted in a variety of social interests. All these phenomena manifested themselves in the politics of San Francisco's urban development plans.[31]

Urban renewal was proposed in the 1950s for San Francisco, as in other American cities, as an adequate instrument to provide a favourable setting for the new service economy, to renovate blighted areas, to displace the poor and minorities, to improve the urban environment, to keep middle class residents, and to reduce the flight of high income taxpayers to the suburbs.

The first serious move towards urban renewal came in the late 1950s when Mayor George Christopher, a Republican businessman, backed the efforts of the Redevelopment Agency, and began the first phase of the Western Addition project (A-1), planned the second phase (A-2), prepared the programme for the Yerba Buena Center (in the South of Market Area), and supported plans for BART.[32] The effort was too great for a political coalition relying solely on business support and Federal grants. Organized labour opposed the Yerba Buena Center on the grounds that it would displace industrial jobs. The conservationist movement stopped the highway programme.[33] The black minorities, stimulated by the Civil Rights Movement and suffering the first displacement in the Western Addition, started to mobilize (a development that eventually led to the Hunter's Point riot in 1966). A politically significant incident was the picketing, in 1963, of Mel's Drive-In, a chain of restaurants owned by conservative supervisor Harold Dobbs, during the period in which he was running for mayor, supported by the business community. The isolation of the conservative group led to a narrow victory by the labour-backed candidate, John Shelley, a Democratic congressman and former president of the San Francisco Labour Council. It was time for negotiation. In the midst of increasing black militancy, particularly in the A-2 section of Western Addition, where 8,000 families were about to be displaced, the business community understood the need to reach a compromise with labour, as well as to make some concessions to ethnic minorities.

In the next election a new coalition was formed which, due to the death of the nominated candidate shortly before the election, came to have Joseph Alioto, a Democrat millionaire lawyer, as its candidate. He succeeded in defeating both the conservative Republican and the liberal Democrat opponents in 1967. Thereafter the city took on the development strategy but now the pie had to be shared. Labour received the promise of construction jobs, as well as more public employment, wage increases, and social benefits. The port of San Francisco came under city control, and Harry Bridges, the historic leader of the 1934 strike, was appointed to its board.[34] Labour now backed redevelopment. As we shall see with the Latino Mission District, the minorities succeeded in stopping any attempt of a new redevelopment project in 1966. Although the black-dominated Western Addition was almost entirely demolished, 1,300 new public housing units and 2,600 subsidized units were subsequently built to curtail the displacement.[35]

The Mission District, with the black ghetto, Hunter's Point, became part of the Model Cities Programme which, although it caused continuous conflicts, also allowed Mayor Alioto an increasing control over the minorities' autonomous organizations. In sum, by bringing together business groups and organized labour, Alioto established a strong basis from which he was able to negotiate with protesters, and, although conceding on some points, he went on to lay the foundations for San Francisco's service economy. During his two terms from 1967 to 1974, skyscrapers multiplied, most urban renewal was accomplished, rehabilitation and beautification programmes were begun. BART was constructed, downtown business boomed, the port was reorganized, and new tourist and commercial facilities were built along the waterfront.[36] To be sure, some projects had their problems – particularly the port – and others, like BART, were begun for reasons that were not only related to the city. But Alioto's time in power saw the higher point of the pro-growth coalition. Nevertheless, the victory of this coalition was not complete. The Yerba Buena Centre was paralysed for many years because of the mobilization of elderly tenants supported by neighbourhood groups.[37] Conservationists expanded their influence, although they were defeated in their legal initiative to limit the height of new buildings.[38] But the main counterbalance was the stimulation of neighbourhood associations which developed in a variety of urban and social situations to control their own development.[39]

The brutality of redevelopment policies triggered local self-defence, particularly because the success of the pro-growth policies undermined labour's presence in the city by bringing in new professional and clerical workers employed in the service-orientated organizations. The pro-growth coalition's final disintegration came in 1974 under the combined impact of fiscal austerity and public employee demands. Richard Nixon's decision in 1973 to cut off

Federal programmes including Model Cities and urban renewal programmes, deprived the coalition of the patronage that fuelled it. The tightening of fiscal policies led, in 1974, to a confrontation between public labour unions asking for wage increases, and a fiscally conservative board of supervisors. Alioto backed labour efforts while business sided with the supervisors. The social basis of the coalition disappeared while the economic crisis seriously limited growth. In the 1975 election, the successful liberal candidate, George Moscone, apparently inherited the Democratic machine, but in reality gained his support from very different sources, of which the business sector only represented a tiny proportion.

Moscone tried to put together a new coalition comprising labour, the black community, and the new neighbourhood associations, led mainly by middle class activists. The leader of the Western Addition's resistance to urban renewal, Hannibal Williams, had already been appointed to the board of the Redevelopment Agency, provoking the resignation of its director. Another prominent black leader, Willie Brown, was given influence over the Housing Authority, and blacks found better opportunities in the public sector.[40] But the most important initiative was the support given by the mayor to the attempt by neighbourhood associations and left wing activists to change the electoral system of the board of supervisors, from city-wide elections to district representation. This initiative meant a major effort to bypass the control of the elections by business interests through media advertising as well as to decentralize city government by direct contact between each supervisor and his or her constituency. In November 1976, a referendum approved the reform, and the subsequent elections provided a much more liberal board of supervisors. San Francisco's business circles became seriously concerned and called for another referendum in 1977. In spite of a major financial effort led by the chamber of commerce, a very militant grassroots campaign by neighbourhood groups succeeded in maintaining the district elections system. In 1980, however, a new referendum, held at the same time as Ronald Reagan's landslide conservative victory, reinstated the system of city-wide elections. Nevertheless, most of the incumbent supervisors were re-elected, maintaining a liberal majority on the board. Among the 11 members were two pro-labour black women, two progressive white women, a socialist gay leader, and a well-known civil rights lawyer.

The recurring issue of district elections revealed not only the variations of San Francisco's political moods but also the emerging coalition behind San Francisco's local power, with minorities and middle class neighbourhoods incorporating a weakened, organized labour into an alliance from which corporate business was largely excluded. One of the most striking changes was the election to the board of supervisors, in 1977, of the leader of the gay community, Harvey Milk, who ran as a gay candidate. Mayor Moscone welcomed his presence in the city government and collaborated closely with him. The gays, who constituted the best organized and most mobilized single voting block of the new coalition, became the most solid supporters of progressive initiatives in the city government.

The reversal of local power relationships in a very short time was as dramatic as the crisis it prompted. In November 1978 a conservative supervisor, former policeman Dan White, shot and killed Mayor Moscone and Supervisor Harvey Milk. When, several months later, he was sentenced to a mild seven year term, the sentence provoked violent protest from the gay community which was answered in kind by the police. Mayor Moscone's death meant the end of his unusual, loose, and personalized coalition. Diane Feinstein, an upper class moderate Democrat, was elected mayor with the support of the same constituencies, but her ties with the business circles were much closer, and between 1979 and 1981 San Francisco's local government became, once again, open so that each group could negotiate only on an *ad hoc* basis.

The significance of such a political evolution for the urban process was that the disintegration of the pro-growth coalition prevented the city from continuing on the path of development at all costs, even if the projects already programmed were to be completed. Instead, the growing strength of the neighbourhood groups, both in social influence and in their presence in the local government, shifted the emphasis toward rehabilitation, environmental conservation, and revitalization of urban life. Ethnic minorities preserved their status quo, albeit in a very defensive manner, potentially threatened, as they were, by individual gentrification and new waves of Asian immigrants. Local cultures organized their territories. The gay community presented the most striking symbol of the search for an alternative life style. San Francisco increasingly fragmented into different worlds: the downtown business centre; the tourist and recreational areas; the different ethnic neighbourhoods; the gay territory; corridors of gentrified houses; the established areas of middle class-based alternative life styles; the defensive pro-family home owned residences; and the aristocratic hills of old San Francisco.

Since no single group was able to dominate the city's development, and no stable coalition came into existence, the city became a space of co-existing interests and cultures, unthreatened by any major project although isolated from any great collective enterprise. Leaving the banks to deal with the rest of the world, most San Franciscans concentrated on their local existence, on their neighbourhood's life, and on their home's comfort and beauty. Perhaps the absence of central urban policy is the secret of the new urban quality attained in San Francisco, along with the maximization of the neighbourhoods' autonomy in a situation where cultural values tend to match market pressures and where community organizations still are a deterrent to any kind of heavy-handed political authority.

In order to explore this major hypothesis, the formulation of which suggests the theme of our analysis without indicating the full complexity of its implications, we must be a good deal more specific. So we will try to understand the urban dynamics of San Francisco through the detailed analysis of two community mobilizations that appear to have provided major contributions to the city's evolution. They are the Latino-based Mission District's process of community organization and the San Francisco gay community. They represent, in their own distinct ways, the main social trends underlying San Francisco's urban quality: the search for cultural identity and for political self-reliance.

URBAN POVERTY, ETHNIC MINORITIES AND COMMUNITY ORGANIZATION: THE EXPERIENCE OF NEIGHBOURHOOD MOBILIZATION IN SAN FRANCISCO'S MISSION DISTRICT

Introduction

The largest urban popular mobilization in San Francisco's recent history took place between 1967 and 1973 in the predominantly Latino Mission District. The movement brought together a variety of social interests and ethnic groups into a multi-issue community organization, the Mission Coalition Organization (MCO), whose structure and tactics were largely inspired by the Alinsky model of community action. At the peak of its power, in 1970–1, the MCO probably involved up to 12,000 people[41] (in a neighbourhood of 50,000), who participated in over 100 grassroots committees of various types. Although the organization disbanded in 1973, after a highly significant and self-destructive process, it brought to the neighbourhood a series of improvements as well as a constellation of neighbourhood organizations and social agencies that survived the crisis and transformed the Mission into a vital urban scene.

The observation of the Mission's social dynamics, the reconstruction of the MCO's history, the analysis of its crisis, and the study of its social and urban outcomes provide privileged ground for the consideration of some major research questions suggested by the American urban experience: the relationship between community organizations and public programmes of social reform; the intertwining of poverty and ethnicity; and the complex articulation between neighbourhood self-reliance and local politics. These are all major themes of the social practice we observed, or reconstructed, in the Mission. On the basis of both existing historical records and our field work in 1980 (see the Methodological Appendix, pp. 231–43), we have been able to provide some tentative answers to the question, fundamental to American life, relating to the interaction between ethnic minorities and urban structure. Let us first recall the social profile of the experience before undertaking its theoretical analysis.

The Background

San Francisco's Mission District has been, for the past 30 years, the gateway to a new world of promises and fears for most Latino immigrants arriving in the Bay Area.[42] The sunny flatland of this old working class neighbourhood was the location of the first Spanish Mission settlement in 1776 and is now the setting for one of the most diverse, ethnic scenes of urban America[43] (see figure 5.1 for its location in San Francisco). It was one of the few areas preserved from the fire that followed in the wake of the 1906 earthquake. The Mission housed the Irish and Italian working class families displaced by the disaster, as well as many of the retail stores which moved away from the downtown area. The working class emigration to the suburbs during the 1940s and 1950s freed a considerable amount of old, though sound, housing

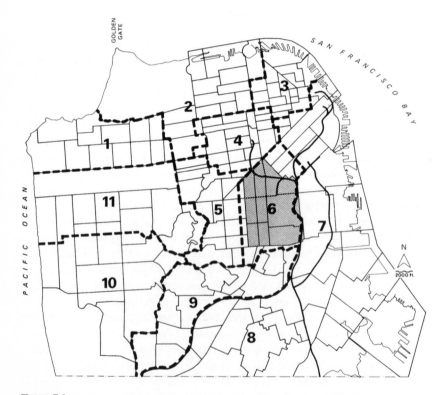

Figure 5.1 Location of the Mission neighbourhood in the city of San Francisco. The thick dotted lines indicate supervisorial districts (which are numbered) and the thin lines census tracts

Source: Mission Housing Development Corporation

units that became a shelter for the incoming Latin and Central American population, migrating for the most part from Nicaragua and El Salvador. During the 1960s and 1970s, Mexicans, Puerto Ricans, Cubans, South Americans, Samoans, American Indians, and Filipinos also moved into the Mission transforming its 50,000 population into a "world city" of many cultures.[44] By 1980, young middle class whites were also settling in the area, renovating some of its Victorian buildings,[45] upgrading its social status, and changing the local ambiance somewhat.

But the Mission still is the *Barrio* (the Latino ghetto): the family income is far below the city's average;[46] the educational[47] and occupational[48] status is at the bottom of the scale; the public services do not equal those available elsewhere in San Francisco;[49] and the proportion of overcrowded and dilapidated housing, although relatively low, is much higher than in most areas of the city.[50] The Latino culture is present all over the neighbourhood, particularly in the Inner Mission sections, from restaurants to cinemas, from bookshops to grocers, from night bars to political posters. The current process of limited gentrification and the exodus of second generation Latinos to the suburbs is largely compensated for by the continuous arrival of new immigrants.[51] The neighbourhood is also the scene for various deviant behaviour and social protest – a mix of prostitution, drugs, "street kids," joyful celebrations and political demonstrations. In 1980, on Friday and Saturday evenings, the low riders slowly paraded along Mission Street filling the night with their music, stopping to arrange parties or to share drugs and drinks.[52] On the pavements, usually around the BART stations,[53] flags and banners call for solidarity with the revolutionaries in Nicaragua and El Salvador. They also protest police brutality, often anticipating their arrest by police officers who constantly patrol the streets of the Mission, particularly during the evenings. And yet, unlike most American ghettos, this agitated ambience has not discouraged white middle class people from walking around the Mission, enjoying its colourful life and even looking forward to their own life in the district.

This urban vitality is not stage managed and organized behind the lights of the bars and Mexican restaurants, but is the expression, in spite of poverty and deficient public services, of a very diverse network of neighbourhood-based activities, of a continuous flow of newcomers, and of an active community of small businesses. In the same way that Chinatown highlights the Asian roots of San Francisco, so the Mission underscores the city's deep Latin American connection. As in most major American cities, the reality of the international social and economic system emerges from behind the curtains of San Francisco's old-fashioned bourgeois charm. And the Mission, like Chinatown, is a combination of slums and lights, remodelling and overcrowding, drugs and politics, real estate speculation and community organization, middle class gentrification and the open door to Latin American immigrants. That evolution, we should note, does not hold true for the black community in San Francisco (either displaced or disorganized in the Western Addition, or kept isolated in the ghetto areas of Hunter's Point and Ingleside), for the East Oakland ghetto, or for San Jose's predominantly *chicano* popular wards.[54]

The Mission presents a unique case of a *Barrio* that remains a centre of attraction for urban life, improving the real estate values while still maintaining most of its character as a neighbourhood for immigrants and the poor. Some of the trends of this urban achievement (the characteristics of which will be presented in our study) seem to be related to the popular mobilization that has taken place in the Mission District since the mid-1960s. At least, this is the argument we will try to develop in the following pages.

Furthermore, the characteristics of neighbourhood mobilization account not only for the urban revival but also for the shortcomings of this urban situation, as a consequence of the contradictions and pitfalls of the grassroots movement. In other words, the community struggles and organization in the San Francisco Mission District account both for the persistence of an autonomous Latino culture and for the incipient process of middle class gentrification. They are also at the basis of the improvement of social services as well as at the roots of the housing crisis. The complexity of the Mission's urban reality is in fact the result of the tortuous path undertaken by the neighbourhood's mobilization.

The Mission Story

The MCO was, between 1967 and 1973, one of the most successful examples of an Alinsky-style community movement, showing a remarkable capacity to combine grassroots organization with institutional social reform. In a different but simultaneous initiative, Latino radical youth, searching to establish Brown Power, united in 1969 to defend *Los Siete de la Raza* in a notorious trial against a group of youth accused of killing a police officer.[55] Behind the activist front, day-to-day social and political work by a variety of agencies and neighbourhood-based groups built up a community network of activities, solidarities, conflicts, and debates. The fragmented and contradictory character of such a powerful and diversified movement resulted in an equally contradictory social outcome. Its internal diversity, its incapacity to become associated with the new local political coalition around George Moscone in 1975, and, above all, the difficulty of bringing some cohesion to demands for improved conditions, class issues, and ethnic identity, led to a highly differentiated social situation where failure and success, co-opted reformism and confused social change, interwined in a pattern as complex as the Mission's urban scene.

This is the theme of our story, one that we must give in full before we can analyse its components so that we may understand how ethnic revolt and urban protest affect society and politics.

The beginnings

As in most American inner cities the first grassroots mobilization in the Mission was triggered, in 1966, by the potential threat of an urban renewal programme. The urban renewal project was initially presented as a study proposed by the San Francisco Redevelopment Agency (SFRA) to foresee, and possibly encourage, urban change induced by the construction of the BART line along Mission Street, with two major stations in the very core of the neighbourhood. Quite apart from the fact, however, that some private development projects were being considered as extensions of the adjacent downtown area, the concern of the Mission residents was more than understandable given the SFRA's record as a major instrument of demolition and displacement, and the future context of increased accessibility to the Mission from the entire Bay Area as a result of the new mass transit system. A conservative Anglo[56] Home Owners Association and a radical Mission Tenants Union[57] simultaneously called the attention of the neighbourhood to the potential danger. But neither of them had the power or the political legitimacy to mobilize and represent the community. The churches, particularly the Presbyterians, the Episcopalians, and the Roman Catholics, seized the chance to lead a vast coalition to stop the urban renewal study. To do so, they relied on the organizational web already existing in the Mission, including at least four different types of neighbourhood groups:

1 Social service orientated agencies, like *Obeca-Arriba Juntos*, initially funded by the Roman Catholic charities and managed by a group of liberal Mexican-Americans with connections with the poverty fighters of the Democratic party.
2 The Latino wing of the San Francisco labour movement organized around the *Centro Social Obrero*, connected to the Construction Workers Union (AFL-CIO Local 261).
3 The church-supported groups, particularly the Roman Catholic council for the Spanish speaking residents.
4 Local chapters of socio-political traditional Latino organizations such as the Mexican American Political Association (MAPA), and League of United Latin American Citizens (LULAC).

Additional support eventually came from the Economic Opportunity Council (EOC) organizers[58] who were at the same time trying to attract popular constituencies to implement the Federal social programmes under the classical premise of "maximum feasible participation."[59] So, from the very beginning, the two major triggers of the American urban movements of the 1960s, urban renewal and the war on poverty, were the underlying causes of social mobilization in the Mission.

After some argument with the labour group, initially attracted to a redevelopment project by the possibility of obtaining construction jobs, a coalition was formed in the neighbourhood to stop urban renewal. This was the Mission Council on Redevelopment (MCOR) which successfully opposed the approval of the study project, organizing a major campaign of grassroots protest and public opinion support that swayed, in December 1966, the board of supervisors of the city of San Francisco to a six to five vote, overriding the mayor's approval of the SFRA's proposal. After its victory, the *ad hoc* coalition dispersed, proving too diverse to agree on anything but the preservation of the neighbourhood. Yet the success of this coalition realized the idea that urban renewal could be stopped and that an alternative pattern of social and urban policies could be developed in opposition to the one inspired by the usually predominant downtown interests. Under these circumstances, the ground was laid for the potential convergence, into an umbrella community organization, of the three powerful groups already active in the Mission's turbulent scene in the late 1960s:

1   The urban-based churches, struggling to maintain their influence among the popular sectors, threatened by spatial displacement as well as by the growing influence of radical ideologies.
2   The radical political groups, formed in the anti-war movement and the campus revolts, and identifying with the involvement of ethnic minorities in the process of Third World liberation.
3   The traditional Latino organizations (both the ones that were service-orientated as well as those politically motivated) trying to benefit from the war on poverty and aware of the challenge presented by the new Latino radical nationalism, one of whose most extreme expressions, the Brown Berets,[60] began to make themselves evident on the streets of the Mission.

Nevertheless the crucial event in the formation of a broadly supported community organization came from high-up the institutional ladder. In February 1968, the newly elected mayor Alioto – probably looking to consolidate his influence among the city's ethnic minorities – unexpectedly announced his intention to apply for a Federally-funded, multi-million dollar Model Cities Programme.[61] The two basic target areas (model neighbourhoods) were going to be Hunter's Point (a black ghetto), and the Inner Mission (the Latino *Barrio*). The choice of these two areas was a striking demonstration of the implicit synonymity between troubled ethnic minorities and urban problems in the terminology of American social policy.

A very broad coalition was formed out of the existing organizations, both to qualify for a series of programmes that would meet the pressing demands of Mission residents and to develop new, more relevant grassroots groups that would control and/or administer the funds, jobs, and institutional resources to be delivered by the Model Cities Programme.

Thus two major factors appear to have been decisive in the process of formulating of the incipient MCO:

1   Although grassroots mobilization against urban renewal predated the Model Cities proposal, the organization was formed to represent the residents' interests in the Federally-funded urban programmes, administered by city hall. The MCO was, therefore, a carefully thought-out project of citizen participation, even though some of its leadership tried to use it to build a powerful and autonomous grassroots organization. Most participating organizations and agencies intended to preserve their autonomy and saw the MCO as a coalition of existing organized constituencies, without any capacity for initiative beyond the mandate of each participating organization.

2   However the MCO leadership saw in this process a chance to build up a new grassroots movement that could expand to be a multi-issue, multi-ethnic community organization representative of the entire neighbourhood, and would eventually bypass the indigenous leaders who they considered to be too close to the public bureaucracies and too narrowly defined as Latino notables.

These two conflicting views of the MCO's role led to continuous internal fighting in the neighbourhood mobilization, many of the differing interests finding expression in the electoral tactics for the annual MCO convention, and in the bureaucratic manoeuvring to win control of the key committees within the coalition. The movement was, from its inception, dominated by an organizational schizophrenia: on the one hand, the attempt to create an autonomous grassroots movement took place within the framework of mandated citizen participation in the local bureaucracies; and on the other hand, the political will to become a multi-issue, single-structure organization was confronted, again and again, with the reality of the MCO's origin as a coalition comprising many organizations, structured around a single issue – the control and management of a Model Cities Programme.

The first conventions

The fragile unity of the MCO, as well as the complexity of the movement it expressed, were apparent at the organization's very first convention, held on 4 October 1968. Although the attendance of 600 delegates on behalf of 66 neighbourhood-based groups established the representativeness of the organization, the convention was disrupted from the opening session. Some delegates, led by the black youth Mission Rebels, accused the Alinskyite leadership of secretive manoeuvring to ensure the control of the coalition's elected board, denied the necessity of an umbrella organization, and called for a more radical stand on truly political issues. In the midst of the shouted confrontations and at a point when many delegates were beginning to leave, a telephone call came from Cesar Chavez[62] praising the founding of the new organization. Order was restored and the convention was saved by being adjourned for one month to repair the damage. The MCO was born, but not, however, with all the participants who had been present at the opening session of the convention. The Mission Rebels, the Marxist–Leninist Mission Tenant Union, *La Raza* (a radical Nationalist Latino party), and other radical Latinos walked out of the organization. The predominantly white middle class Home Owners Association never joined the MCO, distrustful of the Latino predominance. So although the MCOR had provided the organizational drive, the MCO came out with a more community-orientated strategy that went far beyond a merely defensive reaction to urban renewal.

When the first convention was finally reconvened, in November 1968, only 250 delegates appeared. Nevertheless the organization began to progress. By-laws were approved, *ad hoc* committees were set up, a budget was established with contributions coming largely from the churches, and a president was elected: Ben Martinez, a 24-year-old *chicano* college student working in one of the EOC programmes in the Mission. He soon became the charismatic leader of the Community (too charismatic for some of the member organizations). A limited staff was hired and a staff director appointed.[63] He was Mike Miller, an experienced community organizer, trained by Saul Alinsky himself, and introduced to the Mission by the Presbyterian church. Miller it was who developed the strategy of the neighbourhood mobilization.

So as to remain open to the radical wing of the community, the convention took a very firm stand on the future relationship with public urban programmes and city hall, voting 13 non-negotiable demands to be fulfilled by the Model Cities Programme as a prerequisite for the MCO's participation. The most important demand was to reserve the MCO the right to veto any initiative coming from the Model Cities Administration. The most apparent reason for such an extreme position was the popular feeling that Model Cities would slip in a new programme of urban renewal. But also implicit in this stand was the ideology of community control, predominant among most grassroots committees: the feeling that the community itself should take care of the management of the urban programmes, removing them from the bureaucrats' hands. Neither Mike Miller nor Ben Martinez was convinced that the strategy would work and favoured what they called institutional change, that is, forcing the public institutions to modify their policies under pressure from the grassroots, but without actually involving the community organization in the daily management of the urban programmes. The conflicting approaches of community control and institutional change introduced an additional split into the jungle of feuds and alliances that already underlay the MCO.

Before it could debate its strategy, however, the coalition had to prove its capacity to mobilize and organize people, to solve problems, to win demands, and to establish a favourable power relationship *vis-à-vis* city hall, business, and real estate interests. Throughout 1969 a series of actions in the neighbourhood started to root the organization to its constituency. Actions were initiated such as creating new playgrounds, installing community representatives in the new Mission Mental Health Centre, and banning pawnshops in the neighbourhood. Unable to take a clear stand in relationship to the strike at San Francisco State College[64], the coalition lost its appeal for the most radical Latinos and blacks, but reconciled itself with some of the predominantly moderate working class families in the Mission. The controversy between different Latino nationalities was handled by establishing *ad hoc* representation in the executive committee for each national or ethnic group.[65]

So, thanks to some internal and external groundwork, the second convention, in October 1969, was able to provide the image of a mature, broadly representative, and well-martialled grassroots organization. Some 800 delegates attended the meeting on behalf of 81 organizations, including national and ethnic groups, churches, block clubs, tenants unions, youth committees, civil rights organizations, labour unions, social service agencies, business circles, merchants associations, and a few home owners associations. The MCO came into its own from this time, mainly through the militant activities and successful demands of its issue-orientated committees. The two most prominent issues that triggered social struggles were housing and employment. Absentee landlords were singled out, picketed in their suburban homes, and forced to sign fair agreements with their tenants on rents, repairs and maintenance. In one year the housing committee was able to win upward of 100 such actions. So other landlords refrained from indiscriminate rent increases or from the use of eviction. This campaign contributed, with similar struggles in other neighbourhoods in the early 1970s, to the legislation of a mild form of rent control in San Francisco. Another major outcome of the MCO housing campaign, which was instrumental in organizing the community, was a network of building stewards to handle the tenants' complaints on behalf of, and supported by, the entire coalition.

The major field of action for the MCO was, however, to fight discrimination against minorities and youth in the workplace. The coalition forced companies and shops to provide jobs for unskilled workers and special summer jobs for youth by picketing or disrupting normal operations, sometimes with an imaginative and humorous display. For instance, the Hibernia Bank in the Mission was forced to hire Latinos after its Latino clients started to withdraw their funds by writing one dollar cheques on a *tortilla*,[66] a perfectly legal device in California. Once again the emphasis was on simultaneously

obtaining jobs and organizing people through carefully planned job allocation. People were given points according to their commitment to work, and
committee activities (attendance at the meetings, picketing, leaflet distribution, etc.). On the basis of the number of accumulated points, they were
entitled to apply for a job on behalf of the coalition. The companies were
supposed to hire the person proposed by the MCO, as selected by the employment committee, regardless of the persons' professional qualifications,
and the employer had to provide the job and the training. This scheme could
obviously work only on a limited basis and relied on the strong bargaining
position of the community. In fact, during the peak of the MCO's mobilization, the practice did work, and hundreds of jobs were obtained from Pacific
Telephone and from Sears. This approach to employment, however, created
serious friction with the more cautious and traditional manpower and employment programmes used by the established Latino social agencies, which
were also important members of the coalition.

In a parallel development, a community maintenance committee took care
of a variety of local issues such as obtaining stop signs and traffic lights; seeing
that burned and abandoned buildings were torn down to avoid squatting;
improving mail deliveries; and picketing a cinema on Mission Street that
showed pornographic films, forcing it to close, and then coming to an agreement with the theatre whereby it would only show films for the family and
that the MCO members could obtain 25 cents discount on all tickets. The
activities of this committee ensured the good reputation of the coalition among
the conservative home owner's sector in the Mission.

A planning committee, on which the Anglo middle class was well-rep-
resented, collaborated with the city planning department in the formulation
of a new land-use plan for the District.

The MCO tried to establish a broad base across the community at the
price of losing the support of the more radical youth groups, as well as at the
cost of playing down specific Latino cultural demands, an issue that soon
caused major criticism from some of the coalition's more important members.
The major task, however, still had to be undertaken – to obtain a substantial
Model Cities Programme and to make sure that it would benefit the whole
community.

The Model Cities Programme

The mayor had supported, in principle, the provision of a Model Cities
Programme for the Mission, but the important issue under discussion was the
power relationships that it would create. Model Cities was for the mayor the
channel through which funds and jobs could be distributed to the blacks and
Latinos in exchange for their political allegiancy. For the MCO, the first
convention had instructed the leadership to exercise a veto over the pro-

gramme and to administer it autonomously in relation to city hall. The conflict took the form of a major disagreement over the new institution to be set up to operate the programme. The mayor wanted a Community Development Administration, located within city hall, but allowing participation of blacks and Latinos on its board of directors. The MCO felt it should be created as a neighbourhood-based, private corporation, controlled by the community and operated with funds directly allocated to it from the Model Cities Programme. Mayor Alioto refused to give away control of the operation. The MCO engaged in battle and mobilized strong support for its position. In addition to demands from its grassroots committees, it obtained favourable public statements from a very broad spectrum of religious, business, labour, and political leaders ranging from San Francisco's Archbishop to a top aide of Governor Reagan. After the MCO organized a massive march on city hall, the mayor accepted the coalition's proposal. The board of supervisors confirmed the agreement after a public hearing where the MCO impressed the audience with its display of support and discipline, when each representative of 78 local organizations gave a one and one-half minute speech presenting a co-ordinated and scheduled collective presentation of the coalition's position.

Nevertheless, the state does not stop at the city hall level, not even in America. The Federal funding agency, Housing and Urban Development (HUD), refused to allow community control over public funds, arguing that the MCO's insistence on veto power was illegal because it constituted power without commensurate responsibility. In spite of the MCO's momentum, HUD's declared position to reject Model Cities under the conditions already accepted by city hall rekindled the debate among the MCO leaders over the notion of community control. Both the president, Ben Martinez, and staff director, Mike Miller, feared the loss of organizational autonomy and of the transformation of the movement into a high-powered social agency, which would involve them in managing what would be a private, neighbourhood-based corporation. They had previously agreed, however, on the strategy of involvement in the administration of the programmes under pressure from a variety of members of the coalition as well as from the widespread opinion of a community distrustful of public bureaucracies. Now that they were faced with a "choice," as suggested by HUD, of "Take it or leave it," the social agencies and the majority of the membership were ready to accept a compromise that would provide access to the desperately needed public resources. In the formula that was finally established, and approved by city hall, the legal requirements imposed by HUD were respected, but the MCO was allowed to designate 14 of the 21 members of a new public agency, Model Mission Neighborhood Corporation (MMNC), in charge of the administration of Model Cities Programmes in the Mission. A similar public agency was created to manage the urban programmes for the black community in Hunter's Point.

A Model Cities grant was approved in June 1971 for the Mission neighbourhood, respecting these conditions and allocating a sum of 3.2 million dollars per year for a period of five years. The MCO, however, was given only six months to draft the proposal, with little technical expertise and serious internal fighting. Grassroots participation was thus minimal in the elaboration of the goals and procedures that were settled upon for the urban programmes by the MCO's leadership. But the proposed organizational model for the new neighbourhood corporation turned out to be a very sophisticated scheme that basically tried to ensure the objectives of community organization and grassroots enforcement through the resources provided by the programmes.[67] Power and independent organization were considered the most important resources to be obtained from Model Cities.

The organizational scheme was based upon the principle that the MMNC would be tightly controlled by the MCO, whose 14 delegates would meet at a caucus before each meeting and vote as a single group on each issue. Priority would be given to low-income housing programmes and job-finding efforts for the Mission's residents. The main activities of the MMNC would be governed by the main targets already set by the MCO: employment, housing, education, and child care. The main purposes of the programme would be to transform the local power system by asking local governments to be more responsive to people's demands, and to encourage grassroots mobilization and organization centered on the use and control of the granted public resources. A series of procedures were designed to infuse this spirit into the programmes. For instance, a hiring hall was set up to ensure that employers hired job candidates from the Mission on the basis of the non-discriminatory criteria established by the MMNC and with reference to the recommendations of the MCO's employment committee. The educational programme proposed to give money to the school district to improve the schools' facilities on the condition that the school district board would encourage parents' participation in the schools' management, and introduce a series of pedagogic reforms in the schools' curricula. On housing, given the difficulty of obtaining approval for low-income housing projects, the MMNC established a seed-money fund to influence local bank grants, in an effort to end red-lining loans in the Mission.[68]

The reality of managing urban programmes and simultaneously fostering community organizations proved even more difficult than foreseen in spite of the leadership's awareness of the problems. Bureaucratic routine slowed down the programmes at the moment when expectations and demands were mounting. HUD turned down several proposals for housing projects, limiting the total of new constructions to 89 housing units. The strategy of the educational programme was made obsolete when the city desegregation programme through busing broke the relationship between the school district and Mission residents. Additional difficulties came from the insensitivity of the Model Cities

Agency to requests by the Latino cultural associations for bilingual education and bi-cultural programmes. The child care programme, although successful, fell under the management of city hall and so lost its close ties to the MCO. Finally, the innovative hiring practices used by the employment committee were declared illegal, and the companies refused to honour them as soon as they felt strong enough to resist the community's pressure.

Throughout the formation of the MMNC, most of the MCO's original leaders were absorbed into managing the programmes. When cultural, political, and personal divisions developed within the coalition, the internal split took the form of a confrontation between the MCO and its supposedly controlled public agency, legally responsible for the administration of the resources aimed at improving the neighbourhood. The social agencies that existed in the Mission before becoming a part of the MCO were particularly bitter about the new public agency that bypassed them to take over control of the funds that they had been awaiting for such a long time. As a result, the confrontation between the MCO, now controlled by the Latino social agencies, and the MMNC, now managed by the Alinskyite cadres, replaced the anticipated confrontation between Mission residents and city hall. The MCO militants started to picket their fellow MMNC representatives, as they had formerly done against the speculative landlords. Mayor Alioto, reassured by his re-election in 1971, and having carried the Mission vote with the MCO's support, presented himself as a mediator between the rival factions, taking advantage of the community's division to reject the requests for neighbourhood improvement from both groups. When Richard Nixon made the decision in 1974 to shut down all Model Cities Programmes, funds were cut off in San Francisco. The Model Cities Programme in the Mission had, however, already died from wounds inflicted by internal conflicts whose social logic we shall try to explain.

The coalitions' fifth convention, held in November 1972, had the largest attendance, at least on paper, in the organization's history with 1,600 delegates representing 202 neighbourhood groups and agencies. In fact, many of these organizations were only labels prepared for the convention to increase the voting power of the different quarrelling factions. Instead of a social movement, the MCO had become an organizational battleground. Every formal or informal caucus was struggling to win power within the MCO which would then grant them access to the resources of Model Cities as well as to the power centre of city hall.

The first major conflict in the leadership had appeared in the third convention in 1970 when the president decided to run for a third term, at the cost of changing the MCO's by-laws that had forbidden more than two terms. As a result he faced the opposition of one of the founders of the movement, a Puerto Rican woman, outraged by the personalization of the leadership. After her candidacy was defeated, she withdrew from the movement, pulling out with her several grassroots committees.

At the same 1970 convention, Ben Martinez also faced more substantial opposition in the shape of the Latino national groups dominated by the middle class, such as LULAC, arguing that in spite of Martinez's ethnic background, the coalition was dominated by an Anglo Alinsky-inspired staff, insensitive to the Latino culture: the MCO was using a Latino image, so the argument ran, to win power in city hall for a non-Latino organization.[69] Although they lost the 1970 contest, the Latino nationalists received a major boost in 1971 when the chicano-based social agencies in the Mission sided with them to join the Alianza Caucus within the MCO for the purpose of taking control of the organization which up until then was in the hands of the Alinsky cadres, themselves organized as the Unity Caucus.

In 1971, Ben Martinez finally stepped down from the presidency to become staff director.[70] The Unity Caucus, supported by church groups, Latino youth groups and tenants, managed to choose his successor and obtain a majority on the coalition's steering committee in 1971 and again in 1972. But the new president was unable to hold together the complex, effective puzzle that the MCO had become over the previous three years. Meanwhile the Alianza Caucus gained the support of the Latino-based labour groups, the Obreros, as well as social agencies, the powerful Mission Language and Vocational School, and the Latino Nationalists. The result was one of organizational paralysis and self-destructive in-fighting. The Alinskyite cadres used their position of control over the Model Cities Agencies to fire several prominent members of the Alianza Caucus from the staff. Then internecine war broke out amongst the various factions of the MCO including personal attacks, lawsuits, and militant tactics. The tension was heightened by the withdrawal of funds, particularly by the churches that had become sceptical about the character of such a strife-ridden movement. In its last active year, 1972, the MCO only survived with the help of a 42,000 dollar grant from Stanford University, to train its students in community development so that they might write their PhD theses on urban social movements. In January 1974, after a final series of conflicts and personal attacks had been gleefully reported in the local press, the MCO, to all intents and purposes, collapsed.

Yet the entangled network of social interests and neighbourhood-based organizations that had formed the MCO survived and expanded on its own, sometimes coming together for a particular event, but more often competing for political power, social representation, or financial resources.

Further mobilizations

The Alinskyite-branch of the MCO survived through the activity of the Mission Planning Council (MPC), whose opinions and demands were seriously considered by city hall in all decisions concerning the neighbourhood's urban development. In 1975, allied with *La Raza*, the MPC mobilized hundreds of residents to oppose the zoning of a section of the Mission, a change that would have permitted the conversion of family residences into commercial areas, making the displacement of low-income families legal. The zoning was halted as a result of the pressure brought to bear by the neighbourhood and the residential areas were preserved. Nevertheless, the MPC had by 1980 really come to represent the Anglo middle class residents, to the point that the founder, Luisa Ezquerro, a highly respected schoolteacher and leader of the Latino community, left the Council to avoid being identified with its increasingly anti-Latino stand. The last spin-off from the MCO had faded.

The traditional Nationalist–Latino organizations went through serious difficulties to mobilize support for themselves, torn as they were between cultural identity and middle class interests, against the background of the Latino poor. LULAC concentrated on administering some educational programmes, and its membership declined to about 35. MAPA, in spite of good connections with the broader political system, did not have enough strength to take the initiative single-handed, and its only successes came as a result of joint efforts with other community forces, such as the effective campaign against racial discrimination with Latinos for Affirmative Action.

In the late 1970s the two basic grassroots related activities in the Mission District were, on the one hand, the social programmes orientated towards the community, and, on the other, the political solidarity with liberation struggles in Latino America.

Among the social agencies, *Obeca-Arriba Juntos* established itself as a dynamic multi-purpose corporation with a one million dollar a year budget, largely used on manpower programmes. The Mission Hiring Hall, developed on the basis of the Model Cities Programmes, specialized in obtaining jobs for the Latinos. The Mission Language and Vocational School expanded, employing a staff of over 200 people, and was the major channel through which the continuous waves of Latin American immigrants passed, enabling them to integrate into the Mission and subsequently settle in northern California. The Mission Community Legal Defense, also a spin-off of Model Cities, provided free legal assistance to Mission residents who faced criminal charges, and made a point of protecting Latino youth against unjustified police harassment. The Mission Health Neighborhood Centre, funded by Federal programmes, became an important and well-equipped public health facility, although its work was continually interrupted by violent conflicts between the board, speaking for the Latino community organizations, and the centre's staff and health workers, who were influenced by a radical left wing group called The Rebel Workers.

In 1979 the Latino Unity Council (LUC) was established, along the lines of the most prominent social agencies and with the support of some notable people in the Latino community. The council functioned through a network of reciprocal support, including 12 community-based agencies and about 100 individuals. The interactions, organization, and tactics of this coalition radically and deliberately departed from the model incarnated by the MCO. The LUC avoided any by-passing of its member organizations and fully represented its fragmented interests so that its activities were highly dependent upon volatile but evenly-weighted compromises.

Another set of social programmes, mainly funded through United Way,[71] tried to deal with the problems experienced by Mission youth. Real Alternatives Programme (RAP) articulated an effort to meet youth demands on jobs, education, recreation, and counselling, with a strong socio-political commitment expressed through hard day-to-day work to serve the people. Given the increasing incidence of hard-drug abuse among the Mission youth, RAP introduced specialized programmes to deal with this sensitive issue. They created *Centro de Cambio*, a rehabilitation programme partly managed by youths who had formerly been drug addicts. They also built *La Casa*, a residential drug-free centre for youths wanting to escape drug dependency, obtain a high school education and find a job with the staff's support.

The youth-orientated social programmes also had to cope with the friction between the youth, challenging the status quo, and the police, who reacted harshly to that challenge. Efforts such as the Mission Community Alliance emerged to protest police beatings of youths and the juvenile courts' attempts to impose Anglo, middle class social and cultural standards on Latino youths.

While dealing with the problems of poverty and unemployment, those residents of the Mission who were Latino, particularly the youth, tried to emphasize their cultural identity and their ties with political activity in Latin America. They had left behind them the extreme romanticism of the 1960s, best exemplified by the Brown Berets who wanted to expel both Anglos and blacks from America, and to then negotiate the sharing of the country with the American Indians. In San Francisco the effort to provide a political content to the ideology of Latino solidarity was made easier by the Mission's strong Central American connections, at a time when that region was exploding. The revolutions in Nicaragua and El Salvador provided an opportunity for self-affirmation for hundreds of immigrants attracted by a series of activities and events co-ordinated by *La Casa de Nicaragua* and *La Casa del Salvador*. But their stand was too political to obtain massive support from a community living, in many cases, with an uncertain legal status. The convergence between Latin American solidarity and the cultural identity of the San Francisco's Latinos was actually provided by the Mission Cultural Centre, created and funded by city hall in 1975 under pressure from community groups and Latino personalities. Since that time it has become one of the most controversial institutions of the Mission District given its consistent support for left wing politics in Latin America, as well as its campaign for the fostering of the Latino and Chicano cultures in California. This search for such a new source of identity has seemed to be the most fruitful axis of development for the Latinos in San Francisco, since, paradoxically, the movement for political solidarity was undermined by the successes of the revolutions in Central America. The arrival in 1979–80 of so many Nicaraguans escaping the Sandinista Revolution, as well as terrified middle class Salvadorenos, and the newly exiled anti-Castro Cubans, was reversing the political atmosphere in the Mission, forcing the Latino community in California to face up to the reality of their own social and political background.

The old Marcusian dream, incarnated in the San Francisco State College strike of 1969, of bringing together the revolt of the American minorities with the Third World liberation movements had faded. The Brown Berets did not survive their model, the Black Panthers. The solidarity movement organized around *Los Siete de la Raza* disappeared in time to avoid witnessing the personal failure of its defendants who were unable to escape the clash between police and individual, violent revolt. Significantly enough, the main leader of the solidarity movement organized around *Los Siete de la Raza* was a brilliant poet who became an organizer of *La Casa de Nicaragua*. He tried to join the Sandinista army and finally became the first cultural attaché in Washington of the Nicaraguan revolutionary government. Many realized, as he did, that the Latin American revolution had to be accomplished in Latin America, although support for it could be voiced in the streets of the Mission.

Perhaps one of the most significant developments of the radical Latino student movements, formed in the late 1960s, was its gradual transformation into what, in 1980, seemed to be one of the most active community organizations in San Francisco: *La Raza en Accion Local*. Its name clearly expresses its two-fold character: an ethnic-cultural community (*La Raza*) orientated towards local action, and the social demands of a territorially defined group. Coming, as it did, after the San Francisco State College strike, and the early split with the MCO, *La Raza* took a careful stand, concentrating on its legitimacy as defenders of the Latino community – both on cultural grounds and on the basis of their urban demands – and only confronting the system step by step. We should note that they did not follow the model of a grassroots organization, but built social programmes which were funded by the Catholic and Baptist churches and some liberal-minded foundations. Militant groups were formed around these programmes and each group in each programme elected the programme's board, that in turn, elected the general board. The organization was extremely careful in selecting its membership, and required each voting member to have been an active participant in one of the programmes for at least two years. From 1970 onwards, the realm of *La Raza's* activities expanded steadily, to include the La Raza Information Centre, a tutorial programme to improve the education of Latinos, a legal centre for counselling, a silkscreen centre, a credit co-operative, and a housing development corporation which supported co-operative housing, its first venture being to build a 50 unit housing project for low-income residents, solar-heated and built above a public parking area in the very core of the Mission.

The driving force behind this long term effort – maintained in spite of so many failures – was that the community had to learn to rely on its own economy and organization before it could engage in wider confrontations that might bring general acceptance. From time to time, however, the networks established by the programmes were used to mobilize people on specific issues. The 1975 campaign in collaboration with the Mission Planning Council, for example, succeeded in preserving residences for some 4,000 people, and protecting family life along the way, closing down some bookshops and theatres trading in pornography. They attacked, and ran out of business, a bar on 24th Street in order to prevent gentrification of the neighbourhood. They were also influential in redirecting city hall funds for beautifying the urban landscape into more pragmatic uses such as sanitation, public transportation, and traffic regulations. And finally *La Raza* participated effectively in a coalition with all the neighbourhoods in San Francisco to obtain approval for a new zoning ordinance that would preserve the residential character of the city.

All these actions were, nevertheless, skirmishes from *La Raza's* point of view. They were waiting for the moment when the city would be ready for such a large mobilization by all the poor neighbourhoods that it would be capable of imposing a new strategy for urban development. This situation would, however, require the transformation of the local political system. So *La Raza* members were much in evidence in the 1976 and 1977 referendums that modified the way the board of supervisors were elected. Once district elections were established in 1977, *La Raza* began a drive to have its candidates elected as representatives of District 6 which included the Mission. They tried to form a broadly-based Latino coalition around one of its leaders, Gary Borvice, a *chicano*, who was running as a Latino candidate, and they succeeded in obtaining widespread support within the community. Most of the social agencies and several of the former leaders of the MCO sided with Borvice. His opponent was Carol Ruth Silver, a liberal, white lawyer. She ran with the double support of the Anglo middle class and the growing lesbian and gay population of the district, particularly those voters from the section that was not part of the Mission neighbourhood. A few minor Latino candidates diverted some votes from *La Raza* but the race looked as if it would be close run.

In the month before election, however, Larry Del Carlo entered the competition – a former vice president of the MCO and a respected and well-known community leader with a mixed Anglo-Latino background. He ran on a fairly conservative platform and was backed by some of the remaining MCO constituency. He came third in the election[72] but his presence was enough to split the Latino vote, so that Gary Borvice lost to Carol Ruth Silver. Our sources suggest that it was quite possible Del Carlo's candidacy may have been encouraged by Mayor Moscone who wanted both to support the candidate backed by the gay community and to fight the *La Raza* candidate, who was considered politically too radical but culturally too conservative.

Two years later Bob Gonzales, the last Latino supervisor and one of the last vestiges of Alioto's political machine, was defeated by a black woman in the district's election, and with him went the last of the Latino power in the local political arena. Many of the Mission leaders, particularly in *La Raza*, adopted a different strategy to recover some of the power. In the 1979 mayoral election, they supported the conservative challenger to the incumbent mayor, the moderate liberal, Diane Feinstein, in exchange for promises of programmes and positions favouring the Latino community. The conservative lost and the Latino influence declined still further, in a city where they represented approximately 15 per cent of the population. To be sure, they accounted for much less of the actual voters (perhaps as low as 6 per cent), an example of the key difference between a people's existence and their political representation.

A time of uncertainty

The failure of all the Latino-based political initiatives, as well as little grassroots mobilization in the Mission, heralded a period of social uncertainty in the late 1970s. The number of community-based organizations, however, was still high (approximately 60), and most remained quite active. Their achievements nonetheless have been relatively limited and the preservation of the neighbourhood has not been able to alleviate seriously the poverty of its residents. So the contradictions became increasingly acute between the quality of the neighbourhood and the day-to-day survival of immigrants and poor Latinos. Disenchantment set in and drugs swept through the Mission, with hundreds of teenagers swallowed in a "storm of angel dust."[73] A more positive attempt at self-affirmation, though, began to express itself in a new form of Latino youth culture: the low riders. Latino youths bought old cars, installed hydraulic jack-up devices, lowered the bodies, modified the engines and painted the exteriors in pink, green, silver and blue with religious and hippie motifs. They stayed in groups, listening to rock music. On Friday and Saturday nights groups of low riders paraded their cars slowly down Mission Street between 24th and 20th Streets, revving the engines, raising and lowering the chassis, playing their stereos, and stopping from time to time to exchange passengers. Surrounding them on the pavements and in the adjacent streets were hundreds of teenage *cholitos* and *cholitas* (young Latinos), each carrying a radio tuned into the same station. Beer drinking, dancing, smoking, and the urgent need to express pent-up violence was apparent everywhere. From time to time a car, taking advantage of a traffic jam, would stop, the windows open and a dozen youths would run over to grab plastic bags, hand over a few dollars and disappear into the crowd before the police could react. Violence erupted occasionally, encouraged rather than prevented by an overwhelming police presence.

In fact, most of the low riders did not live in the Mission. They were the sons of the Latino immigrants who came to the Mission and were then dispatched to the suburbs of the Bay Area, predominantly to the Southern Peninsula. But the second generation returned to the Mission, and, although they did not grow up there, claimed it as their territory (analogous to the American Indians claiming the Alcatraz Island in the San Francisco Bay). An Anglo-based conservative group (the Mission Action Team) asked for police protection and the mayor quickly provided it so that today the Mission is continuously patrolled by police cars, and frequently visited by the "tactical" squad. On Friday and Saturday nights, traffic is diverted and police cars block the entire street, and arrests and confrontations have become more and more frequent.

Almost the entire Latino community, including the mainstream social agencies and the progressive Mission Cultural Centre, sided with the low riders and vowed to protect their youth in their territory. Hundreds of youths united to "stop police brutality" and to seek new forms of autonomous organizations. The merchants were split on the issue. The Mission Street Merchant's Association, representing Anglo absentee owners, called for police reinforcement and asked for the closing of the Centre. The 24th Street Merchants Association, stronghold of the Latino-owned retailers, supported the dialogue with the youth, looking for solutions to such an explosive situation.

Ten years after the Mission coalition experience, the community organizations have largely failed to solve the social problems or to change the political system. But they have improved the neighbourhood and have succeeded in keeping Latino culture alive in its own territory. The minority youth, because they have been denied the right to the memory of their community's struggles, have revived the process of revolt in their own way, finding new forms to express their cultural identity and their social demands. History does not repeat itself, but when contradictions remain unsolved, they become more acute.

The Rise and Fall of a Neighbourhood Movement: An Analytical Model to Explain the Social Process Underlying the Evolution of the Mission Coalition Organization

The MCO's legacy in the Mission District and the Latino community of San Francisco will be evident for a long time. When we conducted our research, almost eight years after its disintegration, traces of the MCO were everywhere, like a meteorite that has exploded in the sky over San Francisco leaving pieces scattered in the streets of the *Barrio*. People continue to argue over the issues that the MCO raised and its leaders discuss over and over again what happened. Many of them, along with the most active participants, have suffered severe exhaustion from their involvement as frustration mounted. For the ones who have remained politically active, the old divisions that define friends and enemies still exist which goes to show that the MCO was the most intense social experience for those men and women who were part of it, besides being a major urban mobilization. This experience is common to any significant social movement which has sudden and glorious life and death.

Part of the continuing obsession with the MCO lies in the mystery surrounding both its startling surge and its relatively rapid crisis, at the very peak of its achievements. To be sure, every witness of the movement has his or her own interpretation, but most of them point to the clashes in character; to bitter internal fighting to obtain money, jobs and power; to organizational manoeuvring; and to the lack of leadership. And yet we know that these factors are present in all social mobilizations, without, necessarily, the same results. Personal conflicts and ambitions are only a precipitating factor in the crisis of a movement, the underlying causes of which must be found, as we will try to show with the MCO, in the process itself. Furthermore we will seek an explanation for both the success and failure of the MCO, since only a comprehensive scheme can provide us with some understanding about the formation and decline of urban social movements. Only then will we be able to understand why "heroes" become "villains," that is, why the social context allows people to more easily express one or the other of the many contradictory dimensions we all carry in ourselves.

The context of the MCO and a first theoretical construction

Certain factors created a very favourable atmosphere for the emergence of the MCO in 1968, but when reversed in 1972, provided a more difficult framework for community organization and progressive urban policies. As we have pointed out, the MCO appeared as a simultaneous response to two major public programmes that acted as a trigger for most community mobilizations in America during the 1960s: urban renewal and the social programmes funded by the Federal government. The fear that the San Francisco Redevelopment Agency (SFRA) would transform the Mission into another field of action for its bulldozers and developers first motivated people to form a coalition. Once the threat of displacement had been removed, the possibility of obtaining a variety of urban programmes and social benefits through the Model Cities grant pushed the movement onto the offensive. In this sense, the MCO was an archetypical movement arising from the urban heritage of the 1960s. By 1972, the picture had changed greatly with respect to Federal policies. Urban renewal had been stopped because of the neighbourhood opposition and the shrinking resources and influence of the San Francisco Redevelopment Agency. Furthermore, the cutting of social programmes, including Model Cities, by President Nixon's administration dried up the Federal funds, and severely limited the majority of programmes. The channelling of social demands through Model Cities was no longer possible and the MCO, in order to survive and develop had to find other resources and targets. It failed to do so. Thus, it is clear that there was a strong connection between public policies and the formation of neighbourhood movements. Community organizations developed to improve people's living conditions by taking advantage of the Federal social programmes. However, the conservative stand of the Nixon administration prompted a backlash in those programmes, most of which were severely reduced and submitted to tighter controls; and funds dried up, limiting the organizational capacity and undermining the political legitimacy of the urban poor. The new policy emphasized the role of city hall over the grassroots organizations.[74]

So, in spite of the MCO's strength and militancy that by 1972 had gained the respect of its adversaries and of public authorities, it was unable to operate within the relatively open institutional context that had supported its development. However it did not have consequently to fall apart. For the new conservative urban policies to have caused the MCO's collapse, the MCO could only have been a camouflage set up to receive money from the Model Cities programmes (an accusation in fact levelled at the organization by its critics). All available evidence, however, disproves this interpretation.[75] The MCO had hundreds of active members and dozens of grassroots committees, and, although they did take advantage of public funds and programmes, generally took a militant stand on their demands. In fact, even given the favourable situation in 1968, the MCO was created because a group of neighbourhood activists, supported by the churches, wanted to transform the defensive MCOR into an autonomous grassroots organization. It is true, nevertheless, that by 1972 most of the original Alinskyite leaders had become deeply involved in the management of the Model Cities programmes, forgetting, for the most part, the grassroots committees, except to support their own election onto them in the MCO's annual convention. But why? How could the same persons with the same ideas, who had successfully imposed a tight control by the people over the content and management of public programmes for the neighbourhood, allow themselves to become lost in a bureaucratic jungle and consequently isolated from their community? We must try to find a social explanation of the process that led to the precipitating factor in the MCO's crisis – its absorption into social programmes, and its subsequent disarray once the social programmes were dismantled by a Federal administration recovering from the assaults it had suffered in the 1960s.

We need, first, to introduce a few elementary concepts which will enable us to understand the structure and dynamics of an urban movement with the characteristics of the Mission-based mobilization.

Urban movements, and indeed all social mobilizations, happen when, in their collective action and at the initiative of a conscious and organized operator, they address one or more structural issues that differentiate contradictory social interests. [. . .] These issues, or their combination, define the movement, the people they may mobilize, the interests likely to oppose the movement, and the attitude of institutions according to their political orientation. So the issues encapsulate the potential significance of a movement to its society. We call these social issues "goals" of the movement's structure and, to be so, they must be present in its practice. For example, if a movement is to be defined as "Latino," it must act in such a way that there is an affirmation of "Latino ethnicity" with a set of corresponding demands and goals that are defined and put into practice. Of course, the movement's "goals" do not entirely determine its development, outcome, organization, success, or failures. Social mobilization includes the organizational arrangement of these "goals" and the operators – their interaction and their interplay with larger social structures and with other social actors. These "goals" constitute the raw material of a movement, and the understanding of their basic structure affects the explanation of the movement, making it a social process that extends beyond its history and social circumstances.

The social issues providing the "goals" of an urban movement represent the connection in action between the movement and the whole society. The issues are the translation of one into the other, and therefore they are specific to each society as it is historically determined. In the American experience of urban mobilization there seem to have been three main structural issues underlying the popular movements:

1 *Neighbourhood*   The preservation and improvement of residential neighbourhoods at the level of their physical space, at the level of their urban services, and at the level of their economic value. (We exclude from the meaning of *neighbourhood* the social networks or subcultures that are sometimes attached to neighbourhoods. We prefer to describe these as a *community*, to distinguish the urban and cultural dimensions of a neighbourhood.)

2 *Poverty*   The economic and social demands of the most deprived sectors of the population in terms of jobs, income, education and social benefits. We also include in this category a diversity of social problems that (it can be demonstrated) are systemic consequences of the socio-economic deprivation, such as street crime, juvenile violence, and widespread drug traffic and consumption (different from the "drug problem" which is socially broader).

3   *Oppressed ethnic minority*   The specific demands of oppressed ethnic minorities who, besides suffering poverty and urban decay, have problems linked to racial and cultural discrimination. (We do not therefore
consider ethnicity in general here, since Irish or Italians do not face
similar problems in American society. We would, however, have proceeded differently at the turn of the nineteenth century . . .)

If we want to relate these three basic issues to the overall social structure,
we have to remember, first, that specific *neighbourhoods* express the general
dynamics of the *city*; second, that *poverty* is the consequence, at the distribution
level of a basic pattern of relationships of production organized by *class*; and,
third, that the oppression of ethnic minorities originates in an asymmetrical
social structure differentiated by *race*. So the immediate experience of an
urban movement concerns only the first level of a broader structure, along
three different but interrelated dimensions:

Dimensions	*Level of local experience*	*Level of social structure*
Urban–spatial	Neighbourhood	City
Socio-economic	Poverty	Class
Socio-cultural	Minority	Race

What generally characterizes the American experience of *social mobilization*
is that:

1   It tends to happen at the level of immediate experience without relating to the corresponding level of a broader social structure (so that
"poor people" will mobilize to obtain more welfare benefits without
challenging the general employment policy or the taxation system).
2   It tends to isolate each element which means, therefore, that a single
objective is pursued. (Mexican Americans, for example, will try to
obtain social benefits for themselves as Mexican Americans without
considering other ethnic minorities. This pattern of behaviour is defined, in sociological terms, as that of an *interest group*).

What generally characterizes the experience of *social movements*[76] in America,
and even more so in Europe, is that they develop one-dimensionally according to a pattern that we would describe as "horizontal."

From	*Neighbourhood*	to	*City*
From	*Poverty*	to	*Class*
From	*Minority oppression*	to	*Racial liberation*

In addition, social movements tend, on the basis of each mobilization, to challenge the overall social structure by attempting to change the political institutions. Thus their dynamics affect a fourth, and most important, dimension of the social structure: *state power*. Specific to and original in the "community mobilization" model found in the Alinsky-inspired ideologies and tactics[77] is that the elements on which the movement relies are deliberately confined to the immediate experience while, at the same time, they are connected to a multi-dimensional movement dealing with all aspects of the social structure by virtue of bringing together all sorts of popular organizations; and they base their counter-power on this wide support, a power that is called a *community organization*. A community organization theoretically remains autonomous from the political system; yet by mobilizing the grassroots and politicizing the immediate experience, it brings about institutional change that puts pressure on the state. If we represent in our diagram the dynamics of the three theoretical models of social mobilization (interest group, social movement, Alinsky-inspired community movement) we obtain the following:

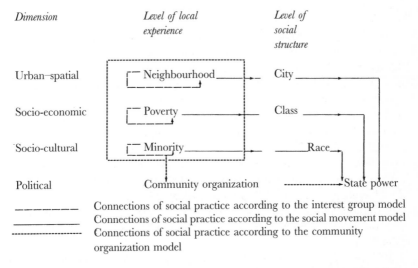

Dimension	Level of local experience	Level of social structure
Urban–spatial	Neighbourhood	City
Socio-economic	Poverty	Class
Socio-cultural	Minority	Race
Political	Community organization	State power

————— Connections of social practice according to the interest group model
Connections of social practice according to the social movement model
-------------------- Connections of social practice according to the community organization model

However simple this theoretical construction may be, it is a helpful tool for deciphering the mystery of the brilliant life and dramatic death of the MCO. It is our hypothesis that the development of the MCO as a community organization came from a successful combination in its practice of *neighbourhood, poverty* and *minority* (Latino) issues yet without reference to the higher elements of *city, class* and *race*. Its failure can be blamed on the relationship established between the MCO (*community organization*) and city hall and Model Cities (*state power*) – this crucial relationship failed precisely because of the MCO's refusal to challenge the higher levels of the social structure. The sources of its strength were also the factors that determined its crisis. Let us develop our interpretation, try to prove it and elaborate on its meaning.

Deciphering the rise and fall of the MCO

The methodology of this demonstration requires a somewhat complex mechanism that organizes in a systematic way the detailed information we gathered on the actions, organization, and evolution of the MCO. (See the Appendix, pp. 231–43, for this formal analysis.) If our hypothesis is true, then:

1   The different elements of the proposed model had to be present in the practice of the Mission mobilization.
2   The elements will have varied during the evolution of the MCO, so that different combinations will have developed compared to the original matrix and the permutations will have been meaningful, and able to have been coded in terms of the basic elements.
3   There will have been a system of significant correspondences between the variations in the structure of the MCO and the variations in its outcomes and functioning.

To observe the evolution of the movement in a systematic way, we have chosen to observe the interests that were present and the positions taken during the five annual conventions of the MCO. Far from being pro-forma meetings, the conventions were the source of power for the leadership and openly expressed the interests and programmes of each member organization. We will be able to test our hypothesis (and to base the proposed analytical model on the experience under observation) by examining the clustering and splits between the different interests and by assessing the impact upon the process of urban mobilization of the new structure that the MCO formed in each convention. Since we have already described the sequence of events in the Mission, and since we will present a systematic summary of information in our Methodological Appendix (see pp. 231–43), the analysis here will concentrate on the synthetic theoretical explanation of the social process under consideration.

In defending the neighbourhood against urban renewal before the MCO existed, MCOR called on the broadest possible range of interests and elements. Many home owners, tenants unions, block clubs, and churches defended the neighbourhood, particularly the Mission Tenants Union, and challenged the urban policy for the entire city. Social agencies, administering Federal programmes, were basically interested in the poverty issues. The Latino branch of the labour unions tried a coalition of class, poverty and Latino elements. The Latino Nationalist groups of different countries introduced the consideration of the Latino minority, and some of them went on to call for Third World liberation and Brown Power. The coalition tried to rest almost everything on a single issue – the arresting of urban renewal. But once this fight was won, the coalition fell apart. The first convention of the MCO in 1968 tried to bring together all these elements and ended in total disruption. The best formula for a movement to begin in the Mission District did not appear to lie with the combination of all dimensions at all levels. The formula that finally worked was one that the MCO put together between 1968 (first convention) and 1970 (third convention), the period in which specific demands were won, a community-controlled Model Cities grant was obtained, and a series of committees and grassroots organizations got underway. During this period it was formed by:

1 MCO-inspired grassroots committees addressing a variety of social issues: employment, education, housing, in the Mission (*neighbourhood* and *poverty*).
2 Church organizations playing a very similar role to the grassroots committees (*neighbourhood* and *poverty*).
3 Latino-based social agencies (*minority* and *poverty*).
4 Latino national groups emphasizing the Latino culture (*minority* and *race*).
5 Latino branch of the labour movement (*minority* and *class*).
6 Strong staff organization such as the MCO (*community organization*).

Reduced to its basics, this structure reproduces the model of community organization as postulated, with the addition of a second order element such as class, and a strong component of racial self-affirmation on the basis of the Latino culture. (In fact the *Centro Social Obrero*, although a part of AFL-CIO Local 261 (construction workers), was much more significant as the Latino branch of the union, than as the union. Its strength came from the language school which was basically a social agency.)

The latter "goal" became the breaking point for some organizations in the third convention, in 1970. Although the MCO fully recognized the Latino's self-affirmation as a major component of the movement, it was not and did not want to be a Latino organization. In the third convention, the fourth "goal" split from the MCO, both in its moderate (*minority*) and radical (*race*) components.

The immediate result was a weakening of the MCO's influence, but this was largely compensated for by the boost given to the organization by the beginning of the Model Cities programmes in 1971. So a seventh "goal" was added: MMNC's staff representing, as it were, a portion of state power. This staff was, significantly enough, headed by the Alinskyite leaders who, in so doing, left behind them the sixth "goal" (*community organization*) that was then operated by the remaining MCO forces.

The major split came at the fourth convention in 1971. The Latino-based social agencies, joining forces with all recipient Latino-orientated groups opposed the candidate from the Alinskyite circles. Although he was elected, with the support of the grassroots committees and churches, the two blocs became warring factions: on the one hand, *neighbourhood and poverty* and on the other hand, *minority and poverty*.

Latino labour found itself in the middle. The two blocks organized. The first one, the Unity Caucus, had 50 per cent Latino members while the second one, the Alianza Caucus, was 100 per cent Latino. In the fifth convention (1972), Latino labour finally switched to the Alianza Caucus and the Latino president of the MCO changed loyalty to be re-elected this time against his former supporters. While the Alinskyites still retained control over the Model Cities institution, the Latino-based organizations and agencies won the leadership of the MCO. The result was conflicting structures as follows:

Unity Caucus	Alianza Caucus
Neighbourhood	Latino culture (*minority*)
Poverty	Latino *poverty*
Some *state power*	Latino *labour*
	Community organization (staff)

The split between neighbourhood issues and minority issues was fatal for the MCO. When, finally, "community organizers" picketed "city hall bureaucrats," and "city hall bureaucrats" fired "Latino militants," the end of the movement had arrived.

Thus, apparently, ethnic divisions and absorption into bureaucracy account for the disintegration of the movement. But why? After all, the MCO was supposed to control MMNC, and the Alinskyite leaders always supported Latino culture. Is it impossible, in America, for a movement to bring together poor people, neighbourhood problems and oppressed minorities in the same community organization? The answer must be "No" by nature, but "Yes" in this particular case. The disintegration came not so much because of the split between Latino and non-Latino people as the use of this real difference to represent more fundamental and contradictory interests.

In truth, the MCO experienced three different but successive splits, apparently related to the division between urban poor (including Latinos) and the Latino cultural self-definition.

The first one, at the initial stage of the organization, clearly distinguished the MCO from the radical nationalists identified with the Third World Liberation Movement. The "reformist" stand of the MCO – trying to "come down to people's real issues" – preferred to distance itself from an ideological radicalism that might compromise its chances of becoming a widely supported grassroots movement.

The second split was more embarrassing. The middle class Latino cultural and political organizations, such as LULAC or MAPA, largely cut the MCO off from the traditional political elites of established Latinos, until they finally eroded its ethnic minority component.

But the real blow came when the Latino-based social agencies, dealing with the poverty issues on behalf of a Latino constituency, opposed the "All People United" stand of the Alinskyites and took over the MCO, regaining control over the grassroots organization. In this context we can state that although the Latino versus non-Latino division was a real one, it only became a disruptive one when it was used as the flag to rally support in the battle over the control of the Model Cities programmes, and beyond, over the representation of Latinos and Mission residents *vis-à-vis* the public social policies. This self-definition of the community-based poverty agencies was not a matter of tactics: it was their very essence. Only by being the socio-political brokers of an ethnic minority, defined in the terms of the dominant culture as "Latinos" or "Spanish-speaking," could they maintain their institutional existence, economic resources, and political influence. And, anyway, their Latino identity was not only organizational self-interest but also the expression of basic distrust towards the artificial uniformity of a culture in which all citizens are equal, except that the decision-making bodies comprise male, white privileged groups as against a constellation of fragmented minorities.

If the economy and institutions discriminate against a particular group, like the Latinos, the reaction will be one of self-preservation, which in this case was to organize a group based around the Latino culture and to address the demands of this group to the powers that be. This is the process by which social needs are converted into *interest groups*, and this was the way the Mission's social agencies were born and grew up. "Mission district" in San Francisco was the code word for the "Latino minority," and this was why they obtained a Model Cities Programme and why the MCO had an immediate impact on the city's social policies. Thus, when the Alinskyite leaders, with a broader vision that stretched across ethnic lines and poor people's interests, took over the social programmes provided by Model Cities, the established Latino agencies felt threatened and decided to end the MCO in favour of the old system of being the intermediaries between their ethnic constituency and the public institutions. Their behaviour was motivated, at one and the same time, by the will to keep their position as broker and by the defence of the borders that would guarantee them at least the share that Latinos could obtain in American society. In other words, once people are institutionally segmented in different interest groups, it is impossible to reconcile the different demands competing for the distribution of increasingly scarce resources.

The confrontation was made more sudden and more acute by the Alinskyite cadres seizing power in the Model Cities agencies, the very same people who were advocating the construction of grassroots organizations as the only real source of help for the poor people. The reason had nothing to do with personal corruption or unrestrained ambition, but was related to the strategy underlying the Alinsky model of community organization which was systematically implemented in the Mission. On the one hand, the community's activists had to rely in the initial stages on the existing social agencies, whose constituency was based upon patronage and who provided the natural ground on which community organizations could grow. On the other hand, if the activists intended eventually to bypass the influence of the agencies and build up autonomous militant organizations, it was necessary to establish their own legitimacy with the neighbourhood residents, including the Latino majority. The legitimacy of the new community organization would only replace the old ties from clients using one of two premises: either people's consciousness would be raised to a higher level so that the defence of their immediate economic interests was not the first and only concern, or they would have to satisfy their immediate demands through new organizational channels that would become the new source of legitimacy.

The MCO's leadership chose the second way, and decided to take over the programmes themselves on the basis of their influence on the grassroots committees to prevent Latino social agencies from reinforcing their power through the resources obtained by grassroots struggles. To keep their influence they needed to fulfil the condition of satisfying people's immediate material needs through the delivery of jobs, services, and money. So, ultimately, they became a "super service" agency, and the MCO was transformed into a battleground between the two sets of agencies fighting over the resources that would buy people's allegiance, once "people" had been reduced to a definition in terms of immediate economic interests. In a case like this, once the driving force of an interest group is accepted, the self-definition of each group tends to be stated in terms of the cultural categories of the dominant ideology. So "Latinos" ended up fighting "non-Latinos" over the control of resources that finally disappeared once the community organizations had become too weak to impose a redistributive policy on the representatives of the state.

But why was it that the community organizers, who had a clear awareness of the need both to respect the identity of different popular sections and to bring them all together in their common interests, were unable to raise the level of self-definition and organization to a point that would have created unity? The reasons for such a crucial outcome are most significant for our understanding of the relationship between urban poverty and ethnicity, and they mainly concern the obstacles existing in most American cities, and certainly in San Francisco, against raising the practice of an urban movement over and above one of the four dimensions we have previously differentiated.

For the neighbourhood issues posed in the Mission to be transformed into an urban policy for the entire city, it was necessary to seek an alliance with a middle class-based neighbourhood movement whose emphasis on urban conservation, environmental quality, and low-density zoning was far removed from the basic concerns of poor Latinos – decent housing and construction jobs. The demand for rent control was the only clear, common ground but it was insufficient to establish an alternative model of urban development taking into consideration both urban quality and living conditions. Thus neighbourhood demands in the Mission remained narrowly defined to local issues.

To connect the poverty problems with a broader strategy of class struggle stronger ties were needed to the labour movement. But the Latino component of the labour movement was dependent on the construction workers, who were only interested in redevelopment and the construction of new high-rise buildings as a source of jobs and income. When the Latino leader of the *Centro Social Obrero* tried to play a major role in the Construction Workers' Union, he ran into bitter conflict with the established union leaders and had to leave San Francisco in 1971 (at gun point, so the story goes).

To shift from defence of Latinos against economic and social discrimination to the self-affirmation of Latino culture as a process of national liberation connected with the Third World was unthinkable for a community organization based on the unification of poor people's interests in a given city. Therefore all self-definition that might alienate other ethnic groups was to be excluded.

Finally, to transform the community organization into a political force (as the gays did in San Francisco) was impossible for a neighbourhood where at least 20 per cent of the residents were not legal residents, and where the majority of the poor people, particularly Latinos, were not registered voters. The lack of confidence in the responsiveness of the political institutions encouraged political alienation, which in turn increased the likelihood of discriminatory practices in public policies which, as ever, sought to reinforce the status quo.

So, constrained to limit their initiatives to the level of people's immediate interests, the community activists who created the MCO were very successful in establishing the link between urban demands, grassroots organizations, and social programmes. Distrustful of radical ideologies, and believing only in what they could take into their own hands, the neighbourhood populists were able to establish themselves as the citizens' representatives and genuinely speak for the poor and minorities. But, having established their legitimacy exclusively on the basis of their capacity to deliver immediate rewards, they reproduced the social fragmentation of different interest groups fighting for the diminishing pieces of an unquestioned pie of dubious taste.

People's unity does not result from an ideological statement. It has to be built, as the MCO activists rightfully argued, through a common collective practice originating from the different situations of its participants. Nevertheless, people's unity neither results from the piecemeal satisfaction of different demands that are taken for granted nor by excluding any process of cultural transformation aimed at the redefinition of needs. The social logic of interest groups is not superseded by their coalition. The Mission community organizers learned too late the crucial historical distinction between popular unity and political trade-offs.

And yet, in its life and death, the MCO decisively shaped the Mission district as well as San Francisco's social policies. As we shall see, the profile of this transformation closely follows the characteristics and shortcomings of a major neighbourhood mobilization, the social logic of which we tried to discover behind the façade of the discourse of its social actors.

A Place to Live: The Urban Impact of Grassroots Mobilization in the Mission District

Urban decay in the Mission district was, as in most American inner cities, the consequence, not the cause, of the white working class flight to the suburbs during the 1950s. Tables 5.1 and 5.2 show a parallel evolution of an increasing Latino population in an urban environment whose quality was consistently below the San Franciso average, and which deteriorated as the landlords were able to avoid repairs and maintenance due to the weak bargaining position of the new Latino immigrant-renters.[78]

Similar downward trends could be observed in most public services and physical facilities, according to the study prepared by the Mission Housing Development Corporation:

> Compared to San Francisco's averages, the Mission District public schools show lower student learning achievement, and serious reading problems; higher drop-out rates; lack of innovative teaching methods and less parents' participation in secondary school activities. Child care centres have waiting lists totalling about 1,000 children; preventive mental and dental health care are insufficient.[79]

Also, while the Inner Mission accounted for 7 per cent of the city's population

Table 5.1 Evolution of Spanish-surname population in the Mission District of San Francisco, 1940–1970

	1940	1950	1960	1970
Total population	52,000	53,000	51,000	51,870
Spanish-surname population	n.a.	5,530	11,625	23,183
% over total population of the district		10.4	22.8	44.7

n.a., not available.

Source: Noelle Charleston, Robert Jolda, and Judith Waldhorn, *Summary of Trends in Housing and Population in the Mission Model Neighbourhood, 1940–1970* (Stanford: Stanford University Community Development Study, 1972, mimeo)

Table 5.2 Housing trends, Mission Model Neighbourhood (MN) and San Francisco (SF), 1940–1970

	1940		1950		1960[a]		1970	
	MN	*SF*	*MN*	*SF*	*MN*	*SF*	*MN*	*SF*
Total units	18,379	222,176	19,288	265,726	21,330	331,000	21,000	310,383
Vacancy rate (%)	5.8	7	1.3	2	4.7	5	4.6	3
Owner-occupancy rate (%)	17	29	19	36	16	33	14	31
Average value	$4181	$5503	$9646	$12,209	$15,913	$17,300	$25,877	$30,600
Renter-occupied (%)	83	71	81	64	84	67	86	69
Average rent	$25	$32	$34	$44	$66	$68	$105	$135
Crowded (1.01+ persons per room) (%)	10	7	9	8	9	6	13	7
Un-sound housing units (%)	4	n.a	9	n.a.	16	n.a.	16	n.a.

[a] A different definition of "unfit" was used in 1960 (see study).

n.a., not available.

Source: Stanford University Community Development Study (as table 5.1)

in 1970 and 9 per cent of the city's youth, they only had 0.004 per cent of San Francisco's 3,452 acres of open and recreational space.[80]

Community organizations in the Mission mobilized to halt the trend towards housing dilapidation and to obtain better urban facilities for the neighbourhood. At the same time they tried to prevent the classic process of a deteriorated area being improved for new residents once the poor and minority families have been displaced, either by redevelopment, "code enforcement" programmes,[81] or higher rents.[82] In fact, the movement started, as we have noted, as a mobilization to prevent the threat of an urban renewal programme.

Thus, the first and major urban impact of neighbourhood mobilization in the Mission was to preserve the neighbourhood physically. The grassroots' opposition to any potential course of displacement prevented future projects from being implemented or even formulated. Such was the case for the Okamoto Plan prepared by the City Planning Department, or with the attempt to re-zone the district to change it from residential to commercial uses. When speculators tried to use "other methods" to make gain out of increasingly valuable land, taking advantage of fires in the 16th Street area in 1974–5 for example, block clubs were formed, in this case to prevent arson and to (successfully) counter their tactics.[83] The impact that BART was supposed to have materialized in terms of increasing accessibility to and from the Mission, as well as upgrading its potential as a commercial and leisure centre. But it did not trigger any major private development projects or even gentrifying renovation on a scale large enough to change the social or physical character of the neighbourhood.

A good indication of the extent of the preservation of housing stock in the Mission is its very high stability compared to the number of housing units demolished or constructed. According to a survey of the City Planning Department between 1968 and 1971 (that is just before and after the mobilization we have studied) only 283 units were demolished in the Mission, and only 461 new units were built. Related to the 21,000 housing units in the Mission in 1970, this represents a low 1.3 per cent and 2.1 per cent of the housing stock. Relative figures for the rest of San Francisco are much higher: 6,657 demolitions out of 310,383 units represents a 2.1 per cent demolition rate, and 16,588 new constructions out of 310,383 units a 5 per cent construction rate. As a point of contrast, in the black Western Addition area, for the same period, 3,119 housing units were demolished and 3,450 constructed; and in the other major black area (South Bayshore) for the same period 1,161 units were demolished and 757 new units built. Thus it seems that community mobilization prevented the Mission from undergoing the physical destruction that other minority residential areas in the city suffered. The reason, again, was that the impressive community organization of the early 1970s, widely publicized by the media, discouraged many realtors and developers from risking investment in an overly volatile, although desirable urban spot. In the words of a realtor, "unless the Latinos get rich or we get rid of them, there is no way to make money there."[84]

In fact this was not true. The Mission preserved its physical setting[85] and its cultural identity, while attracting a growing number of Latino immigrants,[86] and improving the economic vitality of small business. Even in the midst of the disruption caused over several years by the construction of BART, the Mission kept its place as the second major retailing centre in the city. A survey of the 24th Street merchants (the core of the small Latino businesses) at the end of 1975, in a period of economic decline, showed that 50 per cent were making profits similar to those of 1973, and that 20 per cent actually improved their benefits.[87] The housing quality seems at least to have been maintained and probably upgraded.[88] The evaluation of the Stanford University research team on the evolution of the housing stock indicates a proportion of 85 per cent sound housing units for 1972, up from the 1970 figure of 84 per cent, and therefore reversing for the first time the downward trend that started during the 1950s. The property values also improved and by 1979 an average three bedroom unit in the Mission was valued at over 100,000 dollars.[89] To be sure, some gentrification had occurred but by all accounts it was less important than the reinforcement of ethnic minorities with Filipinos, Cubans and Peruvians joining the Central Americans and Mexicans in the late 1970s. How was this possible?

It was certainly not the direct result of the housing demands and policies supported by the MCO, the major result of which was the creation of the Mission Housing Development Corporation (MHDC) in 1971, supposedly aimed at constructing and managing low-rent housing units and providing affordable loans for rehabilitation and home buying in collaboration with the local banks. In fact, as soon as the MCO fell apart, the MHDC suffered all kinds of limitations from HUD, including the rejection of a proposal for a low-income housing project in the Mission on the grounds that there were already too many low-income housing units in that area and more units of this type would encourage urban segregation. Caught between rising prices of land and construction costs and little financial or institutional support, the MHDC, reassigned to the mayor's office, barely survived with a budget of 200,000 dollars per year. In its nine years of existence it could only build 101 housing units (39 for elderly), provide house ownership loans to 80 families, and help with the rebuilding of 331 units using loans that totalled an average of 3,000 dollars each. Even these modest achievements, however, seemed dubious successes to the MHDC's director given the problems of drugs, violence and delinquency that plagued its main achievement, the 50-unit Betel Apartments. He felt that this overall failure was attributable to the fact that the MHDC's only source of strength was the MCO. Once the community was disorganized, the MHDC could not challenge the prevailing housing policy.

What preserved the Mission, both from redevelopment and housing dilapidation, was the neighbourhood's capacity to organize defensively and to take
care of its inner space. On the one hand, any major attempt of widespread
displacement was tackled, albeit with a confused but firm defence that resisted
with equal spirit the redevelopment plans, a re-zoning proposal, or a lesbian
bar. On the other hand, the neighbourhood was cared for on a point-to-point
basis, through individual rehabilitation, maintenance by families, or, sometimes, co-operative housing projects. One such project that *La Raza en Accion
Local* was trying to build in 1980 used solar energy technology for the first
time in a low-income housing project. With this pattern of behaviour, the
settlement of young middle class couples or even of lesbian households did
not meet with open hostility, as long as they fitted into the neighbourhood,
collaborated on its upgrading and got along well with the predominant Latino
culture, keen on its family life. As one neighbourhood group in the Mission
put it,

> We choose to live here because there are more positives than negatives. Our
> neighbourhood is a lively place rich with sounds, the colours, the scents, the
> languages and styles of many cultures, a warm place of sunshine almost every
> day, where neighbours talk to each other on the street and look out for one
> another, a dynamic place where people are actively working towards collective
> improvement and community pride, where change is always in evidence and
> stagnation is impossible.[90]

This was the major contribution of the community mobilization of the Mission, the transformation of a decaying ghetto into a vital neighbourhood. The
improvement of the urban quality was the result of the day-to-day action of
many groups and individuals that had needed a place to live, found it, kept it
and cherished it.

The Mission experience demonstrated that there was a third way out of the
conservative-inspired dilemma between free-market and urban decay: a combination of defensive organization and care for the neighbourhood. But in
spite of the success, there were dark clouds on the horizon. The Mission was
not only a neighbourhood but also a poverty-stricken area, with the usual
characteristics of low-income, unemployment, drugs and violence.

Community and Poverty

A major issue underlying community mobilization in the Mission was poverty. The struggle for economic well-being was the driving force behind the
residents' motivations. Once the neighbourhood had been protected against
renewal, employment became the main concern, and the movement succeeded in obtaining thousands of jobs, either by bargaining with firms (from

Pacific Telephone to local shops) or through training programmes that made low-level service jobs accessible to people without education or without English language skills. The struggle was for the extension of the right to work to deprived ethnic minorities. In a parallel effort, the residents claimed, and largely retained, a variety of social services (health, child care, cultural and recreational facilities, youth centres, drug-counselling programmes), and they improved the quality of the schools, also adding some bilingual educational programmes. Out of the MCO experience came an array of social programmes and non-profit community agencies, initially funded and administered by Model Cities, and later on kept alive by Federal and local funds. Existing agencies, such as *Obeca-Arriba Juntos* or the Mission Language and Vocational School, expanded tremendously throughout the 1970s. An impressive list of social programmes were still alive in 1980 as can be seen in the Appendix on p. 243. Thus community action considerably improved the living conditions of the Mission residents.

The particular organizational form through which improvement was channelled is very significant from the point of our research. Instead of changing the employment policies, expanding bilingual education, providing for public health care, taking care of the specific problems of incoming immigrants, or controlling police brutality, the Federal government and city hall reacted in the traditional American way: they created a piecemeal constellation of *ad hoc* programmes, funded on a year-to-year basis, in those areas or for those problems where the community was strong enough to command a response to its dramatic needs. Furthermore, the management of all these programmes was left in the hands of community leaders who obtained jobs and funds for becoming a cushion between the people they represented and the public administration responsible for the social policies.

This practice had a devastating effect on the community's capacity to preserve its unity and strength since it encouraged corruption, personal power, and the formation of cliques, and divided people's energies with fights between different groups to win control over narrowly defined programmes that framed popular needs into bureaucratic categories. In the final stages, once the community was divided, demobilized and disorganized, many programmes were suppressed or severely curtailed. In 1979, the Mission-based social agencies tried to defend themselves by organizing a Latino Unity Council, representing 12 programmes and a network of local "notables." However they did not have any organized popular support behind them and so had little voice in the administrations' offices. With blue collar jobs disappearing in San Francisco, the public schools deteriorating, and social services reduced, the drug culture found a susceptible population in the late 1970s. Many young Latinos began dropping out of the incomprehensible educational programmes, and, without opportunities to find jobs or invest their energy constructively, they reverted to hanging around on the street corners of the Mission in groups that the police hastily named "gangs." Poverty again became associated with "street crime," depriving any potential revolt from the community of a legitimate name. Unable to foster institutional change, the limited improvement obtained by community mobilization faded with the exhaustion of the neighbourhood militants, allowing poverty and despair to increase in a dramatic, vicious circle.

And yet, in spite of all, life goes on in the Mission today in a continuous self-affirmation of neighbourhood vitality and Latino culture.

Community, Ethnicity, and Culture

The physical preservation of the urban environment and the maintenance of the poor minority population through a variety of social programmes kept the Mission as a very distinctive ethnic community, filled with street life, social contact, and activities of all kinds. In spite of the crisis of the MCO, literally dozens of voluntary associations, with interests ranging from art and music to Latin American liberation or urban planning, maintained the neighbourhood as a strongly self-organized community. The CORO Foundation listed 91 community organizations in the Mission in 1974, more than double the average figure for other San Francisco districts.[91] In 1980 we discovered some 60 grassroots organizations that were active in their own specific field, as shown in the list presented in our Appendix (p. 243), an astounding figure for an area with slightly over 50,000 inhabitants. It is very significant, however, that this grassroots vitality followed a highly fragmented pattern, covering precisely those issues that the MCO failed to put together: neighbourhood, poverty, labour, and Latino culture.

Of the variety of splintered neighbourhood organizations, the Mission Planning Council and Operation Upgrade were the most active ones in the period from 1975 to 1980. They tried to follow up the issues concerning housing, rehabilitation and urban equipment. The 24th Street Merchants Association also developed some new ideas for neighbourhood life by organizing public events, such as the Annual Street Fair which attracted 25,000 people to its first celebration in 1979.

In a separate action, the social agencies (including *Obeca*, the Mission Language and Vocational School, the Mission Neighbourhood Health Center, the Mission Hiring Hall, the Mission Legal Community Defense, etc.) were mostly co-ordinated through the Latino Unity Council, and continued to alleviate poverty in an exhausting daily struggle to solve, at the individual level, the wider social problems of inequality and discrimination.

Latino labour changed its influence and its orientation in the late 1970s. With industrial and construction jobs rapidly disappearing in San Francisco, the *Centro Social Obrero* lost most of its former grip on the local unions. On the other hand, the public employees union (Local 400-AFL-CIO) became the pivotal element between organized labour and the political system, as a result of the shift of the job market towards the service sector. Therefore the main problem of the Latinos was how to take advantage of the new public jobs whilst fighting ethnic and language discrimination in job allocation. A new coalition of organizations and individuals was formed, under the label of Latinos for Affirmative Action, to overcome the employment–ethnicity problem.

The cultural dimension of the Latino community developed very strongly on its own along three different though inter-related paths:

1   National groups preserved their identity through their kin networks, customs, and internal fights, something they continue to do today. The Mission is probably the only place in the world where the daily newspapers of Nicaragua or El Salvador are sold outside those countries; organizational expressions of such national identity, such as *La Casa de Nicaragua* or *La Casa del Salvador* are, at once, a reminder to the immigrants of their origins and a major source of division and rivalry in the emerging local society.

2   There was and is a very strong tendency, particularly among the youth, to relate to Latin American revolutionary movements, encouraging a culture of liberation in which themes from Latin America and the Third World prevail. In this sense some attempt is made to convert the Mission into an enclave within the "enemy's territory." This utopia, however, finds itself contradicted by a growing flow of conservative political refugees from Latin America as the process of liberation goes on in the homeland . . .

3   This is why a third cultural trend becomes increasingly significant in the Mission – the new culture of Latino–San Franciscan teenagers who cannot sympathize with liberation movements of countries that have become foreign to them, but also realize that they are different from other Americans. Symbolized by the low rider phenomenon, prone to drink alcohol and take drugs, and under constant pressure from the police, the "kids" try to maintain a street life and make the Mission their real home. Social programmes for the youth, like *Centro de Cambio*, provide support for the most desperate cases. The Mission Cultural Center tries to relate their experience to the broader Latino liberation through the arts, music, and the organization of the new Mission Carnival. The Mission Community Alliance mobilizes the street culture of the young, socially and politically, around its basic social issue of police harassment.

Thus, the explosion of the MCO has left a new heritage of community action, whose dynamics explains the preservation today of the ethnic identity and cultural vitality of the neighbourhood. But such an intense local life follows a fragmented pattern that strikingly mirrors the divisions of the earlier grassroots mobilization.

Only one effort was made in the late 1970s to co-ordinate urban demands, poverty programmes, and Latino culture in the form of a community organization – *La Raza en Accion Local* which we have already described. But no major movements followed, partly because of unhealed wounds resulting from the in-fighting during the MCO-led mobilizations, and partly because of the very political stand of *La Raza*, which contradicted the weakness of the Latino community in San Francisco's local politics.

The Powerlessness of a Mobilized Community

The experience of the Mission offers the paradox of a highly mobilized community that achieved substantial changes at the urban, social and cultural levels, while being totally unable to become politically influential in the local power system. The only Latino supervisor appointed by Alioto's patronage system was defeated in 1979 and was not re-elected. In the 1977 district elections, the liberal woman lawyer who defeated the several Latino candidates relied on the support of the gay and lesbian communities on the fringes of the Inner Mission. Very few Latinos now hold public positions in the local government, and the Latino community appears to be the most deprived of access to municipal power of all ethnic minorities, considering that they make up about 15 per cent of the city's resident population.

The most usual explanation for such an anomaly concerns the high proportion of non-American citizens among the Latinos (probably around 50 per cent of the adult Latino residents) which considerably weakened their electoral chances. But there were more important factors. A major reason for the defeat of Latino candidates in 1977 and 1980 was the split in the votes among different candidates on the lines of the split observed in the community mobilization. In 1977 the two Latino candidates opposed ethnic self-definition as an issue in the representation of the neighbourhood. Also many of the Latino-American citizens did not register as voters. This sceptical attitude diminished the chances of the community becoming an influential element in the city's coalition politics. What are the roots of such scepticism? The general answer, common to other countries, is the demoralizing experience of not obtaining anything substantial through electoral mobilization.[92] But in San Francisco this has not been the reaction of other oppressed minorities who have suffered similar defeats, such as the blacks and gays. Why, then, should Latinos have behaved differently?

The answer lies, again, in the history of the MCO mobilization. In spite of the low registration by voters, Latinos (and the Mission neighbourhood) had a strong influence on the political system in the 1970s because of their capacity for grassroots organization and militancy. But this strength was devoted not to changing the political system or the social policies, but to obtaining programmes or services whose delivery became the only proof of the Latinos' political effectiveness that could maintain popular support. When the community organization suffered a crisis, it lost momentum and allowed the programmes to be phased out. And without any benefits to deliver, the crisis of the grassroots organizations deepened. But the people did not retire. They continued to mobilize and organize themselves around a variety of issues ranging from land-use planning to mural painting. But they had lost the only established connection with the political system. Deprived of their citizenship, many of them also distrusted the potential of their citizenry, given the frustrating experience of having their needs channelled into the bureaucratic labyrinth of the local welfare state. The power of the grassroots missed its chance of transformation into grassroots power.

Conclusion: The Limits to Urban Change

The threat of urban renewal, the injuries of urban poverty, the suffering of ethnic discrimination: all triggered a powerful grassroots mobilization in the San Francisco *Barrio*, where a team of community organizers supported by the churches took advantage of the favourable atmosphere provided by the Federal programmes of social reform. The neighbourhood-based collective action preserved the physical space of the Mission District and improved the urban quality while keeping its cultural identity as the main focal point of the Latino minority in San Francisco.

This process of urban revival was more the indirect consequence of a very dense network of community organizations than the result of public housing programmes or of planning initiatives. The network acted both as a deterrent against displacement and as a stimulus for individual rehabilitation and collective maintenance of the urban environment. Through grassroots pressure a variety of community-controlled, Federally-funded social programmes directly benefited thousands of residents. Nevertheless, the absorption of most of the leadership into the management of the programmes and the subsequent infighting within the community over the control of public resources, decisively weakened the grassroots organizations, allowing a gradual shrinkage both in the funds and in the scope of the social programmes.

From the beginning, the dilemma of whether to define the community as a poor neighbourhood or as a Latino minority introduced the major division which was deepened when it became necessary to establish the social criteria determining how much of the public resources each faction of the community should receive. The subsequent divergence of the various lines of action in response to urban problems, poverty needs, and ethnic liberation, considerably weakened the social pressure brought to bear on the urban policies dealing with the Mission District. The political marginality of the Latino community, both as a result of the immigrant status of most Latinos and as an expression of their frustrating relationship with the political system, increased the distance between the potential of popular mobilization in the neighbourhood and its actual impact on public policies and living conditions.

The Mission's urban scene expresses the two-fold outcome of this contradictory urban mobilization: on the one hand, a valuable space whose residential quality, cultural vitality, and economic dynamics have considerably improved while preserving its original physical form; on the other hand, the occupation of this space by a deprived and segregated ethnic minority, proud of its culture, although subjected to the increasing pressure of poverty, drugs, crime and police surveillance. The tensions and contradictions between these two realities, both defining the Mission's urban dynamics, became unbearable and remain so today.

Thus the contradictory neighbourhood mobilization that we observed decisively contributed to the preservation of a particular spatial form and the definition of specific urban issues: it shaped the urban scene of the *Barrio* and influenced the urban policies dealing with it. In the Mission, city lights and urban darkness emerge from a common matrix: the achievements and failures of the people.

CULTURAL IDENTITY, SEXUAL LIBERATION AND URBAN STRUCTURE: THE GAY COMMUNITY IN SAN FRANCISCO

Introduction

San Francisco has become the world's gay capital, a new Mecca in our age of individual liberation where homosexuals migrate for a few hours or for many years to find themselves and to learn a language of freedom, sexuality, solidarity, and life – to "come out" and to become gay. Numbers are significant but not crucial. An estimated 115,000 gay men and women, about 17 per cent of the city's population,[93] they represent a much less important number than the large concentration of gay people in New York or Los Angeles. Furthermore, the modern gay liberation movement was triggered by the Stonewall Revolt in New York, on 27 June 1969.[94] Although the gay experience of New York has been more radical and militant, San Francisco has been the city where gays have uniquely succeeded in building up a powerful, though complex, independent community at spatial, economic, cultural, and political levels. And, on such a basis, gay people, particularly gay men, have been able to achieve a certain amount of power within the institutional system. Because of their age, level of education, and militancy, gays represent about 25 per cent of registered voters, and in decisive elections their high turn out may approach 30 per cent of the voters. Since 1977 San Francisco has elected a supervisor who publicly ran as a gay candidate and no mayor can afford to risk openly opposing gays in the election. Also, they have come to have some influence through public appointments – the police department, for example, now recruits gay men and lesbians in informal consultation with the gay community.

However striking these developments may be in the context of our homophobic culture,[95] it is only the expression of a deeper and more significant social process: the emergence of a social movement and its transformation into a political force through the spatial organization of a self-defined cultural community.

Spatial concentration, as the basis of a search for self-reliance, is a fundamental characteristic of the gay liberation movement in San Francisco, which makes it more than a human rights movement trying to end legal discrimination on the basis of sexual preferences. (In our interviews with Harry Britt the political leader of San Francisco's gay community, he went on record as saying that "When gays are spatially scattered, they are not gay, because they are invisible.") The crucial step for gay people was, as the movement said, to "come out of the closet," to publicly express their sexuality, and on the basis of such recognition (namely on the basis of a social stigma), to reconstruct their socialization.[96] But how is it possible to be openly gay in the middle of a hostile and violent society increasingly insecure about its fundamental values concerning virility and family? And how can one learn a new behaviour, a new code, and beyond that a new culture, in a world where sexuality is implicit in everybody's presentation of self and where the general assumption is heterosexuality?

In order publicly to express themselves, gays have always met together – in modern times in night bars and coded places. When they became conscious enough and strong enough to "come out" collectively, they have earmarked place where they could be safe together and could develop new life styles. But this time they selected cities, and within the cities they traced boundaries and created their territory. These boundaries were to expand with the increasing capacity of gay people to defend themselves and to build up a series of autonomous institutions.[97] Levine has shown the systematic patterning of spatial concentrations of gay people in the largest American cities.[98] He, and others, consider such a culturally significant cluster to fit the traditional sociological definition of a ghetto.[99] But whatever coincidence there may be between the characteristics of the ghetto, as defined by the Chicago School, and the gay experience of spatial organization, the argument is a purely formal one and, in any event, misleading. Instead, gay leaders tend to speak of "liberated zones," and there is a major theoretical difference between the two notions, the difference being that gay territories, unlike ghettos, are deliberately constructed by gay people.[100] Of course, they cannot choose the urban space they want because of discrimination against them and because of the limited income of many gays. But they do choose to live together as a cultural community settled in a well-defined territory.

Two major consequences follow for the relationship between the gay movement and the city:

1   The gay territory is not the consequence of forces usually dominating the social and functional patterning of space, particularly the urban land market. Although constrained by economic factors, the gay territory develops according to the relationship between the emerging movement and the counteracting forces, a relationship that reshapes the whole urban fabric.
2   Gays need a spatially defined community for a long period, where culture and power can be reformulated in a process of experimental social interaction and active political mobilization. By virtue of an alternative life style in a spatial sub-set of the urban system, a "city" emerges within the city (not outside the existing city and not necessarily against other communities) in a process that transforms established cultural values and existing spatial forms.

This is the process we want to understand as a major step in our intellectual journey across the web of connections between social movements and urban forms. Why San Francisco? What made this city so attractive to gay people and how did they manage to survive the repression in a setting that was not always tolerant of them, until they established a relatively self-protected territory? What are the social and spatial profiles of this territory? What are the cultural themes of the community, the forms of its social organization, the waving flags of its political battles? And, above all, what are the effects of the process, as triggered by the gay liberation movement, on the city's spatial forms, urban policies, cultural values, and political institutions? Is the gay movement, as reflected by the experience in San Francisco, an agent of urban social change, or on the contrary, does it exhaust itself behind the walls of an artificial paradise? What are the elements favouring one direction or the other in such a dramatic dilemma?

These are the questions we are about to answer by using the results of the field work we conducted in San Francisco between 1980 and 1981 with the collaboration of the gay community, the characteristics and methodology of which are presented and justified in the Appendix to this chapter (pp. 244–52). Let us point out two major and deliberate limits of our analysis:

(1) We do not discuss the origins, evolution, organization or orientation of

the gay movement as such. Although we have obviously tried to understand it in order to be able to establish a significant connection between gay liberation and urban change, it is this latter question that concerns us in this book. Thus all our general understanding of gay culture as a social movement is directed towards the study of its relationship to the city as a social construction.[101]

(2) Our analysis solely concerns gay men. The reason is a profoundly theoretical one. Lesbians, unlike gay men, tend not to concentrate in a given territory, but establish social and interpersonal networks.[102] On the whole they are poorer than gay men[103] and have less choice in terms of work and location, and their politics is less directed towards the established political system. For all these reasons lesbians do not acquire a geographical basis for their political organization and are less likely to achieve local power. And there is a major difference between men and women in their relationship to space. Men have sought to dominate, and one expression of this domination has been spatial. (The same desire for spatial superiority has driven male-dominated cultures to send astronauts to the moon and to explore the galaxy.) Women have rarely had these territorial aspirations: their world attaches more importance to relationships and their networks are ones of solidarity and affection. In this gay men behave first and foremost as men and lesbians as women. So when gay men try to liberate themselves from cultural and sexual oppression, they need a physical space from which to strike out. Lesbians on the other hand tend to create their own rich, inner world and a political relationship with higher, societal levels. Thus they are "placeless" and much more radical in their struggle. For all these reasons, lesbians tend not to acquire a geographical basis for their political organization and are less likely to achieve local power. As a consequence of all these trends, we can hardly speak of lesbian territory in San Francisco as we can with gay men, and there is little influence by lesbians on the space of the city. The situation is, in fact, the consequence of a more fundamental reason for not analysing the experiences of gay men and lesbians as a similar social process. The man/woman distinction as a source of oppression is largely reproduced within the gay universe, and although male gay leaders are clearly anti-sexist and seek alliances with lesbians, the cultural, economic, and political status of gay men and lesbians is clearly unequal, and results in paths of liberation specific to each situation. While spatial communities and local power seem to be fundamental to gay mens' liberation, in San Francisco at least, they are clearly not so for lesbians who are more concerned with the revolution of values than with the control of institutional power. Since our research purpose concerns the relationship between socio-cultural revolt and the city, we will deal only with the experience of gay men in San Francisco. It is an experience with long-standing historical roots that must be recounted in order to understand the role of the city as a potential source of personal freedom.

Why San Francisco? The Historical Development of the Gay City

An instant city, a settlement for adventurers attracted by the gold fields, San Francisco was always a place where people could indulge in personal fantasies and a place of easy moral standards.[104] The city's waterfront and Barbary Coast were a meeting point for sailors, travellers, transients, and lonely people – a milieu of casual encounters and few social rules where the borderline between normal and abnormal was blurred. San Francisco was a gateway city on the western limits of the Western world, and in the marginal zones of a marginal city homosexuality flourished. But in the 1920s San Francisco decided to become respectable, to emerge as the moral and cultural capital of the West, and to grow up gracefully, under the authoritative shadow of the Catholic church, fuelled by its Irish and Italian working-class legions. So "deviants" were repressed and forced into hiding. The reform movement reached the police in the 1930s[105] and forced a crackdown on prostitution and homosexuality, the twin evils in the eyes of puritan morality.

Thus the pioneer origins of San Francisco are not enough to explain its destiny as the setting for gay liberation. The major turning point seems to have been the Second World War.[106] San Francisco was the main port of embarkation and disembarkation for the Pacific front. An estimated 1.6 million men and women passed through the city: young, alone, suddenly uprooted, living on the edge of death and suffering, and living with people of their own sex. The average 10 per cent of homosexuals found in all human populations[107] found themselves more easily and rapidly in this context, and others discovered their bisexuality. Many service men and women were discharged from the military for homosexuality. Many of them were serving in the Pacific area and were ordered to disembark in San Francisco. Since they did not wish to return home bearing what society deemed to be the stigma of homosexuality, they stayed in the city, and were joined at the end of the war by many others who had discovered their sexual and cultural identity. They met in bars, particularly in the Tenderloin area. Bars were then the focal points of social life for gay people;[108] and networks were constructed around these bars: a specific form of culture and ideology began to emerge.[109]

One particular bar has become a legend in San Francisco – The Black Cat (situated on Montgomery Street). It played a major role in the early stages of the gay movement because of the initiative, courage, and imagination of its entertainer, Jose Sarria, a famous drag queen, and a living symbol of the gay movement. Jose Sarria was born in San Francisco. His mother, a Nicaraguan, was a descendant of the Counts of Sarria, from Barcelona, Spain. He worked as a waiter in The Black Cat, a bohemian bar owned by a straight Jewish man. One night he played "Carmen" for a few minutes, with some variations on the theme. In his rendition, Carmen appeared as a drag queen hiding from the police in the bushes of Union Square (the main, fashionable public square in downtown San Francisco). The performance was very successful and Sarria was hired to perform his show on Sunday afternoons because this was the quiet time of the week. For 15 years, each Sunday afternoon, 250 people would pack themselves into The Black Cat to watch Sarria dressed as Madam Butterfly, and listen to his "sermon" about homosexual rights, after which they would end the show by joining hands and singing "God Save the Nelly Queens."

However remote such an image might seem from a liberation movement, the bars and the drag queens were fundamental to the creation of networks, making gay people visible, and stating their right to gather in public places. The Black Cat was, in fact, under continual threat from the police and had to defend its existence through many lawsuits which were finally settled in 1951 when the California Supreme Court declared that it was illegal to close down a bar simply because homosexuals were the usual customers. The first right to a public space had been won. However, after continual harassment from the Alcoholic Beverage Commission, The Black Cat was finally closed in 1963, but not before it had established a tradition, a network, and a fundamental dimension of the gay culture – fun and humour. (This is something that many hardline gay militants seem to be ashamed of, but both Jose Sarria and Harry Britt consider it a crucial aspect of the cultural transformation still to be undertaken. They relish the capacity to enjoy life, turn oppression into creation, and subvert established values by emphasizing their ridiculous aspects. Bars, feasts, and celebrations should be, they believe, the nest of gay culture, as they are one of the primary sources of a vibrant city life.)

The critical moment, nevertheless, was the transition from the bars to the streets, from nightlife to daytime, from "sexual deviance" to an alternative life style. Gays were able to negotiate this change on the basis of another specifically San Franciscan experience: the Beatnik culture and the literary networks through which it expressed itself in the 1950s. Allen Ginsberg's *Howl*[110] provoked a legal action in 1957 against City Lights, the most famous "beat" bookstore, accused of selling "obscene" publications. Kerouac's *On the Road*[111] won an international audience, and the Black Mountain poets were becoming well known to the literary critics. A beat culture emerged as a reaction against several things: McCarthyism, the institution of the family, and suburbanism.[112] This culture concentrated spatially in the old Italian North Beach area near the red light tourist zone of Broadway, and gays were accepted in this tolerant, experimental ambience, and were able to find common interests in an alternative milieu that was concerned with broader issues than sexual differences and boundaries. When the media focused its attention on the San Francisco beatniks, it pinpointed tolerance of homosexuals as evidence of their deviance. In so doing, the media reinforced the attraction to the city for thousands of isolated gays all over the country. On the basis of the bar networks and of the counter-cultural movement, the human rights orientated, respectable gay associations, with an interest in legal rights, found a favourable environment in San Francisco. The conservative, well-to-do Mattachine Society moved its headquarters from Los Angeles to San Francisco in 1955, and some time later began to publish *The Advocate* which became the only gay magazine with a national audience. Also in 1955 the first openly lesbian organization, The Daughters of Bilitis, was founded in San Francisco, and started *Ladder Magazine*. These open expressions of the taboo subjects of sexuality and homosexuality, coinciding as they did with the ideological rebellion of the beatniks, caused much consternation among the conservative sectors of San Francisco. In the 1959 mayoral race, conservative candidate Russell Wolden accused the incumbent, Mayor George Christopher, of allowing the city to become "the national headquarters of organized homosexuals in America." But the establishment and local press criticized Wolden for harming the image of the city and he was defeated.

The newly acquired fame of their growing community gave the gay bar owners the resolution to challenge police harassment by publicizing some cases of corruption and intimidation to which they had been subjected. After minor sanctions, the police responded during 1961 with more repression, including massive raids against gay bars and the revoking of licences for 12 of the city's 30 gay bars, including that of The Black Cat. But the movement was already strong enough to develop its own autonomous organization, reinforced not long afterwards by the anti-war and counter-cultural movements. In 1962, in order to protect themselves against police harassment, the owners of the gay and bohemian bars organized the Tavern Guild which became one of the basic financial and political supporters of all gay activities in San Francisco, and had well over 100 members in 1980. To protect gay rights in law, the same network of bar owners and some prominent gay figures such as Jose Sarria and Jim Foster founded, in 1964, the Society for Individual Rights. This organization soon had over 1,000 members. The hippy culture of the 1960s, which was particularly strong in the Bay Area, was also a sympathetic milieu for gays and influenced their developing cultural identity.

The single event, however, that marked the development of a gay liberation movement in San Francisco, as it did in the rest of the country, was the Stonewall Revolt of 27 June 1969. On that day the police raided, with customary violence, the Stonewall, a gay bar in New York's Greenwich Village. The gays resisted, fighting the police in a three-day battle. The entire gay network reacted across the nation. In 1969 there were only 50 gay organizations; in 1973, there were over 800. In San Francisco the movement grew even faster because of the existing foundations. From the Circle of Loving Companions, created in 1966 as a spin-off of the hippy movement, many organizations evolved into more militant forms, such as the Pink Panthers, the Gay Liberation Front, and the Gay Activist Alliance. In 1971, the movement was strong enough in California to organize a march on Sacramento in defence of gay rights.

In an effort to connect with the extremely powerful current of lesbian liberation, the major theme of the movement was to overcome "invisibility" by "coming out." The objective was to force society to revise standards on sexuality and individual behaviour: homosexuality not only had to be tolerated by a liberal culture, but also accepted as normal and legitimate behaviour by a society that was already questioning fundamental values and institutes such as the family, heterosexuality, and patriarchal authority. Superseding the human rights movement represented by the traditional homophile organizations, gays were asking for their identity to be recognized, and for dominant societal values to change, rather than being forced to adapt to such values. The more radical wing of the movement suffered the same crisis as the political movement of which it was a part. Confronted, after the Cambodian Spring, with stern repression from President Nixon's administration, and divided and weakened by in-fighting and dogmatic ideologies, the student-based organizations ceased. The gay movement, however, continued, and made an exception of itself on the basis of spatial concentration and social networks, building up its own institutions, and discovering its own collective identity as well as the consciousness of its individuals. The gay movement realized that between liberation and politics it first had to establish a community in a series of spatial settings and through a network of economic, social, and cultural institutions. It also discovered that such a community could not be built up as a new utopian phalanstery. Some gays tried to start a new society in a rural environment by buying property in Alpine County in the California Sierra area. They quickly abandoned the project after several homes were destroyed by arson.

Major metropolitan areas such as New York, Los Angeles, Toronto, Seattle and the Bay Area became places of freedom that other cities could not equal. Yet San Francisco was traditionally the most liberal environment where years of struggle by labour, minorities, students and counter-culture movements, as well as a concentration of gay people, had created the conditions for a gay community. So they created a gay community by living in certain neighbourhoods, by operating businesses, by meeting in bars (numbers jumped from 58 in 1969 to 234 in 1980), by inventing feasts and celebrations; in short by organizing socially, culturally and politically. It was against this background that Harvey Milk decided in 1973 to express the political strength of gay people by running for supervisor. A graduate of New York State University at Albany, he was not able to teach because of his discharge in 1956 from the navy for homosexuality. Like many other gays, he migrated in 1969 to San Francisco. After leaving his job as a financial analyst, he opened a photography business, Castro Camera, on Castro Street which soon became the unofficial headquarters for the new political force growing up in San Francisco. When Jose Sarria ran for supervisor in 1961 in his drag queen dress, he obtained 7,000 votes. The goal for Sarria was not to win, but to show that gays were citizens. For Harvey Milk, however, the point was more than self-affirmation. His plan was to go from community, to business, to power. He called for "gays to buy gay," so that Castro would not just be a cruising place, as Greenwich Village in New York, but a space owned by gays, lived in by gays, and enjoyed by gays. If gays could "buy gay" and "live gay," they would also vote gay. And they did. In his first election race, in 1973, Harvey Milk attracted 17,000 votes and came eleventh in a field of 33 candidates. Although it was an excellent showing, it was, at the same time, a sign that he also had to address a broader liberal constituency. In his second electoral attempt, in 1975, while he was still a gay candidate, he also dealt with the more general issues, particularly emphasizing the need to control real estate speculation. He assumed a "straight image," and his support jumped to 53,000 votes, but he still lost.

In spite of these defeats, it was nevertheless clear that the gay vote had become decisive in the city. In the 1975 mayoral election, liberal California Senator George Moscone was elected in favour of his conservative opponent by the very narrow margin of 3,000 votes. Moscone, who was politically astute, appointed Harvey Milk to an important city hall post as a member of the Board of Permit Appeals. For the first time an openly gay leader became a public official. At the same time the neighbourhood movement, boosted by the new progressive coalition emerging around Moscone, was attempting a major drive to make local government more democratic. In 1975, over 50 neighbourhood groups, including representatives of the gay community, met in a San Francisco Community Congress, to promote a programme of social change for the city. A major objective was to make it politically possible to effect urban and social reforms advocated by the grassroots, and to establish an electoral system ensuring accountability of supervisors to local constituencies. A campaign was initiated for district elections which were approved in two referendums (in 1976 and 1977), in spite of the multi-million dollar campaign that the Chamber of Commerce launched against the neighbourhoods' initiative.

Then, on the basis of the territory that the gay community had organized in the Castro area, Harvey Milk was elected supervisor in the 1977 election as a representative of District 5. It was just in time. The homophobic backlash was gaining momentum all over America. A campaign orchestrated by fundamentalist conservatives and publicized by Anita Bryant (an ex-Miss America and a Florida-based singer who appeared in orange-juice advertisements) had succeeded in winning a popular referendum to retain legal discrimination against homosexuals in Miami. Other cities followed suit. Other people expressed their homophobia in a different way. In June 1977 Bob Hillsborough was murdered in San Francisco by a gang of youths who stabbed him repeat-edly, shouting "Faggot. Faggot." Even in California the conservatives believed the moment had come to regain control over public morality. In June 1978 Senator Briggs put on the state ballot a proposition banning homosexuals from teaching in public schools. The gay movement mobilized all its support and Harvey Milk became a major political figure due to his success with the media in this campaign. With the help of liberal Democrats, left-wing militants, and neighbourhood activists, gays won a major victory against conservative forces. In November 1978 Briggs' proposition was rejected by 58 per cent of the Californian voters and by 75 per cent of San Franciscan electors (the prop-osition being defeated in almost all precincts of the city). The local political culture had thoroughly supported the cause of gay rights. In April 1978 the board of supervisors approved a very liberal Gay Rights Ordinance. At the same time, two lesbian leaders, Del Martin and Phyllis Lyon, holding city hall posts, received from the city of San Francisco a certificate of honour for their civic services – including support for lesbians – and for their 25 years of living together. The beginnings in The Black Cat seemed far away: the gays had come a long way, from bar culture to political power. But such power proved precarious. On 27 November 1978 a conservative supervisor, Dan White, an ex-policeman who had campaigned against the tolerance towards "sexual de-viants," shot and killed Mayor George Moscone and Supervisor Harvey Milk in their offices at city hall. He later surrendered to his former colleagues in the police department. The mourning of Moscone and Milk was the most impres-sive political demonstration ever seen in San Francisco: 20,000 people marched with candles, in silence, after listening to speakers who called on the move-ment to pursue the struggle in the way shown by Harvey Milk.

The new mayor, Diane Feinstein, appointed another gay leader, Harry Britt, a socialist, to replace Harvey Milk, following instructions Milk had left recorded on a cassette in case he was murdered.[113] A few months later, on 21 May 1979, a jury sentenced Dan White to seven years in prison, the lowest possible penalty. As *Playboy* reporter Nora Gallagher wrote: "What the jury stands for, in this unfolding drama, are the people who, like White, are growing invisible in San Francisco."[114] Gay visibility had made "invisible" the open will to repress sexuality and life styles not centred on the family. The sectors representing conservative moral values had cause to be alarmed and when the dominant forces in a system become frightened, violence is their most likely response. But, as in New York ten years before, the gays reacted with rage, and after a public meeting in front of city hall to condemn the verdict, they smashed the building's windows, burned police cars, and there followed violent clashes with the police. A new stage of the gay movement had begun. Society was responding to the threat posed by gay values to the fundamental institutions of our civilization, such as family life and sexual repression. And so, in turn, the gay territory could not remain a cultural, utopian community; either walls had to be elevated around the free city or the entire political system had to be reformed. This dilemma was still facing gays at the time of our research.

The gays' power was apparently most uncertain but nonetheless they possessed it, based on a spatial, cultural community whose profile and formation, and relationship to the political process, we will now examine.

The Social Making of a Gay Territory

Space is a fundamental dimension for the gay community.[115] Social prejudice, legal repression, and political violence have forced homosexuals throughout history to be invisible. Such invisibility is a major obstacle to finding sexual partners, discovering friends and leading an unharassed, open life. To overcome this obstacle, gays have always tended to establish their own space where encounters would be possible on the assumption of common sexual and cultural values. Bars were usually where gay social networks developed, the bars themselves being located in certain urban areas where police zoning would implicitly allow some "deviant entertainment" under close surveillance. During the cultural revolts of the 1960s, when certain traditional values began to break down, the gays of San Francisco took advantage of the greater latitude to broaden their space. From bars and street-cruising, their spatial organization shifted to specific neighbourhoods, and from there to larger areas of the city that became, in the mid-1970s, gay free communes.

The urban residential structure was profoundly altered. The gay territory expanded according to a logic the understanding of which will be a key element for establishing the relationship between cultural transformation and urban form.

To proceed with this analysis we had to determine the spatial areas of gay residences and activities in San Francisco at different points in time. Such information was not reported and no empirical research had been done on this matter, so we were forced to find out for ourselves. The Methodological Appendix carefully describes this particular research (pp. 246–50). Let us at this point say what the data bases are and on which ones the following observations and analyses are based.

Given that we could not rely on a single source of information, we established five different means of determining the areas where gays were concentrated in San Francisco:

1   A map drawn by a team of key informants from the gay community on the basis of their experience as pollsters for gay electoral campaigns (figure 5.2). The map was established according to the sequential development of gay residence at different points in time.

Figure 5.2   Gay residential areas
Source: Gay community informants

2   A map representing the proportion of multiple male households on the
    resident population in the area (figure 5.3) in 1977. (The Census does
    not have such information, so we obtained it from the San Francisco
    voter registration files. Therefore, the adequate description of the indi-
    cator is the proportion of registered voters living in multiple male
    households, by precincts; see Methodological Appendix (pp. 246–50).
    Remember that in San Francisco, a high proportion of gays are regis-
    tered voters. Obviously the assumption was not that all such house-
    holds are formed by gays or that all gays lived in such a way. But the
    assumption is that the spatial distribution of adult males living together
    should follow the spatial distribution of gay residences. The fact that
    figure 5.3 closely follows figure 5.2 in its basic trends rather confirms

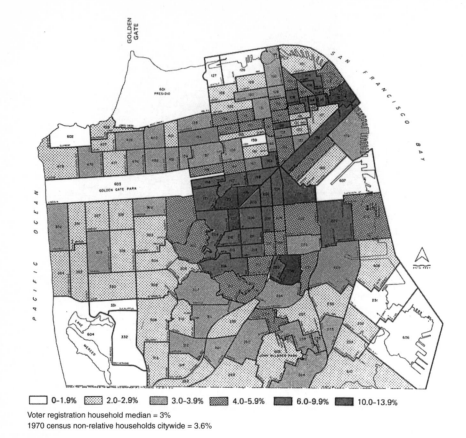

□ 0-1.9%   ▦ 2.0-2.9%   ▨ 3.0-3.9%   ▦ 4.0-5.9%   ■ 6.0-9.9%   ■ 10.0-13.9%

Voter registration household median = 3%
1970 census non-relative households citywide = 3.6%

Figure 5.3   Gay residential areas as indicated by the proportion of multiple male households over the total of registered voters in each census tract, 1977
Source: 1977 voter registration tape/computer programme prepared by Doug De Young

our hypothesis. Thus, we only kept figure 5.3 as a reasonable quantitative indicator of the gay territory, after it had been reinforced by cross-checking from our additional sources of information.

3   A map representing the gay bars and other gay social gathering places (figure 5.4).
4   A map representing self-defined gay businesses, stores and professional offices (figure 5.5).
5   A map representing the highest concentration of votes for Harvey Milk, the gay candidate in the 1975 supervisorial election (figure 5.6).

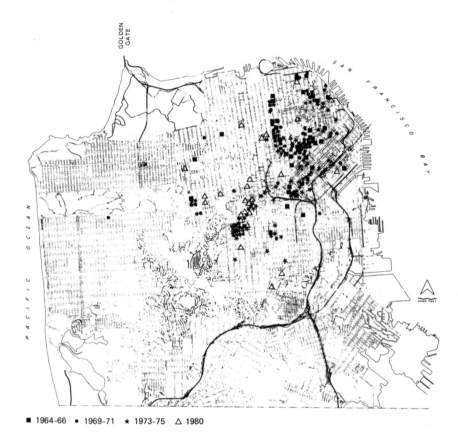

■ 1964-66   ● 1969-71   ★ 1973-75   △ 1980

Figure 5.4   Places where gays gather, 1964–1980 (including bars and social clubs) showing a sequential and cumulative development
Source: Bob Damron's address book. The map is based on a series of maps by Michael Kennedy

Observation of these maps leads to two conclusions:

1   The general spatial pattern tends to evolve along the same lines in all five maps obtained from five different sources, so there is reciprocal reinforcement as to the value of each indicator. While each one by itself would be doubtful as an expression of gay residential areas, the similar spatial distribution in the five maps strongly supports the validity of the residential profile we have obtained. Rank correlation coefficients confirm the covariation between the different indicators of the spatial distribution of gays as shown by figures 5.2, 5.3, and 5.6 (see Methodological Appendix).

Figure 5.5   Golden Gate Business Association members, 1979
Source: GGBA *Buyers' Guide/ Directory,* Autumn 1979–Autumn 1980

2   If (1) is accepted, then there is a gay territory that includes residences, social places, business activities, as well as the ground for political organizing.

We are now able to define the spatial boundaries of San Francisco's male gay community *as of 1980.* Also, given the verification as to the accuracy of our key informants, we may, unless contrary evidence is provided, consider the spatial sequence described by the boundaries over time.

Having established the spatial profile of the gay community, we are also able to relate it to the social and urban characteristics distributed across the city, so that we may understand the factors fostering or counteracting the patterns of settlement inspired by gay culture. On the basis of the 1970 US Census and of the 1974 US Bureau of the Census' *Urban Atlas,*[116] we selected 11 variables considered to be relevant to our analysis (see table 5.3).

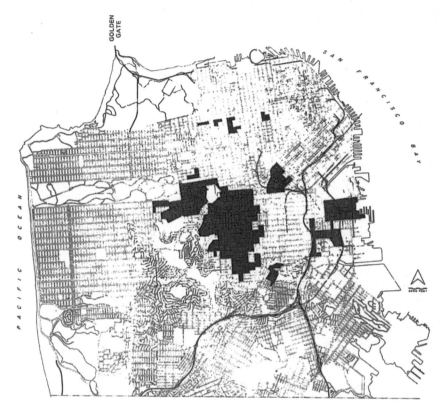

Figure 5.6 Gay voting pattern that indicates two top ranking precincts in support of Harvey Milk in the 1975 supervisorial race
Source: Harvey Milk campaign office

Yet we must keep in mind that all we have is a series of converging indicators of gay location and that the only thing this particular data basis tells us about gayness is where gays are or tend to be. We do not have any indicator of gayness and we are therefore unable to infer anything about gay individuals. In sum, we can only analyse gay versus non-gay spatial units and to proceed in such a way we have carried out two different analyses:

1 On the basis of our key informants' map (figure 5.2) we have divided the city into two categories of spatial areas: those with gay presence and those without. For each selected variable we have calculated the mean value of its distribution in the census tracts corresponding to each of the two categories of space. The *t*-test provides the statistical significance of the differences observed for the mean value of each

Table 5.3 Statistical difference in the values of selected variables for spatial areas with significant gay residence and without significant gay residence, San Francisco, c.1970

| | | | | Pooled variance estimate | | |
Variable	Cultural–spatial area	Mean	s.d.	t	d.f.	2-tail probability
Family % of the resident population under 18	Non-gay	22.8	10.56	4.25	146	0.000
	Gay	15.9	8.43			
Property % of housing units owner-occupied	Non-gay	40.54	31.51	4.41	146	0.000
	Gay	20.93	18.02			
Education % of high-school graduates among residents aged 25 and over	Non-gay	57.21	20.05	−1.55	145	0.123
	Gay	61.73	13.08			
Housing rents Median contract rent (dollars, 1970)	Non-gay	135.04	44.36	1.37	144	0.174
	Gay	126.16	29.76			
Housing value Median housing value (dollars, 1970)	Non-gay	26,886	12,003	−0.26	122.5	0.795
	Gay	27,384	9,360			
Income Median family income (dollars, 1970)	Non-gay	9,858	3,989	0.82	144	0.415
	Gay	9,322	3,804			
Blue collar % of blue collar employed among residents	Non-gay	22.73	12.44	0.54	146	0.588
	Gay	21.72	9.32			
Black population Blacks as % of total population	Non-gay	16.17	25.98	1.10	146	0.273
	Gay	11.96	17.98			
Elderly % of total population over 65	Non-gay	14.66	9.51	0.15	146	0.879
	Gay	14.45	6.29			
Housing dilapidation % of housing units lacking some or all plumbing	Non-gay	7.68	18.09	−0.39	145	0.695
	Gay	8.75	13.81			

Housing decay	Non-gay	7.66	18.45		
% of housing units				−1.07	145	0.288
lacking kitchen facilities	Gay	10.89	17.60		

s.d., standard deviation; d.f., degrees of freedom.
Basic criterion for the statistical significance of the observed differences between mean values of each variable has been the 2-tail probability threshold as provided by the *t*-test. *P* < 0.000 has been considered significant; *P* values between < 0.100 and < 0.200 have been considered moderately significant; *P* values > 0.200 have been considered randomly produced, although they do exist as trends of the urban reality of San Francisco.
Sources: (1) US Census, 1970, San Francisco
       (2) Gay and non-gay areas have been defined by classifying in two separate categories all census tracts, according to information provided by key informants of the gay community, and checked with four other sources as described in the Methodological Appendix (pp. 246–7)
       (3) Our own calculations

    variable in each one of the two categories of spatial units. The extent and direction of such differences will provide the clue for the social and urban specificity of the gay territory.

2   We have tried to establish some measures of correlation between the spatial distribution of the gay community and the spatial distribution of selected social and urban variables. Since we are looking for correspondence between spatial organization in relationship to two series of criteria (rather than co-variation of characteristics across space), the usual regression analysis is inadequate for our purpose. Instead we have proceeded to calculate rank-correlation coefficients (Spearman test) between, on the one hand, the distribution of all census tracts in a six-level scale of "gay space," constructed on the basis of the proportion of multiple male households; and, on the other hand, the distribution of all census tracts in a series of six-level scales on the basis of selected variables. Only variables that the first step of the analysis (as described in 1) showed to be discriminatory were considered in the construction of the scales of social and urban differentiation in San Francisco. Furthermore, one of the findings of our analysis is that these selected variables are likely to affect gay location patterns jointly, instead of having individual effects, since their spatial distribution does not overlap. To test our analysis we constructed an additional special scale, classifying the census tract units in a scale that built into its criteria the three variables considered to have some effect on gay location. The Spearman coefficient between the ranks obtained by the census tracts units in this scale and the ranks they obtained in the multiple male households scale provided the final test for our tentative interpretation of the social roots of gay location patterns.

The most important result of this study is the definition of the spatial organization of the gay community as presented in figures 5.2–5.6. All converge towards a largely similar territorial boundary. Thus, the first finding is that there is a gay territory. Furthermore, it is not only a residential space but also a space for social interaction, for business activities of all kinds, for leisure and pleasure, for feasts and politics. It was on this spatial basis that the gay community succeeded in electing both Harvey Milk and Harry Britt with the largest and best organized single voting block, using the decentralized electoral system by districts that existed in San Francisco between 1976 and 1980.

What were the characteristics of this space? Table 5.3 provides a tentative answer according to the methodology just described.

Of the 11 selected variables examined only two appear strongly negatively associated with the presence of gays: the proportion of owner-occupied housing units and the proportion of the resident population under 18 years. In other words, property and family were the major walls protecting the "straight universe" against the gay influence. It is our hypothesis that fundamental to this relationship was the cultural dimension of the rejection and the capacity of a given neighbourhood to oppose gay immigration either because of the control over real estate property or because of the local organization of a family-orientated community. The latter has been the case, for example, in the Latino Mission District and in the black Bayview–Hunter's Point areas – they have remained outside gay location patterns. Variables in housing value, family income, or blue-collar occupation have not differentiated gay and non-gay areas. Neither gay location nor gay rejection have directly appeared as economic processes: these seem to have come basically from cultural distances. Two other variables show some significant differences between the city and the gay city: gay areas have tended to carry a concentration of more educated population; and non-gay areas have tended towards higher rents. It should be remembered that San Francisco's housing stock was 65 per cent rental and that the areas of highest social status included the likes of Pacific Heights where the proportion of owner-occupied housing was below the average. Thus a new barrier was established in areas exclusive enough to keep gays out through high rents.

These findings are reinforced by the second method we have used to measure our observations. Table 5.4 shows that, as expected, the rank-correlation between the spatial distributions of our indicator of gay residence and each one of those for the four variables obtained by our previous analysis is very weak.

A simple observation of figure 5.7 provides the reason for such a result: gays have not resided in the western zone of the city because of the nature of the property; in the eastern side because of the predominance of the family-orientated community; and in the northern hills because of the high rents. Only when we combine the effects of the three variables in one scale (property, family, and high rents) do we obtain a significant −0.38 rank-correlation

Table 5.4   Spearman correlation coefficients between the rank of census tracts of
San Francisco ordered in a six-level scale according to the proportion of multiple
male households among registered voters resident in 1977, and five other scales as
indicated

	Spearman R
1 Scale according to the proportion of residents under 18 in 1970 (*family*) 6 levels	−0.11
2 Scale according to the proportion of owner-occupied housing units in 1970 (*property*) (6 levels)	−0.16
3 Scale according to the proportion of high-school graduates among residents over 25 in 1970 (*education*) (6 levels)[a]	−0.18
4 Scale according to the median contract rent, in dollars, in 1970 (6 levels) (*high rent*)	−0.17
5 Scale of *family*, *property* and *high rent* (scale in 6 levels constructed by combination of scores of census tracts in scales number 1, 2, and 4. It reads as follows: top level in scale 5 = top level in scale 1 *or* in scale 2 *or* in scale 4, and so on throughout all the levels of the scale)	−0.38 ($P < 0.001$)

[a] The ranking for *education* has been inversed in order and in relationship to the
other scales, to be consistent with the hypothesis of a *direct* correlation with gay
presence.
Source: Our own calculations on the basis of scales constructed by us; see the
Methodological Appendix, pp. 246–50

between this scale and the scale constructed on the basis of the indicator of
gay residence.

   To provide a clearer expression of these results we have constructed figure
5.7 where the three variables and the proportion of multiple male households
(indicator of gay residence) are mapped *together* according to the description in
the figure's caption. Figure 5.7 shows a striking autonomy between the territories defined by the four variables, with only limited overlapping. We are in
the presence of four spaces: property land, family land, rich land (defined by
the proportion of high-rent housing), and gay land. Gay settlement was opposed by property, family, and high class: the old triumvirate of social conservatism. Figure 5.8 provides confirmation of this conclusion. Our informants
(the accuracy of whose information was established through cross-checking
with four other sources) forecasted the expansion of the gay community throughout the 1980s in the areas presented in figure 5.8, without any previous
knowledge of our analysis. They are precisely the zones that appear to be

:::: Top rank in the proportion of multiple male households (indicator of *gay residence*)

▓▓ High proportion of population under 18 (*family*)

|||| High level of high rent in rental housing (*high rent*)

≡≡ High proportion of house ownership (*property*)

▦▦ Overlap of *property* and *high rent*

Figure 5.7   Family, property, high rents, and gay residential areas
Source: Our study on the basis of US Census data and the voter register

contiguous to the gay territory and where the three variables proposed as
deterrents to gay location score relatively low values.

Before proceeding towards any further elaboration of these results, we need
to introduce a historical perspective into the analysis. The spatial setting of
the gay community in San Francisco has developed along a series of progressions
whose dynamics are the clearest way to understand the connection between
alternative culture and spatial form. We have two sources, expressed in figures 5.3 and 5.4 to study the sequence of expansion of the gay territory after
the Second World War: on the one hand, the areas established for each

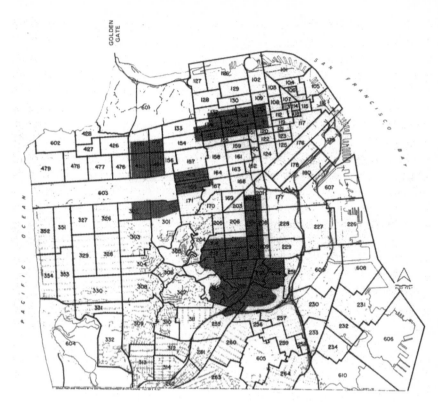

Figure 5.8 Informant basemap: gay residential expansion areas (1980s)
Source: Key informants mapping, February 1980

period by the same team of informants whose information appeared accurate when contrasted to other indicators; and on the other hand the sequence of expansion of gay bars at four points in time on the basis of our reliable source, as cited in the Methodological Appendix. From the observation of these maps, and on the basis of the knowledge of the characteristics of the city as expressed in the US Census Urban Atlas and the Coro Foundation Districts' Handbook,[117] we can propose the following spatial history of San Francisco's gay community.

The spatial history of San Francisco's gay community

At the "beginning," in the 1940s, gays still had to be invisible, and for the most part met in bars, particularly concentrated in the Tenderloin area, a red light zone adjacent to downtown. So gays were forced to be a part of the (relatively) tolerated milieu of individual "deviant" behaviour. There were networks, but no community-places, and no territory. In the 1950s an alternative life style and culture flourished in the cafes and bookshops of North Beach, that of the beatniks. Gays found there a receptive, tolerant atmosphere and they became a part of the rebel residential community that established itself in that area. Without developing a community themselves, gays enjoyed relative freedom as a sub-set of a highly intellectual, fashionable counter-culture. In the 1960s gays' network expanded and took advantage of the atmosphere of liberalism imposed by the anti-war and civil rights movements. In addition to Tenderloin and North Beach, bars flourished around a new axis, Polk and Van Ness, that were more integrated into the city. For the first time, an independent gay residential area developed around the meeting places opened on Polk Street. The adjacent ghetto of the Western Addition was designated for redevelopment and some gay households started buying property in the renewed area in the late 1960s.

The gay liberation movement was given a dramatic impetus by New York's Stonewall Revolt of June 1969. Gays "came out," and many of them migrated from all over the country to the cities where they could express themselves, especially New York, Los Angeles, and San Francisco. The new militants were not content just to be close to social places where there were sexual networks, but tried to develop, symbolically and politically, a life style defined as gay. They tried to establish a community. Others joined the effort in a somewhat confused frame of mind, to be socialized in a new culture more suitable to their needs and behaviour, a culture that they needed to feel part of by being, physically, in a given neighbourhood, for only then would they be able to rub their old classroom slates clean and learn for the first time about themselves in their rightful surroundings. So a collective movement, informally organized, began to take over a well-defined area (the Castro Valley in the geographical centre of San Francisco), an area characterized by two main features: it was traditionally a beautiful Victorian neighbourhood partly vacated by its Irish working-class dwellers moving to the suburbs; and it was a very middle-level area in terms of income and education with much affordable housing to rent. Gays purposely started businesses and shops in the area and neighbourhood associations that forced other businesses in the area, particularly banks, to collaborate with them. Bars and social places followed the residential concentration, so reversing the usual sequence.

At the same time, in the 1970s, two very different trends were expressing other spatial and social orientations of gay people, trends that attracted less attention than the garish lights of the Castro territory. While sharing the aspirations to a self-controlled "private territory," many gays could not afford the high rents that landlords were forcing them to pay if they were to have that kind of freedom. So they started another colonization in the much harsher area, South of Market, where transient hotels, warehouses, and slums waited for redevelopment. Their marginality to the gay community was not only

spatial, but social: they tended to reject the politicization and positive counter-culture of the new liberation movement. Instead, they emphasized the
sexual aspects of gay life, and the more the gay community strove for legitimacy the more an individualistic minority, who were generally poorer and
less-educated, evolved new sexual codes, many of them joining the sado-
masochist networks. The South of Market area became the headquarters of
the leather culture.[118]

A growing proportion of middle-class gays, however, rejected the militant
stands of the liberation movement and ridiculed the idea of setting up in a
ghetto. They believed it was necessary to obtain personal freedom and legal
rights without challenging a system that was otherwise highly favourable to
their sex, class, and race. This orientation, which we will examine as one of
the main debates within the community, has also a distinct spatial expression.
Since the early 1970s, according to our informants, some middle-class gays
had wanted to live in a friendly gay neighbourhood, but not in the Castro
ghetto, and they began to locate themselves, in a very pointed move, in the
lower sections of the fashionable Pacific Heights, literally on the threshold of
San Francisco's elite.

In the mid-1970s, two major spatial developments characterized the gay
community:

1 The Castro ghetto grew and expanded dramatically in all adjacent
   areas. A very dense gay network of bars, health clubs, stores, businesses, and activities developed on the basis of a growing population.
   Immigration from the rest of the country accelerated the rate that gay
   households bought property in the neighbourhood, taking advantage
   of the conversion of rented buildings into condominiums. They moved
   westward to more affluent sections. The expansion also reached the
   Dolores Corridor on the border with the Latino Mission District. Friction developed and there was some anti-gay violence from the Latino
   youth.
2 In a different development, gay households (particularly lesbian) developed in the working-class areas of Bernal Heights and Potrero Hill,
   within what we have called "familyland," taking advantage of relatively sound, cheap housing. The major reason for the tolerance shown
   towards the households was the existence in those areas of very large
   counter-cultural communities established by young white students and
   professionals who maintained a good relationship with working-class
   families – their common ground being the strength of feeling about the
   neighbourhood. Gay men and lesbians were generally welcomed into
   this milieu of 1960s rebels, with which they had associated from the
   outset.

In the late 1970s, on the basis of the newly acquired (though uncertain) protection through political power, a new expansion of gay residences took place on the borders of the middle-class areas such as Inner Richmond and Inner Sunset in the western part of the city, where home ownership was generally required. While still preserving their basic territory, gays had started to dismantle the last barriers to their spatial presence. The contradiction implicit in this move was that either gays would lose their identity to adapt to prevailing patterns of behaviour, or they would have to obtain from the entire city a degree of tolerance that would have demanded society to change its fundamental values with respect to the family and sexual repression – demands that were unlikely to be met without fundamental social change. For the moment we can only point to this question since we will have to introduce additional analytical elements to answer it. But suffice to say now that it is significant that a historical overview of the expansion of gay territory should introduce this debate.

The evolution and characteristics of gay residential space cannot answer the basic research questions we have asked about the relationship between alternative cultures and the production of urban forms. But because spatial structures do show the trace of social processes we are able to introduce some of the basic themes of our analysis on the basis of the results presented here.

The gay community expressed (and continues to express) a diversity of interests and social situations that always overlapped in reality and that we are only able to separate analytically. At the same time it represented a sexual orientation, a cultural revolt, and a political "party." In the case of San Francisco, young professionals and small businessmen who emigrated to the city because of its cultural tolerance and character as a headquarters of an advanced service economy comprise a very important sector of gay people. In fact all these aspects were present in the spatial history of the gay community but with different weights for each period.

When the gay identity had to be reduced to its hard core because of fierce social repression, sexually orientated networks were the basic instrument of communication and solidarity. But gayness is more than a sexual preference: it is an alternative way of life, characterized by the domination of expressiveness over instrumentalism and by human contact over impersonal competition. Such values were very close to the beatnik and hippy cultures of the 1950s and 1960s, and this is why gays moved into the territories of these alternative life styles. But gays were different and represented more than a counter-culture. Not only did they have a sexual network to preserve, they had also to win their right to exist as citizens; they had to engage in political battles, change laws, fight the police, and influence government. But how could they organize within the political institutions only on the basis of bars and of the marginal counter-cultures? To be a society within a society, they had to organize themselves spatially to transform their oppression into the organizational setting of political power. This is why the building of the Castro ghetto was inseparable from the development of the gay community as a social movement. It brought together sexual identity, cultural self-definition, and a political project in a form organized around the control of a given territory. This is why those who rejected the idea of a social movement left the "commune," either to rejoin conventional society in exchange for some tolerance, or to cut all communication and attempt instead to affirm the potency of individualistic sexual pleasure. The ghetto preceeded the movement towards institutionalization and provided the basis, particularly through the decentralized district elections, to obtain enough power to live in the city instead of having to seek self-protection within a community. But as long as gays are beaten and killed because of whom they love, even in a city where they share institutional power, they will need the ghetto. The territorial boundaries of a cultural community are required for the same reasons that Jewish people in Europe, black people in America, and oppressed ethnic minorities all over the world have always needed them – for everyday survival.

The Renovation of Housing and Urban Space by the Gay Residential Communities

Every incoming urban group has an impact on its housing and physical space. The gays of San Francisco definitely improved the quality of housing through repairs, remodelling, and excellent maintenance.[119] Most gay households established themselves by renting or buying houses in middle-level neighbourhoods, worked on them, and upgraded both the buildings and the surrounding environment. The process of urban renovation in San Francisco has been largely, although not exclusively, triggered by gay people. As a result, property values in gay residential areas have been considerably improved, far above the already impressive average for the entire city. Commercial and business development has spread effortlessly through the gay residential areas.[120] The aesthetic quality of most houses renovated by gays has greatly helped San Francisco to preserve its historical heritage of beautiful old Victorian buildings, many of which had been condemned during the 1960s by the technocratic San Francisco Redevelopment Agency (SFRA). The gay community opposed the renewal strategies presaged by the SFRA's bulldozers during the period of the pro-growth coalition with an alternative model – that of rehabilitating the existing city – in which housing stock was to be reused and valuable architectural structures remodelled.[121] In fact, the spectacular urban renovation in San Francisco during the 1970s, with the new gay households as the driving force, was the result of a more complex pattern (as is clearly shown by the typology of renovation agents established by Don Lee on the basis of his study of gay realtors).[122] Three different types of interventions appear to have contributed:

1   Affluent gay professionals, desiring to move into the gay territory, hired
     skilled renovators to do the job for them once they had bought the
     inexpensive houses, the basic structure of which was sound and whose
     old Victorian shape offered a great potential for architectural beauty.
2   Gay realtors and interior decorators discovered the possibilities of a new
     housing market and decided to use it as a way to earn a living. Using
     their commercial and artistic skills, they bought property in low-cost
     areas, and repaired and renovated the buildings in order to sell them for
     a high profit. (This, incidentally, is the process that accounts for some of
     the renovation taking place in the predominantly black area of the West-
     ern Addition.)[123] It would be simplistic to label this activity as "real
     estate speculation." What in fact happened was that gays, discriminated
     against in the labour market, discovered the hard way how to survive
     the tough San Francisco housing market, and then decided to use their
     newly learned skills as a means of earning a living. A few of them
     became realtors and greatly contributed to urban rehabilitation and
     gentrification, most of them taking part as hired, skilled workers, carpen-
     ters, decorators and painters. Don Lee estimates that "the gay commu-
     nity provides 90 per cent of labour in renovation and restoration in
     central San Francisco neighbourhoods."[124] Some of the most prominent
     restoration enterprises, such as the San Francisco Victoriana and the
     San Francisco Renaissance, are spin-offs of initiatives by gays.
3   At the same time, the majority of the gay community could not afford
     to buy a house in San Francisco.[125] So they formed collectives to either
     rent or buy inexpensive buildings, and fixed them up themselves. This
     practice was not only an expression of an economic need but a tra-
     dition initiated by the counter-cultural collectives of the 1960s, in an
     attempt to supersede the role of the family in the traditional household
     structure.[126] These collectives have probably accounted for a large pro-
     portion of San Francisco's housing rehabilitation and maintenance in
     recent years.[127]

The impact of the gay community on the urban space went far beyond the
walls of the restored buildings. The adjacent streets burgeoned with stores,
bars, public places and miscellaneous businesses from clinics to launderettes.
The monograph by Don Lee, "Castro Street commercial district" has clearly
established the decisive commercial, physical, and aesthetic improvement of a
neighbourhood that was being abandoned by its Irish working class who were
moving to the suburbs. To be sure, Castro Valley was – and still is – the core
of the gay community and has therefore had much higher chances of urban
improvement because of the high expectations in terms of real estate. But this
is precisely the argument: unlike other oppressed communities, gay people
have raised the physical standards and economic value of the space they have

occupied. Are we then in the presence of typical gentrification? Were gay people the middle-class vanguard pushing urban poor and minorities out of a newly discovered space picked out by the well-to-do in the so-called "back to the city" movement?[128] This has been the accepted wisdom. Analysts, including Don Lee, have tried to dissociate the gay community from the renovation process, saying that renovation was going on independently of the gays and they took their opportunity. Furthermore, the reference to the contribution by gays to the aesthetics of renovation is rejected as a "sexist prejudice" on account of the supposed "femininity" of gays.[129]

Reality is more complex, but the issue must be discussed because it is fundamental for our research purposes. Has there been a contribution by the gay community to the quality of their urban space or has it been a more general gentrification and a "back to the city" movement by the middle class, part of which happened, in San Francisco, to be gay? Have gays been improving the city or gentrifying the working-class neighbourhoods? Our answers to these questions contain several findings.

First, it is a fact that gays improved the quality of housing and urban space, mainly through renovation and maintenance.[130] Secondly, it is clear that most neighbourhoods that are now residential areas for gays were in a declining condition. Gay location in those neighbourhoods (particularly in the Western Addition, Haight Ashbury, Potrero Hill, Bernal Heights, Castro) was a decisive element in improving the housing stock and the neighbourhoods' commercial vitality. Thirdly, it is not true that all gays, or even a majority of them, were high-income, middle-class professionals. In addition there were poor gay people who lived in the marginal areas, particularly in the South of Market and Tenderloin areas (San Francisco's skid row).

Many gays were able to live in their neighbourhoods because they organized collective households and they were willing to make enormous economic sacrifices to be able to live autonomously and safely as gays. Besides, many gays were more likely to be able to choose their space because they were single men, did not have to sustain a family, were young, and connected to a relatively prosperous service economy. All of these characteristics together made it easier for them to find a house in a tight housing market.

What the gays have had in common with some non-family heterosexual groups is an alternative life style that had close ties with gay culture – a middle-class movement that preferred residence in San Francisco, not because they were predominantly middle class, but because they valued personal experience and an active, social street life. In this sense, gays appear to have been a cultural vanguard for these people. Other groups and institutions started upgrading their neighbourhoods as a result of the renovation initiated by gays. In this context the new policy from the banks located in the Castro area was particularly significant: not only did they lend money to would-be private renovators but they remodelled their own buildings, to improve the physical image of the street. The decision of the Surf Theatre Chain to renovate the Castro Theatre building, the main cinema in the gay territory, was the most symbolic at the time; a very old-fashioned structure in the Hollywood–Babylon tradition, the theatre was declared a Registered Landmark in the city after its renovation in July 1977.

Urban renovation in San Francisco reached proportions far above those of any other American city. Unlike other cities, the "back to the city" movement has not just been the wealthy people inhabiting the central city on the basis of new profitable trends in the housing market.[131] Most renovators have been gay people who have come to San Francisco in the past decade. They have intentionally located themselves, individually or collectively, to build up a new community at a financial and social cost that only "moral refugees" are ready to pay. They have paid for their identity, and in doing so have most certainly gentrified their areas. They have also survived and learnt to live their real life. At the same time, they have revived the colours of the painted façades, repaired the shaken foundations of the buildings, lit up the tempo of the street and helped to make the city beautiful and alive, all in an age that has been grim for most of urban America.

Gay Society and the Urban Culture

When we use the phrase "gay community" we are implying something more than a gay territory and an open gay life style. We are referring to a deliberate effort by gay people to set up their own organizations and institutions in all spheres of life.[132] The first efforts, such as the Tavern Guild, came from the bar networks, mainly as a defensive reaction against harassment, violence and legal intimidation. During the 1970s, when gays felt relatively safe in their space and in their city as a result of the political influence they had acquired, they founded a whole range of gay organizations. Many of these were artistic expressions of a culture struggling to emerge: the Gay Freedom Marching Band, The Lavender Harmony Band, the Lesbian Chorus, the Chrysanthemum Ragtime Band, the Quattro Quartet, and a whole series of dancing groups, orchestras, poetry clubs, and art galleries, most of which were co-ordinated and supported by an umbrella organization, the Golden Gate Performing Arts Inc. At another level, counselling clinics and institutions were started, offering psychological support. Operation Concern tried to provide the necessary milieu for people to adapt to their new social milieu, particularly for the young gays who had just arrived in the city. Gay groups were also placed in different churches according to their beliefs. There was even an openly gay church, the inter-denominational Metropolitan Community Church, started by a former Pentecostal pastor. Even with spiritual experiences, such as EST,[133] gays organized their own circle with the support of *The Advocate*, the major national gay magazine.

The most visible and sometimes most controversial of the attempts to re-build the society on the basis of gay institutions was and remains the Golden Gate Business Association (GGBA), a federated network of more than 500 businesses (in 1980), only five years after its foundation.[134] Since it was able to mobilize some financial support for gay activities and celebrations, as well as for political campaigns, the GGBA has become the target of gay radicals who see it as the symbol of a desire by the more affluent gays to win acceptance within the established capitalist order, instead of furthering the transforma-tion of that order's fundamental values. In fact, a look at the membership[135] reveals that a great majority are small firms and individual businesses such as lawyers, business consultants, realtors, small merchants, bars, financial con-sultants, decorators, advertising specialists, photographers, tourist agents, en-tertainment organizers, and so on. This in no way represents the world of San Francisco's financial establishment. The real business elite is, and will con-tinue to be, profoundly homophobic, and while a few individuals are toler-ated as homosexuals they will not be accepted as gay, namely, as involved in the promotion of an alternative life style. The GGBA has very little possibil-ity, therefore, of allowing the takeover of the gay movement by capitalist forces, and, in fact, expresses the profound desire for individual autonomy and personal freedom that gays feel are the basis of their own development. Such autonomy in American society relies on the ability to earn a living by being self-employed, and there is a real chance for the more educated gays of finding such positions in the changing margins of San Francisco's character-istic service economy. They tend to specialize in providing services for the growing middle class of the city, and in taking intellectually demanding jobs for the government and private corporations. They work also in the expand-ing market of the gay community. Thus we are in a merchant world and in a world of urban freedom, in a world of autonomy, exchange, interaction, and cultural experimentation. We are almost in the world of the Renaissance city where political freedom, economic exchange, and cultural innovation, as well as open sexuality, developed together in a self-reinforcing process on the basis of a common space won by citizens struggling for their freedom.

To push this image even further, we are also in a world of merchant fairs and street feasts. The gay community is one of the main organizers of popular celebrations in San Francisco, some of which come from the merchants' interests that provide the economic support for the community, such as the Annual Castro Street Fair, initiated in 1972 by Harvey Milk, and which attracts over 100,000 people each year to exhibitions, songs, eating, drinking, playing, and meetings to debate politics. Other feasts are gay versions of traditional customs like Christmas carolling, the Beaux Arts Ball, and Hallow-een. Halloween in particular has become a major festival where straight and gay people share their fantasies of "crossing over," dressing as in a contest of imagination, aesthetics and humour, and parading along Polk and Castro streets in a night of joy, drinking, laughing and dancing in the streets under the outraged eyes of a nervous police force that must trust the gay community's autonomous security service to take care of its own people. Costumes and witchcraft are precisely what people need to walk happily on the uncertain edge of blurred identities. But the interesting phenomenon is not only the appropriation by gays of a tradition usually associated with children, but the joy and pleasure of tens of thousands of Bay Area residents who participate in the event in the Castro area, happy to celebrate the gays' sense of humour and life by joining in the fun, dressing in drag or just enjoying the spectacle.

Other major gay celebrations are new, created by the tradition of the movement itself and established to commemorate major social struggles, one of the most important of which is the Gay Freedom Day Parade, a week-long programme of activities to celebrate the anniversary of the Stonewall Riot of 27 June 1969. Initiated by a spontaneous demonstration in 1970, it has become an institution, the major social event for the gay community, when all cultural and political tendencies meet to express the power, joy, and contradictions of an increasingly liberated community. But the colour, imagination, and verve of the celebration are so strong that many people from San Francisco, as well as from other parts of the world, come to join the gays in what has become the major popular event in San Francisco. (In recent years, between 200,000 and 300,000 people have attended the parade.) Other commemorations have another dimension, such as the yearly Memorial March for Harvey Milk and George Moscone, when thousands of mourners march, carrying candles; or the Harvey Milk Birthday Party celebrated in Castro Street since 1979. The gay community has done more through this increasingly diverse array of events than project its values or have fun: it has shown the city that streets are for people, that urban culture means gathering together to play in public places, and that music, politics and games can intertwine in a revitalizing way, creating a new media for messages and establishing new networks of communication. At the Columbus Day Parade (a non-gay celebration) the Gay Marching Band and Twirling Corps appear to be the most cheered performers. This is not only because there are many gays in the city or because of the truly exceptional quality of their performance; it is also because there is a vague consciousness that gays have greatly reinforced the San Francisco tradition of urban life, largely missing in most American cities, such as feasts in the streets and public celebrations – the feeling that a city is not just a combination of capitalist functions and empty streets patrolled by police cars.

Of course, the recognition of this fundamental contribution stops short of the acknowledgement that life could be better if lived their way. But there is the beginning of a connection between gay values and a more general cultural transformation. To consider gay society as a short-sighted, separatist ideology would be misleading. The building of a gay community with its own institutions in the midst of a heavily heterosexual, central city is itself a major transformation, and is highlighted by the fact the gay celebrations have become San Francisco's most popular and brilliant events. But such feasts do not come only from the free expression of a rich culture. They are, as their origins show, symbols of political battles and demonstrations of the strength and militancy of the gay community in its own territory. This is the other side of the parade. Each time there is a major defeat of gay rights in the voting polls of middle America, gays take to the streets in San Francisco chanting "Civil Rights or Civil War." The streets of San Francisco continue to be public places, unlike most American urban streets, partly because of the impact of the gay culture. But for public places to be public, political rights have to be heightened. The gay culture has been able to enrich the urban culture because it has been able to substantially modify the political system. Gay culture is inseparable from gay politics.

Gay Power? The Transformation of the Local Political System by the Gay Community

On a warm spring evening of 1980, middle America was shocked to learn through a CBS nation-wide special report that gays were about to seize power in San Francisco, "everybody's favourite city."[136] It is true that a disciplined and mobilized block of about 20–25 per cent of the city's registered voters[137] was making a difference in the local political system. But the process of power-building was far more complex than just adding gay immigrants to San Francisco's declining population. To understand this process may also explain the profound impact that gays had on city politics and the fragility of that power.

The first apparent connection between the emerging gay community and the political system came in 1972, when George McGovern's presidential campaign opened the way for the expression in an election of many of the social issues arising from the movements of the 1960s. Gay rights were among them.

In the drive to obtain support for McGovern in California, a group of gay, liberal organizers of the homophilic Society for Individual Rights, under the leadership of Jim Foster, founded a gay-orientated political organization affiliated to the Democratic Party, the Alice B. Toklas Democratic Club.[138] It was a very effective campaign organization: the club was rapidly recognized as the responsible gay connection to democratic politics, and prominent straight San Francisco Democrats such as John Burton and the black leader, Willie Brown, joined it. Using the club's influence, Willie Brown sponsored, and obtained approval for, a bill in 1975 that legalized homosexuality in California. The basic political understanding was that the California Democrats would protect the gay community from discrimination and repression in exchange for its votes, channelled through the Democratic Party. This was not, as it transpired, how the majority of the gay community behaved politically in San Francisco. In a parallel effort, Harvey Milk had initiated his own campaign to establish an autonomous political platform for gays. Coming from the anti-war movement, he was distrustful of the national political parties, and was anyway orientated towards grassroots support from the community as the only way of insuring the political accountability of representatives. Taking his Castro Village as a base and using the tactics of a ward politician, Milk attended neighbourhood meetings, shook hands at the bus stops, and spent hours in the local bars.[139] His Castro Camera store became the political meeting place for the local gay community. He obtained 17,000 votes in the 1973 supervisorial election, and 53,000 in 1975. The first major confrontation with the Democratic Party, supported by the Alice B. Toklas Democratic Club, came in 1976. Harvey Milk, a registered Democrat, ran for a State Assembly seat against the official Democratic candidate; he lost the election having received only 45 per cent of the votes cast but carried District 5 which was his territory.

In the midst of this confrontation, the most militant wing of the Alice B. Toklas club seceded to form a new Gay Democratic Club, where explicit gayness became the symbol of their manifesto. The club stressed the importance of gays organizing themselves within the political system and the Democratic Party. In 1979, the club became the Harvey Milk Gay Democratic Club; with a membership of over 1,400 and a militant core of over 200, it was the largest and most active single political organization in San Francisco.

But the key to Harvey Milk's political success in 1977, and with him an autonomous gay community, was the connections he established with the emerging political system. On the one hand, he could only be elected because of the new district-based electoral procedure, itself the expression of the growing influence of neighbourhood associations and grassroots politics of which the gay community was a significant component. On the other hand, he exercised some influence (and so the gay community could win some respect) in the local governing coalition, since it was being reorganized around Mayor Moscone. To replace declining labour presence in the city and to confront pro-growth conservative policies from business, middle-class progressive neighbourhoods and blacks needed the support of the gay community which leant politically to the left. Several supervisors elected in the period from 1975 to 1980 (Carol Silver was one) relied on the gay vote as did Moscone himself. Thus the rise of gay influence represented a total recomposition of local power provoked by grassroots pressure, including the gay community, in which the gay community would be a significant member of the new local alliance, relying on its territorial and cultural constituency.

Harvey Milk's political testament, tape-recorded ten days after his election, was a clear expression of the continuing conflict between gay politics as an expression of the local community and gay politics as a subordinate wing of the Democratic Party. He clearly designated the names of four persons who could replace him as supervisor in the event of his murder. They were, in order of priority: Frank Robinson, a writer and a close friend; Anne Kronenberg, a lesbian militant; Bob Ross, publisher of the BAR[140] and 1978's Emperor of San Francisco;[141] and Harry Britt. Of even greater importance was his naming of the people who should not be nominated to his post. All of them were prominent, established Democrats who would be the most likely appointees of a moderate Democratic mayor such as Diane Feinstein. Harry Britt, who was the more politically experienced of the four, was appointed.

A declared socialist, close to the left of the Democratic Party, Harry Britt became one of the most active supervisors on a variety of progressive issues, always trying to establish his platform on a broader base. Although highly respected by the gay community and clearly representing gays, Britt did not have the charisma of Harvey Milk which was the crucial element for the political self-definition of the community since the Harvey Milk Club was supported by the bar culture and the Tavern Guild. The club's systematic support and endorsement allowed Britt to be easily elected in 1979 and re-elected in 1980.[142] In spite of his presence on the board of supervisors, the influence of gays in the political system did not correspond to its political strength, as measured by the number of appointees nominated by the mayor to city hall posts. Their main influence was in terms of the threat of their opposition. In the 1979 mayoral race, the incumbent, Diane Feinstein, was forced into a run-off against her conservative opponent because of the presence of a gay candidate, and she was elected only when gay leaders called in their votes for her in exchange for a series of promises, noticeably to give them some influence in the recruiting within the police department.

This cautious attitude was symptomatic of the unstable political situation in San Francisco following the assassinations in 1978 of Harvey Milk and George Moscone. The incipient new coalition disappeared at the same time that a right-wing current was sweeping the national political scene. A new coalition of neighbourhood groups, ethnic minorities, women's organizations, gays, and public employees unions was formed, under the name of Action for Accountable Government (AAG). Although influential through its contacts with various communities as well as with Democratic Party leaders, AAG could not control the mayor nor field a new political candidate. So San Francisco became an example of coalition politics, with alliances between different groups forming and disappearing according to the political issues of the moment. In this situation, the initiatives of the gay representatives were consistently progressive, defending social programmes and neighbourhood conservation against the proposals of the downtown business sector and fiscal conservatives. The importance of the gay's contribution to the formation of progressive urban policies in

San Francisco is demonstrated by the series of proposals presented by Harvey Milk and Harry Britt to the board of supervisors including the suggestions to favour rent control, fight real estate speculation, oppose high-rise developments, and defend the city's urban quality. (See the list of these initiatives presented in the Methodological Appendix, pp. 250–2.) Significantly enough, Dan White, Harvey Milk's murderer, was the strongest advocate of redevelopment programmes, and a defender of the controversial and speculative development for tourists known as Pier 39.[143] In this sense, gay leadership sought to establish a broader political legitimacy by embracing the defence of popular interests in urban development, sometimes at the expense of a significant gay real estate sector which was opposed to rent control. We can therefore say that gay political influence in San Francisco has been a major factor since 1975 in undermining the control of business interests over city politics.

Nevertheless, the inability of the various components of this alternative political scheme to establish one platform and a common leadership led to a succession of *ad hoc* alliances and compromises between interests that were not always easy to reconcile when very narrowly defined. For instance, the neighbourhood opposition to high-rise development was criticized by labour unions looking for jobs, both in the construction process and in future office buildings. Gays' desire for urban restoration was viewed by blacks as a threat of intensified gentrification. Police control of anti-gay violence was often considered as a potential source for a crackdown on Latino youth. The protection of family-orientated public services was often met with indifference by the predominantly single gay population, and so on. Thus, in spite of conscious efforts by the leadership to establish strategic alliances, the reduction of the groups' interests to the logic of interest groups led to an increasing fragmentation and to the weakening of the emerging urban popular alliance at a time when it had to face up to a powerful offensive from business interests.[144]

The difficulty that the gay community has had in articulating its interests to a heterosexual society pinpoints the fragility of gay power, even in a city that so clearly wears its political imprint.

The Transformation of the City by the Gay Community and the Limits of Gay Self-determination

The development of a gay community, in support of a political movement to defend civil rights and to foster an alternative life style, has been a major factor of urban change in San Francisco during the 1970s. Most of the changes triggered by the expansion of gay culture have been major contributions to the improvement of the city's quality of life. New gay households account for a significant proportion of the renovation of old buildings, for the repair and maintenance of many sections of the city, for the upgrading of property values, and for the dynamism of the real estate market. Although gay people have operated in a very attractive urban environment, they have also been pioneers in taking unusual risks to live in decaying areas, as well as making innovations in collective co-habitation, enabling an intensive residential use of the city that has resulted in a definite improvement in housing maintenance. Although some of this action took place within the broader context of middle-class, childless professionals desiring to live in the city, a very significant proportion of housing renovation and neighbourhood improvement seems to have been the result of moderate-income gays making a special effort to invest their own work and time to share a limited dwelling space in exchange for the feeling of freedom, protection, and self-expression provided by a gay territory.

Furthermore, the artistic talents of many gays has accounted for one of the most beautiful urban renovations known in American cities. The effects on urban aesthetics have gone beyond the careful painting of the original Victorian façades. Apart from the impressive interior decoration of the imaginatively remodelled flats the impact can be seen in the well-designed treatment of semi-public spaces – between the front door and the pavement for example; in all, a very unusual architectural improvement in the highly individualistic world of American cities.

Some gays have denounced this evaluation of their talent as renovators and of their care as urban dwellers, perceiving in it a typical prejudice of heterosexual culture. It is clear, however, that gay culture has this particular talent, a talent that constitutes an invaluable resource in the preservation of urban beauty. Besides which, there is nothing wrong with recognizing artistic ability, as long as the judgment is not used to maintain a social stigma associated with that image.

There is, in fact, a theoretical social explanation for such a talent. Gay men are in the midst of two processes of socialization, each one leading to a specific set of values. On the other hand, they grow up as men, and therefore are taught to believe in the values of power, conquest, and self-affirmation, values that in American society tend to be expressed through money or, in other words, through the dominance of exchange value. At the same time, because of the feelings that many have had to hide for years, and some for their entire life, they develop a special sensitiveness, a desire for communication, a high esteem of solidarity and tenderness that brings them closer to women's culture. This is not, however, because gays are "feminine," but, like women, their oppression and discrimination creates a distance from the values of conquest and domination which they are supposed to share as men. Thus, they tend to consider the use value of their personal lives as important, or worth more than the exchange value that could be acquired without even obtaining the greatest reward of all – to be themselves. And yet power and money still matter for many gay men. The spatial expression of this two-fold desire for exchange value and use value is, in our opinion, housing renovation. On the one hand they occupy a building, and make it distinctive and valuable. On the other hand, there is something else going on in the restored building: it has beauty, comfort, and sensuality, and it is saying something to the city while expressing something to its own dwellers. And when a space becomes meaningful, exchange value is no longer the dominant issue. This is perhaps the most important contribution of the gay community to the city: not only housing improvement but urban meaningfulness.

As often happens in the process of social change, groups inconvenienced by the progress of another are not properly recompensed. So there has been little urban improvement for the black families forced to move out from the Hayes Valley,[145] or help for the Latinos suffering high rents along the Dolores corridor because of real estate speculation from the increasing influx of gays. These hardships have been at the root of the hostility of ethnic minorities against gay people, a hostility often translated into violence. Class hate, ethnic rage, and fear of displacement by the invaders have clearly held greater sway than prejudices from family traditions or machismo ideology. This contradiction cannot be solved by contacts between the communities. There is too much need on both sides and too much self-definition as interest groups to enable people to relate to broader social perspectives. There have been exceptions. Willie Brown, a black political leader, was the sponsor of the Gay Rights Bill in California. Harry Britt is one of the most active defenders of low-income housing on the board of supervisors. But to really make the interests of gays and ethnic minorities compatible a new urban policy would be needed, emphasizing the use value of residential communities, imposing the public interest before the profit of real estate interests, as well as allowing downtown business to provide non-skilled jobs through construction work, services, and so on. Since ethnic minorities actually need these downtown jobs and many gays are involved in real estate speculation, the limits of the alliance are increasingly narrow, and the feeling of hostility increasingly bitter. The improvement of the urban space by the gay community might therefore represent a new form of residential displacement and social inequality.

There seems to be a parallel contradiction in the improvement by the gay community of urban culture. We have pointed out how decisively street life, popular celebrations, and joyful feasts have increased during the 1970s as a direct consequence of the gay presence. Although the appreciation could be somewhat subjective, most urbanists seem to value public life, street activity, and intense social interaction as one of the most distinctive positive dimensions of city life. Cities, all through history, have been spaces of diversity and communication. When communication ends, or when diversity is swallowed by social segregation, as in the uniform backyards of American suburbs, the urban culture is endangered – the sign, perhaps, of a sick civilization.[146] Thus the intensity of San Francisco's urban culture, certainly highlighted by gays' sense of urban theatre, seems to be an effective antidote against meaningless-ness and broken communication. And yet this urban culture is incomprehen-sible to the elderly people who feel like strangers in their own sedate neighbourhoods. For straight San Franciscans, the Castro ghetto, as well as many of the gay celebrations, seem to be from another world with a distinc-tive dress code[147] aimed to isolate and exclude the "voyeur." The visibility that gays have created has had very positive consequences for the community, including the defensive device of identifying almost immediately who is and who is not gay. But what for gays increases their protection and communica-tion creates for straights a major barrier, limiting the effects that gays may have on urban culture. If only gays benefit from the revival of street life and urban happenings, San Francisco will become a functional and impersonal city like most other American cities, the only difference being that in addition to Chinatown or the Fisherman's Wharf, tourists will be able to visit the gay territory as another curiosity, spatially segregated and culturally distant from the rest of the city. A major barrier to the gay community being heard in a broader urban culture seems to be the necessary emphasis on sexual libera-tion. Western society in general, and the American society in particular, is based on sexual repression. Individuals and institutions are deeply fearful of, and profoundly disturbed by, sexuality. For gays on the other hand, it is a major element of self-definition. We could say that the encouragement that the gay movement gives to the assumption and expression of sexuality is in fact a major contribution to the values of society. And yet, the issue is made more complex by the fact that sexual liberation is continually challenged by the predominance of heterosexuality. So both sexuality and homosexuality have to be affirmed against the psychological frontier between "normal" and "abnormal," as well as against basic rules of social interaction implicit in all organizations and institutions. The daily contradiction is so untenable that gays tend to live more and more within their own walls. But this limit, the need to continuously reinforce relationships, the difficulty of learning new values, and their self-discovery make a fertile ground for the development of esoteric sub-cultures, severing ties with society to explore alternative sources of meanings and feelings through a new sexual code, based on the continual crossing of whatever borders become established. The sado-masochist culture was the most rapidly growing component of the gay community in 1981 and also the most ideologically committed, attacking the gay leaders because they were trying to define norms that were "socially acceptable." For the sado-masochists the journey had no limits. So violence, humiliation, slave auctions, leather dress, Nazi uniforms, chains and whips were much more than sexual stimuli or games. They were cultural expressions of the need to destroy what-ever moral values straight society had left them with since these values have traditionally been used to exploit and repress homosexuality. Although it is true that S-M culture represents a tiny part of the gay community and that most S-M practitioners are heterosexuals, the considerable embarrassment that this issue causes to most aware, gay people is revealing, suggesting that this is an important issue.

Left to itself, in its cultural ghetto, the gay community is unlikely to accomplish the sexual revolution which is, implicitly, its major social project. To make homosexuality acceptable, society has first to accept its own sexuality, and such a cultural transformation provokes panic in most minds and institutions. This is why gay celebrations, no matter how brilliant and humorous they are, can only be city celebrations in part. There is always an underlying sexual dimension that is untenable for many people, not only because of its homosexuality but its sexuality. Unable to build bridges towards a broader and deeper cultural transformation, the gay community is in danger of internal destruction by introspective forces that might cause the community to forget that human experience has to be a social experience if it is going to last and grow. Between the transformation of the city's culture and the sado-masochists' back rooms, the gay community still hesitates and confines itself within the spatial limits of its free village.

It would appear that the bridges between the gay community and social change could be built by the political movement. And we have observed how the power obtained by the gay leadership through the community's capacity for electoral mobilization and social organization was used to contribute to and to support many politically progressive causes, particularly in the field of urban policies. As figure 5.9 shows, District 5 (the Castro area) appears to have been by far the most liberal in terms of political attitudes and voting behaviour. Gays were the backbone of left-wing initiatives in San Francisco's political system. So the gay community transformed the local political system, making it very difficult for conservatives to control the city, and creating an alternative power base relying on neighbourhood associations, public workers' unions, and oppressed ethnic communities. At the same time, as we have already pointed out, the obstacles to such an alliance were conflicting immediate interests between groups defined by very different social situations.

In fact there were two possible forms of political collaboration between these groups. One was the American custom of coalitional politics in which interests are defined and everybody tries to benefit from the political bargain. The experience of San Francisco made it almost impossible for the gay community to reconcile its interests to those of all the other organizations and institutions. The daily contradiction was also apparent within the other groups, producing the stalemate in local politics that we have observed in 1979 and 1980. On the other hand, a political alliance could have been established on the basis of long-run political interests, for instance based on the common and essential concern of transforming a cultural-economic structure which was at

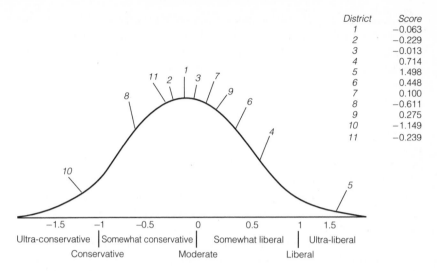

District	Score
1	−0.063
2	−0.229
3	−0.013
4	0.714
5	1.498
6	0.448
7	0.100
8	−0.611
9	0.275
10	−1.149
11	−0.239

Figure 5.9 San Francisco supervisorial districts ranked by liberal/conservative scores (see figure 5.1 on p. 140 for the location of the supervisorial districts). District 5 is the predominantly gay district
Source: Computronics Research, 1977

the same time sexist, homophobic, sexually repressed, racist, and capitalist. Only in such a long-term perspective could gay men and Latinos, for instance, have common interests.

But the gay community in San Francisco has not proceeded in such a direction. Instead of building a new hegemonic culture, including homosexuality, based on an ideologically and politically led transformation, it tried to develop autonomous power to negotiate its demands within the institutional and political system. This strategy could have been successful if the demands and interests of the gays were compatible with the dominant American culture. They have not been so because they implicitly attack a basic social institution: the family. Only if gays are strong enough to replace the family with another form of human organization would they be able to expand at a social level. But to do so, they would need to articulate their struggle to the only major social movement that is oppressed by the family and ready to replace it: the women's movement. And yet lesbians have tended to be excluded from most positions of power within the gay community, and the community has remained dominated by gay men's problems and perspectives. The reason is not only that gay men are first of all men. It is also because lesbians tend to be politically much more radical and willing to make the connection of personal issues to the transformation of society, to be the marching wing of the women's liberation movement. Lesbians know that there is no way they can accommodate this society. Gay men still have some illusions, particularly if class and race join their sex as a potential source of privilege. Harry Britt, in the interview he gave us, considered gay liberation as a 500 year process. So thinking, he clearly associated himself with a process of social transformation, in which gay men would play a major part. But this is not the perspective of the community as a whole. The lack of any clear connection to the women's movement as well as the secondary role that lesbians play within the community are clear signs of a separatist male mentality that severs any link with the major agent of cultural transformation in our society, the women's movement.

Given these conditions, self-destructive tendencies have appeared in San Francisco's gay community, and a very serious homophobic backlash is developing in the media and amongst the family orientated, popular sectors. The improvement of San Francisco's urban quality by the gay community will last only if gays are able to articulate their interests concerning social transformation instead of bargaining specific issues within an incompatible scheme of interest groups. They will have to shift from the coalition politics to strategic and historic alliances, particularly with lesbians and with the women's movement, if they are to transform society. If they ignore these alliances they will overcrowd a ghetto instead of enhancing a city.

The last weeks of Harvey Milk's life were a dark period for him. His friend, Jack Lira, committed suicide. His reasons were apparently not related to Milk or to other people, but caused mainly by his own reflections on the gay universe. When he decided to die, he left at his side the book that he had been obsessed with for months: *Holocaust.* This was not Harvey Milk's message. His efforts, on the contrary, were based upon hope – upon the capacity of gays to free themselves from oppression and while doing so, to free society. This was the profound reason for his commitment to improve the city. The transformation of the city into a space of freedom was a major element in the creation by the gay community of social hegemony. But gays cannot forget that a free city is also everybody's place. The survival of the gay community is closely tied to the overall process of social change.

NOTES

1   From a letter from San Francisco's Planning Director, Mr Dean Macris to Supervisor Harry Britt, chairman of the Board of Supervisor's Planning Committee, 10 May 1981.
2   Jerry Carroll, "San Francisco charming and changing," *San Francisco Chronicle*, 16 May 1980.
3   Economic Research Division, Security Pacific National Bank, 1971.
4   1970 US Census.
5   For 1950, US Census; for 1980, US Census, Preliminary Count; for 1975, California Department of Finance, Population Research Unit.

6   Charles Lockwood, *Suddenly San Francisco: The Early Years of an Instant City* (San Francisco:.The San Francisco Examiner, A California Living Book, 1978).

7   Mel Scott, *The Future of the San Francisco Bay Area* (Berkeley, CA: University of California, Institute of Governmental Studies, 1963).

8   John Mollenkopf, "Community organization and city politics" (Cambridge, MA: Department of Government, Harvard University, unpublished PhD thesis, 1973).

9   Chester Hartman, *Yerba Buena: Land Grab and Community Resistance in San Francisco* (San Francisco: Clide, 1974).

10 Melvin Webber, "The BART experience – what have we learned?" *The Public Interest*, 45 (1976), pp. 79–108.

11 Association of Bay Area Governments, *Census Data Bulletin No. 1* (Berkeley, CA: ABAG 1981).

12 For an analysis of the new forms of urbanization in America, sometimes referred to as the post-industrial city, see John Mollenkopf, *The Politics of Urban Development in the US* (Princeton: Princeton University Press, 1983).

13 Mel Scott, *The San Francisco Bay Area: A Metropolis in Perspective* (Berkeley, CA: University of California Press, 1959); J. Vance, *Geography and Urban Evolution in the San Francisco Bay Area* (Berkeley, CA: Institute of Governmental Studies, University of California, 1969). For an intelligent analysis of recent data concerning the Bay Area, see James M. Simmie, *Beyond the Industrial City?* (Berkeley, CA: Association of Bay Area Governments, 1981, mimeo).

14 Frederick M. Wirt, *Power in the City, Decision-making in San Francisco* (Berkeley, CA: University of California Press, 1974, particularly ch. 10).

15 Census data on ethnic minorities in San Francisco, as everywhere in America, are rather confusing and subject to caution. First of all, since definitions of racial and ethnic categories were changed for the 1980 Census, race and ethnic totals for 1980 are not comparable to previous totals. Thus, although the decade 1970 to 1980 seems to show a spectacular upward trend for Asians and for other races, as well as a moderate downward trend for blacks, nothing conclusive can be said on it, given the lack of comparable figures. Even more complex – and very important for our study – is the size of the Latino population. In 1980 there were in San Francisco, according to the US Census, 83,373 people of "Spanish origin," but since their ethnic definition was considered different from their racial definition, they were included either as whites or as "others." In any case, they represented 12.3 per cent of the total population. Since they can only be included as whites or as "others," we have made two hypotheses: (1) all "others" are Hispanic – that would maximize the proportion of non-Hispanic whites in the total population; under this hypothesis, whites are scaled down to 359,213 people or 52.9 per cent of the total population. (2) San Franciscans of Spanish origin follow the same pattern that was observed by the US Census at the national level, i.e. 40 per cent of those counted classified themselves as "others." This second hypothesis appears to be more likely. It is worth remembering that Hispanics have consistently claimed that they are undercounted. To be sure, illegal immigrants escape the Census. On the basis of our field work, we have estimated that in the Mission District about 20 per cent of Latino residents were workers who had not been counted. Therefore it seems plausible that Latinos account for at

least 15 per cent of San Francisco's population and that ethnic minorities make up about 50 per cent of the city's residents.

16 For an analysis of the patterns of evolution of American central cities, see Roger Friedland, *Power and Crisis in the City: Corporations, Unions and Urban Policy* (London: Macmillan, 1982).

17 Harvey Zorbaugh, *The Gold Coast and the Slum* (Chicago: University of Chicago Press, 1927).

18 See Citizen Housing Task Force (CHTF), *The San Francisco Housing Dilemma: What Can be Done?* (San Francisco: San Francisco Mayor's office, typewritten report, 62 pages, November 1980).

19 John Mollenkopf summarizes all existing studies on the matter in his report, *The San Francisco Housing Market in the 1980s: An Agenda for Neighbourhood Planning* (San Francisco: Report to the San Francisco Foundation, 1980, mimeo).

20 San Francisco Department of City Planning, based on the 1950–80 US Census.

21 CHTF, *Housing Dilemma*.

22 Ibid.

23 There are no reliable comparative data of housing quality that rank San Francisco in relationship to other central cities of large metropolitan areas. This is because existing studies combine San Francisco and Oakland as one metropolitan area, completely distorting the data. But it is almost generally held by experts in the field, such as Professor Allan Jacobs, formerly Director of City Planning in San Francisco, that the city's housing stock is very well maintained.

24 For an analysis of the influence of the "pro-growth coalition" in urban politics, see John Mollenkopf, "Neighbourhood mobilization and urban development: Boston and San Francisco, 1968–1978," *International Journal of Urban and Regional Research*, 5(1) (1981).

25 For analyses of minority neighbourhoods in San Francisco, see Ralph M. Kramer, *Participation of the Poor* (Englewood Cliffs, NJ: Prentice Hall, 1969); Arthur E. Hippler, *Hunter's Point: A Black Ghetto in America* (New York: Basic Books, 1970); Marjorie Heins, *Strictly Ghetto Property: The Story of "Los Siete de la Raza"* (Berkeley, CA: Ramparts Press, 1972); Mollenkopf, *Community Organization*.

26 For the analysis of the emergence of a middle class as a major social basis for neighbourhood movements, see Mollenkopf, "Neighbourhood mobilization."

27 See the very detailed analysis of San Francisco's local government presented in Wirt, *Power in the City*.

28 See Walton Bean, *Boss Ruef's San Francisco: The Story of Union Labor Party, Big Business and the Craft Prosecution* (Berkeley, CA: University of California Press, 1972).

29 Wirt, *Power in the City*, pp. 114–22.

30 Paul Eliel, *The Waterfront and General Strikes, San Francisco, 1934* (San Francisco: San Francisco Industrial Association, 1934), cited by Stephen E. Barton, "Understanding San Francisco" (1979) (see note 31).

31 We have benefited from the thorough and well-documented, unpublished analysis of the history of San Francisco's local politics by Stephen E. Barton, "Understanding San Francisco: social movements in headquarters city" (Berkeley, CA: Department of City Planning, University of California Berkeley, 1979).

32 For an explanation of BART, see Peter Hall, *Great Planning Disasters* (Berkeley, CA: University of California Press, 1982, ch. 4).

33 Personal interview with Professor Jack Kent, founder of "People for Open Space," San Francisco.

34 Harry Bridges, a communist during the 1930s, who was the leader of the Longshoremen's Union, and the historical labour figure in San Francisco.

35 Mollenkopf, "Community Organization," pp. 257–320.

36 See the book fundamental to understanding San Francisco's urban policies: Allan Jacobs, *Making City Planning Work* (Chicago: American Society of Planning Officials, 1978).

37 Hartman, *Yerba Buena*.

38 See "Highrise, housing and politics in San Francisco," in Jim Shoch (ed.), *Where Has All the Housing Gone?* (San Francisco: New American Movement, 1979).

39 Mollenkopf, "Neighbourhood mobilization."

40 Jim Jones, the leader of the People's Temple, whose mystical exodus ended tragically in Guayana, put his constituency's vote behind Moscone, receiving in exchange some influence in the operation of the Housing Authority – an example of the unlimited deals afforded by coalition politics.

41 The evaluation comes from several convergent sources that estimate between 12,000 and 20,000 as the number of people who were involved in the coalition (interviews with Ben Martinez, Mike Miller, Juan Pifarre, among others; the Stanford University Study; and the local press – for instance the *San Francisco Sunday Chronicle and Examiner*, dated 19 July 1970, cites the figure of 12,000). It has to be noted that these were people organized by all kinds of voluntary organizations, all members of the coalition, including churches and social agencies. Active militants on the MCO committees probably numbered around 1,000 in the 1970–71 period. There is no doubt that, relative to the population of the Mission District, it was one of the most widely supported urban mobilizations in America within the past 20 years.

42 An approximate reconstruction of the resident population in 1970 of the Mission District (including Mission and Inner Mission) is provided in the Methodological Appendix (pp. 239–41).

43 For a documented summary of the urban and social history of the Mission District, see *A Plan for the Inner Mission* (San Francisco: Mission Housing Development Corporation, March, 1974), pp. 6–14.

44 The total population of the Mission neighbourhood has had little variation for 30 years: 52,000 in 1940; 53,000 in 1950; 51,000 in 1960; 51,870 in 1970. But the Spanish-surname population jumped from 5,530 in 1950, to 11,625 in 1960, to 23,183 in 1970. Although there are no available figures for the 1980 Census all experts expect that there will be a slight increase of Latinos and Filipinos in the context of a fairly stable population. The data have been collected by the Stanford University Research Team: Noelle Charleston, Robert Jolda and Judith Waldhorn, *Summary of Trends in Housing and Population in the Mission Model Neighbourhood, 1940–1970* (Stanford: Stanford University Community Development Study, 1972, mimeo).

45 According to the Stanford Community Development Study, the Mission contains 10 per cent of San Francisco's 2,000 historic buildings.

46 The mean of salary distribution in the Mission in 1969 was around 8,000 dollars, while in San Francisco as a whole it was 10,908 dollars. Some 11 per cent of the

families were on welfare, against 5 per cent in San Francisco (Stanford Research Team, *Mission Model Neighbourhood*).

47 The percentage of the residents over 25 years old who did not have junior high school education was 41 per cent in the Mission, compared to 23 per cent in San Francisco. The percentage that did not have a high school degree was 82 per cent compared to 67 per cent in San Francisco. College-educated adults represented only 7 per cent of the population against 17 per cent of the San Francisco residents. (Data collected from the 1970 Census by the San Francisco Department of City Planning.)

48 For data on this trend, see the Methodological Appendix, p. 240.

49 San Francisco Department of City Planning, *The Mission: Policies for Neighbourhood Improvement* (January 1976, mimeo); also the extensive data provided by, *A Plan for the Inner Mission* (San Francisco: Mission Housing Development Corporation, March 1974, two volumes).

50 *Mission 1970 Census: Population and Housing* (San Francisco Department of City Planning, January 1973, mimeo; and esp. Roger Herrera, *Inner Mission Housing Strategy* (draft document for Citizen Review, San Francisco Department of City Planning, January 1980).

51 See the evaluation of overcrowding as a consequence of recent immigration flows, as established by Herrera, *Housing Strategy*.

52 For a description of the low riders phenomenon, see pp. 157–8.

53 BART has two much-used stations at the meeting of Mission and 24th Street, and Mission and 16th Street; both are favourite meeting places.

54 *Chicano* – an American with Mexican origins.

55 See the brilliant and well-informed, although passionately partisan, account of this protest: Marjorie Heins, *Strictly Ghetto Property: The Story of "Los Siete de la Raza"* (Berkeley, CA: Ramparts Press, 1972).

56 In the terminology of the ethnic minorities in California, the "Anglo" are the English-speaking whites. The "Latinos" (many of whom only speak English) are considered white by the Census but are not "Anglo." "Anglo" is thus a category of social experience more than a statistical boundary.

57 Founded and controlled by the Progressive Labour Party, an American Maoist group, formed by ex-members of Students for a Democratic Society (SDS).

58 A Federal agency – the executive branch of the war on poverty.

59 According to the Federally required mandate, the formula for which became notorious because of the attacks on it by conservative critics of the programme, e.g. Daniel P. Moynihan, *Maximum Feasible Misunderstanding: Community Action in the War on Poverty* (New York: The Free Press, 1969).

60 A radical Latino youth group that tried to emulate the Black Panthers. Heins, *Ghetto Property*, provides some information on them. They were a minor element in the district but acquired symbolic value by pointing out the spectrum of Latino riots . . . that never came.

61 For an analysis of the meaning of the Model Cities Programme in America, see Peter Marris and Martin Rein, *Dilemmas of Social Reform: Poverty and Community Action in the United States* (New York: Atherton Press, 1967).

62 Cesar Chavez is the leader of the California Farm Workers, most of them of Mexican origin. He became a nationally prominent figure by the heroic and

successful struggle of his union against the agricultural employers. His role was often compared to the one played by Martin Luther King in the very early stages of the black movement.

63 One of the basic elements of the Alinsky model of community organizing is the difference between the president (elected by the grassroots) and the staff director, selected because of his capability and experience. As a consequence, the staff director must change very rapidly to avoid becoming hidebound by bureaucracy. Mike Miller followed the rule to his great regret.

64 San Francisco State College, a well-known university located in San Francisco and funded by the State of California, went on strike for several months in 1969 to support special measures to increase admission for minority students and to design new academic programmes better adapted to their needs. The movement became highly radicalized when faced by stiff opposition and many of the Mission cadres, as well as other minorities, became politicized as a result of their experience in that movement.

65 As a result of such an open representation, the board of the MCO was composed of the following positions: 1 president; 25 executive vice-presidents for: Mexican-Americans, Central Americans, Latin Americans, Puerto Ricans, Afro-Americans, Filipino Americans, Anglo-Americans; Pacific Islanders; Nicaraguans; Salvadorians, Cubans; Europeans, Americans; Mexican Nationals; American Indians; Irish Americans; Italian Americans; Colombians; business, labour, and national sectors; clergy; blacks; senior citizens; and youth.

66 Cornbread cooked in thin slices – typically Mexican.

67 Stanford University researchers and students played a major role in advising the MCO and designing the Model Cities Proposal. The basic elements of the strategy can be deducted from the analysis of the report presented to the National Science Foundation by the Joint MCO–Stanford Research Team, *Mission Model Neighbourhood.*

68 Red-lining; the practice of most banks refusing loans for housing improvement or home ownership in poor urban areas. For a thorough analysis of red-lining in the Bay Area, see Martin Gellen, "The dynamics of institutional mortgage disinvestment in the central city" (Berkeley, CA: University of California, 1979, unpublished PhD thesis in the Department of City and Regional Planning).

69 Significantly enough, a similar conflict developed between black militants and the leadership in another successful Alinsky-inspired organization: the Woodlawn Organization in the Chicago ghetto. At least such is the argument developed in the careful research monograph by John Hall Fish, *Black Power, White Control: The Struggle of the Woodlawn Organization in Chicago* (Princeton, NJ: Princeton University Press, 1973).

70 After leaving the presidency, Ben Martinez was severely injured in a motorcycle accident and was unable to work for a long time. His sudden disappearance from the Mission's political scene aggravated the confusion. He subsequently left the Mission and went to live and work in Los Angeles.

71 A federation of charitable agencies.

72 See data in the Methodological Appendix, pp. 239–41.

73 "Angel dust" is a cheap chemical drug, widely used by the Mission youngsters, prolonged use of which induces irreparable and grave brain damage.

74 For an appraisal of the interaction between neighbourhood movements and Federal policies in America, see John M. Goering, "The national neighbourhood movement," *Journal of the American Planning Association*, 45 (4) (1979), pp. 506–14.

75 Particularly the records of meetings, list of participants, and press accounts of militant actions, as kept in the archives of the MCO which we consulted, and as noted in the independent study by the Stanford University Research Team, which was, in turn, confirmed by our own interviews with a broad range of informants.

76 The difference established between *social movement* and *social mobilization* or *struggle* is important here.

77 For a description of the Alinsky model of community organization, see Michael P. Connolly, "A historical study of change" in Saul D. Alinsky, "Community organization: practice and theory, 1939–72" (Minneapolis: University of Minnesota, 1976, unpublished PhD thesis; and Joan E. Lancourt, *Confront or Concede: the Alinsky Citizen-Action Organizations* (Lexington, MA: Lexington Books, 1979).

78 Stanford Research Team, *Mission Model Neighbourhood*.

79 Mission Housing Development Corporation, *A Plan for the Inner Mission*, p. 14.

80 Ibid. (We should point out to those who know San Francisco that Dolores Park is not included in the Inner Mission.)

81 This is a programme that provides public aid to improve the building to minimum legal standards. The programme requires a significant financial effort from the occupants, and generally results in the upgrading of the building while moving out a high proportion of the poor people.

82 In 1975, 85 per cent of Inner Mission residents were renters. The market for rental housing in San Francisco is a busy one. Yet the rents paid in the Mission in 1970 remained within the range of low and moderate rents.

83 Operation Upgrade and Mission Planning Council, *16th Street: A Neighbourhood Study* (San Francisco: The Mission Planning Council, 1977, mimeo); the information was confirmed by our own interviews, as reported in the Appendix, pp. 233–4).

84 Comment transmitted by a *La Raza en Accion Local* staff member during our interview.

85 San Francisco Department of City Planning, *Changes in San Francisco Housing Inventory, 1977* (San Francisco, 1979, mimeo report, NB table 19).

86 Reliable statistical information on recent immigration flows does not exist on the Mission. Nevertheless, there is general agreement amongst experts that there was an increase of immigrants from Central America, particularly during the period from 1975 to 1980. This is the opinion of Obeca, of a specialist in the San Francisco Planning Dept, of *La Raza*, of the Latino Unity Council, of Latinos for Affirmative Action . . . and it is also our opinion.

87 Mission Planning Council, *24th Street Problems and Possibilities* (San Francisco: MPC, 1976, mimeo report).

88 Such is the judgment of the Mission Housing Development Corporation, as recorded in our interview.

89 Interview with the Mission Liaison Expert of the San Francisco City Planning Department. Prices went up sharply in 1981, putting the minimum ceiling at about 126,000 dollars.

90 Memo from *Operation Upgrade: Citizens for a Cleaner Mission,* "*A Position Statement*" (San Francisco, 15 December 1976, typewritten document).

91 San Francisco Consortium, *Community Organizations in San Francisco* (San Francisco: SFC, 1974).

92 This does not mean electoral mobilization cannot obtain progress. It means that in the event of repeated frustrations, working-class people tend to drop out of the electoral system.

93 Estimates of the San Francisco gay population (obviously unrecorded in the Census data) vary according to different sources. Deborah Wolf, in her book, *The Lesbian Community* (Berkeley, CA: University of California Press, 1979) affirms that "it has been estimated that by 1977 about 200,000 homosexual women and men, out of a total population of 715,000 live in San Francisco at any one time" (p. 74). Besides the fact that San Francisco's population in 1977 had gone down to 672,700, the figure for the gay population seems overestimated. Claude Fischer, on the basis of several sources including his own survey, considers a more accurate estimate to be that 12–15 per cent of all voting-age population adults in the city are homosexual. Nevertheless, the visibility and power of homosexuals far exceeds this figure: "They probably represent 20 per cent or more of the white, Anglo population, and may comprise 25 to 30 per cent of all white Anglo *men* living in the city"; C. S. Fischer, *Dwelling among Friends* (Chicago: University of Chicago Press, 1981), pp. 237–49 and p. 424.

Most political analyses, including Richard Schlachman, specialist on gay-voting, believe gays represent 25 per cent of the voters in San Francisco. While gays tend to be active in the political system, a large proportion of the city's ethnic minorities (including foreigners) do not register as voters, and yet there is *some* gay presence among them, which would slightly increase the numbers. In fact, the only serious way of obtaining a reliable estimate would be to ask a representative sample of the population what their sexual preference is. We only know of one properly designed survey in 1980 which included such a question in its poll. It is the *unpublished* survey conducted by Professor Richard De Leon, of the Political Science Department at San Francisco State University, for the City Charter Commission of the City of San Francisco, on a representative sample totalling 1,377 individuals. The findings are presented in the Methodological Appendix (see p. 248).

According to this source the total gay population would be much higher: 24.4 per cent for men, and 17 per cent of the total. If we stay at the level of the total population, where more estimates are made, 17 per cent of the estimated 678,974 population in 1980 represents 115,675 individuals, which corresponds, very roughly, to the commonly cited figure of about 100,000 and to a somewhat higher figure of the estimated registered voters. We can therefore reasonably say that the gay population in San Francisco must be between 110,000 and 120,000 individuals, two-thirds of them being gay men and one-third lesbians. (If we extrapolate the proportions of De Leon's survey, this figure actually fits with Dr Wolf's more informed estimate of the lesbian population of about 35,000 women.)

94 Barry D. Adam, "A social history of gay politics," in Martin Levine (ed.), *Gay Men: The Sociology of Male Homosexuality* (New York: Harper and Row, 1979), pp. 285–97.

95 See Nora Gallagher, "The San Francisco experience," *Playboy*, January 1980. *Homophobic* (and *homophobia*) is used in this sentence and elsewhere in the book to mean "gay-hating."

96 One of the most perceptive theoretical analyses of the relationship between gay culture and social organization, particularly developing the two themes about the importance of visibility and resocialization for gay people, is Jeffrey Escoffier, "Stigmas, work environment, and economic discrimination against homosexuals," *The Homosexual Counseling Journal*, 2 (1) (1975). See also Erving Goffman, *Stigma: Notes on the Management of Spoiled Identity* (Englewood Cliffs, NJ: Prentice Hall, 1963).

97 See Sol Licata, "Gay power: a history of the American gay movement 1970–1975" (Los Angeles: University of Southern California, 1978, unpublished PhD thesis).

98 Martin Levine, "The gay ghetto," in Levine, (ed.), *Gay Men*.

99 As defined by Louis Wirth, *The Ghetto* (Chicago: University of Chicago Press, 1928).

100 Laud Humphreys, "Exodus and identity: the emerging gay culture," in Levine (ed.), *Gay Men*, pp. 134–47.

101 For such an analysis we refer to books such as Levine (ed.), *Gay Men*; Alan P. Bell and Martin S. Weinberg, *Homosexualities: A Study of Diversity among Men and Women* (New York: Simon and Schuster, 1978); and Laud Humphreys, *Out of the Closets: The Sociology of Homosexual Liberation* (Englewood Cliffs, NJ: Prentice-Hall, 1972).

102 See the research monograph by Deborah G. Wolf, *The Lesbian Community* (Berkeley, CA: University of California Press, 1979), p. 72 and following for this particular point.

103 Jack H. Hedblom, "Social, sexual and occupational lives of homosexual women," *Sexual Behavior*, 2 (10) (1972).

104 Howard Becker, (ed.), *Culture and Civility in San Francisco* (New Brunswick: Transactions, 1971).

105 See Frederick M. Wirt, *Power in the City*, p. 122 onwards.

106 In what follows a basic source is the extraordinary work done by the Gay History Project Collective in the Bay Area. Some of this work has been summarized in an article by John d'Emilio, "Gay politics, gay community: San Francisco's experience," *Socialist Review* 11, (1) (1981), pp. 77–104. Much of the information and ideas in our text are inspired by this work, although we have considerably broadened the base of our information as a result of our own interviews.

107 As established by A. Kinsey et al., *Sexual Behaviour in the Human Male* (Philadelphia and London: W. B. Saunders, 1948), and *Sexual Behaviour in the Human Female* (Philadelphia and London: W. B. Saunders, 1958).

108 Barbara Weightman, "Gay bars as private places," *Landscape*, 25 (1) (1980).

109 Karla Jay and Allen Young, *Lavender Culture* (New York: Harcourt, Brace, Jovanovich, 1980).

110 Allen Ginsberg, *Howl* (San Francisco: City Light Books, 1956).

111 Jack Kerouac, *On the Road* (New York: Viking 1957 and London: André Deutsch 1958; Penguin 1972).

112 See Paul Goodman, *Growing up Absurd: Problems of Youth in the Organized System* (New York: Random House, 1960).

113 Harvey Milk, aware of the possibility of being murdered (as were John and Robert Kennedy, Martin Luther King, and other political reformers in America) tape recorded his political testament, citing the names of people whom he wanted to take his place on the board of supervisors, and those whom he did not want nominated.

114 Gallagher, "The San Francisco experience."

115 See William Ketteringham "Gay public space and the urban landscape: a preliminary assessment" (a paper delivered to the Association of Pacific Coast Geographers' Conference, June 1979).

116 Bureau of the Census, *Urban Atlas* (Washington, DC: Government Printing Office, 1974).

117 Meriel Burtle et al., *The District Handbook: A Coro Foundation Guide to San Francisco's Supervisorial Districts* (San Francisco: Coro Foundation, 1979).

118 The leather culture is that of sado-masochist circles, most of which are made up of heterosexuals.

119 Most of the information on the process of gay renovation in San Francisco was obtained by interviews and documentary research carried on by our former student Don Lee, for his master's thesis "The gay community and improvements in the quality of life in San Francisco" (Berkeley, CA: University of California, 1980, MCP Thesis, Department of City Planning). It is worth saying that we do not share the same interpretation. We did not use his original files but did study written public information. For Don Lee's version of his own findings, we refer the reader to his thesis.

120 Don Lee, "Processes of spatial change in the San Francisco gay community," (Department of Urban Planning, Berkeley, CA: University of California, 1979, paper for CP 298E).

121 Richard Gorman, "Casing out Castro," *After Dark* (June 1979), pp. 38–50.

122 See Don Lee, "Real estate and the gay community in San Francisco," (Berkeley, CA: University of California, paper for Business Administration 280, 1979).

123 Kathy Butler, "Gays who invested in black areas," *San Francisco Chronicle* (1 September 1978).

124 Don Lee, "Castro street commercial district: a preliminary survey" (Berkeley, CA: University of California, 1978, Department of City Planning, paper for I.D.S. 24).

125 David Taylor, "The gay community, and Castro Village: who's oppressing whom" (Berkeley, CA: University of California, 1978, Department of City Planning, paper for CP 229).

126 Jerry Carroll, "San Francisco – charming and changing," *San Francisco Chronicle* (16 May 1980).

127 This is even recognized by the national magazines such as *Time*. See George Church, "How gay is gay?" *Time* (23 April 1979), pp. 72–6.

128 See S. Laska and D. Spain (eds) *Back to the City* (New York: Pergamon Press, 1980).

129 Don Lee, "Changing community structure and the gay neighbourhood" (Berkeley,

CA: University of California, 1980, Department of City Planning, paper for CP 211).

130 Karen A. Murphy, "The gay community and urban transformations: a case study of San Francisco" (Berkeley, CA: University of California, 1980, master's thesis, Department of City Planning).

131 Neil Smith, "Toward a theory of gentrification: a back to the city movement by capital, not people," *Journal of the American Planning Association,* 45 (4) (1979).

132 For detailed information on the social organization of San Francisco's gay community, and a very good report by an outsider, see the interesting book by A. E. Dreuilhe, *La Société Invertie où Les Gais de San Francisco* (Ottawa: Flammarion, 1979). However most of the analysis presented here originates from our own interviews and observations.

133 EST is an institution that organizes sessions of collective spiritual meditation and communication which hundreds of thousands of Californians have attended.

134 Joe Flower, "Gays in business: the prejudice and the power," *San Francisco Magazine* (September 1980).

135 See data reported in the Methodological Appendix, p. 249.

136 CBS, *Gay Power, Gay Politics,* special report, (26 April 1980).

137 According to political analyst Richard Schlachman and confirmed by other specialized pollsters in San Francisco.

138 Alice B. Toklas and Gertrude Stein lived and worked together for most of their adult lives. Only Stein obtained recognition from straight society by always keeping secret her personal life.

139 In the best tradition of the political bosses that had controlled, among many others, the Castro Valley of San Francisco which was actually called the "Capp Corner" in old Irish times. For a good, political chronicle of Harvey Milk's activity, see Randy Shilts, *The Mayor of Castro Street: The Life and Times of Harvey Milk* (New York: St Martins Press 1982) published after we had written these pages.

140 A Berkeley-based, gay activist magazine.

141 According to the coronation ceremony typical of northern California's transvestites.

142 Harry Britt was easily re-elected as supervisor in the 1980 election, in spite of the fact that the election was held under the new city-wide system. The result confirmed the fact that gays had become an electoral force in the city at large, encouraging dreams of a gay mayor in San Francisco.

143 A private "renovation" of the old harbour pier that converted it into a complex of restaurants, shops, and tourist attractions, all in very bad taste; the last place to visit in San Francisco.

144 In August 1980, after a heavily financed media campaign, the business groups led by the Chamber of Commerce, won a referendum in San Francisco, re-establishing the city election procedures for the board of supervisors. This was a major political defeat for neighbourhood groups, blacks, and gays.

145 According to studies commissioned by the Department of Housing and Urban Development, as cited by Mollenkopf, *The San Francisco Housing Market.*

146 See Lewis Mumford, *The Culture of Cities* (New York: Harcourt Brace Jovanovich, 1938).

147 A typical gay around the Castro area may be characterized as having short hair and a moustache, and dressing in a T-shirt, jeans, and leather jacket. This "code" serves to increase visibility and communication amongst gays as well as helping to identify intruders and potential attackers.

METHODOLOGICAL APPENDIX

Research Strategy in San Francisco

Our analysis of San Francisco focuses on the interaction between cultural identity and urban mobilization in the production of the city's functions and forms. The subject matter of this part explains why we selected San Francisco as the urban scene to observe such a problem. Few cities in the industrialized world had such a diversity of urban sub-cultures, and few American cities were so neighbourhood-orientated and so prone to community organization. Within San Francisco we selected two communities that were very different but shared their emphasis on the affirmation of a cultural identity as the most important goal of their mobilization. (Here we use the word "community" in a descriptive, non-theoretical sense, following the actors' own definition. Yet the term implies a self-proclaimed will of establishing cultural boundaries.) The study of the gay community was an obvious choice as it was the most visible, active, organized, and politically influential socio-cultural group in San Francisco. Besides, its experience was most unusual at the world level. On the other hand, we studied the Latino community in order to introduce a new, crucial element of the American scene: the poverty-stricken ethnic minorities. Although the black community in San Francisco was even more active and mobilized than the Latinos in the past two decades, it was unique to the Mission Neighbourhood mobilization of the period 1967–73 that we could observe the interaction between grassroots protest and the self-affirmation of an autonomous, largely immigrant culture. The purpose of the study was not to compare both communities, but to observe the interplay between culture and urban protest for two different cultures within the same city.

The methodology followed to study the two communities was very different. In the case of the Latino-based Mission Neighbourhood mobilization, we tried to reconstruct in all its details the process of urban protest and to understand the evolution of its internal structure through a formalized analytical model on which we could build, using information from one neighbourhood. By contrast, the main effort for the gay community focused on the analysis of its spatial organization and the role played by a culturally defined territory and the impact gays made on urban forms and local politics. We present in this appendix the research operations and databases on which our analysis is founded.

Methodological Appendix to the Study of Urban Mobilization in the Mission District

Research strategy

The study of the Mission was an in-depth case study of a relatively small neighbourhood whose experience of mobilization and community organization we examined in detail. The strategy of proof consists in reconstructing a 14-year span of social mobilization in such a way that the specific interpretation of the process became theoretically significant, logically consistent, and empirically sustained by a body of rich and detailed information.

To fulfil these goals we combined three different approaches:

(1) The analysis of the neighbourhood, both in its urban and social dimensions, through the analysis of existing documentation and personal observation during one year of field work and research from November 1979 to December 1980.

(2)   The study of the community mobilization and organization in the Mission through a series of in-depth interviews by key informants.
(3)   The actual objective of the study was to understand the emergence and crisis of the Mission Coalition Organization (MCO) as well as to measure its impact on the city, in accordance with our theoretical concerns. This purpose was reinforced by the first two steps of the study, since it soon became apparent that the MCO's experience was the social background to which we were referring most of the current community-based activities. Besides, unlike the situation in 1980 when the Mission was not a particularly active community and even less an effective agent of urban change, the MCO used to be *the* large urban movement in San Francisco and its impact was still evident in the neighbourhood when we were there. Thus, understanding the MCO's history was the most fruitful contribution to the study of the relationship between minority neighbourhoods' protest and urban change.

To analyse the MCO experience we had, at the same time, a great problem and a major asset. We could not observe the process but only reconstruct it by calling on the memories of its actors, some of whom were impossible to locate. The asset was that, precisely because of time that had elapsed, we could reconstruct in our interviews the debates, alliances, conflicts, and projects that formed and destroyed the MCO. However, these interviews could only take place successfully if we could obtain the basic information about the MCO from an independent source so that we could talk to its actors with a good deal of the information at our fingertips about the events which we wanted to debate, rather than just learn what happened. At this level we were extraordinarily fortunate to benefit, through Professor John Mollenkopf, from extensive documentation accumulated by Stanford University on the MCO, including very detailed research, in the form of an unpublished PhD thesis by Robert A. Rosenbloom. Later on, Mike Miller, the main organizer of the MCO, gave us access to all his files.
Thus we combined two approaches: reconstruction of events on the basis of existing information, and analyses of the process on the basis of in-depth, carefully planned, interviews with key actors who could provide their part of the truth, and their view of the process. (Naturally they all were aware of the nature and purpose of this research.) Afterwards, it took months to assemble the pieces of such a small but incredibly complex world, by connecting information that previously had not been in one place since communication had broken down between the different sectors of the movement. Furthermore, the different views were exposed to us, free of implications, since the battle was over and we were an outsider. So we could check basic information from various independent sources, and we could also appreciate the different logics at work within a movement whose shadow was still present. Why were people so open to us? Besides the fact that they were nice people and had nothing to hide, we think they realized that what really mattered for us was to understand the process, and nothing else. And they too wanted to understand, since one of the great traumas of the experience was that the MCO fell apart without their people really knowing why, since they were totally involved in their struggle. On the basis of their trust and support, we could collect the most complete set of information and self-analyses we have ever had on any single urban movement. And on such a data basis, we developed our own analysis through the procedures described below.

Data basis

The research on the Mission Neighbourhood mobilization was based on seven different, although inter-related sources, of unequal importance in terms of time and personal work, but equally crucial for the construction of the final picture:

(1)   Basic urban, economic, and social data, facilitated by the special collection of documents on the Mission, gathered by the San Francisco City Planning Department. Its Mission Liaison Planner, Roger Herrera, generously provided me with all the information existing in 1980 on the Mission District. Most of the documents are cited as references in the notes to the chapter.

(2) The reading and analysis of 10 years of the Mission-based Latino magazine, *El Tecolote*, as well as of collections of local press clippings.

(3) The analysis of an important fraction of the MCO's archives, which we could consult in the files still kept at the Organize Training Centre, in San Francisco.

(4) The vast amount of information produced by the Stanford Community Development Study, and, particularly the extraordinary study by Rosenbloom on the Mission Coalition: Robert Arthur Rosenbloom, "Pressuring policy making from the grassroots: the evolution of an Alinsky-style community organization" (Stanford: Department of Political Science, Stanford University, August 1976 unpublished PhD thesis). In addition to the thesis itself, Professor Mollenkopf gave us access to internal memos of the MCO, budget documents, transcripts of interviews etc., which were kept in the Stanford study files.

(5) Unpublished personal accounts of the process written by some of the main participants in the MCO, particularly, Mike Miller, *An Organizer's Tale* (San Francisco: 1976, 160 typewritten pages); and Leandro P. Soto, *Community Economic Development: More Than Hope for the Poor* (San Francisco, 1979, 76 typewritten pages). Of course, they were provided for us by their authors.

(6) Personal observation of Mission's social life for five months, in a systematic way (January–May 1980) and for a year in a more casual manner. This included physical knowledge of the neighbourhood, meeting with the people, being around in the streets, spending time in the public agencies, drinking in the bars, eating in the restaurants, shopping in the area, low riding, attending community meetings, etc.

(7) Yet, the core of our data basis came from 26 selected interviews with key community actors and informants in the period January–June 1980. The criteria for selecting the interviewees was: first all key actors and leaders in the Mission Coalition; second, leaders and members of other community organizations, particularly of *La Raza*, the only important community network that remained independent of the MCO experience; third, the most important community services and social agencies in the Mission; and fourth, experts with

some crucial knowledge of the neighbourhood. Interviews were held in offices, people's homes, or bars. Some were accompanied by wonderful dinners, others were given during tours on foot, most took the form of a heated discussion on the past experience. Their average length was 70 minutes; 20 of the 26 interviews were tape-recorded, the others transcribed and summarized on tape. It was not an easy task to find the key actors of a movement extinguished eight years before, but most were interviewed and, in fact, all the key tendencies of the MCO were represented. Of the leadership, only one major name was missing: Abel Gonzales, the boss of the Latino Labour Union (we were told that he was "somewhere in Texas"). Yet we did discover the key actor, Ben Martinez, and went to see him in his house in the Los Angeles area. So, we give below the list of interviews that represent the basic material behind our analysis of the Mission. We have kept the names of the persons because the vagueness of their institutional role is more than balanced by their popularity in the San Francisco local scene. Thus, by giving the names we publicly guarantee the diversity and accuracy of our sources of information. To be sure, all agreed to have their names cited; the list is as follows:

List of interviews related to the process of community mobilization in the Mission District, San Francisco

(1) Mr Lee Soto, Director, OBECA-Arriba Juntos, founder of MCOR and of the MCO.

(2) Mr Herman Gallegos, founder of MCOR and MCO, active leader of Community Services Organization, California.

(3) Mr Ben Martinez, President of the MCO.

(4) Mr Al Borvice, Director, *La Raza Centro Legal*.

(5) *La Raza en Accion Local*, staff members.

(6) Mr Celso Ortiz, *La Raza* law student, advocate planner.

(7) Ms Luisa Ezquerro, Mission Planning Council, former MCO leader, former Model Cities manager.

(8) Mr Juan Pifarre, Director, Mission Model Cities Neighbourhood.

(9) Mr Larry del Carlo, Mayor's Office of Community Development, Vice-president of the

MCO, Candidate to Supervisor for District 6 (Mission).

(10) Mr Mike Miller, Director, Organize Training Centre, Staff Director of the MCO.

(11) Mr Manuel Larez, former president of LULAC (San Francisco), candidate for the presidency of the MCO, organizer of 24th Street Merchants' Association.

(12) Mr Ed Sandoval, State President, MAPA.

(13) Ms Flor Maria Crane, Vice-president, MCO, candidate for the presidency of the MCO.

(14) Ms Rosario Anaya, Director, Mission Language and Vocational School.

(15) Mr Bob Bustamante, MAPA (San Francisco), Latinos for Affirmative Action.

(16) Mr Pedro Rodriguez, President of LULAC, San Francisco Chapter.

(17) Mr Bob Dwight, Director, Mission Community Legal Defense.

(18) Ms Norma Galvan, Real Alternatives Programme.

(19) Staff, *Centro de Cambio*.

(20) Mr Ricardo Hernandez, President, Latino Unity Council.

(21) Ms Betty Anello, Operation Upgrade.

(22) Mr Alfonso Maciel, Director, Mission Cultural Center.

(23) Dr Paul O'Rourke, Mission Neighbourhood Health Center.

(24) Mr Roger Herrera, Mission Liaison Planner, Department of City Planning, City of San Francisco (1980).

(25) Mr Juan Gonzales, Director, *El Tecolote*.

(26) Mr Jack Bourne, Director, Mission Development Housing Corporation.

An analytical model to explain the social logic underlying the urban mobilization in the Mission

The interpretation of the Mission neighbourhood mobilization [. . .] relied on a systematic analysis of the information we collected, guided by the conceptual mechanism we constructed to understand this particular process. We explain this model below to communicate the research tools we have used. By presenting the model in a somewhat more formalized way, we do not add any explanatory value to what has already been demonstrated [. . .] but we emphasize the main logical and empirical argument for the sake of clarity.

The logic of the demonstration can be summarized in two steps:

(1) The choice of propositions implicit in our analysis, as formulated in terms of the categories proposed in our theoretical construction (neighbourhood, poverty, minority, city, class, race, community organization, and state power, from now on abbreviated as: N, P, M, CY, CL, R, CO, and SP).

(2) The sequence of observed events in the community mobilization, whose logic should closely follow all the propositions on which our interpretation relies.

Let us consider both levels of the demonstration.

The system of theoretical propositions on urban mobilization as related to the Mission study

Before stating the system of propositions, let us keep in mind that:

(1) Our theoretical construct, at this point of the analysis, is an *ad hoc* approach to the movement observed in the Mission. Although it obviously relates to a broader theoretical framework, any generalization of the propositions requires a series of transformations, as formulated in Part 6 [of *The City and the Grassroots*].

(2) The justification of the categories employed here (as well as of the relationships they are supposed to hold) have already been provided [. . .] We only deal here with the formal expression of such relationships. The same argument applies to any substantive analysis of the proposed relationships.

Our analytical model of the Mission neighbourhood mobilization can be summarized by the following nine propositions:

(1) The basic elements structuring the practice of the movement are N, P, M, CY, CL, and R. In fact they are intimate connections between pairs of elements: CY is the upgrading of N at the level of the overall social structure; so are CL for P, and R for M.

(2) To relate to the overall social organization, movements organized around these elements have to relate to SP in its different levels. Such a relationship must be mediated by organizational operators. When an organizational operator expresses N, P, and M, separately, we name it an interest group (IG); when they integrate N, CY, or P, CL, or M, R, to challenge SP, we name it a social movement (SM); when they integrate N, P, M, we name it a community organization (CO).

(3) In the specific context of American inner cities, a direct articulation of N, P, M, CY, CL, R, cannot generate any CO, and therefore cannot jointly address SP, except for purely defensive single-issue purposes on which a coalition of interest groups may be formed.

(4) A successful combination of N, P, and M, in the practice of a movement, creates a dynamic CO that will expand under two conditions:

(a) N, P, and M stick together.

(b) CO relates to SP in such a way that it affects SP's behaviour without coming under SP's control. (It should be noted that condition (a) commands condition (b).

(5) Although N, P, and M, may come together in a shared collective practice, they will not be able to stay together if they do not upgrade their social level (although consciousness raising) in the practice of the movement. Namely, N has to expand to CY, or P to CL, or M to R. If any one of the dimensions expands separately, CO becomes a social movement which integrates in its basic definition the other two dimensions under a subordinate form: an urban social movement (based upon CY), or a class struggle (based upon CL) or an ethnic social movement (based upon R). If all dimensions simultaneously expand, CO becomes the basis for a multi-dimensional social movement challenging SP: it is what we used to name revolutions.

(6) If neither element reaches the higher level of social practice, the basic structure of the movement disintegrates, and therefore CO falls apart, and SP takes over.

Under the conditions of the Mission, neither N, P, or M were present as pure elements. There was actually a combination of NP and MP, with N and M as elements. Thus N could

not rise to the CY level because of its P component that isolated itself from the mainstream of the N-based movement in the city. M was limited to shift towards a racial movement both by its P component (excluding broader M alliances) and by its specific ethnicity as *Latinos* (so that M in the Mission was actually M_1, within a potential $M_1 \ldots M_n$ range representing a variety of ethnic minorities). Under the two conditions described, the elements N, M, P, should split. Since P was a common element to NP and MP combinations, the split, according to our rules, should be between N and M components. Given the particular structure of the movement their opposition should take two forms:

(a) N versus M.

(b) Competition between N and M to appropriate the definition of P, as NP or as MP.

(7) The more N and M oppose each other, through successive steps, the more CO is weakened, and the more SP tends to dominate CO. In the last stage the split between N and M (defined as conflicting NP and MP) is mirrored by the split between CO and SP: M is absorbed within CO and N is absorbed within SP. Under these conditions, the movement disintegrates.

(8) The disintegration of a complex, powerful, and multi-segmented urban movement leaves its trace in the urban scene where it took place, in the form of community-based, single-purpose organizations that represent the different dimensions of the movement, N, NP, P, M, MP. None of them becomes CO, and therefore all of them are submitted to SP without any real capacity of challenging its power.

(9) The social outcomes of the movement express its articulation and the changing relationships between its elements. Thus, a movement whose pattern would follow the sequence as described (according to the logic we proposed), it should:

(a) Have a strong defensive relationship to SP because of the wide range of its interests groups (therefore, opposing those policies hostile to the neighbourhood's status quo).

(b) Be successful on poverty issues given the common ground between this element and

Table 5A.1 Analysis of the elements of the MCO's process of mobilization

	1967–68 (formation of MCO)	1968–69 (1st–2nd Convention)	1969–70 (2nd–3rd Convention)	1970–72 (3rd–5th Convention)	1972–74 (Process of disintegration)
Issues present in the movement	• Defence of the neighbourhood against the potential threat of urban renewal • Search for funding from the Federal social programmes (Model Cities) • Emergence of a Latino culture as a source of identity and protest	• Jobs for minorities (especially Latinos) • Educational programmes • Housing for the poor • Preserving family life • Building of a community organization • Emergence of student-based Third World radicalism	• To expand programmes • To win a Model Cities Programme controlled by the community • To clearly separate from radicals	• To run Model Cities under the strategy of community control (MMNC) • To improve neighbourhood conditions • To obtain more jobs for minorities by expanding the city's economic activity • To support Aliotto's power	• Internal battle over control of public funds; access to the mayor; control of apparatus, of MMNC and MCO
Elements of the movement	• Neighbourhood preservation and improvement (N) • Remedies against poverty (P) • Latino culture (L) • Youth counter-culture (Y)	• Neighbourhood (N) • Poverty (P) • Latino labour (LLB) • Third World liberation radicals (TW) • Community organization (CO)	• Neighbourhood (N) • Poverty (P) • Latino labour (LLB) • Community organization (CO) • Latino culture (L) • Radicals (R)	• Neighbourhood (N) • Poverty (P) • Community organization (CO) • Power (PW) • Latino culture (L) • Latino labour (LLB)	• Neighbourhood (N) • Poverty (P) • Community organization (CO) • Latino culture (L)

Operators of the movement	• MCOR (N, P, L, R) (no interaction) • Brown Berets and other groups (Y, R, P)	• Agencies (P, L) • Churches (N, P) • Latino nationalists (L) • Blockades and tenant unions (N, P) • *Centro Social Obrero* (LLB) – MCO, (CO) – • *v.* Latino radicals • *v.* Homeowners	• Agencies (P, L) • MCO (N, P, CO) • *Centro Social Obrero* (LLB) *v.* • Latino culture (L) • Third World (LR)	• Unity Caucus – MMNC (N, P, CO, PW) *v.* • Alianza Caucus – MCO (L, P, LLB)	• N, CO → MPC • L, P → Agencies • L (Latino culture) • LR (Mission Cultural Centre) • L, P, N, R (*La Raza*) • LLB (Labour Union, *Centro Obrero*)
Effects of the movement	• Stop urban renewal	• Neighbourhood improvement • Building grassroots organization and winning legitimacy in the institutional system	• Obtaining Model Cities • Winning battles over jobs, housing, education	• Obtaining the programmes of Model Cities • Split in leadership • Organizational crisis	• Disintegration of MCO • Active community organizing in the Mission • Planning-orientated activities

Source: Our study

the other components of the structure of the movement.

(c) Basically fail on urban or ethnic issues, given the contradictory relationship between N and M.

(d) Become powerless in relationship to SP, given the collapse of CO.

(e) Have the potential to prevent major disruptive initiatives in the neighbourhood because of the possible coming together of the multiple fragments of the movement as a new defensive reaction against an open threat from business, government, or other social group.

Let us now consider the correspondence between this theoretically meaningful, logically coherent chain of propositions, and the empirical observations we have gathered.

A formalized record of the sequence of events in the process of urban mobilization in the Mission
The method we followed to observe the correspondence between the recorded information and the postulated model was the following:

(1) We divided the process in several periods, according to major breakpoints of urban mobilization:

(a) The pre-MCO period (MCOR mobilization).

(b) The period between MCOR and the second half of MCO's First Convention (1968).

(c) First MCO Convention to Second MCO Convention (1968–1969).

(d) Second MCO Convention to Third MCO Convention (1969–1970).

(e) Third MCO Convention to Fifth MCO Convention (1970–1972).

(f) Process of Disintegration of MCO (1972–1974).

(g) Fragmented community mobilization in the Mission (1974–1980).

Remember that MCO conventions were the occasion to openly express the strength and alliances of the different components of the movement.

(2) For each period we established the basic internal structure of the movement, according to our theoretical codes. We also recorded, for each period, the strength of the community organizations, the relationships to the state, and the outcomes of the movement on urban, social, ethnic, and political issues.

Table 5A.1 summarizes some of the basic information corresponding to each period. It is presented in this highly schematic way to better outline the argument, but the reader should be referred to the text (pp. 139–80) for additional information on the events of each period.

(3) On the basis of such a periodized sequence of events, we can now compare each one of the propositions of our theoretical construct, with the recorded information:

(a) Propositions 1 and 2 are mere definitions.

(b) Proposition 3 is supported by three facts:
   (i) N, P, M, CY, CL, R came together in a defensive coalition (MCOR), to obtain a defensive victory against SP, preserving the *status quo* of the neighbourhood.
   (ii) Yet, as soon as this victory was achieved, MCOR disappeared.
   (iii) In the First Convention of the MCO, in October 1968, the MCO tried to put together the same combination that underlay MCOR, and the effort failed. The MCO could only start on a narrower basis one month later.

(c) Propositions 4, 4a and 4b are positively supported by the structure of the MCO, its successful outcomes, and its advantageous power relationship in the periods 1968–1969 and 1969–1970.

(d) Proposition 5 does not apply empirically to the movement observed in the Mission, although it must be kept in our theoretical construct as a logical step. Let us observe that it does not apply because of the verification of Proposition 6, whose premises exclude those of 5.

(e) Propositions 6 and 7 are verified by:
   (i) The gradual split between N and M in the periods 1969–1970, 1970–1972, and 1972–1974.
   (ii) The particular form of the split:
   In 1969–1970 N, NP and MP versus M.
   In 1970–1971 N, NP versus M, MP.
   In 1971–1972 N, NP versus M, MP, and MCL.

In 1972–1974 SP and NP versus M, MP, MCL, and CO.

(f) Proposition 8 is verified by the composite, fragmented scene of the Mission in 1974–80, along the separate dimensions of N, NP, M, MP, CL, and R, as described in the text. In addition to it, the failure of *La Raza* to bring together again all the dimensions seems to indicate that each element resulting from the disintegration of the MCO was still alive on its own, so that the dimension it represented in the Mission could be combined in a new collective practice by another operator (*La Raza*, for instance) until the genuine fragments coalesced again through a new social process.

(g) Proposition 9 is verified by the outcomes resulting from the social dynamics in each period, as expressed in Table 5A.1, as well as from the presentation of urban, social and political effects, as exposed in [the text].

here some basic data concerning the specificity of the urban setting where it took place (tables 5A.2–5A.9). Notice that data are organized for District 6, which was broader than the Mission. Our study area concerned both the Mission and the so-called Inner Mission (the core of the Latino community), as shown in figure 5.1, p. 170 that locates the neighbourhood within the city of San Francisco. We have kept the district-basis for the data in order to make comparisons easier with other areas of the city. All data come from Coro Foundation, *The District Handbook* (San Francisco, 1979), the most up-to-date synthesis on urban–social data on San Francisco's neighbourhoods at the time of our research. In fact most data are originated from the 1970 American census.

Also, as proof of the vitality of grassroots organization in 1980 – testament to the lasting effects of the earlier period of active mobilization – we include a list of neighbourhood groups and locally based agencies present in 1980 in the Mission (table 5A.10).

The social and urban profile of the Mission neighbourhood

As a way of contributing to the understanding of the mobilization that we studied, we present

Statistical Profile of District 6 and Mission Neighbourhood, 1970

Table 5A.2   Ethnic composition of neighbourhoods

Ethnic category	South of Market (%)	Mission (%)	Inner Mission (%)	Total District 6 (%)	City-wide (%)
White	39	49	26	39	57
Black	10	2	7	6	13
Latin	33	37	55	42	14
Chinese	4	2	2	2	8
Japanese	–	1	–	–	2
Filipino	10	6	6	7	4
American Indian	1	1	1	1	0.5
Other	3	2	3	3	1.5
Foreign stock[a]	51	55	60	56	45
Spanish-speaking	28	32	50	37	12

[a] Foreign born and persons of foreign born and mixed parentage.

Table 5A.3 Family income levels (annual income in thousands of dollars)

Neighbourhood	Total families	Under $4 (%)	$4–10 (%)	$10–15 (%)	$15–25 (%)	Over $25 (%)
South of Market	2,957	29	44	18	8	1
Mission	6,169	20	42	24	12	2
Inner Mission	5,021	24	42	23	9	2
Total District 6	14,147	23	43	22	10	2
City-wide	165,295	14	33	26	20	7

Table 5A.4 Employment category

Neighbourhood	All workers	Managerial/ professional (%)	Skilled (%)	Semi- and unskilled (%)
South of Market	5,811	13	57	30
Mission	11,675	15	60	25
Inner Mission	7,612	10	59	31
Total District 6	25,098	13	59	28
City-wide	318,324	25	55	20

Table 5A.5 Educational level

Neighbourhood	No school (%)	Less than high school (%)	High school only (%)	Some college (%)	College graduate (%)	Adults surveyed
South of Market	4	52	24	11	9	9,854
Mission	2	47	30	11	10	16,837
Inner Mission	5	58	23	8	6	11,796
Total District 6	3	52	25	11	9	38,487
City-wide	3	35	29	16	17	458,887

Table 5A.6 Land use

Neighbourhood	Residential (%)	Commercial (%)	Industrial (%)	Other use (%)	Net area (acres)	Gross area (incl streets)
South of Market	14	24	40	21	420	634
Mission	66	19	4	10	321	483
Inner Mission	49	11	13	27	474	698
Total District 6	42	18	20	20	1215	1815
City-wide	39	6	6	49	23,367	30,329

Table 5A.7 Owners and renters

Neighbourhood	Owner occupied (%)	Renter occupied (%)	Vacant	Total
South of Market	5	89	6	7,744
Mission	17	79	4	11,629
Inner Mission	26	71	3	7,259
Total District 6	16	80	4	26,632
City-wide	31	64	5	311,457

Table 5A.8 Distribution of the Mission neighbourhood active resident population by occupational category, 1970

Type of occupation	No. of people (employed, 16 years or over)	%
Professional, technical, kindred	1,571	7.8
Managers and administrators	753	3.8
Sales workers	758	3.8
Clerical and kindred	5,101	25.9
Craftsmen, foremen and kindred	2,263	11.5
Operators	2,282	14.3
Transport equipment operators	742	3.8
Labourers	1,385	7.0
Service workers	3,591	20.1
Private household workers	347	1.8
Total	18,793	100

Source: 1970 American Census

Table 5A.9   Votes for supervisor in 1977 election, District 6

Candidate	Total votes	% of votes	Mission	Inner Mission	South of Market[a]
Silver (liberal white woman)	4,225	35.0	2,091	769	1,220
Borvice (*La Raza*)	2,376	23.0	1,011	897	380
Del Carlo (moderate, supported by some members of MCO)	1,693	16.5	593	726	256
Medina	417	4.0			
Rivera	361	3.5			
Mendelson	334	3.2			
Cullins	314	3.0			
Martinez	166	1.6			
Acido	159	1.5			
Sucheki	144	1.4			
Others	147	7.3			
Total	10,336	100.0			

[a] Non-Latino area within the district.

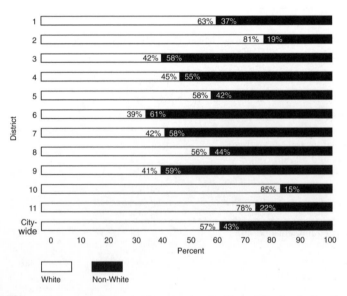

Figure 5A.1   Ethnic composition (white versus non-white) of districts in San Francisco, 1970 (Latinos are here counted as non-white; District 6 includes the Mission)
Source: Coro Foundation on the basis of the 1970 American Census

Table 5A.10   Mission-based community organizations and community-based social agencies identified active in 1980

1 American GI Forum
2 Arriba Juntos
3 Casa Hispaña de Bellas Artes and Casa Editorial
4 Catholic Council for the Spanish Speaking
5 Centro Cultural Guatemalteco
6 Centro de Cambio
7 Centro Latino
8 Centro Social Obrero
9 Centro Social Peruano
10 Club "Alegria"
11 Comite Mexicano Civico Patriotico
12 Communidad Hispano-Americana de Corpus
13 Concilio Mujeres
14 Council of Organizations Pro-Activities of P.R. Affairs, Inc. (COPAP)
15 Defensores de la Juventud
16 Galeria de la Raza/Studio 24
17 Hispanic Educational Congress of the US
18 Horizons Unlimited of SF, Inc.
19 IMAGE
20 *La Raza* Centro Legal
21 *La Raza* Information Center
22 *La Raza* Silkscreen Center
23 *La Raza* Tutorial Center
24 Latin American Fiesta, Inc.
25 Latin American Mission Programme
26 Latin American National Senior Citizens
27 Latin American Republic Assoc.
28 Latin American Veterans Political Assoc.
29 Latino Family Alcoholism Counseling Center
30 Los Mayores de Centro Latino
31 LULAC Educational Service Center
32 Mexican-American Legal Defense and Educational Fund (MALDEF)
33 Mexican-American Political Assoc. (MAPA)
34 Mission Adult Center
35 Mission Cultural Center (MCC)
36 Mission Language and Vocational School Inc.
37 Mission Neighbourhood Health Center
38 Mission Outreach Center
39 Puerto Rican Organization for Women
40 S F Coalition
41 S F Inca Club
42 Spanish-American Political Institute
43 Vetreach Office
44 Centro Communal de Buen Samaritano
45 Children's Rights Group
46 Mission Alcoholic Center
47 Mission Child Care Consortium, Inc.
48 Mission Community Legal Defense
49 Mission Education Center
50 Mission Education Projects, Inc.
51 Mission Head Start
52 Mission Hiring Hall
53 Mission Mental Health Center
54 Mission Neighbourhood Adult Center
55 Mission Neighbourhood Family Center
56 Mission Neighbourhood Physical Development, Inc.
57 Mission Reading Clinic
58 Mission Rebels Health and Nutrition Programme
59 Mission Rebels in Action, Inc.
60 Mission Senior Citizens Center
61 Mission Street Merchants Assoc.
62 Mission YMCA
63 Real Alternatives Programme (RAP)
64 Mission Planning Council
65 Operation Upgrade

This list does *not* include churches, or non-Latino national groups such as Samoans or Filipinos.

Methodological Appendix to the Study of the Gay Community in San Francisco

Research strategy

There were four objectives of this study, in accordance with the theoretical concerns underlying our research:

(1)   To reconstruct the historical origins of the gay community through interviews with key witnesses of the period 1940–1970.
(2)   Given the very crucial role played by the territorial identity of the community, we made a special effort in obtaining information about the non-statistically recorded locational residence of gay people, and identifying the social and urban characteristics of gay residential areas. The goal was to obtain maps of these areas as precise and reliable as possible. Given the potentially sensitive character of this information, we want to emphasize that the research was carried out with the support and approval of the political representatives of the gay community.
(3)   We also tried to evaluate the impact of the gay community on the city through the study of urban innovation, the analysis of the cultural events fostered by the community, and the study of political decisions they supported in local government.
(4)   Finally, since the gay social mobilization largely took the form of winning power within the local political system, we focused an important part of our study on gay politics through selected interviews with key informants and the analysis of available documentation. We should remind the reader that our study is limited to the gay men community, excluding lesbians, for reasons given in [the text].

Data basis

Our study of the gay community relies on three different sets of information:
    The first source and by far the most important, is the field work research conducted jointly by Karen Murphy and the author, from February to December 1980, and pursued later by the author in 1981. Most of the interviews were done by Karen Murphy, although the research design and data analysis, as well as some key interviews, field work observation, and spatial analysis, were done jointly. The research included four different operations:

(1)   A survey of the literature and a review of the main gay publications. The following publications were analysed:
(a)   *The Advocate*, May 1975–1980.
(b)   *Daughters of Bilitis San Francisco Newsletter*, April 1967–November 1968.
(c)   *Gay Sunshine* (San Francisco), Summer 1974–1980.
(d)   *Interim* (Mattachine Society), 1956–1965.
(e)   *Ladder* (San Francisco), 1956–1970.
(f)   *League of Civil Education Newsletter*, 1961–1962.
(g)   *Mattachine Review*, 1966.
(h)   *Vector* (San Francisco), 1965–1968.
(2)   Some personal observations of gay public meetings, social life, and street celebrations, such as the Castro Street Fair, Halloween, the Gay Day Parade, etc., as well as with meetings of the Harvey Milk Gay Democratic Club.
(3)   Information-gathering on the spatial structure of the gay community, as described in the paragraph below, presenting the methodology of our spatial analysis.
(4)   The most important source of information consisted of 27 in-depth interviews with key informants of the gay community as well as with experts in some of the key areas of our research (political consultants for the gay vote; urban geographers for the spatial structure; historians for the evolution of the gay community). Interviews included important gay leaders, such as Harry Britt, Jim Rivaldo, Jim Foster, Bill Krauss, Frank Fitch, Wayne Friday, and others, as well as such historical figures of the gay and lesbian movements as Jose Sarria and Phyllis Lyon. Interviews lasted between 30 minutes and five hours (Jose Sarria) with a median time of 65 minutes. Most of them were given in bars. Ten of the 27 are tape-recorded, the others were transcribed in written notes. The interviews were conducted between February and June 1980. The list of interviews, classified by dominant topics, is as follows:

List of Original Interviews with Key Informants on the Gay Community in San Francisco

Background

(1) Sharon Long, aide to Supervisor Harry Britt.
(2) Gwen Craig, community activist/Vice-president of the Harvey Milk Gay Democratic Club.
(3) Jack Trujillo, community activist/aide to Supervisor Carol Ruth Silver.
(4) Walter Kaplan, community activist/assistant to Supervisor Harvey Milk.
(5) John McEnroe, CHEER, San Francisco State University.
(6) Louis Flynn, Professor, San Francisco State University, Interdisciplinary Social Science Department.

Historical

(7) Jose Sarria, entertainer/First Empress of San Francisco.
(8) Jeff Escoffier, Alan Berube, Gail Rubin, members of the Gay History Project.
(9) Phyllis Lyon, co-author of *Lesbian Women* and co-founder of the Daughters of Bilitis.
(10) Stewart Loomis, Professor of Education, San Francisco State University.

Spatial

(11) Doug DeYoung, private political consultant.
(12) Les Morgan, private consultant/Co-ordinator of San Francisco Police Department's Gay Outreach Programme.
(13) Dick Pabich, community activist/assistant to the Committee to Re-elect Supervisor Harry Britt/community informant.
(14) Jim Rivaldo, community activist/aide to Supervisor Harvey Milk/community informant.
(15) Terry King, community activist/Treasurer, Harvey Milk Gay Democratic Club.
(16) Max Kirkeberg, Professor of Geography, San Francisco State University.
(17) Richard DeLeon, Professor, San Francisco State University Public Sector Research Consultant.
(18) Dick Solem, Jon Kaufman, Solem and Associates Political Consultants.
(19) Bonnie Loyd, Editor, *Landscape* magazine.

Political

(20) Richard Schlachman, political consultant/assistant to the Committee to Re-elect Supervisor Harry Britt/community informant.
(21) Bill Krauss, President of Harvey Milk Gay Democratic Club.
(22) Harry Britt, San Francisco Supervisor.
(23) Jim Foster, community activist/co-founder of Alice B. Toklas Democratic Club.
(24) Frank Fitch, President of Alice B. Toklas Democratic Club/San Francisco Charter Commissioner.
(25) Wayne Friday, President of the Tavern Guild.
(26) Hugh Schwartz, Public Response, Survey Research.
(27) Harry Britt, second interview (1981).

The second source on which we relied is the very important research carried out by Don Lee, for the masters thesis in City Planning, University of California, Berkeley, that he completed under our supervision in June 1980. He particularly focused on the urban impact of the gay community through personal observation, extensive interviewing, press clippings, and data gathering. We did not consult his files, although we used extensively (with his consent) his final written material, summarized in his thesis, but also in a number of course papers. Detailed references for each information provided by his own research can be found in the notes to [this chapter]. Unlike the joint research we did with Karen Murphy (that also led to her masters thesis in City Planning, as well as to a number of joint and individual publications), we do not present the list of interviews or documents collected by Don Lee, since our interpretation does not rely on this material, but only on the summary and analysis provided by Don Lee himself.

The third source was the extensive readings of materials on gay issues and gay politics, both in general, and in San Francisco. The works and sources that have actually been used in our study are cited in the notes [to this chapter].

Methodology for the Spatial Analysis of the Gay Community

There is no statistical source that provides information on sexual preferences of residents of particular urban areas (fortunately enough). Yet, such an obstacle appears overwhelming to the researcher trying to understand the spatial dynamics of the emerging gay culture. Thus, our first and main concern has been to establish, as reliably as possible, the precise spatial boundaries of the gay community in San Francisco. Once gayness is related to certain urban units, on the basis of reliable information, it becomes possible to search for potential associations between gay location patterns and different sets of social and spatial variables. In this section we will start exploring some relationships between the characteristics of population and housing, and the settlement of gays. It is our hope that when the 1980 Census data become available, a more thorough statistical and spatial analysis of the reciprocal influence between the evolution of the city and the affirmation of gay culture will be conducted. This analysis will only be possible if it relies on an accurate estimation of the locational pattern of the gay community in San Francisco. To our knowledge such an estimation has never been attempted on any city in the world: it is an additional reason to be particularly cautious in our approach.

Unable to feel secure enough on any single source of estimation as to the gay spatial distribution, we have used five different sources obtained in an entirely independent manner. The fact that all five sources tend to show a similar spatial pattern of gay residence and activity reinforces the credibility of each particular source, and provides very solid support for the mapping that emerges.

The five sources were as follows:

(1) A map of the concentration of gay residence established on the basis of key informants from the gay community. The main informants were the most qualified political pollsters for gay candidates in San Francisco's local elections. Following our request, informants indicated particular periods of time for gay settlement in each area. Gay residential areas, according to our informants, were cumulative over time. Once they became visible as gay neighbourhoods, they did not reverse their character, and tended, at least in San Francisco, to increase their proportion of gay residents as they consolidated as areas of cultural tolerance. On the other hand, it was impossible to obtain any reliable estimation of the number of gays in each area. Thus, the areas we characterized as gay might be so at very different levels, although it was to be expected that in all these areas there would be a substantial gay residence, and, what is more important, that the gay culture would be evident. Yet it is crucial to keep in mind that we did not quantify the presence of gays in particular areas, and that the entire analysis was based upon the degree of likelihood that each urban unit was a home for gay men, without considering their numbers.

(2) In the second step of our analysis, we looked for a statistical indicator whose different values could be distributed all over the city. On the basis of direct observation of gay life style, we concluded that an accurate indicator would be the proportion of multiple male households in each urban unit. We rejected the proportion of a single male household as an indicator, because of the high percentage of non-gay elderly living alone. Census data did not provide such information, but the voters' registrar for the city of San Francisco did. We used the 1977 Voters' Registrar data files, the most updated source providing such information. Obviously the indicator was the proportion of multiple male households to the total number of registered voters in each urban unit. If we were dealing with an ethnic minority population, we would suffer some uncontrolled statistical bias. But concerning gay men, the source was accurate enough, given their high level of voter registration in their drive to win electoral power in San Francisco. The assumption, of course, was not that all, or the majority, of multiple male households were gay. The assumption was that there would be a strong

correlation between the spatial distribution of gay residence and the spatial distribution of the frequency of multiple male households. The difference was not merely a semantic one; it was to have major consequences for the selection of the statistical techniques suitable to any analysis on this particular data basis.

(3) The third source we selected was the spatial distribution of the vote for the gay candidate in a city-wide local election. It was clear that not all people who vote for a gay candidate were gay. It was also clear that there was a close relationship between the number of gays in an area and the vote for the gay candidate in such an area. And it was equally clear that such a relationship was closer in the early stages of gay mobilization as compared to the time when they had achieved some power on the basis of broader alliances and more diverse constituencies. Thus we selected as gay strongholds the areas of highest electoral support for the late gay leader Harvey Milk in the 1975 supervisorial race, his second attempt at city-wide elected office as a gay candidate and the first in which he obtained a significant number of votes widely distributed across the city (53,000).

(4) The fourth source concerned the location of gay businesses. We mapped 250 businesses (most of them very small) listed in the directory of the Golden Gate Gay Business Association in 1979. Here again, the assumption, relying on our direct observation, was the close connection between gay residence and gay self-proclaimed activities.

(5) The fifth source concerned the location of gay bars and public places as presented in the specialized publications.

To establish relationships between these five indicators of gay territory and all variables provided by the Census, we also transformed the different counting units into census tracts. From now on, these will be our units of observation and analysis.

On the basis of these five different independent sources, we established five maps. The areas of gay concentration that resulted from the observation of the five different maps fitted closely on the whole, into a common spatial location within the city of San Francisco.

To rely on a somewhat less intuitive measure we calculated the zero-order correlation between the spatial distributions of the indicators of gay residence we proposed. To do so, we gave dichotomic values (1,0) to areas with gay presence or absence (figure 5.3, p. 192). We proceeded in a similar way classifying in 1 versus 0, the areas with high or low proportion of multiple male households (levels 6, 5, 4, versus 3, 2, 1, in the scale of census tracts in the city according to the proportion of multiple male households, as shown in figure 5.4 p. 193. We then calculated the correlation for all census tracts distributed in relationship to the values (1,0) of the two indicators. We proceeded in the same manner with the third indicator, namely the importance of gay vote (figure 5.5, p. 194). We also mapped the public places (including bars and social clubs) where gays met (figure 5.6, p. 195) and the location of gay businesses (figure 5.7, p. 200).

The correlations were highly positive; $r = 0.55$ ($P = 0.001$) between the areas designated by the community informants and the ones resulting from the spatial distribution of multiple male households. And $r = 67$ ($P = 0.001$) between the definition proposed by the informants and the distribution of the 1975 vote for Harvey Milk. Statistical measures confirmed what the simple observation of the maps suggested: we had a similar pattern of spatial location provided by different independent indicators whose credibility were mutually reinforced. We now were able to define the spatial boundaries of San Francisco's gay male community as of 1980. Also, given the verification of the accuracy of the estimation provided by our key informants, we could, unless contrary evidence was provided, consider as a probable trend the spatial sequence described by them over time.

Having established the spatial profile of the gay community, we were able to relate it to the social and urban characteristics distributed across the city, in order to understand the factors fostering or counter-acting the patterns of settlement inspired by the gay culture. On the basis of the 1970 American Census and of the 1974 American Bureau of Census' *Urban Atlas*, we selected 11 variables considered to be relevant to our analysis, as presented in table 5.3, p. 196.

Table 5A.11 Sexual preference of a representative sample of San Francisco residents by age and sex (percentages on the total of each sex and age group)

Sexual preference	Total		Male		Female		Age 18–29 (%)		Age 30–49 (%)		Age 50 and over (%)	
	No.	%	No.	%	No.	%	Male	Female	Male	Female	Male	Female
Gay and bisexual	226	17	159	24.4	67	9.6	21	13	37	9	11	7
Heterosexual	1,111	83	483	75.6	628	90.4	79	87	63	91	89	93
Total (no.)	1,337	100	642	100	695	100	243	215	249	222	150	258

Source: Richard DeLeon and Courtney Brown, unpublished research report (San Francisco State University, Department of Political Science, 1980; provided by Professor DeLeon)

Yet we must bear in mind that the only thing this particular data basis told us about gayness is where gays were or tended to be. We did not have any indicator of gayness; the only thing we had was a series of converging indicators of gay location. Thus, we could not infer anything about gay individuals. We were only able to analyse gay versus non-gay spatial units. To proceed in such a way we carried out two different analyses:

(1) On the basis of our key informants' map, we divided the city into two categories of spatial areas: those with gay presence and those without such a presence. We calculated for each selected variable the mean value of their distri-

Table 5A.12 Businesses registered as members of the gay business association by type of activity

	No.	%
Banking and insurance	7	2.8
Real estate	20	8.1
Advertising/public relations	13	5.3
Contractors and building supplies	11	4.4
Retail stores	20	8.1
Restaurants and hotels	10	7.7
Bars, discos, baths, health clubs[a]	18	7.3
Antiques, art galleries, collectors	7	2.8
Hair stylists	9	3.7
Lawyers	11	4.5
Architects and interior designers	9	3.6
Financial, computer, and business consultants	25	10.1
Travel agencies and tourism	10	4.0
Audio-visual and communications	2	0.8
Automobiles sales, repair and service	2	0.8
Printers	10	4.0
Bookstores	1	0.4
Newspapers and magazines	8	3.2
Doctors and health care	7	2.8
Counselling	11	4.5
Personal services (chauffeurs, maids and other)	5	2.0
Business services (secretarial support)	6	2.4
Employment agencies	6	2.4
Miscellaneous	10	4.0
Total	238	99.7[b]

[a] There are over 200 gay bars in San Francisco, although most of them are not members of the Golden Gate Business Association, since they tend to be organized under the Tavern Guild.
[b] Percentages add only up to 99.7% because of rounding up of figures.
Source: Our own study

bution in the census tracts corresponding to each one of the two categories of space. The *t*-test provided the statistical significance of the differences observed for the mean value of each variable in each one of the two categories of spatial units. The extent and direction of such differences provided the clue for the social and urban specificity of the gay territory.

(2) We tried to establish some measure of correlation between the spatial distribution of selected social and urban variables. Since we were not looking for co-variation between characteristics across the space, but for correspondence between spatial organization in relationship to two series of criteria, the usual regression analysis was inadequate to our purpose. Instead we have proceeded to calculate rank-correlation coefficients (Spearman test) between, on the one hand, the distribution of all census tracts in a 6-level scale of gay space, constructed on the basis of the proportion of multiple male households; and, on the other hand, the distribution of all census tracts in a series of 6-level scales on the basis of selected variables. Only variables that the first step of the analysis (as described above, in 1) showed to be discriminatory were considered to construct the scale of social and urban differentiation in San Francisco. Furthermore, one of the findings of our analysis was that these selected variables were likely to affect gay location patterns jointly, instead of having individual effects, since their spatial distribution does not overlap. Thus, to test our analysis we constructed an additional scale, classifying the census-tract units in a scale that combined in its criteria the three variables considered to have some effect on gay location. The Spearman coefficient between the ranks they obtained in the multiple male households scale provided the final test for our tentative interpretation of the social roots of gay location patterns.

Selected Information on the Gay Community

We shall now give some important information to which we referred in the text [. . .] to support our analysis. Such information includes the most accurate unpublished data on sexual preferences of a representative sample of San Francisco's residents (table 5A.11); our classification of gay businesses on the basis of the directory of the Golden Gate Business Association (table 5A.12), and the list of proposals concerning urban policies presented to the San Francisco's board of supervisors by Supervisors Harvey Milk and Harry Britt, political leaders of the gay community. We constructed this list on the basis of information provided by the staff members of the Committee on Planning, Housing, and Development of the San Francisco's board of supervisors.

Legislation introduced and measures proposed by gay representatives in the San Francisco Board of Supervisors on matters of housing and urban policy, 1977–1981

Harvey Milk's sponsored initiatives

- Authored anti-speculation ordinance designed to provide monetary disincentive for trading residential property for speculative purposes. Defeated 9–2 (in 1978).
- Sponsor of Prop. U, an unsuccessful ballot measure designed to force landlords to rebate their Prop. 13 tax savings to tenants (1978).
- Consistent opponent of downtown high-rises (1978).
- 1976–1978 opposed expansion of UC medical centre-related doctor's complexes into residential neighbourhoods; also opposed similar expansion of Franklin Medical Center in Castro area. Both issues were popular and hard-fought and largely successful efforts of neighbourhood activists largely supported by Harvey Milk before he was Supervisor.
- Strong advocate of rent control (1978).
- Introduced moratorium on second-floor conversions from residential to commercial in November, 1978; passed. Preparatory to Special Use District legislation eventually passed under Britt's leadership. Also moratorium on new bars and restaurants in certain areas.

Some legislative background information on Supervisor Harry Britt, appointed to the Board January 1979

Chronology of proposals

1979
- Strongly supported rent control legislation.
- Introduced legislation for strong control on high-rise expansion.
- Supported the settlement of the suit brought against the Police Department by the Officers for Justice, the Chinese for Affirmative Action, the NAACP, NOW, etc.
- Authored the one-year moratorium on bars and restaurants on Haight and 24th Streets.
- Opposed the multi-million dollar sewer project as being too costly and too disruptive to the integrity of the neighbourhoods.

1980
- Introduced legislation to prevent discrimination against the disabled.
- Introduced the Residential Hotel Conversion Act to severely limit conversions of residential hotels to tourist use. This legislation helped to preserve low-income housing for the poor and elderly.
- Sponsored the neighbourhood Special Use District legislation – an ordinance that protects the integrity of neighbourhood commercial areas.
- Introduced legislation to regulate the transportation of toxic chemicals through residential neighbourhoods.
- Introduced legislation to close the loophole in the rent stabilization law, which will result in the elimination of vacancy de-control.

1981
- Re-introduced Mayor George Moscone's proposal for an Office of Citizens Complaints.
- Introduced legislation to establish registration of paid lobbyists.
- Co-sponsored legislation that would strongly regulate the conversion of rental units into condominiums.
- Held hearings regarding the possible need for some type of rent regulation for commercial property occupied by small merchants.
- Called for hearings on the concept of equal pay for comparable worth.
- Introduced resolution to put the City and County of San Francisco on record opposing off-shore oil drillings.

Supervisor Britt's attitude on selected urban issues

Condominium conversion
- Since reappointment to the Board of Supervisors in January 1981, has voted against all proposals to convert rental units to condos. The board regularly must vote on each condo conversion proposal, and Britt's opposition is usually the minority position.
- June 1981 – sponsored a moratorium on condo conversions which was defeated by one vote.
- 1981 – supported a limit on condo conversions of 1,000 per year which passed and is law.

Special use districts
- Sponsor of legislation creating Special Use Districts, now in existence in seven neighbourhood areas, in which merchants and residents set standards for neighbourhood commercial development. Legislation is designed to prevent the excessive intrusion of non-neighbourhood orientated businesses into traditional neighbourhood commercial districts (1980).

Residential hotel conversion ordinance
- Supported successful moratorium on conversion of residential hotel units to tourist use in 1979 – interim measure while long-term legislation was being drafted.
- December 1980 – sponsored Residential Hotel Conversion law – adopted unanimously, which effectively prevented residential hotel units from being converted to tourist use. These units are one of the last remaining sources of low-income housing, particularly for the elderly in the Tenderloin area.
- May, 1981 – resisted the rewriting of this law to weaken its enforcement and other

sections, creating loopholes which make it much easier to convert. This watered-down bill passed with Britt and Supervisor Nancy Walker dissenting, and is now law.

High-rise construction

- Opposition to downtown high-rises has been a long-time neighbourhood cause in San Francisco. They are seen by neighbourhood activists as exacerbating housing problems, impacting negatively on the neighbourhoods, and creating tax and service burdens on the citizens. Britt has followed the tradition of Harvey Milk in opposing excessive high-rise construction.
- Sponsor of the November 1979 ballot proposition placing strict control on high-rises. The measure lost.

Rent control

- May 1979 – sponsored rent control law, which passed and was signed into law, established rent control and fairly strict eviction controls – limited rent increases to 7 per cent yearly and established a Rent Arbitration Board.
- 1979 – supported strong rent control legislation which did not pass at the board.
- November 1979 – strong sponsor of Proposition R ballot measure for stronger rent control. Measure lost.
- Fall 1980 – sponsored an amendment to rent law opposing vacancy de-control which,

in current law, causes vacant apartments to escape rent control. Compromise version passed board and was vetoed by mayor.

Miscellaneous

- 1980 – unsuccessfully opposed use of city redevelopment funds to underwrite Opera Plaza, a condominium development in which units would sell for $100,000 – $350,000.
- May 1981 – opposed Performing Arts Center Garage which would provide below market rate parking for patrons of the Opera and Symphony and result in the tearing down of several dozen low- and moderate-income housing units. Garage approved on 9–2 vote.
- Early 1981 – successfully lobbied for inclusion in Mayor's UDAG proposal for North of Market area of low-cost housing, largely in control of local neighbourhood and housing activists.
- Late 1981 – working with Latino-based community housing corporation to help create first subsidized housing project which integrates housing for the disabled, families, and seniors.
- Late 1981 – sponsor of legislation to create low-cost senior housing on top of Performing Arts Center Garage.

Source: San Francisco Board of Supervisors' internal files, Committee on Planning, Housing and Development, 1981

PART
THREE
The City in the Information
Age

SIX

The Informational Mode of Development and the Restructuring of Capitalism

(1989)

Modes of Production, Modes of Development, and Social Structure

Technological change can only be understood in the context of the social structure within which it takes place. Yet such an understanding requires something more than historically specific description of a given society. We must be able to locate technology in the level and process of the social structure underlying the dynamics of any society. On the basis of a theoretical characterization of this kind we may then go on to investigate the actual manifestations of the interaction between technology and the other elements of social structure in a process that shapes society and, therefore, space. To proceed along these lines it is necessary to introduce some theoretical propositions and to advance a few hypotheses that attempt to place the analysis of technological change and economic restructuring, as presented in this chapter, within the framework of a broader social theory that informs the overall investigation undertaken in this book [*The Informational City*, 1989].

The analytical focus here is on the emergence of a new mode of development, which I will call the "informational mode," in historical interaction with the process of restructuring of the capitalist mode of production. Therefore, definitions are needed of the concepts of mode of production, mode of development, and restructuring. Such definitions, if they are to be theoretical and not simply taxonomic, require succinct presentation of the broader social theory that lends analytical meaning to such concepts as tools of understanding social structures and social change. For the purposes of this book, the presentation of the overall theoretical framework must be reduced to the few elements indispensable for communicating my hypothesis that the interaction between modes of production and modes of development is at the source of the generation of new social and spatial forms and processes.

This theoretical perspective postulates that societies are organized around human processes structured by historically determined relationships of production, experience, and power.[1] Production is the action of humankind on matter to appropriate and transform it for its benefit by obtaining a product, consuming part of it (in an unevenly distributed manner), and accumulating the surplus for investment in accordance with socially determined goals. Experience is the action of human subjects on themselves within the various dimensions of their biological and cultural entity in the endless search for fulfillment of their needs and desires. Power is that relationship between human subjects which, on the basis of production and experience, imposes the will of some subjects upon others by the potential or actual use of violence.

Production is organized in class relationships that define the process by which the non-producers appropriate the surplus from the producers. Experience is structured around gender/sexual relationships, historically organized around the family, and characterized hitherto by the domination of men over women. Sexuality, in the broad, psychoanalytic sense, and family relationships, structure personality and frame symbolic interaction.

Power is founded upon the state, since the institutionalized monopoly of violence in the state apparatus ensures the domination of power-holders over their subjects. The symbolic communication between subjects on the basis of production, experience, and power, crystallizes throughout history on specific territories and thus generates cultures.

All these instances of society interact with one another in framing social phenomena; however, given the particular research interest of this work in the relationship between technological change and economic restructuring, the effort of theoretical definition will here be focused on the structure and logic of the production process.

Production has been defined above as the purposive action of humankind to appropriate and transform matter, thus obtaining a product. It is a complex process because each one of its elements is itself made up of relationships between other elements. Humankind, as a collective actor, is differentiated in the production process between labor and the organizers of production; labor is internally differentiated and stratified according to the role of the producers in the production process. Matter includes nature, human-modified matter, and human-produced matter,[2] the labors of history forcing us to move away from the classic distinction between humankind and nature which has been largely superseded by the reconstruction of our environment through millennia of human action.

The relationship between labor and matter in the process of work is also complex: it includes the use of means of production to act upon matter, on the basis of energy and knowledge. Technology refers to the type of relationship established between labor and matter in the production process through the intermediation of a given set of means of production enacted by energy and knowledge.[3]

The product is itself divided into two main categories, according to its utilization in the overall process of production and reproduction: reproduction and surplus. Reproduction includes three sub-categories: reproduction of labor, reproduction of social institutions (ultimately enforcing relationships of production), and reproduction of means of production and their technological support basis. The surplus is the share of the product that exceeds the historically determined needs for the reproduction of the elements of the production process. It is divided again into two major categories, according to its destination: consumption and investment. Consumption is stratified according to societal rules. Investment is geared toward the quantitative and qualitative expansion of the production process according to the objectives determined by the controllers of the surplus.

Social structures interact with production processes by determining the rules for the appropriation and distribution of the surplus. These rules constitute modes of production, and these modes define social classes on the basis of social relationships of production. The structural principle by which the surplus is appropriated, thus designating the structural beneficiary of such appropriation, namely the dominant class, characterizes a mode of production. In contemporary societies there are two fundamental modes of production: capitalism and statism. Under capitalism, the separation between producers and their means of production, the commodification of labor, and the private ownership of the means of production on the basis of control of commodified surplus (capital), determine the basic principle of appropriation and distribution of surplus by the capitalist class, not necessarily for its exclusive benefit, but for the processes of investment and consumption decided by that class in the specific context of each unit of production under its control. Under statism, the control of the surplus is external to the economic sphere: it lies in the hands of the power-holders in the state, that is, in the apparatus benefiting from the institutional monopoly of violence. In both cases there is expropriation of the producers from their control over the surplus, although criteria for the distribution of consumption and allocation of investment vary according to the respective structural principles of each mode of production. Capitalism is oriented toward profit-maximizing, that is, toward increasing the amount and proportion of surplus appropriated on the basis of the control over means of production. Statism is oriented toward power-maximizing, that is, toward increasing the military and ideological capacity of the political apparatus for imposing its goals on a greater number of subjects and at deeper levels of their consciousness.

Modes of production do not appear as a result of historical necessity. They are the result of historical processes in which a rising social class becomes dominant by politically, and often militarily, defeating its historical adversaries, building social alliances, and obtaining support to construct its hegemony. By hegemony I understand, in the Gramscian tradition, the historical ability of a given class to legitimate its claim to establish political institutions and cultural values able to mobilize the majority of the society, while fulfilling its specific interests as the new dominant class.

The social relationships of production, and thus the mode of production, determine the appropriation and distribution of the surplus. A separate, yet fundamental question is the *level* of such surplus, determined by the productivity of a particular process of production, that is, by the ratio of the value of each unit of output to the value of each unit of input. Productivity levels are themselves dependent on the relationship between labor and matter as a function of the use of means of production by the application of energy and knowledge. This process is characterized by technical relationships of production, defining a *mode of development*. Thus, modes of development are the technological arrangements through which labor acts upon matter to generate the product, ultimately determining the level of surplus. Each mode of development is defined by the element that is fundamental in determining the productivity of the production process. In the agrarian mode of development, increases in the surplus result from quantitative increases in labor and means of production, including land. In the industrial mode of development, the source of increasing surplus lies in the introduction of new energy sources and in the quality of the use of such energy. In the informational mode of development, the emergence of which is hypothesized here, the source of productivity lies in the quality of knowledge, the other intermediary element in the relationship between labor and the means of production. It should be understood that knowledge intervenes in all modes of development, since the process of production is always based on some level of knowledge. This is in fact what technology is all about, since technology is "the use of scientific knowledge to specify ways of doing things in a reproducible manner."[4] However, what is specific to the informational mode of development is that here knowledge intervenes upon knowledge itself in order to generate higher productivity. In other words, while in the preindustrial modes of development knowledge is used to organize the mobilization of greater quantities of labor and means of production, and in the industrial mode of development knowledge is called upon to provide new sources of energy and to reorganize production accordingly, in the informational mode of development knowledge mobilizes the generation of new knowledge as the key source of productivity through its impact on the other elements of the production process and on their relationships. Each mode of development has also a structurally determined goal, or performance principle, around which technological processes are organized:

industrialism is oriented toward economic growth, that is, toward maximizing output; informationalism is oriented toward technological development, that is, toward the accumulation of knowledge. While higher levels of knowledge will result in higher levels of output, it is the pursuit and accumulation of knowledge itself that determines the technological function under informationalism.

Social relationships of production, defining modes of production, and technical relationships of production (or productive forces), defining modes of development, do not overlap, although they do interact in contemporary societies. In this sense, it is misleading to pretend that the informational mode of development (or post-industrial society) replaces capitalism, since, as Alain Touraine, Radovan Richta, and Daniel Bell indicated years ago,[5] these are different analytical planes, one referring to the principle of social organization, the other to the technological infrastructure of society. However, there are between the two structural processes complex and significant interactions which constitute a fundamental element in the dynamics of our societies.

Societies are made up of a complex web of historically specific relationships that combine modes of production, modes of development, experience, power, and cultures. Under capitalism, because of its historical reliance on the economic sphere as the source of power and legitimacy, the mode of production tends to organize society around its logic, without ever being able to exhaust the sources of social reproduction and social change within the dynamics of capital and labor. However, given the structural preponderance of capitalist social relationships in the class structure, and the influence they exercise on culture and politics, any major transformation in the processes by which capital reproduces itself and expands its interests affects the entire social organization. Modes of production – and capitalism is no exception – evolve with the process of historical change. In some instances, this leads to their abrupt supersession; more often, they transform themselves by responding to social conflicts, economic crises, and political challenges, through a reorganization that includes, as a fundamental element, the utilization of new technical relationships of production that may encompass the introduction of a new mode of development. By *restructuring* is understood the process by which modes of production transform their organizational means to achieve their *unchanged* structural principles of performance. Restructuring processes can be social and technological, as well as cultural and political, but they are all geared toward the fulfillment of the principles embodied in the basic structure of the mode of production. In the case of capitalism, private capital's drive to maximize profit is the engine of growth, investment, and consumption.

Modes of development evolve according to their own logic; they do not respond mechanically to the demands of modes of production or of other instances of society. However, since technical relationships are historically subordinated to social relationships of production, experience, and power, they tend to be molded in their structure and orientation by restructuring processes. On the other hand, they do have a specific logic that dominant social interests ignore only at the risk of spoiling their technological potential – as, for example, a narrow orientation toward secretive, applied military technology can frustrate scientific advancement. Modes of development emerge from the interaction between scientific and technological discovery and the organizational integration of such discoveries in the processes of production and management. Since these processes are dependent upon the overall social organization, and particularly upon the dynamics of the mode of production, there is indeed a close interaction between modes of development and modes of production. This interaction occurs in different forms according to the pace of historical change. There is a continuous, gradual adaptation of new technologies to the evolving social relationships of production; there are also periods of major historical change, either in technology or in social organization. When historical circumstances create a convergence between social change and technological change, we witness the rise of a new technological paradigm, heralding a new mode of development. This, I contend, is what has brought the rise of the informational mode of development in the last quarter of the twentieth century.

The New Technological Revolution and the Informational Mode of Development

The new technological paradigm

During the two decades from the late 1960s to the late 1980s a series of scientific and technological innovations have converged to constitute a new technological paradigm.[6] The scientific and technical core of this paradigm lies in microelectronics, building on the sequential discoveries of the transistor (1947), the integrated circuit (1957), the planar process (1959), and the microprocessor (1971).[7] Computers, spurred on by exponential increases in power and dramatic decreases in cost per unit of memory, were able to revolutionize information processing, in both hardware and software. Telecommunications became the key vector for the diffusion and full utilization of the new technologies by enabling connections between processing units, to form information systems. Applications of these microelectronics-based information systems to work processes in factories and offices created the basis for CAD/CAM (computer aided design/computer aided manufacturing) and flexible integrated manufacturing, as well as for advanced office automation, paving the way for the general application of flexible integrated production and management systems. Around this nucleus of information technologies, a number of other fundamental innovations took place, particularly in new materials (ceramics, alloys, optical fiber), and more recently, in superconductors, in laser, and in renewable energy sources. In a parallel process, which benefited from the enhanced capacity to store and analyze information, genetic engineering extended the technological revolution to the realm of living matter. This laid the foundations for biotechnology, itself an information technology with its scientific basis in the ability to decode and reprogram the information em-bodied in living organisms.[8]

Although the scientific foundations of these discoveries had already come into existence, over timescales varying from field to field, the relatively simul-taneous emergence of these various technologies, and the synergy created by their interaction, contributed to their rapid diffusion and application, and this in turn expanded the potential of each technology and induced a broader and faster development of the new technological paradigm.[9] A key factor in this synergistic process relates to the specific nature of this process of innovation: because it is based on enhanced ability to store, retrieve, and analyze infor-mation, every single discovery, as well as every application, can be related to developments in other fields and in other applications, by continuous interac-tions through the common medium of information systems, and communicat-ing by means of the common language of science, in spite of the persistence of specialization in different scientific fields.

Social, economic, and institutional factors have, as I will argue, been decis-ive in the coming together of these different scientific innovations under the form of a new technological paradigm.[10] However, the specificity of the new technologies plays a major role in the structure and evolution of this para-digm, and imposes the materiality of their internal logic on the articulation between the process of innovation and the process of social organization. The new technological paradigm is characterized by two fundamental features.[11] First, the core new technologies are *focused on information processing*. This is the primary distinguishing feature of the emerging technological paradigm. To be sure, information and knowledge have been crucial elements in all techno-logical revolutions, since technology ultimately boils down to the ability to perform new operations, or to perform established practices better, on the basis of the application of new knowledge. All major technological changes are in fact based on new knowledge. However, what differentiates the current process of technological change is that *its raw material itself is information, and so is its outcome*. What an integrated circuit does is to speed up the processing of information while increasing the complexity and the accuracy of the process. What computers do is to organize the sets of instructions required for the handling of information, and, increasingly, for the generation of new informa-tion, on the basis of the combination and interaction of stored information. What telecommunications does is to transmit information, making possible flows of information exchange and treatment of information, regardless of distance, at lower cost and with shorter transmission times. What genetic engineering does is to decipher and, eventually, program the code of the living matter, dramatically expanding the realm of controllable information processing.

The output of the new technologies is also information. Their embodiment in goods and services, in decisions, in procedures, is the result of the application of their informational output, not the output itself. In this sense, the new technologies differ from former technological revolutions, and justify calling the new paradigm the "informational technological paradigm," in spite of the fact that some of the fundamental technologies involved in it (for example, superconductivity) are not information technologies. But the paradigm itself exists and articulates a convergent set of scientific discoveries by focusing on information processing and by using the newly found informational capacity to enable articulation and communication throughout the whole spectrum of technological innovations. Furthermore, with the progress of the new technological revolution, the machines themselves take second place to the creative synergy made possible by their use as sources of productivity. This trend is often referred to in the literature as the growing importance of software over hardware, a theme stimulated by the promise of research in such fields as artificial intelligence. However, this is still an open debate in scientific terms. Better design of integrated circuits, ever larger-scale integration, enhanced telecommunications capability, and the use of new material in the manufacturing of information-processing devices, are in the medium-term perspective probably more important than artificial intelligence as a basis for information-handling and information-generation capacity. The fundamental trend overall seems to depend not so much on the somewhat obsolete idea of the growing dominance of software over hardware, as on the ability of new information technologies to generate new information, thus emphasizing the specific nature of their output *vis-à-vis* former technological paradigms.

The second major characteristic of the new technologies is in fact common to all major technological revolutions.[12] The main effects of their innovations are on *processes*, rather than on *products*.[13] There are, of course, major innovations in products, and the surge of new products is a fundamental factor in spurring new economic growth. However, the deepest impact of innovation is associated with the transformation of processes.[14] This was also the case with the two industrial revolutions associated with technical paradigms organized respectively around the steam engine and around electricity.[15] In both cases, energy was the pivotal element which, by gradually penetrating all processes of production, distribution, transportation, and management, revolutionized the entire economy and the whole society, not so much because of the new goods and services being produced and distributed, but because of the ways of performing the processes of production and distribution, on the basis of a new source of energy that could be decentralized and distributed in a flexible manner. The new energy-based industrial and organizational processes gave birth to goods and services, hence products, that could not even have been imagined before the diffusion of energy-processing devices. But it was the revolution in energy, with its influence on all kinds of processes, that created the opportunity for the surge in new products. Process commands products, although functional, economic, and social feedback effects are crucial to an understanding of the historical process.

Similarly, in the current informational revolution, what new information technologies are about in the first place is process. A chip has value only as a means of improving the performance of a machine for an end-use function. A computer is a tool for information handling, whose usefulness for the organization or individual using it depends on the purpose of the information-processing activity. A genetically modified cell will take on its actual significance in its interaction with the whole body. While all social and biological activities are in fact processes, some elements of these processes crystallize in material forms that constitute goods and services, the usual content of economic products. Technological revolutions are made up of innovations whose products are in fact processes.

These two major characteristics of the informational technological paradigm[16] have fundamental effects on its impact on society. (Society itself, as stated above, frames and influences technological innovation in a dialectical relationship of which, at this point, we are only examining one factor, namely, the influence of new technologies on social organization.)

A fundamental consequence is derived from the essential process-orientation of technological innovation. Because processes, unlike products, enter into all spheres of human activity, their transformation by such technologies, focusing on omnipresent flows of information, leads to modification in the material basis of the entire social organization. Thus, new information technologies are transforming the way we produce, consume, manage, live, and die; not by themselves, certainly, but as powerful mediators of the broader set of factors that determines human behavior and social organization.

The fact that new technologies are focused on information processing has far-reaching consequences for the relationship between the sphere of sociocultural symbols and the productive basis of society. Information is based upon culture, and information processing is, in fact, symbol manipulation on the basis of existing knowledge; that is, codified information verified by science and/or social experience. Thus, the predominant role of new information technologies in the process of innovation is to establish ever more intimate relationships among the culture of society, scientific knowledge, and the development of productive forces. If information processing becomes the key component of the new productive forces, the symbolic capacity of society itself, collectively as well as individually, is tightly linked to its developmental process. In other words, the structurally determined capacity of labor to process information and generate knowledge is, more than ever, the material source of productivity, and therefore of economic growth and social well-being. Yet this symbolic capacity of labor is not an individual attribute. Labor has to be formed, educated, trained, and retrained, in flexible manipulation of symbols, determining its ability constantly to reprogram itself. In addition, productive organizations, social institutions, and the overall structure of society, including its ideology, will be key elements in fostering or stalling the new information-based productive forces. The more a society facilitates the exchange of information flows, and the decentralized generation and distribution of information, the greater will be its collective symbolic capacity. It is this capacity which underlies the enhancement and diffusion of information technologies, and thus the development of productive forces.

In this sense, the new informational technological paradigm emphasizes the historical importance of the Marxian proposition on the close interaction between productive forces and social systems.[17] Perhaps it is only in the current historical period, because of the close connection between information and culture through the human mind, and thus between productivity and social organization, that such inspired anticipation bears its full meaning. However, if this perspective is to be intellectually fruitful it must be purified both from any ideological assumption of historical directionality and from any value judgment. The development of productive forces by the liberation of information flows does not require that capitalism be superseded. In fact, state-planned societies have proved more resistant to the new technological revolution than market-based economies, in contradiction of Marx's prophecy that socialism possessed a superior ability to develop productive forces. Equally unfounded is the opposite ideological position which states that market forces are innately superior in steering development in information technologies. Japan's leadership in the field has been built on strong, systematic state intervention in support of national companies, to raise their technological level in pursuit of the national goal of establishing Japan as a world power on non-military grounds.

The key mechanism for the development of productive forces in the new informational technological paradigm seems to be the ability of a given social organization to educate and motivate its labor force while at the same time setting up an institutional framework that maximizes information flows and connects them to the developmental tasks. The social and political means of achieving such goals vary historically, as do the societal outcomes of the development processes. However, not all these processes are undetermined, and relationships can certainly be found between social structures, technoeconomic development, and institutional goals. Nevertheless, the present purpose is more limited and more focused. It is sufficient here to pinpoint the fact that because the new productive forces are information based, their development is more closely related than ever to the characteristics of symbolic production and manipulation in every society, actually fulfilling the hypothesis proposed by Marx on the relationship between social structure and techno-economic development.

From the characteristics of the process-orientation of information-based technology derives a third fundamental effect of the new technological paradigm on social organization: namely, increased *flexibility* of organizations in production, consumption, and management. Flexibility, in fact, emerges as a key characteristic of the new system taking shape;[18] yet it takes place within a context of large-scale production, consumption, and management, generally associated with large organizations and/or extended organizational networks. What happens is that new technologies build on the organizational capacity resulting from the industrial form of production and consumption, particularly during its mature stage (generally associated with what has been labeled in the literature as "Fordism," a very misleading term);[19] but they contribute both to transforming this system and enhancing that organizational capacity by preserving the economies of scale and the depth of organizational power, while overcoming rigidity and facilitating constant adaptation to a rapidly changing context. In this way, the historical oppositions between craft production and large-scale manufacture, between mass consumption and customized markets, between powerful bureaucracies and innovative enterprises, are dialectically superseded by the new technological medium, which ushers in an era of adaptive organizations in direct relationship with their social environments.[20] By increasing the flexibility of all processes, new information technologies contribute to minimizing the distance between economy and society.

The organizational transition from industrialism to informationalism

The new technological paradigm has fundamental social consequences linked to the specific logic of its basic characteristics. Yet, the new technologies are themselves articulated into a broader system of production and organization, whose ultimate roots are social, but to whose development new technologies powerfully contribute.[21] It is this complex, interacting system of technology and organizational processes, underlying economic growth and social change, that we call a *mode of development*. It is not the product of new technologies, nor are the new technologies a mechanical response to the demands of the new organizational system. It is the convergence between the two processes that changes the technical relationships of production, giving rise to a new mode of development. The previous section presented in summary form the relatively autonomous evolution of technological innovation which has led to the emergence of the informational technological paradigm. This section will examine, even more succinctly, the main organizational and structural trends that characterize the transition from the industrial to the informational mode of development.

The main process in this transition is not the shift from goods to services but, as the two main theorists of the "post-industrial society"[22] proposed many years ago, Alain Touraine in 1969 and Daniel Bell in 1973, the emergence of information processing as the core, fundamental activity conditioning the effectiveness and productivity of all processes of production, distribution, consumption, and management. The new centrality of information processing results from evolution in all the fundamental spheres of the industrial mode of development, under the influence of economic and social factors and structured largely by the mode of production. Specifically, the secular trend toward the increasing role of information results from a series of developments in the spheres of production, of consumption, and of state intervention.

In the sphere of *production*, two major factors have fostered information-processing activities within the industrial mode of development. The first is the emergence of the large corporation as the predominant organizational form of production and management.[23] An economy based on large-scale production and centralized management generated the growing number of information flows that were needed for efficient articulation of the system. The second resides within the production process itself (considering production in the broad sense, that is including production of both goods and services), and is the shift of the productivity sources from capital and labor to "other factors" (often associated with science, technology, and management), as shown by the series of econometric analyses in the tradition best represented by Robert Solow.[24] The hard core of these information-processing activities is composed of knowledge, which structures and provides adequate meaning to the mass of information required to manage organizations and to increase productivity.

In the sphere of *consumption*, two parallel processes have emphasized the role of information. On the one hand, the constitution of mass markets, and the increasing distance between buyers and sellers, have created the need for specific marketing and effective distribution by firms, thus triggering a flurry of information-gathering systems and information-distributing flows, to establish the connection between the two ends of the market.[25] On the other hand, under the pressure of new social demands, often expressed in social movements, a growing share of the consumption process has been taken over by collective consumption, that is, goods and services directly or indirectly produced and/or managed by the state,[26] as a right rather than as a commodity, giving rise to the welfare state. The formation of the welfare state has produced a gigantic system of information flows affecting most people and most activities, spurring the growth of bureaucracies, the formation of service delivery agencies, and consequently the creation of millions of jobs in information handling.[27]

In the sphere of *state intervention*, the past half-century has seen a huge expansion of government regulation of economic and social activities that has generated a whole new administration, entirely made up of information flows and information-based decision processes.[28] Although variations in the mode of production lead to a bureaucratic cycle, with upswings and downturns in the trend toward regulation, state intervention is in more subtle ways a structural feature of the new mode of development, in a process that Alain Touraine has characterized as "la société programmée."[29] This is the process by which the state sets up a framework within which large-scale organizations, both private and public, define strategic goals, which may be geared toward international economic competitiveness or military supremacy, that permeate the entire realm of social activities without necessarily institutionalizing or formalizing the strategic guidance of these activities. To be able to steer a complex society without suffocating it, the modern state relies on a system of "neo-corporatist" pacts, in Philippe Schmitter's terms,[30] which mobilize and control society through a system of incentives and disincentives made up of storage of information, emission of signals, and management of instructions. The state of the informational mode of development, be it under capitalism or under statism, exercises more intervention than ever, but it does so by controlling and manipulating the network of information flows that penetrate all activities. It does not follow that society is doomed to the Orwellian vision, since the intervention of the state will be informed by the political values emerging from the dynamics of the civil society, and thus its enhanced power could be used to counteract the built-in bureaucratic tendencies of state apparatuses.[31] As Nicos Poulantzas wrote ten years ago: "This statism does not refer to the univocal reinforcement of the State, but it is rather the effect of one tendency, whose two poles develop unevenly, toward the simultaneous reinforcing–weakening of the State."[32] The attempt by the state to override the contradiction between its increasing role and its decreasing legitimacy by diffusing its power through immaterial information flows greatly contributes to the dramatic explosion of information-processing activities and organizations. This is because the state sets up a series of information systems that control activities and citizens' lives through the codes and rules determined by those systems.

These structural trends, emerging and converging in a society largely dominated by the industrial mode of development, pave the way for the transformation of that mode, as information processing, with its core in knowledge generation, detracts from the importance of energy in material production, as well as from the importance of goods-producing in the overall social fabric. However, this transformation of the mode of development could not be accomplished without the surge of innovation in information technologies which, by creating the material basis from which information processing can expand its role, contributes to the change both in the structure of the production process and in the organization of society. It is in this sense that I hypothesize the formation of a new, informational mode of development: on the basis of

the convergence through interaction of information technologies and information-processing activities into an articulated techno-organizational system.

The interaction between technological innovation and organizational change in the constitution of the informational mode of development

The convergence between the revolution in information technology and the
predominant role of information-processing activities in production, consumption, and state regulation leads to the rise of the new, informational mode of
development. This process triggers a series of new structural contradictions
which highlight the relative autonomy of technological change in the process of
social transformation. In fact, the diffusion of new technologies under the new
mode of development calls into question the very processes and organizational
forms that were at the basis of the demand for information technologies. This
is because these organizational forms were born within the industrial mode of
development, under the influence of the capitalist mode of production, and
generally reflect the old state of technology. As the new technologies, and the
realm of the possibilities they offer, expand, those same organizational forms
that were responsible for the demand for new technologies are being rendered
obsolete by their development. For instance, the large corporation was critical
in fostering the demand for computers. But as microcomputers increase in
power and become able to constitute information systems in harness with advanced telecommunications, it is no longer the large, vertical conglomerate but
the network which is the most flexible, efficient form of management.

In another crucial development, the old form of the welfare state loses
relevance. Previously, its operation had called for the expansion of information-processing activities: but as information itself becomes a productive force,
so the social characteristics of labor reproduction (and thus of collective consumption: education, health, housing, etc.) become key elements in the development of productive forces, embodied in the cultural capacity of labor to
process information. Thus, the old, redistributive welfare state becomes obsolete, not so much because it is too expensive (this is the capitalist critique, not
the informational challenge), as because it has to be restructured to connect
its redistributional goals with its new role as a source of productivity by means
of the investment in human capital.

A third manifestation of the process of institutional change set in motion by
the new technologies concerns the role of the state. The expansion of state
regulatory intervention underlay the explosion of government-led information
activities, enhancing its dominant role, within the limits of its legitimacy.
However, rapid innovation in information technologies has created the facility for two-way information flows, making it possible for civil society to control the state on democratic principles, without paralyzing its effectiveness as
a public interest agency. In this situation, the persistence of bureaucratic

aloofness, once deprived of its former technical justification, emphasizes authoritarian tendencies within the state, delegitimizes its power, and prompts calls for institutional reform toward more flexible and more responsive government agencies.

The organizational transformation of the mode of development, then, leads to the expansion of information technologies, whose effect triggers pressure for further organizational change. The informational mode of development is not a rigid structure, but a constant process of change based on the interaction between technology and organization. Yet the logic of this process of change does not depend primarily on the interaction between these two planes, for modes of development are conditioned in their historical evolution by the dynamics of specific societies, themselves largely conditioned by the contradictions and transformations of the modes of production that characterize them. More specifically, the evolution of the informational mode of development, with its changing interaction between technology and organizational structures, depends, in our societies, on the restructuring of the capitalist mode of production that has taken place in the past decade. The transition between modes of development is not independent of the historical context in which it takes place; it relies heavily on the social matrix initially framing the transition, as well as on the social conflicts and interests that shape the transformation of that matrix. Therefore, the newly emerging forms of the informational mode of development, including its spatial forms, will not be determined by the structural requirements of new technologies seeking to fulfil their developmental potential, but will emerge from the interaction between its technological and organizational components, and the historically determined process of the restructuring of capitalism.

The Restructuring of Capitalism in the 1980s

When social systems experience a structural crisis, as a result of historical events acting on their specific contradictions, they are compelled either to change their goals, or to change their means in order to overcome the crisis. When the system changes its goals (or structural principles of performance), actually becoming a different system, there is a process of social transformation. When the system changes the institutionalized means by which it aims to achieve its systemic goals, there is a process of social restructuring. Each restructuring process leads to a new manifestation of the system, with specific institutional rules which induce historically specific sets of contradictions and conflicts, developing into new crises that potentially trigger new restructuring processes. This sequence goes on until the social equation underlying both structures and processes makes possible historical change to replace the old system by a new one.

The transformation of the capitalist mode of production on a global scale follows, in general terms, this social logic. The Great Depression of the 1930s, followed by the dislocation of World War II, triggered a restructuring process that led to the emergence of a new form of capitalism very different from the *laissez-faire* model of the pre-Depression era.[33] This new capitalist model, often characterized by the misleading term "Keynesianism,"[34] relied on three major structural modifications:[35]

1   A social pact between capital and labor which, in exchange for the stability of capitalist social relationships of production and the adaptation of the labor process to the requirements of productivity, recognized the rights of organized labor, assured steadily rising wages for the unionized labor force, and extended the realm of entitlements to social benefits, creating an ever-expanding welfare state.
2   Regulation and intervention by the state in the economic sphere: key initiatives in the accumulation process, stimulation of demand through public expenditures, and absorption of surplus labor by increasing public employment.
3   Control of the international economic order by intervention in the sphere of circulation via a set of new international institutions, organized around the International Monetary Fund and under the hegemony of the United States, with the imposition of the dollar (and to some extent the pound) as the standard international currency. The ordering of world economic processes included the control by the center of the supply and prices of key raw materials and energy sources, most of these being produced by a still largely colonized Third World.

This state-regulated capitalism assured unprecedented economic growth, gains in productivity, and prosperity in the core countries for about a quarter of a century. In retrospect, history will probably consider these years as the golden age of western capitalism.

As I have shown elsewhere,[36] these same structural elements that accounted for the dynamism of this model were the very factors that led to its crisis in the 1970s, under the stress of its contradictions, expressed through rampant inflation that disrupted the circulation process, and under the pressure of social movements and labor struggles whose successful social and wage demands lowered the rate of profit. The oil shocks of 1974 and 1979 were precipitant events which, acting on structurally determined inflation, drove the circulation of capital out of control, prompting the need for austerity policies and fiscal restraint, and thus undermining the economic basis for state intervention. Although in strictly economic terms the increase in oil prices was not the cause of the structural crisis, its impact was crucial in calling into question the post-World War II model of capitalism, because of the pervasive effects of energy cost and supply in an economic system relying on an industrial mode of development based upon energy.

The crisis of the system in the 1970s revealed the declining effectiveness of the mechanisms established in the 1930s and 1940s in ensuring the fulfillment of the basic goals of the capitalist economy.[37] Labor was steadily increasing its share of the product. Social movement outside the workplace were imposing growing constraints on the ability of capital and bureaucracies to organize production and society free from social control. The state entered a fiscal crisis brought on by the contradiction between growing expenditures (determined by social demands) and comparatively decreasing revenues (limited by the need to preserve corporate profits).[38] The international order was disrupted by the surge of Third World nationalism (simultaneously opposed, supported, and manipulated by the strategies of the superpowers), and by the entry into the international economy of new competitive actors. The structural difficulty of making hard choices led companies to pass costs on into prices, the state to finance its intervention through debt and money supply, and the international economy to prosper through financial speculation and irresponsible lending in the global markets. After a series of unsuccessful stop-and-go policies, the second oil shock of 1979 revealed the depth of the crisis and necessitated a restructuring process that was undertaken simultaneously by both governments and firms, while international institutions such as the IMF imposed the new economic discipline throughout the world economy.

A new model of socio-economic organization had to be established which would be able to achieve the basic aims of a capitalist system, namely: to enhance the rate of profit for private capital, the engine of investment, and thus of growth; to find new markets, both through deepening the existing ones and by incorporating new regions of the world into an integrated capitalist economy; to control the circulation process, curbing structural inflation; and to assure the social reproduction and the economic regulation of the system through mechanisms that would not contradict those established to achieve the preceding goals of higher profit rates, expanding demand, and inflation control.

On the basis of these premises, a new model of capitalism emerged which, with national variations and diverse fortunes, actually characterizes most of the international system in the late 1980s. Reducing the new model to its essentials, we can summarize it in three major features which simultaneously address the four goals stated above as the fundamental requirements for the restructuring of capitalism to operate successfully.

(1) *The appropriation by capital of a significantly higher share of surplus from the production process.* This is a reversal of the historical power relationship between capital and labor, and a negation of the social pact achieved in the 1930s and 1940s. This fundamental goal is achieved by combining increases in productivity and increases in exploitation, by means of a fundamental restructuring

of the work process and of the labor market which includes the following aspects:

(a) Higher productivity derived from technological innovation, combined with the uneven distribution of the productivity gains in favor of capital.

(b) Lower wages, reduced social benefits, and less protective working conditions.

(c) Decentralization of production to regions or countries characterized by lower wages and more relaxed regulation of business activities.

(d) Dramatic expansion of the informal economy, at both the core and the periphery of the system. By the informal economy is meant income-generating activities that are unregulated by the institutional system, in a context where similar activities are regulated. Much of the development of the informal economy has to do with the dismantling in practice of many provisions of the welfare state, for example, avoiding payment of social benefits and contravening the legislation protecting workers.[39]

(e) A restructuring of labor markets to take in growing proportions of women, ethnic minorities, and immigrants, namely, those social groups which, because of institutionalized discrimination and social stigma, are most vulnerable in society and thus in the marketplace.[40] However, it is important to observe that such vulnerability is socially determined. Should the social context change, this supposedly docile labor would not be incorporated into the new labor markets. For example, while immigration has boomed during the restructuring process in the US, it has been practically halted in western Europe. Although part of the difference has to lie in the ability of the US to create millions of new unskilled jobs, a substantial factor is the unionization and rising consciousness of immigrant workers in Europe during the 1970s, to the point where, in countries such as Switzerland and Germany, they have become the militant vanguard among factory workers.[41] It makes little sense for European management to continue to import labor which, despite its social vulnerability, could turn into a focus for militancy while not being responsive to the same mechanisms of integration that are operative with respect to native workers.

(f) The weakening of trade unions – a fundamental, explicit goal of the restructuring process in most countries, and in fact, probably the most important single factor in achieving the overall objective of restoring the rate of profit at a level acceptable for business. By and large this objective has been achieved. Organized labor in most capitalist countries, with the exception of Scandinavia, is at the lowest point of its power and influence in the past thirty years, and its situation is still deteriorating rapidly. Some of the reasons for this decline are structural: for example, the fading away of traditional manufacturing, where the strength of the unions was concentrated, and the parallel expansion of a weakly unionized service economy. Other factors have to do directly with the transformation of labor markets, as noted under (e) above: women, often because of the sexism of the labor unions, are less unionized; many immigrants do not feel that the unions represent them; the informal economy detracts from the socializing effects of the workplace. However, organized labor has also been weakened as a result of targeted policies by both governments and firms, engaging in a deliberate effort at achieving what is perceived as a historical objective that would dramatically increase the freedom of capital to steer the economy and society.[42] Thus, Reagan's tough handling of the 1981 air traffic controllers' strike in the US, ending up with the de-registration of their union (PATCO), and the placement of the names of all the strikers in a blacklist to ban them from future Federal government employment, sent out a powerful signal that was well heard by business. Similarly, Thatcher's merciless repression of the coal miners' strike in the UK ushered in a new era of management – labor relations that put the British Trades Union Congress on the defensive. The historical reversal of the capital-labor power relationship, encapsulated in the gradual decline of the trade union movement, is the cornerstone of the restructuring of capitalism in the 1980s.

(2) *A substantial change in the pattern of state intervention, with the emphasis shifted from political legitimation and social redistribution to political domination and capital accumulation.*[43] Although in the "Keynesian" model regulation of capitalist growth was also a key objective, the means by which such regulation was exercised included widespread expansion of the welfare state, as well as both direct and indirect creation of public sector jobs, stimulating demand and contributing to the reproduction of labor power. The new forms of state intervention are much more directly focused on capital accumulation, and give priority to domination over legitimation in the relationship between state and society, in response to the emergency situation in which the system found itself in the 1970s. However, in contradiction of the ideological self-representation of the restructuring process by its main protagonists, what we are witnessing is not the withdrawal of the state from the economic scene, but the emergence of a new form of intervention, whereby new means and new areas are penetrated by the state, while others are deregulated and transferred to the market. This simultaneous engagement and disengagement of the state in the economy and society is evident in several mechanisms that express the new form of state support of capitalism:

(a) Deregulation of many activities, including relaxation of social and environmental controls in the work process.

(b) Shrinkage of, and privatization of productive activities in, the public sector.

(c) Regressive tax reform, favoring corporations and upper-income groups.

(d) State support for high-technology R&D and leading industrial sectors which form the basis of the new informational economy. This support usually takes the dual form of financing infrastructure and research, and favorable fiscal policies.

(e) Accordance of priority status to defense and to defense-related industries, combining, in pursuit of the objectives of the new state, the reinforcement of military power and the stimulation of a high-technology dominated defense sector. Following an old formula of Herbert Marcuse, I will call this trend the rise of the "warfare state." Defense spending and the development of new defense industries is also a fundamental way of creating new markets to compensate for retrenchment in other public-sector expenditures, as well as for the loss of demand resulting from the lowering of wages in the production process.

(f) Shrinkage of the welfare state, with variations within and between countries according to the relative power of affected groups.

(g) Fiscal austerity, with the goal of a balanced budget, and tight monetary policy. These are key policies for the new model of capitalism, as the fundamental means of controlling inflation. However, while fiscal conservatism is an integral component of the new capitalism, recent historical experience shows the possibility of huge budget deficits resulting from the contradictions consequent on the implementation of the model in a given country, in particular in the US.

(3) *The third major mechanism of the restructuring of capitalism is the accelerated internationalization of all economic processes, to increase profitability and to open up markets through the expansion of the system.* The capitalist economy has been, since its beginnings, a world economy, as Braudel and Wallerstein have reminded us.[44] However, what is new is the increasing interpentration of all economic processes at the international level with the system working as a unit, worldwide in real time. This is a process that has grown steadily since the 1950s and has accelerated rapidly in the 1970s and 1980s as an essential element of the restructuring process. It embraces capital movements, labor migration, the process of production itself, the interpenetration of markets, and the use of nation states as elements of support in an international competition that will ultimately determine the economic fate of all nations.

The internationalization of capitalism enhances profitability at several levels:

(a) It allows capital to take advantage of the most favourable conditions for investment and production anywhere in the world. Sometimes this translates into low wages and lack of government regulation. In other instances, penetration of key markets or access to technology are more important considerations for the firm. But the fact remains that the increasing homogenization of the economic structure across nations allows for a variable geometry of production and distribution that maximizes advantages in terms of opportunity costs.

(b) By allowing round-the-clock capital investment opportunities world-wide, internationalization dramatically increases the rate of turnover of capital, thus enhancing profit levels for a given profit rate, although at the cost of increasing instability built into the system.

(c) The internationalization process also opens up new markets, and connects segments of markets across borders, increasingly differentiating societies vertically while homogenizing markets horizontally. This expansion of demand through new markets is absolutely crucial in a model that relies on the reduction of wages in the core countries, since the loss in potential demand has to be made up by the incorporation of whichever new markets may exist anywhere in the world. This is particularly important in the transitional period of restructuring, when wages have to be kept at the lowest possible level to increase profits and attract investment, while keeping demand high enough to justify new investment.

The process of internationalization offers dynamic expansion possibilities that could substantially benefit the capitalist system. But it can also pose fundamental problems to individual units of that system, be they firms or countries, which are faced with new, tougher competition from the new actors which are incorporated into the system and quickly learn the ruthlessness of the game. This has been the case for the US which has lost market share, in both its domestic market and the international economy, to Japan and the newly industrialized countries. Given the interdependence of economic processes and national policies, the internationalization process prepares the ground for future major crises: on the one hand, any significant downturn has immediate repercussions worldwide, and is thus amplified; on the other hand, competition constantly provokes the threat of protectionism which could wreck the very basis of the system. A system in which the interests of the totality are not necessarily the interests of each competitive unit in every moment in time could become increasingly disruptive. When the "creative destruction" process[45] takes place at the international level, the intermixing of national interests with competitive strategies becomes explosive.

The overpowering of labor by capital, the shift of the state toward the domination–accumulation functions of its intervention in economy and society, and the internationalization of the capitalist system to form a world-wide interdependent unit working in real time are the three fundamental dimensions of the restructuring process that has given birth to a new model of capitalism, as distinct from the "Keynesian" model of the 1945–75 era as that one was from "*laissez-faire*" capitalism.[46]

These three processes are present in most countries' recent economic policies, but their relative importance may vary considerably according to each country's history, institutions, social dynamics, and place in the world economy. Thus, the UK has emphasized the overpowering of labor as the rallying cry of the Thatcher government; the US has made the emergence of a new "war-fare state," based upon high-technology development, the centerpiece of its economic recovery; Japan has saved itself much of the pain of the restructuring process by riding the crest of the internationalization wave. However, since the capitalist system is a world system at the level of the mode of production (although certainly not at the level of societies), the different dimensions of the restructuring process are interconnected across the various regions of the international economy.

Also, the actual practice of restructuring is full of contradictions. Not only social but economic as well. For instance, in the case of the Reagan administration in the US the dramatic defense build up, combined with a regressive tax reform and the political inability to dismantle social security, led to the biggest budget deficit in American history, under one of the most ideologically committed administrations to fiscal conservatism. The budget deficit was financed to a large extent by foreign capital, attracted by high interest rates, driving up the dollar's exchange rate. Together with declining competitiveness of American manufacturing, this evolution resulted in catastrophic trade deficits that weakened the American economy. The twin mega-deficits have spoiled to a large extent the benefits of restructuring for American capitalism and will, most likely, lead to austerity policies in the 1989–91 period that could trigger a world recession. While our purpose here goes far beyond economic forecasting we want to emphasize that the process of restructuring is by no means exempt of contradictions. While fiscal austerity was a must of the new model, and as such was formulated by its supply-side defenders, it could not actually be implemented because the political support for the boldest extremes of restructuring could not be marshalled. The artificial implementation of the model (on the basis of debt-financed military expenditures, a policy we have labeled "perverted Keynesianism")[47] could lead to its demise or to its sharpening through reinforced austerity policies, ushering in a new crisis.

However, in spite of these contradictory trends, a new model of capitalism has emerged that could outlast the forthcoming crises. One of the reasons for its likely durability, we hypothesize, is that it has encompassed in its expansion the informational mode of development that was bursting into life in a process of historical simultaneity. It is the interaction and the articulation between the informational mode of development and the restructuring of capitalism that creates the framework shaping the dynamics of our society and our space.

The articulation between the informational mode of development and the restructuring of capitalism: reshaping the techno-economic paradigm

The historical coincidence of the restructuring of capitalism and the rise of the informational mode of development has created a structural convergence resulting in the formation of a specific techno-economic paradigm at the very roots of our social dynamics. Because political and organizational decision-makers are always primarily concerned to perpetuate the interests they represent, and therefore concerned with the process of restructuring, it is under the dominance of that process that the merger has taken place. However, the two components of the paradigm are distinguishable only analytically, because while informationalism has now been decisively shaped by the restructuring process, restructuring could never have been accomplished, even in a contradictory manner, without the unleashing of the technological and organizational potential of informationalism.

Given the complexity of the articulation process, I will differentiate between the two dimensions that compose the informational mode of development: the *technological* and the *organizational*. Both have been fundamental in giving rise to a new form of capitalism which, in turn, has stimulated and supported the technological revolution and has adopted new organizational forms.

New *information technologies* have been decisive in the implementation of the three fundamental processes of capitalist restructuring.

(1) *Increasing the rate of profit* by various means:

(a) Enhancing productivity by the introduction of microelectronics-based machines that transform the production process.

(b) Making possible the decentralization of production, and the spatial separation of different units of the firm, while reintegrating production and management at the level of the firm by using telecommunications and flexible manufacturing systems.

(c) Enabling management to automate those processes employing labor with a sufficiently high cost level and a sufficiently low skill level to make automation both profitable and feasible. These jobs happened to be those concentrated in the large-scale factories that had become the strongholds of labor unions, and better remunerated labor, during the industrial era.

(d) Positioning capital in a powerful position *vis-à-vis* labor. Automation, flexible manufacturing, and new transportation technologies provide management with a variety of options that considerably weaken the bargaining position of the unions. Should the unions insist on preserving or improving their levels of wages and benefits, the company can automate or move elsewhere, or both, without losing its connections with the market or with the network of production. Thus, either by using automation to substitute for labor, or by extracting concessions by wielding the threat to automate or relocate, capital uses new technologies to free itself from the constraints of organized labor.

(2) New technologies are also a powerful instrument in weighting the accumulation and domination functions of state intervention. This occurs on two main levels:

(a) On the one hand, rapid technological change makes obsolete the entire existing weapons system, creating the basis for the expansion of the "warfare state" in a political environment characterized by states striving for military supremacy and therefore engaging in a technological arms race that can only be supported by the resources of the state.

(b) On the other hand, the strategic role played by high technology in economic development draws the state to concentrate on providing the required infrastructure, downplaying its role in redistributional policies.

(3) The process of *internationalization of the economy* could never take place without the dramatic breakthroughs in information technologies. Advances in telecommunications, flexible manufacturing that allows simultaneously for standardization and customization, and new transportation technologies emerging from the use of computers and new materials, have created the material infrastructure for the world economy, as the construction of the railway system provided the basis for the formation of national markets in the nineteenth century. In addition, the economic effects of new technologies are also crucial in the formation of an international economy. Their effects on process condition the international competitiveness of countries and firms. Their effects on new products create new markets in which the harshest competitive battles are fought, with new economic actors trying to short-circuit the sequence of development by leapfrogging into state-of-the-art high-technology markets through dramatic efforts of national development. The new technological division of labor is one of the fundamental lines of cleavage in the emerging international economic order.

The *organizational* components of the informational mode of development are also fundamental features in the restructuring process. Three major organizational characteristics of informationalism may be distinguished, each one of them affecting the three dimensions of the restructuring process.

(1) There is a growing *concentration of knowledge-generation and decision-making processes in high-level organizations* in which both information and the capacity of processing it are concentrated. The informational world is made up of a very hierarchical functional structure in which increasingly secluded centers take to its extreme the historical division between intellectual and manual labor. Given the strategic role of knowledge and information control in productivity and profitability, these core centers of corporate organizations are the only truly indispensable components of the system, with most other work, and thus most other workers, being potential candidates for automation from the strictly functional point of view. How far this tendency toward widespread automation is actually taken in practice is a different matter, depending on the dynamics of labor markets and social organization.

This concentration of information power in selected segments of the corporate structure greatly favors the chances of the restructuring process in the three dimensions presented:

(a) Productive labor can be reduced to its essential component, thus downgrading the objective bargaining power of the large mass of functionally dispensable labor.

(b) The rise of the technocracy within the state displaces the traditional integrative functions of the politically determined bureaucracy, establishing a tight linkage between the high levels of the state and the corporate world through the intermediary of the scientific establishment. The rise of the meritocracy, using the notion advanced by Daniel Bell, establishes new principles of legitimacy in the state, further removing it from the political controls and constituencies represented by the diversity of social interests.

(c) As technology transfer becomes the key to competition in the international economy, that process is controlled by knowledge holders in the centers of the dominant scientific and corporate organizations. It follows that the effective accomplishment of the internationalization process requires access to these knowledge centers, ruling out the adoption of an isolationist stance, which would only lead to the technological obsolescence of those economies and firms holding it.

(2) The second major organizational characteristic of informationalism concerns the *flexibility* of the system and of the relationships among its units, since flexibility is both a requirement of and a possibility offered by new information technologies.[48] Flexibility acts powerfully as a facilitator of the restructuring process in the following ways:

(a) It changes capital–labor relationships, transforming a potentially permanent and protected worker status into a flexible arrangement generally adapted to the momentary convenience of management. Thus, temporary workers, part-time jobs, homework, flexitime schedules, indefinite positions in the corporate structure, changing assignments, varying wages and benefits according to performance, etc., are all creative expedients of management that, while they increase tremendously the flexibility and thus the productivity of the firm, undermine the collective status of labor *vis-à-vis* capital.

(b) In the restructuring of the state, organizational flexibility contributes to the formation of public–private partnerships and to the blurring of the distinction between the public and private spheres. Segments of the welfare state are being shifted to the private sector, corporations are being brought into the formulation of public policies, and a selective interpenetration of state and capital is diminishing the autonomy of the state, along the lines of the "recapitalization" of the state, characteristic of the restructuring process.[49]

(c) Flexibility is also a necessary condition for the formation of the new world economy, since it is the only organizational form that allows constant adaptation of firms to the changing conditions of the world market.[50]

(3) A third fundamental organizational characteristic of informationalism is the shift from *centralized* large corporations to *decentralized* networks made up of a plurality of sizes and forms of organizational units.[51] Although networking increases flexibility, it is actually a different characteristic, since there are forms of flexibility that do not require networks. These networks, which could not exist on such a large scale without the medium provided by new information technologies, are the emerging organizational form of our world, and have played a fundamental role in ensuring the restructuring process:

(a) They are the prevalent form of the informal economy, as well as of the sub-contracting practices that have disorganized and reorganized the labor process, enhancing capital's profitability.[52]

(b) They have provided the model for the constitution of the new warfare state [. . .] on the basis of the interaction between different specialized government agencies, the defense industry, high-technology firms, and the scientific establishment.

(c) They are the organizational form used by major multinational corporations that have established variable strategic alliances to compete in the international economy.[53] Unlike the tendency of the industrial mode of development toward oligopolistic concentration, in the informational era large corporations set up specific alliances for given products, processes, and markets: these alliances vary according to time and space, and result in a variable geometry of corporate strategies that follow the logic of the multiple networks where they are engaged rather than the monolithic hierarchy of empire conglomerates.

Networks, on the basis of new information technologies, provide the organizational basis for the transformation of socially and spatially based relationships of production into flows of information and power that articulate the new flexible system of production and management. The restructuring of capitalism has used the adaptive potential of organizational networking to find breathing room for its "creative-destructive" energy, hitherto constrained by the social and political bonds inflicted upon it by a society reluctant to be but a commodity. The libertarian spirit of capitalism finally found itself at home at the last frontier where organizational networks and information flows dissolve locales and supersede societies. Informationalism and capitalism have historically merged in a process of techno-economic restructuring whose social consequences will last far beyond the social events and political circumstances that triggered the decisions leading to its development in the 1980s.

From this historical synthesis, new social forms and new spatial processes have emerged. My inquiry will explore the territory thus constituted. It will take us into the new world being made up from the contradictions of our past and the promises of our future through the conflicts of our present.

NOTES

1   The social theory underlying this analysis cannot be fully presented in the context of this book, which addresses a specific research topic. However, it is intellectually important to relate this study to the overall theoretical framework that informs it. The elaboration of this theory has built upon several classical traditions: Marx for the analysis of class relationships; Freud and Reich for the understanding of personality on the basis of sexual and family relationships; Weber for the analysis of the state. A number of contemporary social scientists have been crucial to my understanding of links and developments not covered in the classical writings: Nicos Poulantzas, for the recasting of the theory of social classes and the state; Alain Touraine for his analysis of post-industrialism; Nancy Chodorow for the intellectual connection between feminist theory and the psychoanalytical tradition; Agnes Heller, for the understanding of the historical creation of social needs; and Michel Foucault and Richard Sennett for the connection between power and culture. In making explicitly known my theoretical sources, I hope to help place this brief summary of my underlying theoretical framework in the ongoing intellectual debates in social sciences.

2   Under the term "human-modified matter" I would include what could be called at the risk of paradox, "immaterial matter," that is, the set of symbols and

communication codes that are generated by the human mind and which, while they are intangible, are a fundamental part of matter, since they are indeed a material force. One way to understand the informational mode of development, that I will not explore at present, could be the shift from physical matter to mental matter in the process of expansion of nature.

3   The definition is from Harvey Brooks, cited in Daniel Bell, *The Coming of Post-Industrial Society* (New York: Basic Books, 1973) p. 29 of the 1976 edition.

4   Ibid.

5   Alain Touraine, *La Société post-industrielle* (Paris: Denoel, 1969); Radovan Richta, *La Civilisation au carrefour* (Paris: Anthropos, 1969); Bell, *Post-industrial Society*.

6   For a summary, informed presentation of the rise and implications of information technology, see, for instance, Tom Forester, *High Tech Society. The Story of the Information Technology Revolution* (Oxford: Blackwell, 1987); also Bruce R. Guile (ed.), *Information Technologies and Social Transformation* (Washington, DC: National Academy Press, 1985).

7   See E. Braun and S. MacDonald, *Revolution in Miniature* (Cambridge: Cambridge University Press, 1982).

8   See Edward J. Sylvester and Lynn C. Klotz, *The Gene Age: Genetic Engineering and the Next Industrial Revolution* (New York: Scribner, 1983).

9   See John S. Mayo, "The evolution of information technologies," in Guile (ed.), *Information Technologies*, pp. 7–33.

10   Nathan Rosenberg, "The impact of historical innovation: a historical view," in Ralph Landau and Nathan Rosenberg (eds), *The Positive Sum Strategy: Harnessing Technology for Economic Growth* (Washington, DC: National Academy Press, 1986).

11   See Melvin Kranzberg, "The information age: evolution or revolution," in Guile (ed.), *Information Technologies*, pp. 35–55.

12   See Melvin Kranzberg and Carroll W. Pursell, Jr (eds), *Technology in Western Civilization*, 2 vols (New York: Oxford University Press, 1967).

13   I. Mackintosh, *Sunrise Europe: The Dynamics of Information Technology* (Oxford: Blackwell, 1986).

14   Nathan Rosenberg, *Perspectives on Technology* (Cambridge: Cambridge University Press, 1976).

15   See Eugene S. Ferguson, "The steam engine before 1830;" John R. Brae, "Energy conversion;" and Harold J. Sharlin, "Applications of electricity;" in Kranzberg and Pursell (eds), *Technology in Western Civilization*.

16   For the notion of "technical paradigm" see the analysis in Carlota Perez, "Structural change and the assimilation of new technologies in the economic and social systems," *Futures*, 15 (1983), pp. 357–75.

17   Marx developed his most far-reaching analysis of the social implications of technology in the *Grundrisse*.

18   See Robert Boyer and Benjamin Coriat, "Technical flexibility and macro stabilisation," paper presented at the Venice Conference on Innovation Diffusion, 17–21 March 1986 (Paris: CEPREMAP, 1986).

19   For an analysis of "Fordism," see Robert Boyer, *Technical Change and the Theory of Regulation* (Paris: CEPREMAP, 1987).

20   Michael Piore and Charles Sabel, *The Second Industrial Divide* (New York: Basic Books, 1984).

21 See the fundamental work on the whole series of issues discussed in this chapter, Peter Hall and Paschal Preston, *The Carrier Wave: New Information Technology and the Geography of Innovation, 1846–2003* (London: Unwin Hyman, 1988).

22 For a discussion of post-industrialism, see Manuel Castells, *The Economic Crisis and American Society* (Oxford: Blackwell, 1980), pp. 164–78.

23 Alfred D. Chandler, *The Visible Hand* (Cambridge: Cambridge University Press, 1977).

24 Robert Solow, "Technical changes and the aggregate production function," *Review of Economics and Statistics*, August 1957. For a summary of the debate on the sources of productivity, see Richard R. Nelson, "Research on productivity growth and productivity differences: dead ends and new departures," *Journal of Economic Literature*, 19 (September 1981), pp. 1029–64.

25 I have relied for this analysis on Nicole Woolsey-Biggart, *Charismatic Capitalism*. (Chicago, IL: University of Chicago Press, 1990).

26 Manuel Castells, "Collective consumption and urban contradictions in advanced capitalism," in Leo Lindberg et al. (eds), *Stress and Contradiction in Modern Capitalism* (Lexington, MA: Heath, 1974).

27 Morris Janowitz, *Social Control of the Welfare State* (Chicago, IL: University of Chicago Press, 1976).

28 Michel Aglietta, *Une théorie de la regulation économique: le cas des Etats-Unis* (Paris: Calmann-Levy, 1976).

29 Alain Touraine, *La voix et le regard* (Paris: Seuil, 1978).

30 Philippe Schmitter, *Interest Conflict and Political Change in Brazil* (Stanford: Stanford University Press, 1981).

31 Gordon Clark and Michael Dear, *State Apparatus* (Boston: Allen and Unwin, 1984).

32 Nicos Poulantzas, *L'etat, le pouvoir, le socialisme* (Paris: Presses Universitaires de France, 1978), p. 226 (my translation).

33 See James O'Connor, *Accumulation Crisis* (Oxford: Blackwell, 1984).

34 Post-Depression capitalism did not actually follow the policies proposed by Keynes: the state acted on supply as much as on demand. It would be more appropriate to refer to this form of capitalism as state-regulated capitalism.

35 See Michel Aglietta, *Regulation et crises du capitalisme* (Paris: Calmann-Levy, 1976).

36 For an analysis of the causes of the economic crisis of the 1970s and of the potential way out of it through the restructuring process, see Castells, *Economic Crisis and American Society*.

37 Samuel Bowles et al., *Beyond the Wasteland* (New York: Doubleday, 1983).

38 See James O'Connor's classic, *The Fiscal Crisis of the State* (New York: St Martin's Press, 1973).

39 See Manuel Castells and Alejandro Portes, "World underneath: the origins, dynamics, and consequences of the informal economy," in Alejandro Portes, Manuel Castells, and Lauren Benton (eds), *The Informal Economy* (Baltimore, MD: The Johns Hopkins University Press, 1989).

40 Michael Reich, *Discrimination in Labor Markets* (Princeton, NJ: Princeton University Press, 1982).

41 Manuel Castells, "Immigrant workers and class struggle in Western Europe," *Politics and Society*, 2 (1975).

42 Joel Krieger, *Reagan, Thatcher and the Politics of Decline* (New York: Oxford University Press, 1986).

43 I rely here on an analysis of the state, adapted from Nicos Poulantzas's work, that sees the state's relatively autonomous actions taking place within a dialectical process of ensuring domination and accumulation on the one hand, while trying to maintain legitimation and redistribution on the other. For an attempt at using these concepts in empirical research, see Manuel Castells and Francis Godard, *Monopolville* (Paris: Mouton, 1974).

44 Fernand Braudel, *Capitalisme et civilisation materielle* (Paris: Armand Colin, 1979); Immanuel Wallerstein, *The Modern World System* (New York: Academic Press, 1974).

45 By the "creative destruction" of capitalism I refer, of course, to the notion proposed by Schumpeter in his *Business Cycles*.

46 Robert Boyer (ed.), *Capitalismes fin de siècle* (Paris: Presses Universitaires de France, 1986).

47 See our analysis of "Reaganomics" in Martin Carnoy and Manuel Castells, "After the crisis?," *World Policy Journal*, May 1984.

48 On the role of flexibility, see Boyer and Coriat, *Technical Flexibility*.

49 The notion of the "recapitalization" of the state has been proposed by S.M. Miller.

50 For an analysis of flexibility in enhancing competitiveness in the international economy, see Manuel Castells et al., *The Shek Kip Mei Syndrome: Economic Development and Public Housing in Hong Kong and Singapore* (London: Pion, 1990).

51 On the analysis of networks, see Piore and Sabel, *The Second Industrial Divide* and Woolsey-Biggart, "Direct sales."

52 For evidence on the fundamental role of networks in the informal economy, see Portes, Castells, and Benton, *The Informal Economy*.

53 See Peter Schulze, "Shifts in the world economy and the restructuring of economic sectors: increasing competition and strategic alliances in information technologies" (Berkeley, CA: University of California, Institute of International Studies, 1987).

CHAPTER SEVEN

Information Technology, the Restructuring of Capital–Labor Relationships, and the Rise of the Dual City

(1989)

Toward the Transformation of the Urban Social Structure: The Dual City

The dynamics of economic dualism in the inner city

The polarization and segmentation of the labor force under the impact of the process of techno-economic restructuring has specific spatial manifestations. Although much attention has been given to the regional disparity of the processes of new growth and decline, often simplified under the summary opposition between the sunbelt and the "rustbelt,"[1] probably the most significant spatial expression of the restructuring of labor is taking place within the largest metropolitan areas, and particularly in the dominant world cities, such as New York and Los Angeles.[2] With the exception of some old industrial cities whose fate has been overwhelmingly determined by the old manufacturing industries (Buffalo, NY, for example)[3] processes of sectoral growth and decline, and the reallocation of jobs and labor, are taking place simultaneously within the same metropolitan areas, in a complex pattern that combines the creation of new, highly paid jobs in advanced services and high-technology sectors, the destruction of middle-level jobs in old manufacturing, the gradual shrinkage of protected jobs in the public sector, and the proliferation of new, low-paid jobs both in services and in downgraded manufacturing. At the same time, three inter-related phenomena add complexity to the emerging urban social structure: the explosion of the informal economy, unregulated income-generating activities in a context where similar activities are government-regulated; the reduction of the rate of participation in the labor force, as officially defined, indicative of a growing surplus population in the formal economy; and the proliferation of the criminal economy, particularly in activities related to the drug trade, which becomes the shop floor for a growing proportion of ethnic-minority youth in the largest inner cities.

Interpretations of these trends vary, according to different intellectual traditions. Two predominant theses, nevertheless, formulate a plausible argument, in terms that are largely complementary, in spite of the ideological and theoretical differences between their respective proponents.

One school of thought points to the mismatching of skills between the jobs that are being created and those being destroyed.[4] Advanced services and high-technology industries require a higher level of education than most of the traditional manufacturing and menial jobs that are being phased out, thus substantially changing and upgrading the skills required to obtain employment in the new labor market. With most of the new jobs being created in the advanced services clusters of the large CBDs,[5] and many of the disappearing traditional jobs being concentrated in the old urban industrial cores surrounding these CBDs,[6] it follows that the new expanding labor markets are concentrated in the nodal centers of the large metropolitan areas, as are the pools of obsolete labor, no longer employable, which are made up predominantly of ethnic minorities. John Kasarda, a leading urban scholar forecasting the rise of the dual city,[7] has analyzed the creation of knowledge-intensive jobs and entry-level jobs for nine major US cities between 1970 and 1980 (see table 7.1). His data show the occupational shift in favor of knowledge-intensive jobs, particularly for the largest north-eastern cities. Such a transition could in fact be beneficial for the upgrading of the social structure were it not for the mismatching of skills determined by inequality in the educational system, itself a result of spatial segregation by class and race. Public schools in the largest inner cities receive proportionally fewer resources than those in the suburbs, and cater to the poorest sectors of the population, with an overwhelming proportion of ethnic minorities with the greatest educational need to overcome a cultural disadvantage in their family background. The majority of the resident population of inner cities, then, cannot match the skill requirements of the new labor market because of the inefficiency and segregated nature of the public school system. In the northeast region in 1982, 42 percent of black males aged 16–64 had not completed high school; the proportion for white males was only 31.4 percent. Adding to this racial discrimination in the labor market, we see that 26.2 percent of those relatively uneducated black males were unemployed in the north-eastern central cities in 1982, against an average of 10.2 percent of white males.[8] For all regions in 1982, 16.5 percent of all black central city residents aged 16–24 were neither in school nor in the labor force, with the same figure increasing to 17.1 percent for the 25–64 age group. The corresponding figures for whites were

Table 7.1 Employment changes by industry's average educational requirements, for nine US cities, 1970–1980 (000s)

City and industrial categorization[a]	No. of jobs (1980)	Change (1970–80)	
		No.	%
New York			
Entry-level	763	−472	−38.2
Knowledge-intensive	462	92	24.9
Philadelphia			
Entry-level	208	−102	−32.9
Knowledge-intensive	91	25	37.8
Baltimore			
Entry-level	108	−52	−32.4
Knowledge-intensive	32	5	20.6
Boston (Suffolk County)			
Entry-level	115	−34	−22.6
Knowledge-intensive	75	19	33.3
St Louis			
Entry-level	103	−23	−18.2
Knowledge-intensive	21	−8	−26.3
Atlanta (Fulton County)			
Entry-level	136	−19	−12.1
Knowledge-intensive	41	11	35.6
Houston (Harris County)			
Entry-level	457	194	73.8
Knowledge-intensive	152	83	119.4
Denver			
Entry-level	110	14	14.5
Knowledge-intensive	44	21	91.4
San Francisco			
Entry-level	142	13	10.2
Knowledge-intensive	65	21	46.8

[a] Entry-level industries are those where mean schooling completed by employees is less than 12 years; knowledge-intensive industries are those where mean schooling completed is more than 14 years.
Sources: US Bureau of the Census, *Current Population Survey* tape, March 1982, and *County Business Patterns*, 1970, 1980. Figures are rounded. (Compiled and adapted by Kasarda, "Urban change and minority opportunities")

only 5.4 percent and 9.2 percent. Of these black males not in the labor force and not in school, 40 percent were on welfare, with the proportion increasing to 82 percent for black females. Central cities in the largest metropolitan areas host the majority of the growth in highly paid jobs, while they come to be inhabited mainly by an ethnic-minority population which is increasingly inadequate to fill these jobs. The dual city, manifested in the spatial coexistence of a large sector of professional and managerial middle-class with a growing urban underclass, epitomizes the contradictory development of the new informational economy, and the conflictual appropriation of the inner city by social groups who share the same space while being worlds apart in terms of lifestyle and structural position in society.

Yet while the mismatching thesis underlines a fundamental trend of the new urban social structure, it has some serious methodological and theoretical shortcomings, as has been argued by Norman Fainstein.[9] It also fails to explain why there has been substantial growth in job creation in general, including low-paying jobs, in the largest inner cities, particularly during the 1980s. Indeed, after the 1980–2 recession, unemployment has steadily reduced in most inner cities, even for ethnic minorities, although it remains very high for the youth of these minorities. Moreover, this increasing employment rate has taken place in a context where hundreds of thousands of new immigrants have arrived in the metropolitan labor markets, attracted in particular to the booming economies of New York and California.

There are in fact four distinct, though inter-related, processes at work here:

1. The decline of some industries and the increasing obsolescence of a segment of semi-skilled labor that is being expelled from the labor force.
2. The dynamism of two macro-sectors, one in advanced services and the other in high-technology industries, both of which also include a substantial number of low-paid, low-skill jobs, such as janitors, low-level secretaries, assembly workers.
3. The growth of new, downgraded manufacturing activities, many of them informal, which recycle some of the surplus labor expelled from the declining sectors, while incorporating some of the new immigrants, particularly women.
4. The expansion of informal and semi-formal service activities spurred on by the overall economic dynamism. These service activities, many of them in consumer services, provided numerous jobs for immigrants, ethnic minorities and women.

This is the analysis put forward by a number of scholars, most notably by Saskia Sassen, in an interpretation that links the thesis of polarization of the occupational structure with the process of restructuring of capital–labor relationships.[10] In this perspective, the dual city is not simply the urban social structure resulting from the juxtaposition of the rich and the poor, the yuppies and the homeless, but the result of simultaneous and articulated processes of growth and decline. Furthermore, according to Sassen's analysis, growth occurs at the same time in the formal and in the informal sectors of the economy, at the top and at the bottom of the newly dynamic industrial sectors, and affects both skilled and unskilled labor, although in segmented labor markets that cater variously to the specific requirements of each segment of capital invested in the different sectors of the local economy. From this follows a highly differentiated social structure, both polarized and fragmented, with segments divided on the basis of class, gender, race, and national origin. Some of the labor surplus is recycled in the dynamic structure of the new informational economy, while the rest leaves the formal labor force, to be distributed among the recipients of welfare, the informal economy, and the criminal economy. This new social dynamics has profound consequences on the spatial organization and processes of the large metropolitan areas. However, since the complexity of these processes makes the analysis hardly comprehensible at a high level of generality, I will introduce here a summary account of the transformation of the urban social structure of New York and Los Angeles in order to clarify the precise meaning of the rise of the dual city as the new urban form linked to the overall process of techno-economic restructuring.

New York, New York! Dreams and nightmares of the restructuring process

After its dramatic fiscal crisis in 1975–7, New York City bounced back in one of the most spectacular cases of local economic development in recent history.[11] In the decade 1977–87, the city added 400,000 new jobs in an expansion interrupted only by the nationwide recession of 1981–2.[12] Of these jobs, 342,000 were in the private sector, with finance, insurance, real estate, and business services accounting for about 70 percent of new job creation. These industries employed in 1987 664,000 workers, amounting to about one-fifth of all private jobs. At the same time, the building boom linked to the upgraded residences for the professional labor force, generated about 64,000 new construction jobs. In addition, growing local revenues and the political needs of the city's patronage system restored, selectively, public services and service jobs, so that by December 1987 local government employment, including education, had risen to 450,000 jobs. However, this process of growth and job creation went hand in hand with a dramatic restructuring process, both among industries and in the labor market. While 153 industries experienced growth in the city in 1977–86, a greater number, 207, actually declined. Most of this decline took place in manufacturing, which shrank in absolute numbers from 539,000 jobs in 1977 to 396,000 in 1986, representing in the latter year slightly over 11 percent of the total labor force (see figure 7.1). In fact, in the 1980s, New York City lost manufacturing jobs at three

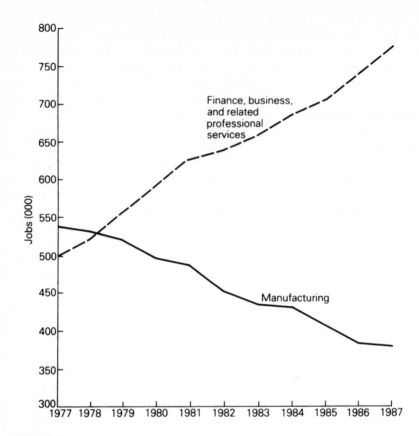

Figure 7.1   Payroll employment in manufacturing and finance, business and related professional services, New York City, 1977–1987
Source: Ehrenhalt, "New York City"

times the national rate of decline. Furthermore, in the 1982–7 period, the US economy recovered about half the manufacturing jobs lost during the 1980–2 recession, but New York lost an additional 100,000 factory jobs in these years with the greatest losses concentrated in apparel, miscellaneous manufacturing and electrical–electronic equipment, and the bulk of them being unskilled and semi-skilled jobs. On the other hand, about half of the new jobs were in professional, managerial, and technical positions. As a result, the overall occupational composition of the labor force in New York City has been upgraded. Executives and managers accounted for 11.7 percent of the labor force in 1983 and 13.3 percent in 1986, while the proportion of professionals also increased from 13.9 percent in 1983 to 15.8 percent in 1986. Including technicians, the upper level of the occupational structure in 1986

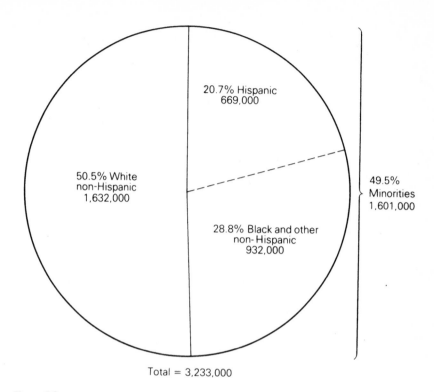

20.7% Hispanic
669,000

50.5% White
non-Hispanic
1,632,000

49.5%
Minorities
1,601,000

28.8% Black and other
non-Hispanic
932,000

Total = 3,233,000

Figure 7.2   Estimated distribution of the New York City resident labor force by race and Hispanic origin, 1987
Source: Ehrenhalt, "New York City"

accounted for 31.3 percent of the total labor force, establishing as a fundamental presence a large group of professional labor that possesses the purchasing power, the demographic weight, and the educational skills to dominate the city economically, culturally, and politically.

This trend is in direct conflict with the changing composition of the New York City population, characterized by a growing proportion of minimally educated minorities, and recent immigrants whose education is hardly marketable in the US. The overall drop-out rate in the city's high schools reached a staggering 37 percent in 1987, 80 percent of which appears to concern ethnic minorities (if we extrapolate the 1980 data for the 16–19 age group). The mismatching of skills is particularly striking in the case of New York. On the one hand, for the American labor force as a whole, one or two years in college seems increasingly to be the norm for obtaining a job: the proportion of the labor force with some college attendance in 1987 stood at 46 percent, double that of 1970, and it continues to rise. On the other hand, ethnic

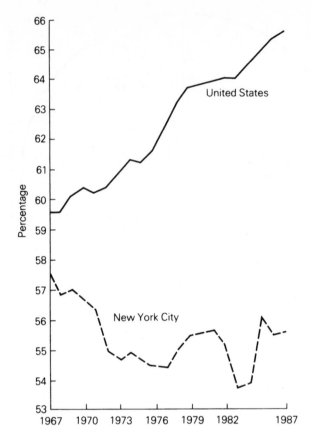

Figure 7.3   Labor force participation rates, United States and New York City, 1967–1987 (total, age 16 years and over)
Source: Ehrenhalt, "New York City"

minorities seem to have accounted for most of the net labor force growth in the 1977–87 period and are projected to continue to do so for most of the net increase in New York City's labor force in the 1990s. They accounted in 1987 for 49.5 percent of the total labor force (see figure 7.2); yet at the same time they exhibit the highest school drop-out rates, and are exposed to the declining quality of the spatially segregated public school system.

Mismatching and racial discrimination in the labor market result in a substantially above-average unemployment level for ethnic minorities, even in the context of sustained economic expansion in the 1980s. In New York in 1987, unemployment levels were 3.1 percent for non-Hispanic whites and 8.5 percent for ethnic minorities. A more important phenomenon, likely to be linked to the inappropriateness of the new labor demand for the urban labor supply, is the low rate of labor-force participation in New York, ten points below the national average, with the disparity increasing over the past 20 years (see figure 7.3). According to Samuel M. Ehrenhalt, New York Regional Commissioner for the Bureau of Labor Statistics: "It would take something on the order of a half million more New Yorkers in the labor force to lift the New York participation rate to the national average. This points to a considerable job deficit in the local economy and a substantial number of New Yorkers outside the mainstream."[13]

Nevertheless, a great number of jobs have been created, as indicated, showing the strength and the vitality of the new economy. Indeed, most of the ethnic minorities, including recent immigrants, have improved their relative position in the economy.[14] However, this is partly a mere statistical construct: a growing economy, creating a large number of office and service jobs in a context of increasing representation of ethnic minorities in the labor market, must necessarily include a higher proportion of minorities in the new service jobs. Yet the tendencies toward polarization described in the preceding sections of this chapter are reflected in an ethnically and gender segregated occupational structure in the new labor force of New York City, as can be seen in the data calculated by John Mollenkopf detailing occupational position by gender and by ethnic group for 1980. As an illustration of these trends, table 7.2 has been constructed on the basis of Mollenkopf's data. Three occupational positions have been selected representative respectively of the top of the occupational scale (managers), of the middle to low position in services (clerical), and of the low-skill manual workers (operatives). For each position, an elementary scale has been built, taking as its zero level the proportion of WASP (white Anglo-Saxon Protestant) males who hold such occupational positions (as a percentage of overall employed WASP males). The difference has been simply calculated in percentage points between the proportion of WASP males in a given occupational position and the corresponding proportion for each ethnic/gender group. Obviously, positive signs indicate over-representation, while negative signs indicate under-representation. Without going into the details of the table, it can be observed that, for managers, Jewish males and WASP males are over-represented, while all women and ethnic minorities are under-represented, with ethnic-minority women being in the most disadvantaged position.

One apparent anomaly merits explanation: Chinese males are over-represented among the managers, even overtaking WASP males. An analysis of the sectoral distribution of Chinese male workers, provided by Mollenkopf's database, dissipates the myth of the Chinese male "already making it in corporate business": 51 percent of Chinese male workers are in "restaurants, hotels, and bars," and thus, they are "managers" of their community-based restaurants. As for employed Chinese women, 67.3 percent are manufacturing workers.

Table 7.2   Ethnic composition of occupations in New York City, 1980, by gender (differences in percentage points between proportion of WASPs in each occupational group and proportion of each ethnic group in the same occupation)

	Occupation				
Ethnicity	Managers and professionals	Managers	Clerical	Operatives	% of male/ female population
Male					
WASP	0.0	0.0	0.0	0.0	2.15
Jewish	+6.0	+1.5	−1.5	−5.9	4.29
Italian	−5.9	−3.1	−1.5	+6.3	16.90
Irish	−5.9	−3.3	+0.9	+2.1	8.18
Black (NY)	−5.9	−4.1	+4.5	+6.1	11.35
Jamaican	−8.4	−4.7	−2.9	+6.5	2.38
Puerto Rican	−10.3	−4.2	−6.5	+14.1	10.46
Dominican	−13.6	−6.2	−10.1	+20.2	3.23
Chinese	−0.6	+0.6	−11.3	−2.6	2.58
Female					
WASP		−2.8	+28.3	−12.3	2.35
Jewish		−3.4	+30.3	−7.7	5.56
Italian		−4.9	+32.4	−14.1	16.14
Irish		−4.2	+33.8	−15.0	9.56
Black (NY)		−5.2	+26.1	−10.0	14.08
Jamaican		−7.7	+9.6	−12.2	3.68
Puerto Rican		−7.7	+7.7	+18.7	8.67
Dominican		−9.5	−6.3	+39.7	3.85
Chinese		−5.4	−6.3	+37.9	2.52

Source: 1980 US Census Public Use Microdata Sample, calculated by John Mollenkopf and elaborated by the author

Concerning clerical work, women in general, but particularly Caucasian women, are overwhelmingly over-represented, while recent immigrant, non-English-speaking women are, as one might expect, under-represented. As for operatives, recent immigrants, both male and, even more, female, are concentrated in these jobs, sharing the joys of industrial working-class life in the informational city with the remnants of Italian, Irish, and black workers in the restructured manufacturing sector. Overall, groups privileged by gender and ethnic background (translated into higher education) occupy the top of the hierarchy; women form the bulk of the new white-collar working class of the service economy; and recent immigrants, along with Puerto Ricans, assume the new positions in downgraded manufacturing and low-skill consumer services. To complete our picture of the emerging occupational structure we should add the expansion of new retail commerce (neighbourhood grocery stores, for example) on the basis of recent immigrants (Koreans, Indians, Chinese), and the growing concentration of blacks in public services: New York blacks in government services (17.1 percent of black males work in public services), and West Indian blacks in health services (11.4 percent of Jamaican males and 29.9 percent of Jamaican females work in health services).

Although the only empirical way of assessing rigorously the polarization of New York City's occupational structure would be to undertake an analysis of income and educational levels for each occupation and industry (which are not available in the published information), the existing data together with most of the specialized research literature on the subject all seem to indicate that the process of growth during the 1980s has generated, at the same time, a significant segment of well-paid professionals and technical jobs, a mass of low-paid, semi-skilled clerical jobs for women, and an insufficient but growing number of low-paid jobs for ethnic minorities and immigrants both in downgraded manufacturing and miscellaneous services.[15]

An important element in connecting the new dynamism of the New York economy and the restructuring of labor is the growth of the informal economy. Saskia Sassen has investigated this topic over several years, combining secondary data analysis, ethnographic research, and interviews with key informants.[16] Without being able to estimate the overall size of the phenomenon, in terms of either regional GDP or employment, she has found enough evidence to indicate that it is a sizeable economic reality and one that is rapidly expanding to become an indispensable element of the local economy as well as of New Yorkers' way of life. Much of these informal income-generating activities concern manufacturing, particularly in apparel, footwear, toys, sporting goods, and electronic components and accessories. For instance, she reports estimates by labor unions that in 1981 there were in New York about 3,000 sweatshops in the garment industry, employing about 50,000 workers, with a further 10,000 workers doing home work in garments. She also reports, on the basis of data provided by the New York State Labor Department and the Industrial Board of Appeals, considerable informal sub-contracting work in the electronics industry, working out of "garage-shops" and "basement-fronts." She observed that while the furniture industry lost 9 percent of its registered labor between 1982 and 1987, at the same time a number of furniture-making shops were opening in areas that were not zoned for this kind of work, such as Ridgewood Astoria in Queens, and Williamsburg in Brooklyn. In addition, construction work on a small scale is also predominantly informal: Sassen estimates that about 90 percent of all interior remodeling in New York is done without a building permit, by craft workers and contractors who are not registered, most of them recent immigrants. "Gypsy cabs" have taken over the transportation business to the numerous areas of the City where regular cabs refuse to go.[17]

The development of the informal economy is connected to two broader trends of which it is an essential, though certainly not a unique, component. The first of these is the downgrading of manufacturing, with the phasing out or relocation of traditional manufacturing activities, for instance in the garment industry, while low-labour-cost, largely unregulated operations open up in New York to cater to the booming retail market represented by the largest and probably most demanding market in the world. Secondly, there is an explosion in customized services, from gourmet grocery stores to laundry and housekeeping, linked to the new lifestyles of the substantial segment of the population made up of professionals and managers, either single or dual-income households, with little time but high purchasing power and increasingly sophisticated tastes (or, at least, with the idea of being sophisticated, and the desire to become so). As Sassen argues, the new consumption pattern, shifting from middle-level suburban families to high-level urbanite professionals, represents a shift from capital-intensive consumer goods to labor-intensive consumer services, thus stimulating a very large labor demand for customized services, both in high-skill occupations (fashion design, *chefs de cuisine*, in-house "artists") and low-skill occupations ("24-hour tailors," waiters, drivers, security guards).[18] While many of these jobs are by no means part of the informal economy, their definition and their working conditions are usually on the border-line, being extremely flexible, and making part-time, overtime, one-time service, and sub-contracting, the working rule rather than the exception. Hence the polarization and segmentation of an increasing pool of activities, and therefore of labor, on the vibrant New York scene.

A largely unexplored segment of New York's economy is linked to booming criminal activities, particularly related to the drug traffic. While these activities do generate income and a kind of employment for some sectors of the ghetto population, particularly for drop-out youths, they are not limited to the underclass. In fact, the money-laundering activities that are a substantial part of the drug economy lie behind the flourishing of many ephemeral businesses, from restaurants to art galleries, that blossom and disappear in the space of a few months, creating and then destroying a number of jobs that are as ephemeral as their source. Ironically, these money-laundering processes epitomize the oft-praised flexibility of the new economy. While the role of the criminal economy must not be exaggerated, it is important to keep in mind its existence, which adds to the complexity of the overall restructuring process.[19]

The informal economy, and more generally the new flexibility of labor relationships, have greatly contributed to the opening up of job opportunities for the new wave of immigration that has hit New York since the late 1970s, ranking it with Los Angeles and Miami as the most ethnically diverse metropolises in the world. In 1980, 24 percent of New Yorkers were foreign-born (excluding of course Puerto Ricans who are US citizens), and this proportion is predicted to rise to about one-third of the resident population by 1990. Most of these foreign-born residents are recent entrants, a substantial proportion of whom are undocumented.[20] It is estimated that there are about 350,000 Asians (Chinese, Koreans, Vietnamese, Cambodians, Indians), at least 400,000 Dominicans (the largest recent group of immigrants to New York), about 500,000 West Indians, about 250,000 non-Puerto Rican Hispanics (from Colombia, Mexico, Ecuador, Peru, etc.), over 200,000 Europeans (most of them Russian Jews and Italians), and a large number of Arabs, particularly from Egypt and the Lebanon. While living conditions are very harsh for most of the immigrants, particularly for those from Latin America and the Caribbean, they have succeeded in integrating themselves into the labor market, generally in the entry-level jobs, although some groups with financial and educational resources have established small businesses in a number of sectors (for example, middle-class Koreans in the grocery business, Indians in the newspaper stands).[21] Bailey and Waldinger have shown how the living conditions of these immigrants improve in the context of an expanding local economy, sometimes exceeding the achievements of local young blacks and New York Puerto Ricans.[22] However, a number of indications point to the fact that racial discrimination and class barriers are likely to prevent these immigrant families attaining social mobility on a similar level to the non-WASP Caucasian immigrants of former generations, with the potential exception of some middle-class groups, particularly among the Koreans and Chinese.[23] In fact, instead of witnessing the expansion of an informal economy, or of flexible manufacturing and customized services, as a consequence of the drive and entrepreneurialism of the new immigrants, we observe the opposite phenomenon: the new economy, with its flexibility and its polarized occupational structure, has been able to integrate an immigrant labor force that because of its greater vulnerability, linked to racial, class, and language discrimination, and often to its uncertain legal status, is ready to accept working conditions that American workers, including native ethnic minorities, do not accept or are not trusted to accede to by their employers. The new immigration provides the labor supply necessary for the restructuring of labor implicit in the polarized occupational structure of the information economy.

The process of labor restructuring in New York, proceeding along the lines presented, has specified spatial manifestations. As Saskia Sassen writes:

> These processes can be seen as distinct modes of economic organization and their corresponding uses of space: the postindustrial city of luxury high-rise office and residential buildings located largely in Manhattan; the old dying industrial city of low-rise buildings and family type houses, located largely in the outer-boroughs; and the Third World city imported via immigration and lo-

Table 7.3 Occupational specialization of the resident labor force in the New York metropolitan region, 1950, 1970, and 1980

Specialization index (NYMR = 100)

Occupation	Manhattan			Rest of core			Inner Ring			Outer Ring		
	1950	1970	1980	1950	1970	1980	1950	1970	1980	1950	1970	1980
Managers	93	112	127	93	77	76	122	120	109	84	114	106
Professionals	128	148	163	82	79	74	113	106	99	106	120	107
Clerical	95	94	82	115	117	122	90	90	96	72	74	85
Sales	93	90	94	104	91	87	102	113	109	88	107	106
Crafts	57	50	43	102	101	96	107	107	103	127	128	119
Operatives	94	77	74	104	114	116	92	96	94	109	83	98
Laborers	92	67	57	94	109	117	99	100	100	133	102	94
Service	190	130	105	84	102	116	81	88	90	93	100	94

Source: Hoover and Vernon, *Anatomy of a Metropolis*, 1962, p.148: Kamer, "The changing spatial relationship between residence and workplaces in the New York metropolitan region," 1977, pp. 448–9; calculated from US Bureau of the Census, *General Social and Economic Characteristics*, Connecticut, New Jersey and New York, table 177 by Richard Harris, "Home and work in New York since 1950"

cated in dense groupings spread all over the city . . . Each of these three processes can be seen to contain distinct income occupational structures and concomitant residential and consumption patterns, well captured in the expansion
of a new urban gentry alongside expanding immigrant communities.[24]

Richard Harris has proceeded to a systematic analysis of the spatial differentiation of the New York metropolitan area as an expression of the tendencies
toward class, race, and gender polarization in the occupational structure.[25] His
data show an increasing functional specialization of the area, with advanced
services concentrated in Manhattan, the rest of the core specializing in transportation and public administration, and the inner and outer rings absorbing a
growing proportion of manufacturing and retailing. In terms of residence, table
7.3 shows the dramatic trend toward the concentration in Manhattan of managers and professionals, while clericals and the lower occupational groups are
over-represented in the inner city outside Manhattan, and the inner and outer
rings oscillate moderately around the average, with a slight over-representation
of managers and of the middle strata, together with an under-representation of
the new and old working classes (clerical, operatives, and laborers). This occupational differentiation of residential patterns is reinforced by distinct lifestyles
derived from different household structures. Thus, while the suburbs continue
to be based on a typical nuclear family, in Manhattan the average household
size (1.7) is lower than in any other country. This single or childless way of life
characterizes the consumption patterns and the cultural models of the new
professional elite in world cities such as New York.

In terms of income, the core of the city exhibits an interesting bimodal
pattern, with the resident population of Manhattan concentrated in the highest and lowest strata of income distribution (see figure 7.4). This stratification
pattern is in contrast to that prevailing in the other spatial components of the
metropolitan area, as can also be observed from the data displayed in figure
7.4. The outer boroughs of the inner city contain a high concentration of low-
income population, while the inner ring is biased toward the upper segments
of the distribution, and the outer ring is the closest to the average of the
overall income distribution. Thus, there is at the same time intra-metropolitan segregation by income (the suburbs being the privileged space), and intra-
urban residential segregation within Manhattan, which hosts both the highest
income group and some of the poorest sectors of the population. Ethnic
residential segregation closely follows this general pattern, with blacks being
the most concentrated and segregated social group, followed by Hispanics.
Immigrants of different ethnic groups find their interstitial space either as
microcommunities within large segregated areas of other ethnic minorities, or
in enclaves inside the predominantly white city, in a symbiotic relationship
that is more successful when they provide services to the higher-income resident population.

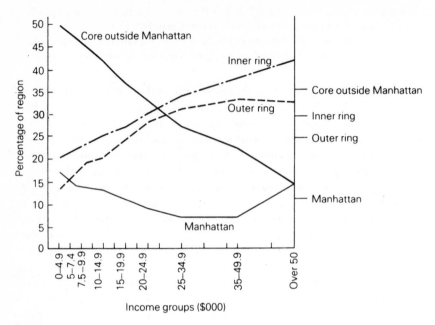

Figure 7.4   Geographical distribution of households by income, New York metropolitan region, 1979
Source: Harris, "Home and work in New York since 1950"

However, the spatial coexistence of very different social groups in an increasingly valuable space in most of Manhattan is increasingly challenged by the skyrocketing of real estate prices and the increasing functional and social attraction of the central urban space for the professional–managerial segment, representing close to one-third of the employed population. The consequent process of widespread gentrification is gradually, but surely, changing the social characteristics of residential space in the inner city, further segregating social groups and pushing the ethnic minorities into increasingly secluded areas, such as Harlem and the south Bronx. Old white ethnic neighborhoods barricade themselves, against both the threat of minorities and their risk of displacement.[26] The urban dynamics resulting from these conflictual processes is characterized both by territorial defensiveness and increasing social and ethnic homogenization of specific neighborhoods. The dual city is a shared space within which the contradictory spheres of the local society are constantly trying to differentiate their territories.

Richard Harris concludes his study on the spatial differentiation of New York with a statement relevant to the present analysis:

The restructuring of New York's economy in the past thirty years has created greater inequality. The contrasts between rich and poor neighborhoods have become greater. Different parts of the metropolitan area have been affected in different ways, and the City most of all. The loss of manufacturing jobs has had greatest impact upon the boroughs while office growth has been especially important in Manhattan. The changing geography of employment has shaped the emerging social geography of the metropolitan area. Substantial parts of Manhattan have been gentrified, while most areas in the boroughs have suffered a decline. In the process, a new and larger pattern of contrasts between Manhattan, the boroughs, and the outer suburban rings has emerged . . . Many kinds of informal work have grown up to serve local needs. In the South Bronx this informal work means survival; in the SoHo it means a fashionable way of life; in new ethnic communities scattered throughout the city it helps people to build a home away from home . . . Life on Long Island or in Fairfield County, as in any American suburbs, depends on a good deal of unpaid domestic labor. But Manhattan, with its towers of apartments and condominiums, more than any place in the continent, is designed to minimize anything but paid work. In this manner, the homes and workplaces of New York together constitute a complex geography of work that embodies the continuing polarities of class and gender, ethnicity and race.[27]

The characterization of New York as a dual city does not simply mean that opposition between executive limousines and homeless people: more fundamentally, it represents an urban social structure that exists on the basis of interaction between opposite and equally dynamic poles of the new informational economy, whose developmental logic polarizes society, segments social groups, isolates cultures, and segregates the uses of a shared space.

The last urban frontier: the restructuring of Los Angeles

Nowhere is the process of urban restructuring more completely manifested than in Los Angeles, the city where, in the image suggested by its urban analyst, Edward Soja, "it all comes together," as in Borges' Aleph.[28] Like New York, in the past two decades Los Angeles has become a leading financial and business center at the international level, second only to New York in the US, constituting itself the corporate hub for trade and investment in the Pacific Basin.[29] In fact, trans-Pacific trade has surpassed trans-Atlantic trade for the US, and almost half of its volume is concentrated on the LA ports of San Pedro and Long Beach. Around this core of internationally oriented corporate services, and a still buoyant entertainment and media industry, a number of producer and consumer services have clustered, leading to a spectacular office boom which, together with the residential demand generated by rapid growth in jobs and residents, has fueled one of the largest and most profitable real estate markets in the country.

In addition to this development of advanced services, and in contrast to New York, Los Angeles' manufacturing sector also expanded dramatically during the 1970s and 1980s, to become, in 1984, the largest manufacturing center in the US, in terms of the absolute number of manufacturing jobs in the greater Los Angeles area. This is in sharp contrast with the popular image of Los Angeles as the postindustrial city. Indeed, Los Angeles saw the creation of 250,000 manufacturing jobs in the 1940s, of another 400,000 in the 1950s, of 200,000 in the 1960s, and, in the 1970s, at a moment of slow manufacturing growth in the US, of another 225,000 manufacturing jobs, almost a quarter of total US manufacturing job creation during the decade. The newest manufacturing growth is based on two very different sectors: on the one hand, aerospace and defense-oriented electronics, constituting a booming high-technology sector, concentrated around Los Angeles International Airport and in Orange County [. . .]; and on the other hand, consumer goods, particularly garments and apparel, which account for about 125,000 manufacturing jobs that are low-paid and frequently filled by immigrant women, most of them undocumented. At the same time, as shown by Soja, Morales, and Wolff in their pioneering study on the restructuring of Los Angeles, traditional manufacturing has been phased out. Los Angeles, once boasting the second largest concentration of automobile assembly industries, in the 1980s lost all its automobile factories but one.[30] The city's entire rubber industry, also the second largest US concentration after Akron, also disappeared in the late 1970s. In the 1978–82 period alone 70,000 manufacturing jobs were lost, three-quarters of them in the auto, tire, steel, and civilian aircraft sectors.

The labor force of Los Angeles has altered correspondingly. Unionized labor has been substantially reduced during the 1980s: in Los Angeles County the level of unionization in manufacturing dropped from 30 percent to about 23 percent, and in Orange County from 26.4 percent to 10.5 percent. While the proportion of craft workers and operatives in the labor force substantially decreased, Los Angeles now holds the largest concentration of engineers and scientists anywhere in the US, fueled by its role as the top location, in absolute terms, for defense contracts. At the other end of the employment spectrum, as in New York, corporate services, particularly in finance and law, have created hundreds of thousands of professional and managerial jobs, while low-paid service jobs have increased by about 500,000 in the past twenty years, pushing the region's total to 5.5 million jobs in the mid-1980s.

As in New York, new immigrants to the area have filled many of the jobs in downgraded manufacturing and consumer and personal services, with probably an even greater proportion than in New York of undocumented workers, particularly from Mexico and Central America. Since the late 1960s Los Angeles has received an estimated number of over 1 million Mexicans, 300,000 Salvadoreans, 200,000 Koreans, and several additional hundreds of thousands of Chinese, Indochinese, Filipinos, Thais, Iranians, Arabs, Armenians, Guatemalans, Colombians, and Cubans, among others. Los Angeles blacks have been discriminated against in the labor market, and their levels of unemployment are often above those of the new immigrants, who are considered less threatening by employers in search of flexibility and acquiescence from a socially and politically vulnerable labor force. Soja, Morales, and Wolff report that the ghetto areas of south-central Los Angeles, including Watts, saw their social condition deteriorate during the 1970s, falling below their level of 1965 at the time of the Watts riots.

This process of economic and social restructuring is also spatially specific. While most of the plants closing were concentrated in Los Angeles County and in the Long Beach industrial area, suburban Orange County picked up most of the new, high-technology-based manufacturing development. Advanced services organized in a multinuclear urban structure in the downtown area, in the Wilshire Corridor toward the affluent Westside, and are increasingly decentralizing toward Orange County (particularly in the booming Irvine Business Complex[31], Pasadena, and Glendale-Burbank (see figure 7.5). Downgraded manufacturing clustered in whichever spaces could escape administrative controls, generally in low-income areas, such as central and east Los Angeles.

A sharply polarized labor force, with large segments of minority youth excluded from it, has led to a highly segregated residential structure, probably the most ethnically segregated of any major city in the US (only tentatively indicated in figure 7.6). Class is also a major factor in residential segregation, as is shown by the clustering of the residences of engineers displayed in figure. 7.7). An important reason for the high level of spatial segregation in Los Angeles is its extreme administrative fragmentation, for the city of Los Angeles represents a much smaller proportion than New York of its metropolitan area. The fragmentation of a very large, extremely decentralized conurbation (home to over 12 million people) makes possible a strict segregation of public services, in particular of public schools, whose quality, dependent upon local revenue per capita, is a primary factor in determining residential location for concerned middle-class parents. Interestingly enough in such a multi-ethnic local society, class is taking over from ethnicity as the primary criterion for residential segregation, although the large black and Chicano ghettos (Watts and east Los Angeles respectively) are substantially homogeneous in ethnic terms, largely because class and race reinforce each other as factors leading to the segregation of the overwhelmingly low-income black and Chicano communities.

In these ghettoized communities many youths have no prospect of making it in an upgraded economy where the low-level jobs are sought after by an increasing pool of downgraded labor coming from all horizons. In the late 1980s, with drop-out rates at an all-time high, these youths often turn to gang

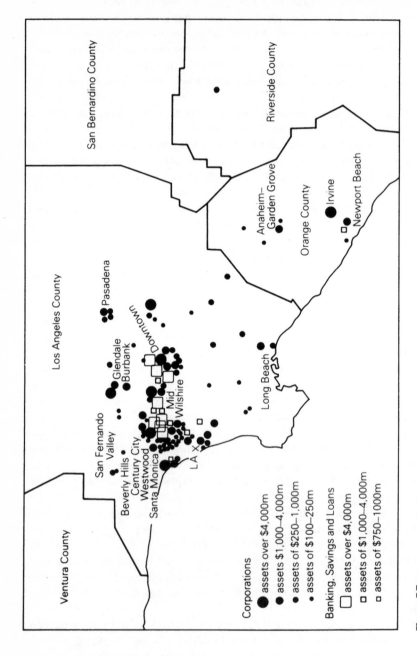

Figure 7.5 Corporate and banking headquarters in the Los Angeles region

Source: Soja, Morales, and Wolff, "Urban restructuring"

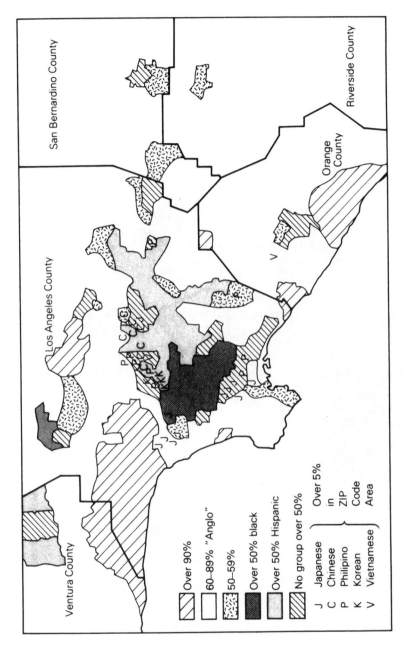

Figure 7.6 Distribution of major ethnic groups in the Los Angeles area, 1980

Source: Soja, Morales, and Wolff, "Urban restructuring"

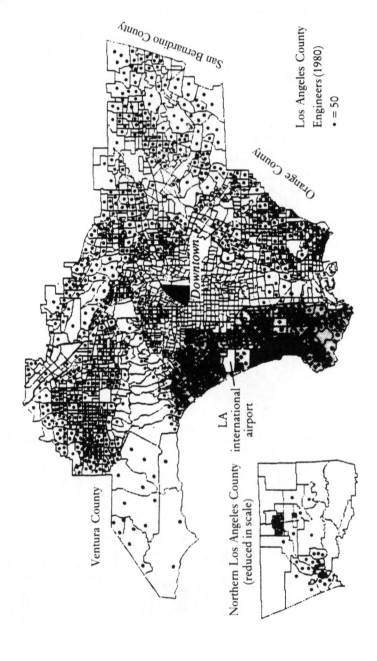

Figure 7.7 Residential location of engineers, Los Angeles County, 1980
Source: Soja, Morales, and Wolff, "Urban restructuring"

formation, most of them simply to build up networks of personal interaction and affirm their identity; too often these gangs also become vehicles for the drug trade, now a multibillion-dollar business. Some of the Los Angeles gangs have won control over national markets for the wholesale distribution of drugs. A surge of violence reminiscent of 1920s Chicago provoked in 1988 a ferocious backlash from public opinion, leading to massive raids by the police, who in several instances arrested hundreds of suspects, detaining them in the Olympic Coliseum Stadium to investigate their gang connections. The police were under instructions to arrest people who could be seen in the streets of some areas (generally in central and south Los Angeles) and who "dressed or acted as gang members."[32] Thus, the boundaries of "normality" and "abnormality" have been traced and enforced. The dual city resorts to policing entire areas of its space that appear to have been lost to social disorder. Although drug trafficking is indeed a murderous activity, the quasi-military occupation by police of large sectors of Los Angeles goes beyond the protection of public order. It indicates alienation between social groups, social norms, and spatial areas. It indicates the outer limits of the restructuring process in the last urban frontier.

The Rise of the Dual City

The dual city is a classic theme of urban sociology.[33] The contrast between opulence and poverty in a shared space has always struck scholars, as well as public opinion. Thus, the coexistence in 1980s' Los Angeles of $11 million condominium apartments, sold with a complimentary Rolls Royce, and 50,000 homeless wandering in the streets and on the beaches of the Californian dream, is but an extreme manifestation of an old urban phenomenon, probably aggravated in the 1980s by the removal of the welfare safety net in the wake of neoconservative public policies. Yet there is a new form of urban dualism on the rise, one specifically linked to the restructuring process and to the expansion of the informational economy. It relates, first of all, to the simultaneous processes of growth and decline of industries and firms, processes taking place most intensely at the nodal points in the economic geography, namely, the largest metropolitan areas where most of the knowledge-intensive activities and jobs are concentrated. This occupational transition, unlike the historical shift from agricultural to industrial societies, is characterized by a mismatching between the characteristics of labor being phased out and the requirements for new labor. This is partly due to the contradiction between the much higher knowledge components of a substantial proportion of the new occupations and the institutional capacities of most societies, and specifically of American society, to adapt the educational system and to enhance the structural conditions that give rise to a higher cultural and scientific level of labor.

Yet given that the majority of new occupations do not require sophisticated skills, most of the new characteristics looked for in labor are a function not of technological change but of social and economic restructuring. What is at stake is the dismantling of the capital–labor relationships that were institutionalized during the long, conflictual process by which industrial society was formed. The transition from industrial to informational production processes overlaps with the rise of flexible production, which, under current historical conditions, tends to be equated with de-institutionalized capital–labor relationships. There follows the general demise of traditional labor, not only in manufacturing, and the conditioning of new labor to new organizational conditions, characterized by its relentless adaptation to the needs of firms and agencies as perceived by management, generally under the rule of market logic. Growth and decline do not compensate each other, as they did during the transition toward the industrial society. Part of the new potential labor force, especially among ethnic minority youth, is not integrated into the new labor market, and becomes surplus population. The majority of labor is restructured, both by the imposition upon it of new working conditions, generally in a different sector of activity, and by changing the characteristics of the labor pool itself, increasing the proportion of women, immigrants, and ethnic minorities in the labor force, taking advantage of the greater social vulnerability of these groups in a social context of gender and racial discrimination. Nevertheless, a significant proportion of labor, recruited from the better educated social groups, is upgraded in skills and social status, and becomes the backbone of the new informational economy, both in advanced services and in high-technology manufacturing. The differential reassignment of labor in the process of simultaneous growth and decline results in a sharply stratified, segmented social structure that differentiates between upgraded labor, downgraded labor, and excluded people. Dualism refers here both to the contradictory dynamics of growth and decline, and to the polarizing and exclusionary effects of these dynamics.

The new dual city can also be seen as the urban expression of the process of increasing differentiation of labor in two equally dynamic sectors within the growing economy: the information-based formal economy, and the downgraded labor-based informal economy. The latter is a highly dynamic, growth-oriented, and often very profitable sector, whose reality is far distant from the survival activities with which it has generally been associated. The informal economy cannot be equated with urban poverty, and in this sense urban dualism does not pertain to the realm of social stratification but to a new socio-economic structure characterized by the different growth dynamics of two distinct, though articulated components. What differentiates the two sectors, as argued in chapter [6 of this volume], is the breakdown of state intermediation between capital and labor, resulting in different production relationships, and ultimately in different characteristics of labor, either because it was molded to the requirements of unregulated relationships or because it was selected (or self-selected) in the first place on the basis of its malleability to new working conditions. The widespread observation concerning the entrepreneurialism of the new immigrants fits this model, but so does the adaptation of clerical women to higher skilled jobs at lower rates of pay and without job security, on a part-time basis and without a contract. The informal economy, being concentrated in the largest and most dynamic metropolitan areas, particularly in the central cities, also contributes to the new urban dualism; two equally dynamic sectors, interconnected by a number of symbiotic relationships, define specific labor markets and labor processes in such a way that the majority of workers are unlikely to move upwardly between them. The economy, and thus society, becomes functionally articulated but organizationally and socially segmented.

A third major process of dualization concerns the polarized occupational structure within the rising sectors of advanced services and high technology, with its impact on a stratification system; because of the shrinkage of its middle levels, the system appears to be less open to occupational mobility than in the recent past. Given the relatively large proportion of labor in the upper levels of the occupational structure, the higher levels of the society are no more a secluded elite inevitably forced to interact with the overwhelming majority of the society, but can be functionally and socially self-contained, while the lower tier loses the attraction of the social role model provided by the higher social strata because the privileges, skills, and values of the upper-level, professional class seem to be unreachable for most of the semi-skilled labor force.

Thus the non-complementary processes of informational growth and industrial decline, the downgrading and upgrading of labor, the differentiation between the formal and the informal sectors, and the polarization of the occupational structure in the new industries, together produce a highly differentiated labor force that crystallizes in very distinct lifestyles in terms of household structure, inter-gender family relationships, and uses of the urban space. In fact, structural dualism, along the series of dimensions we have indicated, does not result in two social worlds, but in a variety of social universes whose fundamental characteristics are their fragmentation, the sharp definition of their boundaries, and the low level of communication with other such universes. The dual city is a multifaceted reality, but structural dualism manifests itself in the transformation of bipolar dialectics into dual dichotomies. It is in this sense, and only in this sense, that we can speak of dualism.

Structural positions in the relationship of production and distribution crystallize in lifestyles that become less and less communicable, as they presuppose radically different financial means and cultural skills, and so lead to the formation of micro-societies through the patterning of space. Residential areas become exclusionary devices where the dynamics of real estate costs tend to impose social homogeneity, both in terms of class and in terms of ethnicity. The adaptation of a desirable space historically occupied by ethnic minorities or working-class families to its new privileged status as residential location for the new urbanites of the informational society takes place through systematic gentrification and displacement that further segregates the city. What results is a spatial structure that combines segregation, diversity, and hierarchy. The upper tier of the society, mostly white, and largely male-dominated, either by single men or through patriarchal relationships, occupies select spaces, both in the inner core and in exclusive suburbs, and maintains them in a separate circuit of lifestyle, services, and leisure, increasingly protected by both public and private security forces. The vast majority of downgraded workers and new laborers share an excluded space that is highly fragmented, mainly in ethnic terms, building defensive communities that fight each other to win a greater share of services, and to preserve the territorial basis of their social networks, a major resource for low-income communities. Downgraded areas of the city serve as refuges for the criminal segment of the informal economy, as well as reservations for displaced labor, barely maintained on welfare. Newcomers to the dual city often pioneer transformations of these areas, increasing the tension between conflicting social interests and values expressed in territorial terms. On the other hand, a large proportion of the population, made up of low-level labor forming the legions of clerical and service workers of the informational economy, insert themselves into microspaces, individualizing their relationship to the city, which becomes reduced, in their living experience, to a tenuous connection between home and work, in the vain hope of not being whirled into the changing dynamics of community structuration and destructuration. Structural dualism leads at the same time to spatial segregation and to spatial segmentation, to sharp differentiation between the upper level of the informational society and the rest of the local residents as well as to endless segmentation and frequent opposition among the many components of restructured and destructured labor.

The territorially based institutional fragmentation of local governments and of schools reproduces these cleavages along the lines of spatial segregation. Since educational and cultural capacity are key elements in labor performance in the informational economy, the system is largely self-reproductive, unless modified by social protest and/or deliberate political intervention.

The social universe of these different worlds is also characterized by differential exposure to information flows and communication patterns. The space of the upper tier is usually connected to global communication and to vast networks of exchange, open to messages and experiences that embrace the entire world. At the other end of the spectrum, segmented local networks, often ethnically based, rely on their identity as the most valuable resource to defend their interests, and ultimately their being.[34] So the segregation of space in one case (for the large social elite) does not lead to seclusion, except regarding communication with the other components of the shared urban area;

while segregation and segmentation for defensive communities of ethnic minorities, workers, and immigrants do reinforce the tendency to shrink the world to their specific culture and their local experience, penetrated only by standardized television images, and mythically connected, in the case of immigrants, to tales of the homeland. The dual city opposes, in traditional sociological terms, the cosmopolitanism of the new informational producers to the localism of the segmented sectors of restructured labor.

The series of processes I have shown to be linked to the spatial dimension of labor restructuring in the informational economy converge toward a fundamental outcome of the dual city: its role in restructuring and destructuring social class formation. On the one hand, the recycling, downgrading, and conditioning of labor leads to the configuration of a number of territorially segregated, culturally segmented, socially discriminated communities that cannot constitute a class because of their extremely different positions in the new production relationships, reflected and amplified in their territorial differentiation in the city. On the other hand, a large proportion of the population (between one-fourth and one-third in the largest metropolitan areas) holds the strategic position of information producers in the new economy, enjoys a high cultural and educational level, is correspondingly rewarded in income and status within the stratification system, and controls the key to political decision-making in terms of its social influence and organizational capacity. This new professional-managerial class, that by and large is white-dominated and male-dominated, is spatially organized, in terms of residence, work, and consumption activities, and tends to appropriate an increasingly exclusive space on the basis of a real estate market that makes location in that space a most valuable asset. This social group is not a ruling class in the traditional sense. It is a hegemonic social class that does not necessarily rule the state but fundamentally shapes civil society. The spatial articulation of its functional role and its cultural values in a very specific space, concentrated in privileged neighborhoods of nodal urban areas, provides both the visibility and the material conditions for its articulation as a hegemonic actor. In contrast, the endless social and spatial fragmentation of the diversified segments of restructured labor at the lower level fixes their cultural and territorial identities in terms irreducible to other experiences, breaking down the pattern of social communication with other communities and among different positions in the work process. And this is probably the essence of the dual city in our society: an urban form that articulates the rise of the new socially dominant category in the informational mode of development, while disarticulating and opposing the fragments of destructured labor as well as the components of the new labor incorporated into the emerging economic structure. The fundamental contemporary meaning of the dual city refers to the process of spatial restructuring through which distinct segments of labor are included in and excluded from the making of new history.

NOTES

1 Larry Sawers and William K. Tabb (eds), *Sunbelt/Snowbelt: Urban Development and Regional Restructuring* (New York: Oxford University Press, 1984).
2 Joe Feagin and Michael Smith (eds), *The Capitalist City* (Oxford: Blackwell, 1986).
3 Diana Dillaway, "The politics of restructuring in a declining city: Buffalo, NY," unpublished master's thesis, Berkeley, University of California, 1987.
4 William Wilson, "The urban underclass in advanced industrial society," in Paul E. Peterson (ed.), *The New Urban Reality* (Washington, DC: Brookings Institution, 1985).
5 Thierry Noyelle and Thomas J. Stanback, *The Economic Transformation of American Cities* (Totowa, NJ: Rowman and Allanheld, 1984).
6 B. Bluestone and B. Harrison, *The Deindustrialization of America* (New York: Basic Books, 1982).
7 John D. Kasarda, "Urban change and minority opportunities," in Paul Peterson (ed.), *The New Urban Reality* (Washington, DC: Brookings Institution, 1985).
8 Ibid., p. 57.
9 Norman Fainstein, "The underclass/mismatch hypothesis as an explanation for black economic deprivation," *Politics and Society*, 15(4) (1986–7), pp. 403–51.
10 Saskia Sassen, "Issues of core and periphery: labour migration and global restructuring," in Jeff Henderson and Manuel Castells (eds), *Global Restructuring and Territorial Development* (London: Sage, 1987); and Saskia Sassen, *The Mobility of Labor and Capital* (New York: Cambridge University Press, 1988).
11 John Mollenkopf, "Economic development," in C. Brecher and R. Horton (eds), *Setting Municipal Priorities: American Cities and the New York Experience* (New York: New York University Press, 1984).
12 I have benefited greatly from the perceptive, well-documented analysis by Samuel M. Ehrenhalt, "New York City in the new economic environment: new risks and a changing outlook" (New York Regional Commissioner, US Bureau of Labor Statistics, 1988) (paper communicated by the author).
13 Ehrenhalt, "New York City," p. 12.
14 Thomas Bailey and Roger Waldinger, "Economic change and the ethnic division of labor in New York City," paper prepared for the Social Science Research Council Committee on New York City, February 1988.
15 See the studies presented in John H. Mollenkopf and Manuel Castells (eds), *Dual City: Restructuring New York* (New York: Russell Sage Foundation, 1991); see also Gus Tyler, "A tale of three cities – upper economy, lower – and under," in *Dissent*, special issue: "In search of New York," Fall 1987, pp. 463–71; Emanuel Tobier, "Population," in Brecher and Horton, *Setting Municipal Priorities*; Roger Waldinger, "Changing ladders and musical chairs: ethnicity and opportunity in post-industrial New York," paper delivered at the International Conference on Ethnic Minorities, University of Warwick, UK, September 1985.
16 Saskia Sassen, "The informal economy in New York City," in Alejandro Portes, Manuel Castells, and Lauren Benton (eds), *The Informal Economy* (Baltimore, MD: The Johns Hopkins University Press, 1989).
17 Saskia Sassen, "New York City's informal economy," paper prepared for the

Social Science Research Council Committee on New York City, February 1988.

18 Saskia Sassen and C. Benamou, "Hispanic women in the garment and electronics industries in New York metropolitan area," research report to the Revson Foundation, New York, 1985.

19 For the whole of the US, estimates of cash flow generated by drug traffic oscillate between $60 billion and $120 billion. This capital has to be recycled in the formal economy through laundering. See Jeff Gerth, "Vast flow of cash threatens currency, banks and economies," *New York Times*, 11 April 1988, p. A8.

20 See Nancy Foner (ed.), *New Immigrants in New York* (New York: Columbia University Press, 1987); Philip Kasinitz, "The City's new immigrants," in *Dissent*, Fall 1987, pp. 497–506.

21 Roger Waldinger, *Through the Eye of the Needle: Immigrants and Enterprise in New York's Garment Trades* (New York: New York University Press, 1986).

22 Bailey and Waldinger, "Economic change and the ethnic division of labor."

23 Alejandro Portes and Robert L. Bach, *Latin Journey: Cuban and Mexican Immigrants in the United States* (Berkeley, CA: University of California Press, 1985); Foner, *New Immigrants in New York*; Sassen, "Issues of core and periphery."

24 Sassen, "New York City's informal economy," p. 1.

25 Richard Harris, "Home and work in New York since 1950," paper prepared for the Social Science Research Council Committee on New York City, February 1988.

26 William Kornblum, "The white ethnic neighborhoods in New York City," paper prepared for the Social Science Research Council on New York City, 1988.

27 Harris, "Home and work in New York," p. 34.

28 Edward W. Soja, "Taking Los Angeles apart: some fragments of a critical human geography," *Environment and Planning: D. Space and Society*, special issue on Los Angeles, 4 (3) (September 1986) pp. 255–73.

29 Edward W. Soja, "Economic restructuring and the internationalization of the Los Angeles region," in Feagin and Smith, *The Capitalist City*.

30 Edward Soja, Rebecca Morales, and Goetz Wolff, "Urban restructuring: an analysis of social and spatial change in Los Angeles," *Economic Geography*, 59 (2) (April, 1983), pp. 195–230.

31 On suburban office development in Los Angeles, as linked to the process of spatial restructuring, see Tamara Phibbs, *Linkages, Labor, and Localities in the Location of Suburban Office Centers: A Case Study of Office Establishments in Orange County, California*, master's thesis in Urban Planning (Los Angeles, University of California, 1989).

32 *Los Angeles Times*, 9 April 1988.

33 It is, of course, a classic theme of the Chicago School of urban sociology. See, for instance, Harvey Zorbaugh, *The Gold Coast and the Slum* (Chicago, IL: University of Chicago Press, 1927).

34 A theme that I have developed in *The City and the Grassroots* (Berkeley, CA: University of California Press, 1983).

EIGHT

The Space of Flows

(1996, 2nd edn 2000)

Space and time are the fundamental, material dimensions of human life. Physicists have unveiled the complexity of such notions, beyond their fallacious intuitive simplicity. School children know that space and time are related. And superstring theory, the latest fashion in physics, advances the hypothesis of a hyperspace that articulates ten dimensions, including time. (Kaku, 1994). There is, of course, no place for such a discussion in my analysis, strictly concerned with the *social meaning of space and time*. But my reference to such complexity goes beyond rhetorical pedantry. It invites us to consider social forms of time and space that are not reducible to what have been our perceptions to date, based upon socio-technical structures superseded by current historical experience.

Since space and time are intertwined in nature and in society, so they will be in my analysis, although for the sake of clarity I shall focus sequentially first on space, in this chapter, and then on time in the next one [chapter 7 of *The Network Society*]. The ordering in the sequence is not random: unlike most classical social theories, which assume the domination of space by time, I propose the hypothesis that space organizes time in the network society. This statement will, I hope, make more sense at the end of the intellectual journey I propose to the reader in these two chapters.

Both space and time are being transformed under the combined effect of the information technology paradigm, and of social forms and processes induced by the current process of historical change [. . .]. However, the actual profile of this transformation sharply departs from common-sense extrapolations of technological determinism. For instance, it appears to be obvious that advanced telecommunications would make location of offices ubiquitous, thus enabling corporate headquarters to quit expensive, congested, and unpleasant central business districts for custom-made sites in beautiful spots around the world. Yet Mitchell Moss's empirical analysis of the impact of telecommunications on Manhattan's business in the 1980s found that these new, advanced telecommunications facilities were among the factors responsible for slowing down corporate relocation away from New York, for reasons that I shall expose below. Or, to use another example on a different social domain, home-based electronic communication was supposed to induce the decline of dense urban forms, and to diminish spatially localized social interaction. Yet the first mass diffused system of computer-mediated communication, the French Minitel, [. . .] originated in the 1980s in an intense urban environment, whose vitality and face-to-face interaction was hardly undermined by the new medium. Indeed, French students used Minitel to successfully stage *street* demonstrations against the government. In the early 1990s telecommuting – that is, working at home on-line – was practiced by a very small fraction of the labor force, in the United States (between 1 and 2 percent on a given day), Europe, or Japan, if we except the old, customary practice of professionals to keep working at home or to organize their activity in flexible time and space when they have the leisure to do so.[1] While working at home part-time seems to be emerging as a mode of professional activity in the future, it develops out of the rise of the network enterprise and of the flexible work process [. . .] not as the direct consequence of available technology. The theoretical and practical consequences of such precisions are critical. It is this complexity of the interaction between technology, society, and space that I shall address in the following pages.

To proceed in this direction, I shall examine the empirical record on the transformation of location patterns of core economic activities under the new technological system, both for advanced services and for manufacturing. Afterwards, I shall try to assess the scarce evidence on the interaction between the rise of the electronic home and the evolution of the city, and I shall elaborate on the recent evolution of urban forms in various contexts. I shall then synthesize the observed tendencies under a new spatial logic that I label *space of flows*. I shall oppose to such logic the historically rooted spatial organization of our common experience: *the space of places*. And I shall refer to the reflection of such dialectical opposition between the space of flows and the space of places in current debates in architecture and urban design. The purpose of this intellectual itinerary is to draw the profile of this new spatial process, the space of flows, that is becoming the dominant spatial manifestation of power and function in our societies. In spite of all my efforts to anchor the new spatial logic in the empirical record, I am afraid it is unavoidable, toward the end of the chapter, to confront the reader with some fundamentals of a social theory of space, as a way to approach the current transformation of the material basis of our experience. Yet my ability to communicate a rather abstract theorization of new spatial forms and processes will, I hope, be enhanced by a brief survey of available evidence on recent spatial patterning of dominant economic functions and social practices.[2]

Advanced Services, Information Flows, and the Global City

The informational, global economy is organized around command and control centers able to coordinate, innovate, and manage the intertwined activities of networks of firms.[3] Advanced services, including finance, insurance, real estate, consulting, legal services, advertising, design, marketing, public relations, security, information gathering, and management of information systems, but also R&D and scientific innovation, are at the core of all economic processes, be it in manufacturing, agriculture, energy, or services of different kinds (Daniels, 1993). They all can be reduced to knowledge generation and information flows (Norman, 1993). Thus, advanced telecommunications systems could make possible their scattered location around the globe. Yet more than a decade of studies on the matter have established a different spatial pattern, characterized by the simultaneous dispersion and concentration of advanced services (Graham, 1994). On the one hand, advanced services have substantially increased their share in employment and GNP in most countries, and they display the highest growth in employment and the highest investment rates in the leading metropolitan areas of the world (Enderwick, 1989). They are pervasive, and they are located throughout the geography of the planet, excepting the "black holes" of marginality. On the other hand, there has been a spatial concentration of the upper tier of such activities in a few nodal centers of a few countries (Daniels, 1993). This concentration follows a hierarchy between tiers of urban centers, with the higher-level functions, in terms of both power and skill, being concentrated in some major metropolitan areas. (Thrift, 1986; Thrift and Leyshon, 1992). Saskia Sassen's (1991) classic study of the global city has shown the joint dominance of New York, Tokyo, and London in international finance, and in most consulting and business services of international scope. These three centers together cover the spectrum of time zones for the purpose of financial trading, and work largely as a unit in the same system of endless transactions. But other centers are important, and even more pre-eminent in some specific segments of trade, for example Chicago and Singapore in futures' contracts (in fact, first practiced in Chicago in 1972). Hong Kong, Osaka, Frankfurt, Zurich, Paris, Los Angeles, San Francisco, Amsterdam, and Milan are also major centers both in finance and in international business services (Daniels, 1993). And a number of "regional centers" are rapidly joining the network, as "emerging markets" develop all over the world: Madrid, São Paulo, Buenos Aires, Mexico, Taipei, Moscow, Budapest, among others.

As the global economy expands and incorporates new markets it also organizes the production of advanced services required to manage the new units joining the system, and the conditions of their ever-changing linkages

(Borja et al., 1991). A case in point which illustrates this process is Madrid, relatively a backwater of the global economy until 1986. In that year Spain joined the European Community, opening up fully to foreign capital investment in the stock exchange markets, in banking operations, and in acquisition of companies equity, as well as in real estate. As shown in our study,[4] in the 1986–90 period foreign direct investment in Madrid and in Madrid's stock exchange fueled a period of rapid regional economic growth, together with a boom in real estate and a fast expansion of employment in business services. Acquisitions of stocks in Madrid by foreign investors between 1982 and 1988 jumped from 4,494 million pesetas (pts) to 623,445 million pts. Foreign direct investment in Madrid went up from 8,000 million pts in 1985 to almost 400,000 million pts in 1988. Accordingly, office construction in downtown Madrid, and high-level residential real estate, went in the late 1980s through the same kind of frenzy experienced in New York and London. The city was deeply transformed both through the saturation of valuable space in the core city, and through a process of massive suburbanization which, until then, had been a somewhat limited phenomenon in Madrid.

Along the same line of argument, a study by Cappelin (1991) on services networking in European cities shows the increasing interdependence and complementarity between medium-sized urban centers in the European Union. He concluded that: "The relative importance of the city–region relationships seems to decrease with respect to the importance of the relationships which interlink various cities of different regions and countries . . . New activities concentrate in particular poles and that implies an increase of disparities between the urban poles and their respective hinterlands" (Cappelin, 1991: 237). Thus, the global city phenomenon cannot be reduced to a few urban cores at the top of the hierarchy. It is a process that connects advanced services, producer centers, and markets in a global network, with different intensity and at a different scale depending upon the relative importance of the activities located in each area *vis-à-vis* the global network. Inside each country, the networking architecture reproduces itself into regional and local centers, so that the whole system becomes interconnected at the global level. Territories surrounding these nodes play an increasingly subordinate function, sometimes becoming irrelevant or even dysfunctional; for example, Mexico City's *colonias populares* (originally squatter settlements) that account for about two-thirds of the megapolitan population, without playing any distinctive role in the functioning of Mexico City as an international business center (Davis, 1994). Furthermore, globalization stimulates regionalization. In his studies on European regions in the 1990s, Philip Cooke has shown, on the basis of available evidence, that the growing internationalization of economic activities throughout Europe has made regions more dependent on these activities. Accordingly, regions, under the impulse of their governments and business elites, have restructured themselves to compete in the global economy, and

Figure 8.1 Largest absolute growth in information flows, 1982 and 1990
Source: Federal Express data, elaborated by Michelson and Wheeler (1994)

they have established networks of cooperation between regional institutions and between region-based companies. Thus, regions and localities do not disappear, but become integrated in international networks that link up their most dynamic sectors (Cooke and Morgan, 1993; Cooke, 1994).

An approximation to the evolving architecture of information flows in the global economy has been obtained by Michelson and Wheeler (1994) on the basis of data analysis of traffic for one of the leading business couriers, Federal Express Corporation. They studied the 1990s' movement of overnight letters, packages, and boxes between US metropolitan areas, as well as between the US major sending centers and international destinations. The results of their analysis, illustrated in figures 8.1 and 8.2 show two basic trends: (a) dominance of some nodes, particularly New York, followed by Los Angeles, increasing over time; (b) selected national and international circuits of connection. As they conclude:

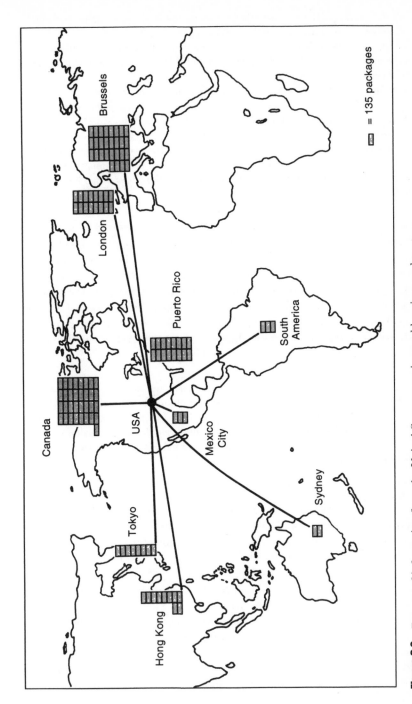

Figure 8.2 Exports of information from the United States to major world regions and centers
Source: Federal Express data, 1990, elaborated by Michelson and Wheeler (1994)

> All indicators point to a strengthening of the hierarchical structure of com-
> mand-and-control functions and the resulting exchange of information . . . The
> locational concentration of information results from high levels of uncertainty,
> driven in turn by technological change, market demassification, deregulation
> and market globalization . . . [However] as the current epoch unfolds, the im-
> portance of flexibility as a basic coping mechanism, and of agglomeration econo-
> mies as the preeminent locational force will persist. The importance of the city
> as a center of gravity for economic transactions thus will not vanish. But with
> the impending regulation of international markets . . . with less uncertainty
> about the rules of the economic game and the players involved, the concentra-
> tion of the information industry will slow and certain aspects of production and
> distribution will filter into lower levels of an internationalized urban hierarchy.
> (Michelson and Wheeler, 1994: 102–3)

Indeed, the hierarchy in the network is by no means assured or stable: it is
subject to fierce inter-city competition, as well as to the venture of highly risky
investments in both finance and real estate. Thus, P. W. Daniels, in one of the
most comprehensive studies of the matter, explains the partial failure of the
major redevelopment project of Canary Wharf in London's Docklands as the
result of the overextended strategy of its developer, the notorious Canadian
firm Olympia & York, unable to absorb the office development glut of the
early 1990s, in the wake of retrenchment of financial services employment in
both London and New York. He concludes that:

> The expansion of services into the international market place has therefore
> introduced a greater degree of flexibility, and ultimately competition, into the
> global urban system than was the case in the past. As the experience with
> Canary Wharf has shown, it also made the outcome of large-scale planning and
> redevelopment within cities a hostage to external international factors over
> which they can have limited control. (Daniels 1993: 166)

Thus, in the early 1990s, while business-led explosive urban growth was
experienced in cities such as Bangkok, Taipei, Shanghai, Mexico DF, or
Bogota; on the other hand, Madrid, along with New York, London, and
Paris, went into a slump that triggered a sharp downturn in real-estate prices
and halted new construction. Then, in the late 1990s, London's and New
York's real estate revalued substantially, while the urban cores of major Asian
cities were severely struck by a financial crisis, partly induced by the bursting
of the bubble of their real-estate markets [. . .]. This urban roller-coaster at
different periods, across areas of the world, illustrates both the dependence
and vulnerability of any locale, including major cities, to changing global
flows.

But why must these advanced service systems still be dependent on agglomeration in a few large metropolitan nodes? Here again, Saskia Sassen, cap-

ping years of field work research by herself and other researchers in different contexts, offers convincing answers. She argues that:

> The combination of spatial dispersal and global integration has created a new strategic role for major cities. Beyond their long history as centers for international trade and banking, these cities now function in four new ways: first, as highly concentrated command points in the organization of the world economy; second, as key locations for finance and for specialized service firms . . .; third, as sites of production, including the production of innovation in these leading industries; and fourth, as markets for the products and innovations produced. (Sassen, 1991: 3–4)

These cities, or rather, their business districts, are information-based, value-production complexes, where corporate headquarters and advanced financial firms can find both the suppliers and the highly skilled, specialized labor they require. They constitute indeed networks of production and management, whose flexibility needs *not* to internalize workers and suppliers, but to be able to access them when it fits, and in the time and quantities that are required in each particular instance. Flexibility and adaptability are better served by this combination between agglomeration of core networks, and global networking of these cores, and of their dispersed, ancillary networks, via telecommunications and air transportation. Other factors seem also to contribute to strengthen concentration of high-level activities in a few nodes: once they are constituted, heavy investment in valuable real estate by corporations explains their reluctance to move because such a move would devalue their fixed assets; also, face-to-face contacts for critical decisions are still necessary in the age of widespread eavesdropping, since, as Saskia Sassen reports that a manager confessed to her during an interview, sometimes business deals are, of necessity, marginally illegal.[5] And, finally, major metropolitan centers still offer the greatest opportunities for the personal enhancement, social status, and individual self-gratification of the much-needed upper-level professionals, from good schools for their children to symbolic membership at the heights of conspicuous consumption, including art and entertainment.[6]

Nevertheless, advanced services, and even more so services at large, do indeed disperse and decentralize to the periphery of metropolitan areas, to smaller metropolitan areas, to less-developed regions, and to some less-developed countries.[7] New regional centers of service processing activities have emerged in the United States (for example, Atlanta, Georgia, or Omaha, Nebraska), in Europe (for example, Barcelona, Nice, Stuttgart, Bristol), or in Asia (for example, Bombay, Bangkok, Shanghai). The peripheries of major metropolitan areas are bustling with new office development, be it Walnut Creek in San Francisco or Reading near London. And in some cases, new major service centers have sprung up on the edge of the historic city, Paris's

La Défense being the most notorious and successful example. Yet, in almost all instances, decentralization of office work affects "back offices"; that is, the mass processing of transactions that execute strategies decided and designed in the corporate centers of high finance and advanced services (see Castells, 1989b: ch. 3; Dunford and Kafkalas, 1992). These are precisely the activities that employ the bulk of semi-skilled office workers, most of them suburbanite women, many of them replaceable or recyclable, as technology evolves and the economic roller-coaster goes on.

What is significant about this spatial system of advanced service activities is neither their concentration nor decentralization, since both processes are indeed taking place at the same time throughout countries and continents. Nor is it the hierarchy of their geography, since this is in fact tributary to the variable geometry of money and information flows. After all, who could predict in the early 1980s that Taipei, Madrid, or Buenos Aires could emerge as important international financial and business centers? I believe that the megalopolis Hong Kong-Shenzhen-Guangzhou-Zhuhai-Macau will be one of the major financial and business capitals in the early twenty-first century, thus inducing a major realignment in the global geography of advanced services (see Henderson, 1991; Kwok and So, 1992, 1995). But for the sake of the spatial analysis I am proposing here, it is secondary if I miss my prediction. Because, while the actual location of high-level centers in each period is critical for the distribution of wealth and power in the world, from the perspective of the spatial logic of the new system what matters is the versatility of its networks. The global city is not a place, but a process. A process by which centers of production and consumption of advanced services, and their ancillary local societies, are connected in a global network, while simultaneously downplaying the linkages with their hinterlands, on the basis of information flows.

The New Industrial Space

The advent of high-technology manufacturing, namely micro-electronics-based, computer-aided manufacturing, ushered in a new logic of industrial location. Electronics firms, the producers of new information technology devices, were also the first to practice the locational strategy both allowed and required by the information-based production process. During the 1980s, a number of empirical studies conducted by faculty and graduate students at the University of California Berkeley's Institute of Urban and Regional Development provided a solid grasp on the profile of "the new industrial space."[8] It is characterized by the technological and organizational ability to separate the production process in different locations while reintegrating its unity through telecommunications linkages, and micro-electronics-based precision and flexibility in the fabrication of components. Furthermore, geographical specificity of each phase of the production process is made advisable by the singularity of the labor force required at each stage, and by the different social and environmental features involved in the living conditions of highly distinct segments of this labor force. This is because high-technology manufacturing presents an occupational composition very different from traditional manufacturing: it is organized in a bipolar structure around two predominant groups of roughly similar size; a highly skilled, science- and technology-based labor force, on the one hand; and a mass of unskilled workers engaged in routine assembly and auxiliary operations, on the other hand. While automation has increasingly enabled companies to eliminate the lower tier of workers, the staggering increase in the volume of production still employs, and will for some time, a considerable number of unskilled and semi-skilled workers whose location in the same areas as scientists and engineers is neither economically feasible nor socially suitable, in the prevailing social context. In between, skilled operators also represent a distinctive group that can be separated from the high levels of high-technology production. Because of the light weight of the final product, and because of easy communication linkages developed by companies throughout the globe, electronics firms, particularly American, developed from the beginnings of the industry (as early as Fairchild's plant location in Hong Kong in 1962) a locational pattern characterized by the international spatial division of labor (Cooper, 1994). Roughly speaking, both for micro-electronics and computers, four different types of location were sought for each one of the four distinctive operations in the production process:

1 R&D, innovation, and prototype fabrication were concentrated in highly innovative industrial centers in core areas, generally with good quality of life before their development process degraded the environment to some extent.
2 Skilled fabrication in branch plants, generally in newly industrializing areas in the home country, which in the case of the US generally meant in medium-sized towns in the Western states.
3 Semi-skilled, large-scale assembly and testing work that from the very beginning was located offshore in a substantial proportion, particularly in South-East Asia, with Singapore and Malaysia pioneering the movement of attracting factories of American electronics corporations.
4 Customization of devices and aftersales maintenance and technical support, which was organized in regional centers throughout the globe, generally in the area of major electronics markets, originally in America and Western Europe, although in the 1990s the Asian markets rose to equal status.

European companies, used to cozy locations on their protected home turfs, were pushed to decentralize their production systems in a similar global chain, as markets opened up, and they started to feel the pinch of competition from Asian-based operations, and from American and Japanese technological advantage (Chesnais, 1994). Japanese companies tried to resist for a long time quitting "fortress Japan," both for reasons of nationalism (at the request of their government) and because of their close dependence on "just-in-time" networks of suppliers. However, unbearable congestion and sky-rocketing prices of operation in the Tokyo-Yokohama area forced first regional decentralization (helped by MITI's Technopolis Program) in less-developed areas of Japan, particularly in Kyushu (Castells and Hall, 1994), and then, from the late 1980s, Japanese companies proceeded to follow the locational pattern initiated by their American competitors two decades earlier: offshore production facilities in South-East Asia, searching for lower labor costs and looser environmental constraints, and dissemination of factories throughout the main markets in America, Europe, and Asia in order to pre-empt future protectionism (Aoyama, 1995). Thus, the end of Japanese exceptionalism confirmed the accuracy of the locational model that, together with a number of colleagues, we proposed to understand the new spatial logic of high-technology industry. Figure 8.3 displays schematically the spatial logic of this model, elaborated on the basis of empirical evidence gathered by a number of researchers in different contexts (Castells, 1989b: ch. 2).

A key element in this locational pattern is the decisive importance of technological innovation production complexes for the whole system. This is what Peter Hall and I, as well as the pioneer in this field of research, Philippe Aydalot, called "milieux of innovation."[9] By milieu of innovation I understand a specific set of relationships of production and management, based on a social organization that by and large shares a work culture and instrumental goals aimed at generating new knowledge, new processes, and new products. Although the concept of milieu does not necessarily include a spatial dimension, I argue that in the case of information technology industries, at least in this century, spatial proximity is a necessary material condition for the existence of such milieux because of the nature of the interaction in the innovation process. What defines the specificity of a milieu of innovation is its capacity to generate synergy; that is, the added value resulting not from the cumulative effect of the elements present in the milieu but from their interaction. Milieux of innovation are the fundamental sources of innovation and of generation of value added in the process of industrial production in the Information Age. Peter Hall and I studied for several years the formation, structure, and dynamics of the main technological milieux of innovation around the world, both actual and supposed. The results of our inquiry added some elements to the understanding of the locational pattern of information technology industry (Castells and Hall, 1994).

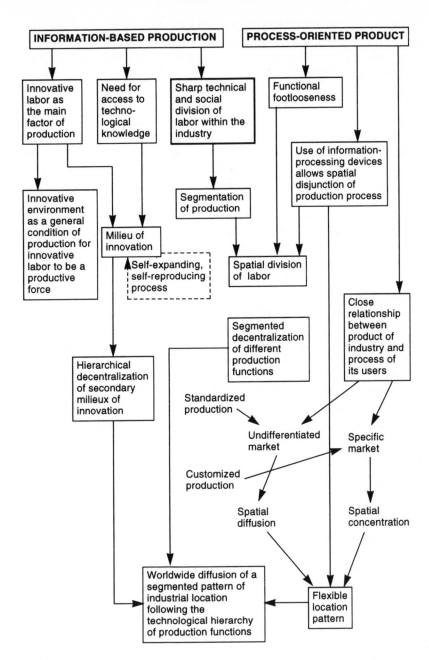

Figure 8.3 System of relationships between the characteristics of information technology manufacturing and the industry's spatial pattern
Source: Castells (1989a)

First of all, high-technology-led industrial milieux of innovation, which we called "technopoles," come in a variety of urban formats. Most notably, it is clear that in most countries, with the important exceptions of the United States and, to some extent, Germany, the leading technopoles are in fact contained in the leading metropolitan areas: Tokyo, Paris-Sud, London–M4 Corridor, Milan, Seoul–Inchon, Moscow–Zelenograd, and at a considerable distance Nice–Sophia Antipolis, Taipei–Hsinchu, Singapore, Shanghai, São Paulo, Barcelona, and so on. The partial exception of Germany (after all, Munich is a major metropolitan area) relates directly to political history: the destruction of Berlin, the pre-eminent European science-based industrial center, and the relocation of Siemens from Berlin to Munich in the last months of the Third Reich, under the anticipated protection of American occupation forces and with the subsequent support of the Bavarian CSU party. Thus, against the excessive imagery of upstart technopoles there is indeed continuity in the spatial history of technology and industrialization in the Information Age: major metropolitan centers around the world continue to cumulate innovation-inducing factors and to generate synergy, in manufacturing as in advanced services.

However, some of the most important innovation centers of information technology manufacturing are indeed new, particularly in the world's technological leader, the United States. Silicon Valley, Boston's Route 128 (rejuvenating an old, traditional manufacturing structure), the southern California technopole, North Carolina's research triangle, Seattle, and Austin, among others, were by and large linked to the latest wave of information-technology-based industrialization. We have shown that their development resulted from the clustering of specific varieties of the usual factors of production: capital, labor, and raw material, brought together by some kind of institutional entrepreneur, and constituted by a particular form of social organization. Their raw material was made up of new knowledge, related to strategically important fields of application, produced by major centers of innovation, such as Stanford University, CalTech, or MIT schools of engineering research teams, and the networks built around them. Their labor, distinct from the knowledge factor, required the concentration of a large number of highly skilled scientists and engineers, from a variety of locally based schools, including those mentioned above but also others, such as Berkeley, San Jose State, or Santa Clara, in the case of Silicon Valley. Their capital was also specific, willing to take the high risks of investing in pioneering high-tech: either because of the military imperative on performance (defense-related spending), or else because of the high stakes of venture capital betting on the extra rewards of risk-taking investments. The articulation of these production factors was generally the fact, at the onset of the process, of an institutional actor, such as Stanford University launching the Stanford Industrial Park that induced Silicon Valley; or the Air Force commanders who, relying on Los Angeles boosterism, won for southern California the defense contracts that would make the new Western metropolis the largest high-technology defense complex in the world. Finally, social networks, of different kinds, powerfully contributed to the consolidation of the milieu of innovation, and to its dynamism, ensuring the communication of ideas, the circulation of labor, and the cross-fertilization of technological innovation and business entrepreneurialism.

What our research on the new milieux of innovation, in the US or elsewhere, shows is that while there is indeed spatial continuity in metropolitan dominance, it can also be reversed given the right conditions. And that the right conditions concern the capacity to spatially concentrate the proper ingredients for inducing synergy. If such is the case, as our evidence seems to support, then we do have a new industrial space marked by fundamental discontinuity: milieux of innovation, new and old, constitute themselves on the basis of their internal structure and dynamics, later attracting firms, capital, and labor to the seedbed of innovation they constituted. Once established, milieux of innovation both compete and cooperate between different regions, creating a network of interaction that brings them together in a common industrial structure beyond their geographical discontinuity. Research by Camagni (1991) and the research teams organized around the GREMI network shows the growing interdependence of these milieux of innovation all over the globe, while at the same time emphasizing how decisive for its fate is the capacity of each milieu to enhance its synergy. Finally, milieux of innovation command global networks of production and distribution that extend their reach all over the planet. This is why some researchers, such as Amin and Robins (1991), argue that the new industrial system is neither global nor local but "a new articulation of global and local dynamics."

However, to have a clear vision of the new industrial space constituted in the Information Age we must add some precision. This is because too often the emphasis of the analysis has been placed on the hierarchical spatial division of labor between different functions located in different territories. This is important, but not essential in the new spatial logic. Territorial hierarchies can be blurred, and even reversed, as the industry expands throughout the world, and as competition enhances or depresses entire agglomerations, including milieux of innovation themselves. Also, secondary milieux of innovation are constituted, sometimes as decentralized systems spun off from primary centers, but they often find their niches in competition with their original matrices, examples to the point being Seattle *vis-à-vis* Silicon Valley and Boston in software, or Austin, Texas, *vis-à-vis* New York or Minneapolis in computers. Furthermore, in the 1990s, the development of the electronics industry in Asia, mainly under the impulse of American–Japanese competition, has complicated extraordinarily the geography of the industry in its mature stage, as shown in the analyses by Cohen and Borrus (1995) and by Dieter Ernst (1994). On the one hand, there has been substantial upgrading of the technological potential of American multinationals' subsidiaries, particularly in Singapore, Malaysia, and Taiwan, and this upgrading has trickled down to their local subsidiaries. On the other hand, Japanese electronics firms, as mentioned above, have massively decentralized their production in Asia, both to export globally and to supply their onshore parent plants. In both cases, a substantial supply base has been built in Asia, thus rendering obsolete the old spatial division of labor in which South-East and East Asian subsidiaries occupied the bottom level of the hierarchy.

Furthermore, on the basis of the review of available evidence up to 1994, including his own company surveys, Richard Gordon (1994) convincingly argues for the emergence of a new spatial division of labor, one characterized by its variable geometry, and its back and forth linkages between firms located in different territorial complexes, including the leading milieux of innovation. His detailed analysis of developments in 1990s' Silicon Valley shows the importance of extra-regional relationships for the most technologically sophisticated and transaction-intensive interactions of regional high-technology firms. Thus he argues that

> in this new global context, localized agglomeration, far from constituting an alternative to spatial dispersion, becomes the principal basis for participation in a global network of regional economies . . . Regions and networks in fact constitute interdependent poles within the new spatial mosaic of global innovation. Globalization in this context involves not the leavening impact of universal processes but, on the contrary, the calculated synthesis of cultural diversity in the form of differentiated regional innovation logics and capabilities. (Gordon, 1994: 46)

The new industrial space does not represent the demise of old, established metropolitan areas and the rising sun of new, high-tech regions. Nor can it be apprehended under the simplistic opposition between automation at the center and low-cost manufacturing at the periphery. It is organized in a hierarchy of innovation and fabrication articulated in global networks. But the direction and architecture of these networks are submitted to the endless changing movements of cooperation and competition between firms and between locales, sometimes historically cumulative, sometimes reversing the established pattern through deliberate institutional entrepreneurialism. What does remain as the characteristic logic of the new industrial location is its geographical discontinuity, paradoxically made up of territorial production complexes. The new industrial space is organized around flows of information that bring together and separate at the same time – depending upon cycles or firms – their territorial components. And as the logic of information technology manufacturing trickles down from the producers of information technology devices to the users of such devices in the whole realm of manufacturing, so the new spatial logic expands, creating a multiplicity of global industrial networks whose intersections and exclusions transform the very notion of industrial location from factory sites to manufacturing flows.

Everyday Life in the Electronic Cottage: The End of Cities?

The development of electronic communication and information systems allows for an increasing disassociation between spatial proximity and the performance of everyday life's functions: work, shopping, entertainment, healthcare, education, public services, governance, and the like. Accordingly, futurologists often predict the demise of the city, or at least of cities as we have known them until now, once they are voided of their functional necessity. Processes of spatial transformation are of course much more complicated, as history shows. Therefore, it is worthwhile to consider the scant empirical record on the matter.[10]

A dramatic increase of teleworking is the most usual assumption about the impact of information technology on cities, and the last hope for metropolitan transportation planners before surrendering to the inevitability of the mega-gridlock. Yet, in 1988, a leading European researcher on telecommuting could write, without the shadow of a joke, that "There are more people doing research on telework than there are actual teleworkers" (Steinle, 1988: 8). In fact, as noted by Qvortup (1992: 8), the whole debate is biased by the lack of precision in defining telework, leading to considerable uncertainty when measuring the phenomenon. After reviewing available evidence, he adequately distinguishes between three categories: (a) "Substitutors, those who substitute work done at home for work done in a traditional work setting" (these are telecommuters in the strict sense); (b) self-employed, working on-line from their homes; (c) supplementers, "bringing supplementary work home from their conventional office." Furthermore, in some cases this "supplementary work" takes most of the working time; for example, according to Kraut (1989), in the case of university professors. By most reliable accounts, the first category, telecommuters *stricto sensu* employed regularly to work on-line at home, is very small overall, and is not expected to grow substantially in the foreseeable future (Nilles, 1988; Rijn and Williams, 1988; Huws et al., 1990) In the United States the highest estimates evaluated in 1991 about 5.5 million home-based telecommuters, but of this total only 16 percent telecommuted 35 hours or more per week, 25 percent telecommuted less than one day a week, with two days a week being the most common pattern. Thus, the percentage of workers who on any given day are telecommuting ranges, depending on estimates, between 1 and 2 percent of the total labor force, with major metropolitan areas in California displaying the highest percentages (Mokhtarian,

1991a, b; Handy and Mokhtarian, 1995). On the other hand, what seems to be emerging is telecommuting from telecenters; that is, networked computer facilities scattered in the suburbs of metropolitan areas for workers to work on-line with their companies (Mokhtarian, 1991b). If these trends are confirmed, homes would not become workplaces, but work activity could spread considerably throughout the metropolitan area, increasing urban decentralization. Increase in home work may also result as a form of electronic outworking by temporary workers, paid by the piece of information processing under an individualized subcontracting arrangement (see Lozano, 1989; Gurstein, 1990). Interestingly enough, in the United States, a 1991 national survey showed that fewer than a half of home telecommuters used computers: the rest worked with a telephone, pen, and paper.[11] Examples of such activities are social workers and welfare fraud investigators in Los Angeles County (Mokhtarian, 1992: 12). What is certainly significant, and on the rise, is the development of self-employment, and of "supplementers," either full-time or part-time, as part of the broader trend toward the disaggregation of labor and the formation of virtual business networks [. . .]. This does not imply the end of the office, but the diversification of working sites for a large fraction of the population, and particularly for its most dynamic, professional segment. Increasingly mobile telecomputing equipment will enhance this trend toward the office-on-the-run, in the most literal sense.[12]

How do these tendencies affect cities? Scattered data seem to indicate that transportation problems will get worse, not better, because increasing activity and time compression allowed by new networking organization translate into higher concentration of markets in certain areas, and into greater physical mobility for a labor force that was previously confined to its working sites during working hours.[13] Work-related commuting time is kept at a steady level in the US metropolitan areas, not because of improved technology, but because of a more decentralized location pattern of jobs and residences that allows easier, suburb-to-suburb traffic flows. In those cities, particularly in Europe, where a radioconcentric pattern still dominates daily commuting (such as Paris, Madrid, or Milan), commuting time is sharply up, particularly for stubborn automobile addicts (Cervero, 1989, 1991; Bendixon, 1991). As for the new, sprawling metropolises of Asia, their coming into the Information Age runs parallel to their discovery of the most awesome traffic jams in history, from Bangkok to Shanghai (Lo and Yeung, 1996).

Teleshopping was slow to live up to its promise, and ultimately was pushed out by the Internet's competition. It supplemented rather than replaced commercial areas (Miles, 1988; Schoonmaker, 1993; Menotti, 1995). However, e-commerce, with billions of dollars of on-line sales in the US over Christmas 1999, is a major, new development [. . .]. Nevertheless, the growing importance of on-line transactions does not imply the disappearance of shopping centers and retail stores. In fact, the trend is the opposite: shopping areas proliferate around the urban and suburban landscape, with showrooms that address customers to on-line ordering terminals to get the actual goods, often home-delivered (*Business Week*, 1999). A similar story can be told for most on-line consumer services. For instance, telebanking (Castano, 1991; Silverstone, 1991) is spreading fast, mainly under the impulse of banks interested in eliminating branch offices and replacing them by on-line customer services and automated-teller machines. However, the consolidated bank branches continue as service centers to sell financial products to their customers through a personalized relationship. Even on-line, cultural features of localities may be important as locational factors for information-oriented transactions. Thus, First Direct, the telephone banking branch of Midland Bank in Britain, located in Leeds because its research "showed West Yorkshire's plain accent, with its flat vowel sounds but clear diction and apparent classlessness, to be the most easily understood and acceptable throughout the UK – a vital element of any telephone-based business" (Fazy, 1995). Thus, it is the system of branch office sellers, automated tellers, customer service-by-telephone, and on-line transactions that constitutes the new banking industry.

Health services offer an even more interesting case of the emerging dialectics between concentration and centralization of people-oriented services. On the one hand, expert systems, on-line communications, and high-resolution video transmission allow for the distant interconnection of medical care. For instance, in a practice that has become usual, if not yet routine, in 1995, highly skilled surgeons supervise by videoconference surgery performed at the other end of the country or of the world, literally guiding the less-expert hand of another surgeon into a human body. Regular health checks are also conducted via computer and telephone on the basis of patients' computerized, updated information. Neighborhood healthcare centers are backed by information systems to improve the quality and efficiency of their primary-level attention. Yet, on the other hand, in most countries major medical complexes emerge in specific locales, generally in large metropolitan areas. Usually organized around a big hospital, often connected to medical and nursing schools, they include in their physical proximity private clinics headed by the most prominent hospital doctors, radiology centers, test laboratories, specialized pharmacists, and, not infrequently, gift shops and mortuaries, to cater for the whole range of possibilities. Indeed, such medical complexes are a major economic and cultural force in the areas and cities where they are located, and tend to expand in their surrounding vicinity over time. When forced to relocate, the whole complex moves together (Moran, 1990; Lincoln et al. 1993; Miller and Swensson, 1995).

Schools and universities are paradoxically the institutions least affected by the virtual logic embedded in information technology, in spite of the foreseeable quasi-universal use of computers in the classrooms of advanced countries. But they will hardly vanish into virtual space. In the case of elementary and secondary schools, this is because they are as much childcare centers and/or children's warehouses as they are learning institutions. In the case of universities, this is because the quality of education is still, and will be for a long time, associated with the intensity of face-to-face interaction. Thus, the large-scale experiences of "distant universities," regardless of their quality (bad in Spain, good in Britain), seem to show that they are second-option forms of education which could play a significant role in a future, enhanced system of adult education, but which could hardly replace current higher-education institutions. What is emerging, however, in good-quality universities is the combination of on-line, distant learning and on-site education. This means that the future higher-education system will not be on-line, but on networks between nodes of information, classrooms' sites, and students' individual locations. Computer-mediated communication is diffusing around the world, although with an extremely uneven geography [. . .]. Thus, some segments of societies across the globe, for the time being concentrated in the upper professional strata, interact with each other, reinforcing the social dimension of the space of flows (Batty and Barr, 1994; Graham and Marvin, 1996; Wellman, 1999).

There is no point in exhausting the list of empirical illustrations of the actual impacts of information technology on the spatial dimension of everyday life. What emerges from different observations is a similar picture of simultaneous spatial dispersion and concentration via information technologies. People increasingly work and manage services from their home, as the 1993 survey of the European Foundation for the Improvement of Living and Working Conditions shows (Moran, 1993). Thus, "home centeredness" is an important trend of the new society. Yet it does not mean the end of the city. Because workplaces, schools, medical complexes, consumer services outlets, recreational areas, commercial streets, shopping centers, sports stadiums, and parks still exist and will exist, and people will shuttle between all these places with increasing mobility precisely because of the newly acquired looseness of working arrangements and social networking: as time becomes more flexible, places become more singular, as people circulate among them in an increasingly mobile pattern.

However, the interaction between new information technology and current processes of social change does have a substantial impact on cities and space. On the one hand, the urban form is considerably transformed in its layout. But this transformation does not follow a single, universal pattern: it shows considerable variation depending upon the characteristics of historical, territorial, and institutional contexts. On the other hand, the emphasis on interactivity between places breaks up spatial patterns of behavior into a fluid network of exchanges that underlies the emergence of a new kind of space, the space of flows. On both counts, I must tighten the analysis and raise it to a more theoretical level.

The Transformation of Urban Form: The Informational City

The Information Age is ushering in a new urban form, the informational city. Yet, as the industrial city was not a worldwide replica of Manchester, the emerging informational city will not copy Silicon Valley, let alone Los Angeles. On the other hand, as in the industrial era, in spite of the extraordinary diversity of cultural and physical contexts there are some fundamental common features in the transcultural development of the informational city. I shall argue that, because of the nature of the new society, based upon knowledge, organized around networks, and partly made up of flows, the informational city is not a form but a process, a process characterized by the structural domination of the space of flows. Before developing this idea, I think it is first necessary to introduce the diversity of emerging urban forms in the new historical period, to counter a primitive technological vision that sees the world through the simplified lenses of endless freeways and fiber-optic networks.

America's last suburban frontier

The image of a homogeneous, endless suburban/ex-urban sprawl as the city of the future is belied even by its unwilling model, Los Angeles, whose contradictory complexity is revealed by Mike Davis's marvelous *City of Quartz* (1990). Yet it does evoke a powerful trend in the relentless waves of suburban development in the American metropolis, West and South as well as North and East, toward the end of the millennium. Joel Garreau has captured the similarities of this spatial model across America in his journalistic account of the rise of *Edge City*, as the core of the new urbanization process. He empirically defines Edge City by the combination of five criteria:

> Edge City is any place that: (a) Has five million square feet or more of leasable office space – the work place of the Information Age . . . (b) Has 600,000 square feet or more of leasable retail space . . . (c) Has more jobs than bedrooms (d) Is perceived by the population as one place . . . (e) Was nothing like "city" as recently as thirty years ago. (Garreau, 1991: 6–7).

He reports the mushrooming of such places around Boston, New Jersey, Detroit, Atlanta, Phoenix, Texas, southern California, San Francisco Bay area, and Washington, DC. They are both working areas and service centers around which mile after mile of increasingly dense, single-family dwelling residential units organize the "home centeredness" of private life. He remarks that these ex-urban constellations are:

tied together not by locomotives and subways, but by freeways, jetways, and rooftop satellite dishes thirty feet across. Their characteristic monument is not a horse-mounted hero, but the atria reaching for the sun and shielding trees perpetually in leaf at the core of corporate headquarters, fitness centers, and shopping plazas. These new urban areas are marked not by the penthouses of the old urban rich or the tenements of the old urban poor. Instead, their landmark structure is the celebrated single-family detached dwelling, the suburban home with grass all around that made America the best housed civilization the world has ever known. (Garreau, 1991: 4)

Naturally, where Garreau sees the relentless frontier spirit of American culture, always creating new forms of life and space, James Howard Kunstler (1993) sees the regrettable domination of the "geography of nowhere," thus reigniting a decades-long debate between partisans and detractors of America's sharp spatial departure from its European ancestry. Yet, for the purpose of my analysis, I will retain just two major points of this debate.

First, the development of these loosely interrelated ex-urban constellations emphasizes the functional interdependence of different units and processes in a given urban system over very long distances, minimizing the role of territorial contiguity, and maximizing the communication networks in all their dimensions. Flows of exchange are at the core of the American Edge City.[14]

Secondly, this spatial form is indeed very specific to the American experience because, as Garreau acknowledges, it is embedded in a classic pattern of American history, always pushing for the endless search for a promised land in new settlements. While the extraordinary dynamism that this represents did indeed build one of the most vital nations in history, it did so at the price of creating, over time, staggering social and environmental problems. Each wave of social and physical escapism (for example, the abandonment of inner cities, leaving the lower social classes and ethnic minorities trapped in their ruins) deepened the crisis of American cities (Goldsmith and Blakely, 1992), and made more difficult the management of an overextended infrastructure and of an overstressed society. Unless the development of private "jails-for-rent" in Western Texas is considered a welcome process to complement the social and physical disinvestment in American inner cities, the "*fuite en avant*" of American culture and space seems to have reached the limits of refusing to face unpleasant realities. Thus, the profile of America's informational city is not fully represented by the Edge City phenomenon, but by the relationship between fast ex-urban development, inner-city decay, and obsolescence of the suburban built environment (Gottdiener, 1985; Fainstein et al., 1992).

European cities have entered the Information Age along a different line of spatial restructuring linked to their historical heritage, although finding new issues, not always dissimilar to those emerging in the American context.

The fading charm of European cities

A number of trends constitute together the new urban dynamics of major
European metropolitan areas in the 1990s.[15] The business center is, as in
America, the economic engine of the city, networked in the global economy.
The business center is made up of an infrastructure of telecommunications,
communications, advanced services, and office space, based upon technology-
generating centers and educational institutions. It thrives upon information
processing and control functions. It is usually complemented by tourism and
travel facilities. It is a node of the inter-metropolitan network (Dunford and
Kafkalas, 1992; Robson, 1992). Thus, the business center does not exist by
itself but by its connection to other equivalent locales organized in a network
that forms the actual unit of management, innovation, and work (Tarr and
Dupuy, 1988).

The new managerial–technocratic–political elite does create exclusive spaces,
as segregated and removed from the city at large as the bourgeois quarters of
the industrial society, but, because the professional class is larger, on a much
larger scale. In most European cities (Paris, Rome, Madrid, Amsterdam),
unlike in America – if we except New York, the most un-American of US
cities – the truly exclusive residential areas tend to appropriate urban culture
and history, by locating in rehabilitated or well-preserved areas of the central
city. By so doing, they emphasize the fact that when domination is clearly
established and enforced (unlike in *nouveau-riche* America) the elite does not
need to go into suburban exile to escape the populace. This trend is, however,
limited in the case of the UK where the nostalgia for the life of the gentry in
the countryside translates into up-scale residence in selected suburbs of metropolitan areas, sometimes urbanizing charming historic villages in the vicinity of a major city.

The suburban world of European cities is a socially diversified space; that
is, segmented in different peripheries around the central city. There are the
traditional working-class suburbs, often organized around large, public housing estates, lately in home ownership. There are the new towns, French,
British, or Swedish, inhabited by a younger population of the middle classes,
whose age made it difficult for them to penetrate the housing market of the
central city. And there are also the peripheral ghettos of older public housing
estates, exemplified by Paris's La Courneuve, where new immigrant populations
and poor working families experience exclusion from their "right to the city."
Suburbs are also the locus of manufacturing production in European cities,
both for traditional manufacturing and for new, high-technology industries
that locate in the newest and environmentally most desirable peripheries of
metropolitan areas, close enough to the communication centers but removed
from old industrial districts.

Central cities are still shaped by their history. Thus, traditional working-class neighborhoods, increasingly populated by service workers, constitute a distinctive space, a space that, because it is the most vulnerable, becomes the battleground between the redevelopment efforts of business and the upper middle class, and the invasion attempts of countercultures (Amsterdam, Copenhagen, Berlin) trying to reappropriate the use value of the city. Thus, they often become defensive spaces for workers who only have their home to fight for, being at the same time meaningful popular neighborhoods and likely bastions of xenophobia and localism.

The new professional middle class in Europe is torn between attraction to the peaceful comfort of boring suburbs and the excitement of a hectic, and often too expensive, urban life. The trade-offs between the differential spatial patterns of work of dual-job families often determine the location of their household.

The central city, in Europe as well, is also the focus for the ghettos of immigrants. However, unlike American ghettos, most of these areas are not so economically deprived because immigrant residents are generally workers, with strong family ties, thus counting on a very strong support structure that makes European ghettos family-oriented communities, unlikely to be taken over by street crime. England again seems exceptional in this regard, with some ethnic-minority neighborhoods in London (for example, Tower Hamlets or Hackney) being closer to the American experience than to Paris's La Goutte d'Or. Paradoxically, it is in the core administrative and entertainment districts of European cities, be it Frankfurt or Barcelona, where urban marginality makes its presence felt. Its pervasive occupation of the busiest streets and public transportation nodal points is a survival strategy destined to be present, so that they can receive public attention or private business, whether it be welfare assistance, a drug transaction, a prostitution deal, or the customary police attention.

Major European metropolitan centers present some variation around the urban structure I have outlined, depending upon their differential role in the European network of cities. The lower their position in the new informational network, the greater the difficulty of their transition from the industrial stage, and the more traditional will be their urban structure, with old-established neighborhoods and commercial quarters playing the determinant role in the dynamics of the city. On the other hand, the higher their position in the competitive structure of the new European economy, the greater the role of their advanced services in the business district, and the more intense will be the restructuring of urban space.

The critical factor in the new urban processes, in Europe as elsewhere, is the fact that urban space is increasingly differentiated in social terms, while being functionally interrelated beyond physical contiguity. There follows the separation between symbolic meaning, location of functions, and the social appropriation of space in the metropolitan area. This is the trend underlying the most important transformation of urban forms worldwide, with particular force in the newly industrializing areas: the rise of mega-cities.

Third millennium urbanization: mega-cities

The new global economy and the emerging informational society have indeed a new spatial form, which develops in a variety of social and geographical contexts: mega-cities.[16] Mega-cities are, certainly, very large agglomerations of human beings, all of them (13 in the United Nations classification) with over 10 million people in 1992 (see figure 8.4), and four of them projected to be well over 20 million in 2010. But size is not their defining quality. They are the nodes of the global economy, concentrating the directional, productive, and managerial upper functions all over the planet: the control of the media; the real politics of power; and the symbolic capacity to create and diffuse messages. They have names, most of them alien to the still dominant European/North American cultural matrix: Tokyo, São Paulo, New York, Ciudad de Mexico, Shanghai, Bombay, Los Angeles, Buenos Aires, Seoul, Beijing, Rio de Janeiro, Calcutta, Osaka. In addition, Moscow, Jakarta, Cairo, New Delhi, London, Paris, Lagos, Dacca, Karachi, Tianjin, and possibly others, are in fact members of the club (see Borja and Castells, 1997). Not all of them (for example, Dacca or Lagos) are dominant centers of the global economy, but they do connect to this global system huge segments of the human population. They also function as magnets for their hinterlands; that is, the whole country or regional area where they are located. Mega-cities cannot be seen only in terms of their size, but as a function of their gravitational power toward major regions of the world. Thus, Hong Kong is not just its six million people, and Guangzhou is not just its six and a half million people: what is emerging is a mega-city of 40–50 million people, connecting Hong Kong, Shenzhen, Guangzhou, Zhuhai, Macau, and small towns in the Pearl River Delta, as I shall develop below. Mega-cities articulate the global economy, link up the informational networks, and concentrate the world's power. But they are also the depositories of all these segments of the population who fight to survive, as well as of those groups who want to make visible their dereliction, so that they will not die ignored in areas bypassed by communication networks. Mega-cities concentrate the best and the worst, from the innovators and the powers that be to their structurally irrelevant people, ready to sell their irrelevance or to make "the others" pay for it. Yet what is most significant about mega-cities is that they are connected externally to global networks and to segments of their own countries, while internally disconnecting local populations that are either functionally unnecessary or socially disruptive. I argue that this is true of New York as well as of Mexico or Jakarta. *It is this distinctive feature of being globally connected and locally disconnected, physically and socially, that makes mega-cities a new urban form.* A form that is

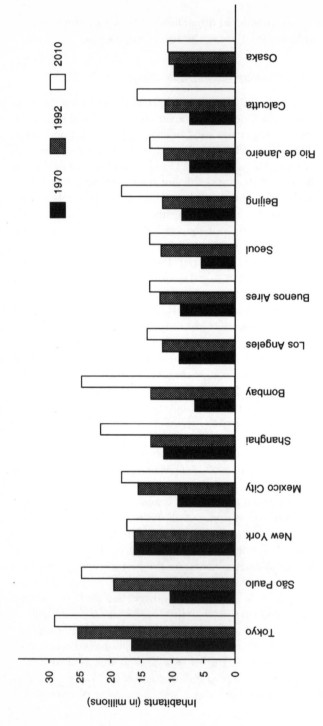

Figure 8.4 The world's largest urban agglomerations (>10 million inhabitants in 1992)

Source: United Nations, 1992

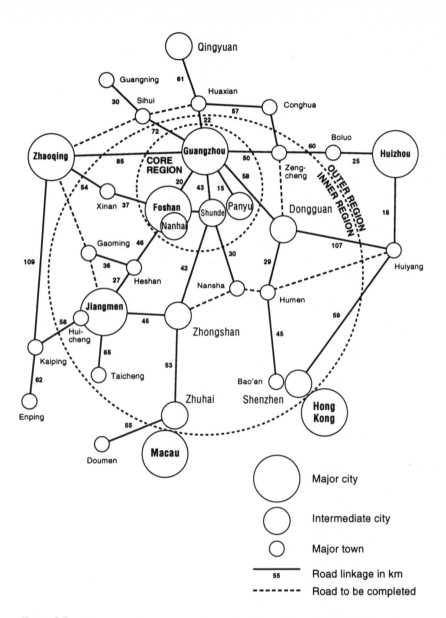

Figure 8.5 Diagrammatic representation of major nodes and links in the urban region of the Pearl River Delta
Source: Woo (1994)

characterized by the functional linkages it establishes across vast expanses of territory, yet with a great deal of discontinuity in land-use patterns. Mega-cities' functional and social hierarchies are spatially blurred and mixed, organized in retrenched encampments, and unevenly patched by unexpected pockets of undesirable uses. Mega-cities are discontinuous constellations of spatial fragments, functional pieces, and social segments (Mollenkopf and Castells, 1991; Lo and Yeung, 1996).

To illustrate my analysis I shall refer to a mega-city in the making that is not even yet on the map but that, in my opinion, will be one of the pre-eminent industrial, business, and cultural centers of the twenty-first century, without indulging in futurology: the Hong Kong–Shenzhen–Canton–Pearl River Delta–Macau–Zhuhai metropolitan regional system.[17] Let us look at the mega-urban future from this vantage point (see figure 8.5). In 1995, this spatial system, still without a name, extended itself over 50,000 km^2, with a total population of between 40 and 50 million, depending on where boundaries are defined. Its units, scattered in a predominantly rural landscape, were functionally connected on a daily basis, and communicated through a multimodal transportation system that included railways, freeways, country roads, hovercrafts, boats, and planes. New superhighways were under construction, and the railway was being fully electrified and double-tracked. An optic fiber telecommunications system was in process of connecting the whole area internally and with the world, mainly via earth stations and cellular telephony. Five new airports were under construction in Hong Kong, Macau, Shenzhen, Zhuhai, and Guangzhou, with a projected passenger traffic capacity of 150 million per year. New container ports were also being built in North Lantau (Hong Kong), Yiantian (Shenzhen), Gaolan (Zhuhai), Huangpo (Guangzhou) and Macau, adding up to the world's largest port capacity in a given location. At the heart of such staggering metropolitan development are three interlinked phenomena:

1   The economic transformation of China, and its link-up to the global economy, with Hong Kong being one of the nodal points in such connection. Thus, in 1981–91, Guandong province's GDP grew at 12.8 percent per year in real terms. Hong Kong-based investors accounted at the end of 1993 for US$40 billion invested in China, representing two-thirds of total foreign direct investment. At the same time, China was also the largest foreign investor in Hong Kong, with about US$25 billion a year (compared with Japan's US$12.7 billion). The management of these capital flows was dependent upon the business transactions operated in, and in between, the various units of this metropolitan system. Thus, Guangzhou was the actual connecting point between Hong Kong business and the governments and enterprises not only of Guandong province, but of inland China.

2   The restructuring of Hong Kong's economic basis in the 1990s led to a dramatic shrinkage of Hong Kong's traditional manufacturing basis, to be replaced by employment in advanced services. Thus, manufacturing workers in Hong Kong decreased from 837,000 in 1988 to 484,000 in 1993, while employees in trading and business sectors increased, in the same period, from 947,000 to 1.3 million. Hong Kong developed its functions as a global business center.

3   However, Hong Kong's manufacturing exports capacity did not fade away: it simply modified its industrial organization and its spatial location. In about ten years, between the mid-1980s and the mid-1990s, Hong Kong's industrialists induced one of the largest-scale processes of industrialization in human history in the small towns of the Pearl River Delta. By the end of 1994, Hong Kong investors, often using family and village connections, had established in the Pearl River Delta 10,000 joint ventures and 20,000 processing factories, in which were working about 6 million workers, depending upon various estimates. Much of this population, housed in company dormitories in semi-rural locations, came from surrounding provinces beyond the borders of Guandong. This gigantic industrial system was being managed on a daily basis from a multilayered managerial structure, based in Hong Kong, regularly traveling to Guangzhou, with production runs being supervised by local managers throughout the rural area. Materials, technology, and managers were being sent from Hong Kong and Shenzhen, and manufactured goods were generally exported from Hong Kong (actually surpassing the value of Hong Kong-made exports), although the building of new container ports in Yiantian and Gaolan aimed at diversifying export sites.

This accelerated process of export-oriented industrialization and business linkages between China and the global economy led to an unprecedented urban explosion. Shenzhen Special Economic Zone, on the Hong Kong border, grew from zero to 1.5 million inhabitants between 1982 and 1995. Local governments in the whole area, full of cash from overseas Chinese investors, embarked on the construction of major infrastructural projects, the most amazing of which, still in the planning stage at the time of writing, was the decision by Zhuhai's local government to build a 60 km bridge over the South China Sea to link by road Zhuhai and Hong Kong.

The southern China metropolis, still in the making but a sure reality, is a new spatial form. It is not the traditional megalopolis identified by Gottman in the 1960s on the north-eastern seaboard of the United States. Unlike this classical case, the Hong Kong–Guandong metropolitan region is not made up of the physical conurbation of successive urban/suburban units with relative functional autonomy in each one of them. It is rapidly becoming an interdependent unit, economically, functionally, and socially, even more so after Hong Kong and Macau rejoined China. But there is considerable spatial discontinuity within the area, with rural settlements, agricultural land, and undeveloped areas separating urban centers, and industrial factories being scattered all over the region. The internal linkages of the area and the indispensable connection of the whole system to the global economy via multiple communication links are the real backbone of this new spatial unit. Flows define the spatial form and processes. Within each city, within each area, processes of segregation and segmentation take place, in a pattern of endless variation. But such segmented diversity is dependent upon a functional unity marked by gigantic, technology-intensive infrastructures, which seem to know as their only limit the amount of fresh water that the region can still retrieve from the East River area. The southern China metropolis, only vaguely perceived in most of the world at this time, is likely to become the most representative urban face of the twenty-first century.

Current trends point in the direction of another Asian mega-city on an even greater scale when, in the early twenty-first century, the corridor Tokyo–Yokohama–Nagoya (already a functional unit) links up with Osaka–Kobe–Kyoto, creating the largest metropolitan agglomeration in human history, not only in terms of population, but in economic and technological power. Thus, in spite of all their social, urban and environmental problems, mega-cities will continue to grow, both in their size and in their attractiveness for the location of high-level functions and for people's choice. The ecological dream of small, quasi-rural communes will be pushed away to countercultural marginality by the historical tide of mega-city development. This is because mega-cities are:

- centers of economic, technological, and social dynamism, in their countries and on a global scale; they are the actual development engines; their countries' economic fate, be it the United States or China, depends on mega-cities' performance, in spite of the small-town ideology still pervasive in both countries;
- centers of cultural and political innovation;
- connecting points to the global networks of every kind; the Internet cannot bypass mega-cities: it depends on the telecommunications and on the "telecommunicators" located in those centers.

To be sure, some factors will slow down their pace of growth, depending on the accuracy and effectiveness of policies designed to limit mega-cities' growth. Family planning is working, in spite of the Vatican, so we can expect a continuation of the decline in the birthrate already taking place. Policies of regional development may be able to diversify the concentration of jobs and population to other areas. And I foresee large-scale epidemics, and disintegration of social control that will make mega-cities less attractive. However, overall, mega-cities will grow in size and dominance, because they keep feeding themselves on population, wealth, power, and innovators, from their extended hinterland. Furthermore, they are the nodal points connecting to the global networks. Thus, in a fundamental sense, the future of humankind, and of each mega-city's country, is being played out in the evolution and management of these areas. Mega-cities are the nodal points, and the power centers of the new spatial form/process of the Information Age: the space of flows.

Having laid out the empirical landscape of new territorial phenomena, we now have to come to grips with the understanding of such a new spatial reality. This requires an unavoidable excursus through the uncertain trails of the theory of space.

The Social Theory of Space and the Theory of the Space of Flows

Space is the expression of society. Since our societies are undergoing structural transformation, it is a reasonable hypothesis to suggest that new spatial forms and processes are currently emerging. The purpose of the analysis presented here is to identify the new logic underlying such forms and processes.

The task is not an easy one because the apparently simple acknowledgement of a meaningful relationship between society and space hides a fundamental complexity. This is because space is not a reflection of society, it is its expression. In other words: space is not a photocopy of society, it is society. Spatial forms and processes are formed by the dynamics of the overall social structure. This includes contradictory trends derived from conflicts and strategies between social actors playing out their opposing interests and values. Furthermore, social processes influence space by acting on the built environment inherited from previous socio-spatial structures. Indeed, *space is crystallized time.* To approach in the simplest possible terms such a complexity, let us proceed step by step.

What is space? In physics, it cannot be defined outside the dynamics of matter. In social theory, it cannot be defined without reference to social practices. This area of theorizing being one of my old trades, I still approach the issue under the assumption that "space is a material product, in relationship to other material products – including people – who engage in [historically] determined social relationships that provide space with a form, a function, and a social meaning" (Castells, 1972: 152; my own translation). In a convergent and clearer formulation, David Harvey, in his book *The Condition of Postmodernity*, states that "from a materialist perspective, we can argue that objective conceptions of time and space are necessarily created through material practices and processes which serve to reproduce social life ... It is a fundamental axiom of my enquiry that time and space cannot be understood independently of social action" (Harvey, 1990: 204). Thus, we have to define, at a general level, what space is, from the point of view of social practices; then, we must identify the historical specificity of social practices, for example those in the informational society that underlie the emergence and consolidation of new spatial forms and processes.

From the point of view of social theory, *space is the material support of time-sharing social practices*. I immediately add that any material support bears always a symbolic meaning. By time-sharing social practices I refer to the fact that space brings together those practices that are simultaneous in time. It is the material articulation of this simultaneity that gives sense to space *vis-à-vis* society. Traditionally, this notion was assimilated to contiguity. Yet it is fundamental that we separate the basic concept of material support of simultaneous practices from the notion of contiguity, in order to account for the possible existence of material supports of simultaneity that do not rely on physical contiguity, since this is precisely the case of the dominant social practices of the Information Age.

I have argued in the preceding chapters [of *The Network Society*] that our society is constructed around flows: flows of capital, flows of information, flows of technology, flows of organizational interaction, flows of images, sounds, and symbols. Flows are not just one element of the social organization: they are the expression of processes *dominating* our economic, political, and symbolic life. If such is the case, the material support of the dominant processes in our societies will be the ensemble of elements supporting such flows, and making materially possible their articulation in simultaneous time. Thus, I propose the idea that there is a new spatial form characteristic of social practices that dominate and shape the network society: the space of flows. *The space of flows is the material organization of time-sharing social practices that work through flows*. By flows I understand purposeful, repetitive, programmable sequences of exchange and interaction between physically disjointed positions held by social actors in the economic, political, and symbolic structures of society. Dominant social practices are those which are embedded in dominant social structures. By dominant structures I understand those arrangements of organizations and institutions whose internal logic plays a strategic role in shaping social practices and social consciousness for society at large.

The abstraction of the concept of the space of flows can be better understood by specifying its content. The space of flows, as the material form of support of dominant processes and functions in the informational society, can be described (rather than defined) by the combination of at least three layers of material supports that, together, constitute the space of flows. *The first layer, the first material support of the space of flows, is actually constituted by a circuit of electronic exchanges* (micro-electronics-based devices, telecommunications, computer processing, broadcasting systems, and high-speed transportation – also based on information technologies) that, together, form the material basis for the processes we have observed as being strategically crucial in the network of society. This is indeed a material support of simultaneous practices. Thus, it is a spatial form, just as it could be "the city" or "the region" in the organization of the merchant society or of the industrial society. The spatial articulation of dominant functions does take place in our societies in the network of interactions made possible by information technology devices. In this network, no place exists by itself, since the positions are defined by the exchanges of flows in the network. Thus, the network of communication is the fundamental spatial configuration: places do not disappear, but their logic and their meaning become absorbed in the network. The technological infrastructure that builds up the network defines the new space, very much like railways defined "economic regions" and "national markets" in the industrial economy; or the boundary-specific, institutional rules of citizenry (and their technologically advanced armies) defined "cities" in the merchant origins of capitalism and democracy. This technological infrastructure is itself the expression of the network of flows whose architecture and content is determined by the powers that be in our world.

The second layer of the space of flows is constituted by its nodes and hubs. The space of flows is not placeless, although its structural logic is. It is based on an electronic network, but this network links up specific places, with well-defined social, cultural, physical, and functional characteristics. Some places are exchangers, communication hubs playing a role of coordination for the smooth interaction of all the elements integrated into the network. Other places are the nodes of the network; that is, the location of strategically important functions that build a series of locality-based activities and organizations around a key function in the network. Location in the node links up the locality with the whole network. Both nodes and hubs are hierarchically organized according to their relative weight in the network. But this hierarchy may change depending upon the evolution of activities processed through the network. Indeed, in some instances, some places may be switched off the network, their disconnection resulting in instant decline, and thus in economic, social and physical deterioration. The characteristics of nodes are dependent upon the type of functions performed by a given network.

Some examples of networks, and their corresponding nodes, will help to communicate the concept. The easiest type of network to visualize as representative of the space of flows is the network constituted by decision-making systems of the global economy, particularly those relative to the financial system. This refers to the analysis of the global city as a process rather than a place, as presented in this chapter. The analysis of the "global city" as the production site of the informational, global economy has shown the critical role of these global cities in our societies, and the dependence of local societies and economies upon the directional functions located in such cities. But beyond the main global cities, other continental, national, and regional economies have their own nodes that connect to the global network. Each one of these nodes requires an adequate technological infrastructure, a system of ancillary firms providing the support services, a specialized labor market, and the system of services required by the professional labor force.

As I showed above, what is true for top managerial functions and financial markets is also applicable to high-technology manufacturing (both to industries producing high technology and to those using high technology, that is all advanced manufacturing). The spatial division of labor that characterizes high-technology manufacturing translates into the worldwide connection between the milieux of innovation, the skilled manufacturing sites, the assembly lines, and the market-oriented factories, with a series of intra-firm linkages between the different operations in different locations along the production lines; and another series of inter-firm linkages among similar functions of production located in specific sites that become production complexes. Directional nodes, production sites, and communication hubs are defined along the network and articulated in a common logic by communication technologies and programmable, micro-electronics-based, flexible integrated manufacturing.

The functions to be fulfilled by each network define the characteristics of places that become their privileged nodes. In some cases, the most unlikely sites become central nodes because of historical specificity that ends up centering a given network around a particular locality. For instance, it was unlikely that Rochester, Minnesota, or the Parisian suburb of Villejuif would become central nodes of a world network of advanced medical treatment and health research, in close interaction with each other. But the location of the Mayo Clinic at Rochester and of one of the main centers for cancer treatment of the French health administration at Villejuif, in both cases for accidental, historical reasons, have articulated a complex of knowledge generation and advanced medical treatment around these two odd locales. Once established, they attracted researchers, doctors, and patients from around the world: they became a node in the world's medical network.

Each network defines its sites according to the functions and hierarchy of each site, and to the characteristics of the product or service to be processed in the network. Thus, one of the most powerful networks in our society, narcotics production and distribution (including its money-laundering component), has constructed a specific geography that has redefined the meaning, structure, and culture of societies, regions, and cities connected in the network (Arrieta et al., 1991; Laserna, 1995). Thus, in cocaine production and trade, the coca production sites of Chapare or Alto Beni in Bolivia or Alto Huallanga in Peru are connected to the refineries and management centers in Colombia, which were subsidiary, until 1995, to the Medellin or Cali headquarters, themselves connected to financial centers such as Miami, Panama, the Cayman Islands, and Luxembourg, and to transportation centers, such as the Tamaulipas or Tijuana drug traffic networks in Mexico, then finally to distribution points in the main metropolitan areas of America and Western Europe. None of these localities can exist by itself in such a network. The Medellin and Cali cartels, and their close American and Italian allies, would have been out of business a long time before being dismantled by repression without the raw materials produced in Bolivia or Peru, without the chemicals (precursors) provided by Swiss and German laboratories, without the semi-legal financial networks of free-banking paradises, and without the distribution networks starting in Miami, Los Angeles, New York, Amsterdam, or La Coruña.

Therefore, while the analysis of global cities provides the most direct illustration of the place-based orientation of the space of flows in nodes and hubs, this logic is not limited by any means to capital flows. The main dominant processes in our society are articulated in networks that link up different places and assign to each one of them a role and a weight in a hierarchy of wealth generation, information processing, and power making that ultimately conditions the fate of each locale.

The third important layer of the space of flows refers to the spatial organization of the dominant, managerial elites (rather than classes) that exercise the directional functions around which such space is articulated. The theory of the space of flows starts from the implicit assumption that societies are asymmetrically organized around the dominant interests specific to each social structure. The space of flows is not the only spatial logic of our societies. It is, however, the dominant spatial logic because it is the spatial logic of the dominant interests/functions in our society. But such domination is not purely structural. It is enacted, indeed conceived, decided, and implemented by social actors. Thus, the technocratic–financial–managerial elite that occupies the leading positions in our societies will also have specific spatial requirements regarding the material/spatial support of their interests and practices. The spatial manifestation of the informational elite constitutes another fundamental dimension of the space of flows. What is this spatial manifestation?

The fundamental form of domination in our society is based on the organizational capacity of the dominant elite that goes hand in hand with its capacity to disorganize those groups in society which, while constituting a numerical majority, see their interests partially (if ever) represented only within the framework of the fulfillment of the dominant interests. Articulation of the elites, segmentation and disorganization of the masses seem to be the twin mechanisms of social domination in our societies (see Zukin, 1992). Space plays a fundamental role in this mechanism. In short: elites are cosmopolitan, people are local. The space of power and wealth is projected throughout the world, while people's life and experience are rooted in places, in their culture, in their history. Thus, the more a social organization is based upon ahistorical flows, superseding the logic of any specific place, the more the logic of global power escapes the socio-political control of historically specific local/national societies.

On the other hand, the elites do not want and cannot become flows themselves, if they are to preserve their social cohesion, develop the set of rules and the cultural codes by which they can understand each other and dominate the others, thus establishing the "in" and "out" boundaries of their cultural/political community. The more a society is democratic in its institutions, the more the elites have to become clearly distinct from the populace, so avoiding the excessive penetration of political representatives into the inner world of strategic decision-making. However, my analysis does not share the hypothesis about the improbable existence of a "power elite" *à la* Wright Mills. On the contrary, the real social domination stems from the fact that cultural codes are embedded in the social structure in such a way that the possession of these codes opens the access to the power structure without the elite needing to conspire to bar access to its networks.

The spatial manifestation of this logic of domination takes two main forms in the space of flows. On the one hand, the elites form their own society, and constitute symbolically secluded communities, retrenched behind the very material barrier of real-estate pricing. They define their community as a spatially bound, interpersonally networked subculture. I propose the hypothesis that the space of flows is made up of personal micro-networks that project their interests in functional macro-networks throughout the global set of interactions in the space of flows. This is a well-known phenomenon in the financial networks: major strategic decisions are taken over business luncheons in exclusive restaurants, or in country house week-ends over golf playing, as in the good old days. But such decisions will be executed in instant decision-making processes over telecommunicated computers which can trigger their own decisions to react to market trends. Thus, the nodes of the space of flows include residential and leisure-oriented spaces which, along with the location of headquarters and their ancillary services, tend to cluster dominant functions in carefully segregated spaces, with easy access to cosmopolitan complexes of arts, culture, and entertainment. Segregation happens both by location in different places and by security control of certain spaces open only to the elite. From the pinnacles of power and their cultural centers, a series of symbolic socio-spatial hierarchies is organized, so that lower levels of management can mirror the symbols of power and appropriate such symbols by constructing second-order spatial communities that will also tend to isolate themselves from the rest of society, in a succession of hierarchical segregation processes that, together, are tantamount to sociospatial fragmentation. At the limit, when social tensions rise, and cities decay, elites take refuge behind the walls of "gated communities," a major phenomenon around the world in the late 1990s, from southern California to Cairo and from São Paulo to Bogota (Blakely and Snyder, 1997).

A second major trend of cultural distinctiveness of the elites in the informational society is to create a lifestyle and to design spatial forms aimed at unifying the symbolic environment of the elite around the world, thus superseding the historical specificity of each locale. Thus, there is the construction of a (relatively) secluded space across the world along the connecting lines of the space of flows: international hotels whose decoration, from the design of the room to the color of the towels, is similar all over the world to create a sense of familiarity with the inner world, while inducing abstraction from the surrounding world; airports' VIP lounges, designed to maintain distance *vis-à-vis* society in the highways of the space of flows; mobile, personal, on-line access to telecommunications networks, so that the traveler is never lost; and a system of travel arrangements, secretarial services, and reciprocal hosting that maintains a close circle of the corporate elite together through the worshipping of similar rites in all countries. Furthermore, there is an increasingly homogeneous lifestyle among the information elite that transcends the cultural borders of all societies: the regular use of SPA installations (even when traveling), and the practice of jogging; the mandatory diet of grilled salmon and green salad, with *udon* and *sashimi* providing a Japanese functional equivalent; the "pale chamois" wall color intended to create the cozy atmosphere of the inner space; the ubiquitous laptop computer, and Internet access; the combination of business suits and sportswear; the unisex dressing style, and so on. All these are symbols of an international culture whose identity is not linked to any specific society but to membership of the managerial circles of the informational economy across a global cultural spectrum.

The call for cultural connectedness of the space of flows between its different nodes is also reflected in the tendency toward the architectural uniformity of the new directional centers in various societies. Paradoxically, the attempt by postmodern architecture to break the molds and patterns of architectural discipline has resulted in an overimposed postmodern monumentality which became the generalized rule of new corporate headquarters from New York to Kaoshiung during the 1980s. Thus, the space of flows includes the symbolic connection of homogeneous architecture in the places that constitute the nodes of each network across the world, so that architecture escapes from the history and culture of each society and becomes captured into the new imaginary, wonderland world of unlimited possibilities that underlies the logic transmitted by multimedia: the culture of electronic surfing, as if we could reinvent all forms in any place, on the sole condition of leaping into the cultural indefinition of the flows of power. The enclosure of architecture into an historical abstraction is the formal frontier of the space of flows.

The Architecture of the End of History

Nomada, sigo siendo un nomada.

Ricardo Bofill[18]

If the space of flows is truly the dominant spatial form of the network society, architecture and design are likely to be redefined in their form, function, process, and value in the coming years. Indeed, I would argue that all over history, architecture has been the "failed act" of society, the mediated expression of the deeper tendencies of society, of those that could not be openly declared but yet were strong enough to be cast in stone, in concrete, in steel, in glass, and in the visual perception of the human beings who were to dwell, deal, or worship in such forms.

Panofsky on Gothic cathedrals, Tafuri on American skyscrapers, Venturi on the surprisingly kitsch American city, Lynch on city images, Harvey on postmodernism as the expression of time/space compression by capitalism, are some of the best illustrations of an intellectual tradition that has used the forms of the built environment as one of the most signifying codes to read the basic structures of society's dominant values (Panofsky, 1957; Lynch, 1960; Tafuri, 1971; Venturi et al., 1977; Harvey, 1990). To be sure, there is no simple, direct interpretation of the formal expression of social values. But as research by scholars and analysts has revealed, and as works by architects have demonstrated, there has always been a strong, semiconscious connection between what society (in its diversity) was saying and what architects wanted to say (see Burlen, 1972).

Not any more. My hypothesis is that the coming of the space of flows is blurring the meaningful relationship between architecture and society. Because the spatial manifestation of the dominant interests takes place around the world, and across cultures, the uprooting of experience, history, and specific culture as the background of meaning is leading to the generalization of ahistorical, acultural architecture.

Some tendencies of "postmodern architecture," as represented for instance by the works of Philip Johnson or Charles Moore, under the pretext of breaking down the tyranny of codes, such as modernism, attempt to cut off all ties with specific social environments. So did modernism in its time, but as the expression of an historically rooted culture that asserted the belief in progress, technology and rationality. In contrast, postmodern architecture declares the end of all systems of meaning. It creates a mixture of elements that searches formal harmony out of transhistorical, stylistic provocation. Irony becomes the preferred mode of expression. Yet, in fact what most postmodernism does is to express, in almost direct terms, the new dominant ideology: the end of history and the supersession of places in the space of flows.[19] Because only if

Figure 8.6   Downtown Kaoshiung
Photograph: Professor Hsia Chu-joe

we are at the end of history can we now mix up everything we knew before (see figure 8.6). Because we do not belong any longer to any place, to any culture, the extreme version of postmodernism imposes its codified code-breaking logic anywhere something is built. The liberation from cultural codes hides in fact the escape from historically rooted societies. In this perspective, postmodernism could be considered the architecture of the space of flows.[20]

The more that societies try to recover their identity beyond the global logic of uncontrolled power of flows, the more they need an architecture that exposes their own reality, without faking beauty from a transhistorical spatial repertoire. But at the same time, oversignificant architecture, trying to give a very definite message or to express directly the codes of a given culture, is too primitive a form to be able to penetrate our saturated visual imaginary. The meaning of its messages will be lost in the culture of "surfing" that characterizes our symbolic behavior. This is why, paradoxically, the architecture that seems most charged with meaning in societies shaped by the logic of the space of flows is what I call "the architecture of nudity." That is, the architecture whose forms are so neutral, so pure, so diaphanous, that they do not pretend to say anything. And by not saying anything they confront the experience with the solitude of the space of flows. Its message is the silence.

For the sake of communication, I shall use two examples drawn from

Figure 8.7   The entrance hall of Barcelona airport
Source: Original drawing by Ricardo Bofill; reproduced by kind permission of Ricardo Bofill

Spanish architecture, an architectural milieu that is widely recognized as being currently at the forefront of design. Both concern, not by accident, the design of major communication nodes, where the space of flows materializes ephemerally. The Spanish festivities of 1992 provided the occasion for the construction of major functional buildings designed by some of the best architects. Thus, the new Barcelona airport, designed by Bofill, simply combines beautiful marble floor, dark glass façade, and transparent glass separating panels in an immense, open space (see figure 8.7). No cover up of the fear and anxiety that people experience in an airport. No carpeting, no cozy rooms, no indirect lighting. In the middle of the cold beauty of this airport passengers have to face their terrible truth: they are alone, in the middle of the space of flows, they may lose their connection, they are suspended in the emptiness of transition. They are, literally, in the hands of Iberia Airlines. And there is no escape.

Let us take another example: the new Madrid AVE (high-speed train) station, designed by Rafael Moneo. It is simply a wonderful old station, exquisitely rehabilitated, and made into an indoor palm-tree park, full of birds that sing and fly in the enclosed space of the station. In a nearby structure, adjacent to such a beautiful, monumental space, there is the real station with the high-speed train. Thus, people go to the pseudo-station, to visit it, to walk through its different levels and paths, as they go to a park or a museum. The too-obvious message is that we are in a park, not in a station; that in the old station, trees grew, and birds nested, operating a metamorphosis. Thus, the high-speed train becomes the oddity in this space. And this is in fact the question everybody in the world asks: what is a high-speed train doing there, just to go from Madrid to Seville, with no connection whatsoever with the European high-speed network, at a cost of US$4 billion? The broken mirror of a segment of the space of flows becomes exposed, and the use value of the station recovered, in a simple, elegant design that does not say much but makes everything evident.

Some prominent architects, such as Rem Koolhas, the designer of the Lille Grand Palais Convention Center, theorize the need to adapt architecture to the process of de-localization, and to the relevance of communication nodes in people's experience: Koolhas actually sees his project as an expression of the "space of flows." Or, in another instance of a growing self-awareness of architects about the structural transformation of space, the American Institute of Architects' award-winning design of D.E. Shaw and Company's offices by Steven Holl in New York's West 45th Street (figure 8.8):

Figure 8.8 The waiting room at D. E. Shaw and Company: no ficus trees, no sectional sofas, no corporate art on the walls
Source: Muschamp (1992)

offers [in Herbert Muschamp's words] a poetic interpretation of . . . the space
of flows . . . Mr Holl's design takes the Shaw offices to a place as novel as the
information technology that paid to build them. When we walk in the door of
D.E. Shaw we know we are not in 1960s Manhattan or Colonial New England.
For that matter, we have left even much of present day New York far below on
the ground. Standing inside the Holl atrium we have got our head in the clouds
and our feet firmly planted on solid air. (Muschamp, 1992)

Granted we may be forcing Bofill, Moneo, and even Holl into discourses
that are not theirs.[21] But the simple fact that their architecture would allow
me, or Herbert Muschamp, to relate forms to symbols, to functions, to social
situations, means that their strict, retained architecture (in rather formally
different styles) is in fact full of meaning. Indeed, architecture and design,
because their forms either resist or interpret the abstract materiality of the
dominant space of flows, could become essential devices of cultural innovation and intellectual autonomy in the informational society through two main
avenues. Either the new architecture builds the palaces of the new masters,
thus exposing their deformity hidden behind the abstraction of the space of
flows; or it roots itself into places, thus into culture, and into people.[22] In both
cases, under different forms, architecture and design may be digging the
trenches of resistance for the preservation of meaning in the generation of
knowledge. Or, which is the same, for the reconciliation of culture and technology.

Space of Flows and Space of Places

The space of flows does not permeate down to the whole realm of human
experience in the network society. Indeed, the overwhelming majority of
people, in advanced and traditional societies alike, live in places, and so they
perceive their space as place-based. *A place is a locale whose form, function, and
meaning are self-contained within the boundaries of physical contiguity.* A place, to
illustrate my argument, is the Parisian *quartier* of Belleville.

Belleville was, as for so many immigrants throughout its history, my entry
point to Paris, in 1962. As a 20-year-old political exile, without much to lose
except my revolutionary ideals, I was given shelter by a Spanish construction
worker, an anarchist union leader, who introduced me to the tradition of the
place. Nine years later, this time as a sociologist, I was still walking Belleville,
working with immigrant workers' committees, and studying social movements
against urban renewal: the struggles of what I labeled *"La Cité du Peuple,"*
reported in my first book (Castells, 1972: 496ff). More than thirty years after
our first encounter, both Belleville and I have changed. But Belleville is still a
place, while I am afraid I look more like a flow. The new immigrants (Asians,
Yugoslavs) have joined a long-established stream of Tunisian Jews, Maghrebian

Figure 8.9   Belleville, 1999: a multicultural, urban place
Photograph: Irene Castells and Jose Bailo

Muslims, and southern Europeans, themselves the successors of the intra-urban exiles pushed into Belleville in the nineteenth century by the Hausmannian design of building a bourgeois Paris. Belleville itself has been hit by several waves of urban renewal, intensified in the 1970s.[23] Its traditional physical landscape of a poor but harmonious historic *faubourg* has been messed up with plastic postmodernism, cheap modernism, and sanitized gardens on top of a still somewhat dilapidated housing stock. And yet, Belleville in 1999 is a clearly identifiable place, both from the outside and from the inside (see figure 8.9). Ethnic communities that often degenerate into hostility toward each other coexist peacefully in Belleville, although keeping track of their own turf, and certainly not without tensions. New middle-class households, generally young, have joined the neighborhood because of its urban vitality, and powerfully contribute to its survival, while self-controlling the impacts of gentrification. Cultures and histories, in a truly plural urbanity, interact in the space, giving meaning to it, linking up with the "city of collective memory" *à la* Christine Boyer (1994). The landscape pattern swallows and digests substantial physical modifications, by integrating them in its mixed uses and active street life. Yet Belleville is by no means the idealized version of the lost community, which probably never existed, as Oscar Lewis demonstrated in his revisit of Tepoztlan. Places are not necessarily communities,

Figure 8.10   Las Ramblas, Barcelona, 1999: city life in a liveable place
Photograph: Jordi Borja and Zaída Muxi

although they may contribute to community-building. But the life of their inhabitants is marked by their characteristics, so that they are indeed good and bad places depending on the value judgement of what a good life is (see figure 8.10). In Belleville, its dwellers, without loving each other, and while certainly not being loved by the police, have constructed throughout history a meaningful, interacting space, with a diversity of uses and a wide range of functions and expressions. They actively interact with their daily physical environment. In between home and the world, there is a place called Belleville.

Not all places are socially interactive and spatially rich. It is precisely because their physical/symbolic qualities make them different that they are places. Thus Allan Jacobs, in his great book about *Great Streets* (1993), examines the difference in urban quality between Barcelona and Irvine (the epitome of suburban southern California) on the basis of the number and frequency of intersections in the street pattern: his findings go even beyond what any informed urbanist could imagine (see figures 8.11 and 8.12). So Irvine is indeed a place, although a special kind of place, where the space of experience shrinks inward toward the home, as flows take over increasing shares of time and space.

The relationships between the space of flows and the space of places, between simultaneous globalization and localization, are not predetermined in their outcome. For instance, Tokyo underwent a substantial process of

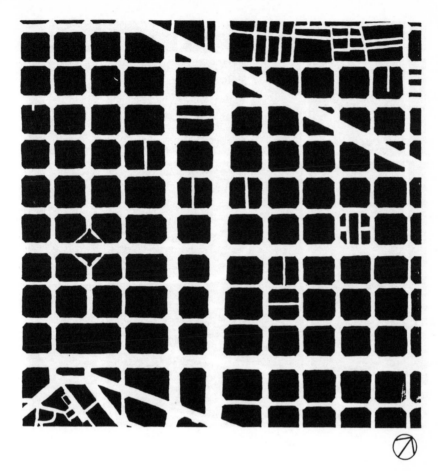

Figure 8.11 Barcelona: Paseo de Gracia
Source: Jacobs (1993)

urban restructuring during the 1980s to live up to its role as "a global city," a process fully documented by Machimura. The city government, sensitive to the deep-seated Japanese fear about the loss of identity, added to its business-oriented restructuring policy an image-making policy of singing the virtues of old Edo, pre-Meiji Tokyo. An historical museum (*Edo-Tokyo Hakubutsakan*) was opened in 1993, a public relations magazine was published, exhibitions regu-

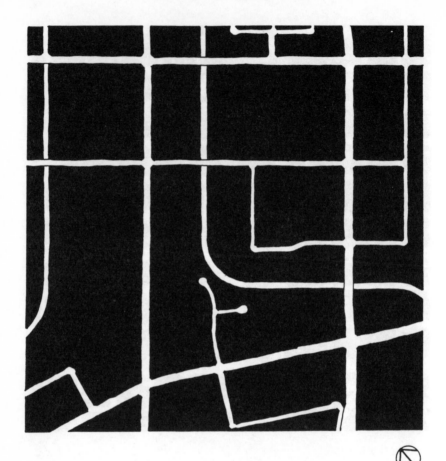

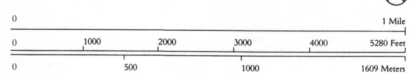

Figure 8.12 Irvine, California: business complex
Source: Jacobs (1993)

larly organized. As Machimura writes, "Although these views seem to go in totally different directions, both of them seek for redefinition of the Western-ized image of the city in more domestic ways. Now, 'Japanization' of the Westernized city provides an important context for the discourse about 'glo-bal city' Tokyo after modernism."[24] Yet Tokyo citizens were not complaining just about the loss of historical essence, but about the reduction of their everyday life's space to the instrumental logic of the global city. A project symbolized this logic: the celebration of a World City Fair in 1997, a good occasion to build another, major business complex on reclaimed land in Tokyo Harbor. Large construction companies happily obliged, and work was well underway in 1995. Suddenly, in the 1995 municipal election, an independent candidate, Aoshima, a television comedian without backing from political parties or financial circles, campaigned on a one-issue program: to cancel the World City Fair. He won the election by a large margin, and became governor of Tokyo. A few weeks later, he kept his campaign promise and canceled the World City Fair to the disbelief of the corporate elite. The local logic of civil society was catching up with, and contradicting, the global logic of international business.

Thus, people do still live in places. But because function and power in our societies are organized in the space of flows, the structural domination of its logic essentially alters the meaning and dynamic of places. Experience, by being related to places, becomes abstracted from power, and meaning is increasingly separated from knowledge. There follows a structural schizo-phrenia between two spatial logics that threatens to break down communication channels in society. The dominant tendency is toward a horizon of networked, ahistorical space of flows, aiming at imposing its logic over scattered, segmented places, increasingly unrelated to each other, less and less able to share cultural codes. Unless cultural, political, *and physical* bridges are deliberately built between these two forms of space, we may be heading toward life in parallel universes whose times cannot meet because they are warped into different dimensions of a social hyperspace.

NOTES

1   For an excellent overview of the interaction between telecommunications and spatial processes, see Graham and Marvin (1996). For evidence of the impact of telecommunications on business districts, see Moss (1987, 1991, 1992: 147–58). For a summary of the evidence on teleworking and telecommuting in advanced societies, see Korte et al. (1988); and Qvortup (1992).

2   To a large extent, the empirical basis and the analytical foundations of this chapter rely on the research work I did in the 1980s, summarized and elaborated in my book *The Informational City: Information Technology, Economic Restructuring, and the Urban–Regional Process* (Castells, 1989b). Although this chapter contains up-dated, additional information on various countries, as well as further theoretical elaboration, I still refer the reader to the cited book for more detailed analysis and empirical support of the analysis presented here. Accordingly, *I shall not repeat here the empirical sources that have been used and cited in the above-mentioned book.* This note should be considered as a generic reference to the sources and material contained in *The Informational City*. For an up-to-date discussion on these matters, see also Graham and Marvin (1996, 2000). For an historical, analytical, and cultural

overview of the evolution of cities, see the masterpiece by Sir Peter Hall (1998). For an international perspective on urbanization, see Borja and Castells (1997).

3   For an excellent overview of current transformations of spatial forms and processes at the global level, see Hall (1995: 3–32).

4   For a summary of the research report, see Castells (1991).

5   Personal notes, reported by Sassen over a glass of Argentinian wine, Harvard Inn, April 22, 1994.

6   For an approximation to the differentiation of social worlds in global cities, using New York as an illustration, see the various essays collected in Mollenkopf (1989); and Mollenkopf and Castells (1991); see also Zukin (1992).

7   For evidence on spatial decentralization of services, see Marshall et al. (1988); Castells (1989b: ch. 3); Daniels (1993: ch. 5).

8   For an analytical summary of the evidence gathered by these studies on new patterns of manufacturing location, see Castells (1988). See also Scott (1988); Henderson (1989).

9   The concept of milieu of innovation, as applied to technological/industrial development, emerged in the early 1980s in a series of exchanges, in Berkeley, between Peter Hall, the late Philippe Aydalot, and myself. We were also influenced by some economic writings on the matter, around the same time, by B. Arthur and by A. E. Anderson. Peter Hall and I, in separate papers, attempted formulations of the concept in 1984 and subsequent years; and in Europe the research network originally organized by Philippe Aydalot, the Groupe de Recherche sur les Milieux Innovateurs (GREMI), undertook systematic research on the matter, published in 1986 and subsequent years. Among GREMI researchers, Roberto Camagni provided, in my personal opinion, the most precise analysis on this topic.

10   For sources on topics covered in this section, see Graham and Marvin (1996); Wheeler and Aoyama (2000).

11   "Telecommuting data form link resources corporation," cited by Mokhtarian (1991b).

12   "The new face of business," in *Business Week* (1994: 99ff).

13   I have relied on a balanced evaluation of impacts by Vessali (1995).

14   See the collection of papers gathered in Caves (1994).

15   For developments on European cities, see Borja et al. (1991); Deben et al. (1993); Martinotti (1993); Siino (1994); Hall (1995); Borja and Castells (1997).

16   The notion of mega-cities has been popularized by several urban experts in the international arena, most notably by Janice Perlman, founder and director of the New York-based "Mega-cities Project." For a journalistic account of her vision, see *Time* (1993), which also offers basic data on the topic.

17   My analysis on the emerging southern China metropolis is based, on the one hand, on my personal knowledge of the area, particularly of Hong Kong and Shenzhen, where I conducted research in the 1980s; on the other hand, particularly for developments in the 1990s, on a number of sources of which the most relevant are the following: Sit (1991); Leung (1993); Lo (1994); Hsing (1995); Kwok and So (1995); Ling (1995).

18   Opening statement of Ricardo Bofill's architectural autobiography, *Espacio y Vida* (Bofill, 1990).

19 I find my own understanding of postmodernism and postmodern architecture very close to David Harvey's analysis. But I shall not take responsibility for using his work in support of my position.

20 For a balanced, intelligent discussion of the social meaning of postmodern architecture, see Kolb (1990); for a broader discussion of the interaction between globalization/informationalization processes and architecture, see Saunders (1996).

21 For Bofill's own interpretation of Barcelona airport (whose formal antecedent, I believe, is his design for Paris's Marché St Honoré), see his book: Bofill (1990). However, in a long personal conversation, after reading the draft of my analysis, he did not disagree with my interpretation of the project of an "architecture of nudity," although he conceived it rather as an innovative attempt to bring together high-tech and classic design. We both agreed that the new architectural monuments of our epoch are likely to be built as "communication exchangers" (airports, train stations, intermodal transfer areas, telecommunication infrastructures, harbors, and computerized trading centers).

22 For a useful debate on the matter, see Lillyman et al. (1994).

23 For an updated social and spatial, illustrated history of Belleville, see the delightful book by Morier (1994); on urban renewal in Paris in the 1970s, see Godard et al. (1973).

24 Machimura (1995: 16). See his book on the social and political forces underlying the restructuring of Tokyo: Machimura (1994).

REFERENCES

Amin, Ash and Robins, Kevin (1991) "These are not Marshallian times," in Roberto Camagni (ed.), *Innovation Networks: Spatial Perspectives*, pp. 105–20. London: Belhaven Press.

Aoyama, Yuko (1995) "Locational strategies of Japanese multinational corporations in electronics," unpublished PhD dissertation, Berkeley, CA: University of California.

Arrieta, Carlos G. et al. (1991) *Narcotrafico en Colombia: dimensiones politicas, economicas, juridicas e internacionales*. Bogota: Tercer Mundo Editores.

Batty, Michael and Barr, Bob (1994) "The electronic frontier: exploring and mapping cyberspace," *Futures*, 26(7): 699–712.

Bendixon, Terence (1991) "El transporte urbano," in Jordi Borja et al. (eds), *Las grandes ciudades en la decada de los noventa*, pp. 427–53. Madrid: Editorial Sistema.

Blakely, Edward J. and Snyder, Mary Gail (1997) *Fortress America: Gated Communities in the United States*. Washington, DC: Brookings Institution Press.

Bofill, Ricardo (1990) *Espacio y Vida*. Barcelona: Tusquets Editores.

Borja, Jordi and Castells, Manuel (1997) *Local and Global: Management of Cities in the Information Age*. London: Earthscan.

Borja, Jordi et al. (eds) (1991) *Las grandes ciudades en la decada de los noventa*. Madrid: Editorial Sistema.

Boyer, Christine (1994) *The City of Collective Memory*. Cambridge, MA: MIT Press.

Burlen, Katherine (1972) "La réalisation spatiale du désir et l'image spatialisée du besoin," *Espaces et sociétés*, 5: 145–59.

Business Week (1994) "The information technology revolution: how digital technology is changing the way we work and live," special issue.

Business Week (1999) The Internet age," October 4.

Camagni, Roberto (1991) "Local milieu, uncertainty and innovation networks: towards a new dynamic theory of economic space," in Roberto Camagni (ed.), *Innovation Networks: Spatial Perspectives*, pp. 121–44. London: Belhaven Press.

Cappelin, Riccardo (1991) "International networks of cities," in Roberto Camagni (ed.), *Innovation Networks: Spatial Perspectives*. London: Belhaven Press.

Castano, Cecilia (1991) *La Informatizacion de la banca en Espana*. Madrid: Ministerio de Economia/Universidad Autónoma de Madrid.

Castells, Manuel (1972) *La Question urbaine*. Paris: François Maspero.

Castells, Manuel (1988) "The new industrial space: information technology manufacturing and spatial structure in the United States," in G. Sternlieb and J. Hughes (eds), *America's New Market Geography: Nation, Region and Metropolis*. New Brunswick, NJ: Rutgers University Press.

Castells, Manuel (1989a) "High technology and the new international division of labor," *Labour Studies*, October.

Castells, Manuel (1989b) *The Informational City: Information Technology, Economic Restructuring, and the Urban-Regional Process*. Oxford: Blackwell.

Castells, Manuel (1991) "Estrategias de desarrollo metropolitano en las grandes ciudades españolas: la articulación entre crecimiento economico y calidad de vida," in Jordi Borja et al. (eds), *Las grandes ciudades en la decada de los noventa*, pp. 17–64. Madrid: Editorial Sistema.

Castells, Manuel and Hall, Peter (1994) *Technopoles of the World: The Making of 21st Century Industrial Complexes*. London: Routledge.

Caves, Roger W. (1994) *Exploring Urban America*. Thousand Oaks, CA: Sage.

Cervero, Robert (1989) *America's Suburban Centers: The Land Use–Transportation Link*. Boston, MA: Unwin Hyman.

Cervero, Robert (1991) "Changing live–work spatial relationships: implications for metropolitan structure and mobility," in John Brotchie et al. (eds), *Cities in the 21st Century: New Technologies and Spatial Systems*, pp. 330–47. Melbourne: Longman and Cheshire.

Chesnais, François (1994) *La Mondialisation du capital*. Paris: Syros.

Cohen, Stephen and Borrus, Michael (1995) *Networks of American and Japanese Electronics Companies in Asia*. Berkeley, CA: University of California, BRIE research paper.

Cooke, Philip (1994) "The cooperative advantage of regions," paper prepared for Harold Innis Centenary Celebration Conference *Regions, Institutions and Technology*, University of Toronto, September 23–25.

Cooke, Philip and Morgan, K. (1993) "The network paradigm: new departures in corporate and regional development," *Society and Space*, 11: 543–64.

Cooper, Charles (ed.) (1994) *Technology and Innovation in the International Economy*. Aldershot, Hants: Edward Elgar and United Nations University Press.

Daniels, P. W. (1993) *Service Industries in the World Economy*. Oxford: Blackwell.

Davis, Diane (1994) *Urban Leviathan: Mexico in the 20th Century*. Philadelphia, PA: Temple University Press.

Davis, Mike (1990) *City of Quartz*. London: Verso.

Deben, Leon et al. (eds) (1993) *Understanding Amsterdam: Essays on Economic Vitality, City*

Life, and Urban Form. Amsterdam: Het Spinhuis.

Dunford, M. and Kafkalas, G. (eds) (1992) *Cities and Regions in the New Europe: the Global–Local Interplay and Spatial Development Strategies*. London: Belhaven Press.

Enderwick, Peter (ed.) (1989) *Multinational Service Firms*. London: Routledge.

Ernst, Dieter (1994) *Networks in Electronics*. Berkeley, CA: University of California, BRIE research monograph.

Fainstein, Susan S., Gordon, Ian and Harloe, Michael (eds) (1992) *Divided Cities*. Oxford: Blackwell.

Fazy, Ian Hamilton (1995) "The superhighway pioneers," *The Financial Times*, June 20.

Garreau, Joel (1991) *Edge City: Life on the New Frontier*. New York: Doubleday.

Godard, Francis et al. (1973) *La Renovation urbaine à Paris*. Paris: Mouton.

Goldsmith, William W. and Blakely, Edward J. (1992) *Separate Societies: Poverty and Inequality in US Cities*. Philadelphia, PA: Temple University Press.

Gordon, Richard (1994) *Internationalization, Multinationalization, Globalization: Contradictory World Economies and New Spatial Divisions of Labor*. Santa Cruz, CA: University of California Center for the Study of Global Transformations, working paper 94.

Gottdiener, Marc (1985) *The Social Production of Urban Space*. Austin, TX: University of Texas Press.

Graham, Stephen (1994) "Networking cities: telematics in urban policy – a critical review," *International Journal of Urban and Regional Research*, 18(3): 416–31.

Graham, Stephen and Marvin, Simon (1996) *Telecommunications and the City: Electronic Spaces, Urban Places*. London: Routledge.

Graham, Stephen and Marvin, Simon (2000) *Splintering Networks, Fragmenting Cities: Urban Infrastructure in a Global–Local Age*. London: Routledge.

Gurstein, Penny (1990) "Working at home in the live-in office: computers, space, and the social life of household," unpublished PhD dissertation, Berkeley, CA: University of California.

Hall, Peter (1995) "Towards a general urban theory," in John Brotchie et al. (eds), *Cities in Competition: Productive and Sustainable Cities for the 21st Century*, pp. 3–32. Sydney: Longman Australia.

Hall, Peter (1998) *Cities in Civilization*. New York: Pantheon Books.

Handy, Susan and Mokhtarian, Patricia L. (1995) "Planning for telecommuting," *Journal of the American Planning Association*, 61(1): 99–111.

Harvey, David (1990) *The Condition of Postmodernity*. Oxford: Blackwell.

Henderson, Jeffrey (1989) *The Globalisation of High Technology Production: Society, Space and Semiconductors in the Restructuring of the Modern World*. London: Routledge.

Henderson, Jeffrey (1991) "Urbanization in the Hong Kong–South China region: an introduction to dynamics and dilemmas," *International Journal of Urban and Regional Research*, 15(2): 169–79.

Hsing, You-tien (1995) *Migrant Workers, Foreign Capital, and Diversification of Labor Markets in Southern China*. Vancouver: University of British Columbia, Asian Urban Research Networks, working paper series.

Huws, U., Korte, W. B. and Robinson, S. (1990) *Telework: Towards the Elusive Office*. Chichester, Sussex: John Wiley.

Jacobs, Allan (1993) *Great Streets*. Cambridge, MA: MIT Press.

Kaku, Michio (1994) *Hyperspace: A Scientific Odyssey through Parallel Universes, Time Warps, and the 10th Dimension*. New York: Oxford University Press.

Kolb, David (1990) *Postmodern Sophistications: Philosophy, Architecture and Tradition.* Chicago, IL: University of Chicago Press.

Korte, W. B., Robinson, S. and Steinle, W. K. (eds) (1988) *Telework: Present Situation and Future Development of a New Form of Work Organization.* Amsterdam: North-Holland.

Kraut, R. E. (1989) "Tele-commuting: the trade-offs of home-work," *Journal of Communications*, 39: 19–47.

Kunstler, James Howard (1993) *The Geography of Nowhere: The Rise and Decline of America's Man Made Landscape.* New York: Simon and Schuster.

Kwok, R. and So, Alvin (eds) (1995) *The Hong Kong–Guandong Link: Partnership in Flux.* Armonk, NY: M. E. Sharpe.

Kwok, Yin-Wang and So, Alvin (1992) *Hong Kong–Guandong Interaction: Joint Enterprise of Market Capitalism and State Socialism.* Manoa: University of Hawaii, research paper.

Laserna, Roberto (1995) "Regional development and coca production in Cochabamba, Bolivia," unpublished PhD dissertation, Berkeley, CA: University of California.

Leung, Chi Kin (1993) "Personal contacts, subcontracting linkages, and development in the Hong Kong–Zhujiang Delta Region," *Annals of the Association of American Geographers*, 83(2): 272–302.

Lillyman, William, Moriarty, Marilyn F. and Neuman, David J. (eds) (1994) *Critical Architecture and Contemporary Culture.* New York: Oxford University Press.

Lincoln, Thomas L. and Ware, Willis H. (1993) "The electronic medical record," *Information Society*, 9(2): 157–88.

Ling, K. K. (1995) "A case for regional planning: the Greater Pearl River Delta: a Hong Kong perspective," unpublished research seminar paper, CP 229. Berkeley, CA: University of California, Department of City and Regional Planning.

Lo, C. P. (1994) "Economic reforms and socialist city structure: a case study of Guangzhou, China," *Urban Geography*, 15(2) 128–49.

Lo, Fu-chen and Yeung, Yue-man (eds) (1996) *Emerging World Cities in the Pacific Asia.* Tokyo: United Nations University Press.

Lozano, Beverly (1989) *The Invisible Work Force: Transforming American Business with Outside and Home-based Workers.* New York: Free Press.

Lynch, Kevin (1960) *The Image of the City.* Cambridge, MA: MIT Press.

Machimura, T. (1994) *Sekai Toshi Tokyo no Kozo* [The structural transformation of a global city Tokyo]. Tokyo: Tokyo University Press.

Machimura, T. (1995) *Symbolic Use of Globalization in Urban Politics in Tokyo.* Kunitachi: Hitotsubashi University Faculty of Social Sciences, research paper.

Marshall, J. N. et al. (1988) *Services and Uneven Development.* Oxford: Oxford University Press.

Martinotti, Guido (1993) *Metropoli. La Nuova morfologia sociale della citta.* Bologna: Il Mulino.

Menotti, Val (1995) "The transformation of retail social space: an analysis of virtual shopping's impact on retail centers," unpublished research paper for seminar CP298I, University of California, Berkeley, Department of City and Regional Planning.

Michelson, Ronald L. and Wheeler, James O. (1994) "The flow of information in a global economy: the role of the American urban system in 1990," *Annals of the Association of American Geographers*, 84 (1): 87–107.

Miles, Ian (1988) *Home Informatics: Information Technology and the Transformation of Everyday Life.* London: Pinter.

Miller, Richard L. and Swensson, Earl S. (1995) *New Directions in Hospital and Health Care Facility Design.* New York: McGraw-Hill.

Mokhtarian, Patricia L. (1991a) "Defining telecommuting," *Transportation Research Record,* 1305: 273–81.

Mokhtarian, Patricia L. (1991b) "Telecommuting and travel: state of the practice, state of the art," *Transportation,* 18: 319–42.

Mokhtarian, Patricia L. (1992) "Telecommuting in the United States: letting our fingers do the commuting," *Telecommuting Review: The Gordon Report,* 9(5): 12.

Mollenkopf, John (ed.) (1989) *Power, Culture, and Place: Essays on New York City.* New York: Russell Sage Foundation.

Mollenkopf, John and Castells, Manuel (eds) (1991) *Dual City: Restructuring New York.* New York: Russell Sage Foundation.

Moran, R. (1990) "Health environment and healthy environment," in R. Moran, R. Anderson and P. Paoli (eds), *Building for People in Hospitals, Workers, and Consumers.* Dublin: European Foundation for the Improvement of Living and Working Conditions.

Moran, R. (1993) *The Electronic Home: Social and Spatial Aspects: A Scoping Report.* Dublin: European Foundation for the Improvement of Living and Working Conditions.

Morier, Françoise (ed.) (1994) *Belleville, Belleville: visages d'un planète.* Paris: Editions Creaphis.

Moss, Mitchell (1987) "Telecommunications, world cities, and urban policy," *Urban Studies,* 24: 534–46.

Moss, Mitchell (1991) "The new fibers of economic development," *Portfolio,* 4: 11–18.

Moss, Mitchell (1992) "Telecommunications and urban economic development," in OECD, *Cities and New Technologies,* pp. 147–58. Paris: OECD.

Muschamp, Herbert (1992) "A design that taps into the 'Informational City'," *Sunday New York Times,* August 9, Architecture View Section: 32.

Nilles, J. M. (1988) "Traffic reduction by telecommuting: a status review and selected bibliography," *Transportation Research A,* 22A(4): 301–17.

Norman, Alfred Lorn (1993) *Informational Society: An Economic Theory of Discovery, Invention and Innovation.* London: Kluwer.

Panofsky, Erwin (1957) *Gothic Architecture and Scholasticism.* New York: Meridian Books.

Qvortup, Lars (1992) "Telework: visions, definitions, realities, barriers," in OECD, *Cities and New Technologies,* pp. 77–108. Paris: OECD.

Rijn, F. V. and Williams, R. (eds) (1988) *Concerning Home Telematics.* Amsterdam: North-Holland.

Robson, B. (1992) "Competing and collaborating through urban networks," *Town and Country Planning,* September: 236–8.

Sassen, Saskia (1991) *The Global City: New York, London, Tokyo.* Princeton, NJ: Princeton University Press.

Saunders, William (ed.) (1996) *Architectural Practices in the 1990s.* Princeton, NJ: Princeton University Press.

Schoonmaker, Sara (1993) "Trading on-line: information flows in advanced capitalism," *Information Society,* 9(1): 39–49.

Scott, Allen (1988) *New Industrial Spaces.* London: Pion.

Siino, Corinne (1994) "La ville et le chomage," *Revue d'économie régionale et urbaine,* 3: 324–52.

Silverstone, R. (1991) *Beneath the Bottom Line: Households and Information and Communication*

Technologies in the Age of the Consumer. London: Brunel University Center for Research on Innovation, Culture, and Technology.

Sit, Victor Fueng-Shuen (1991) "Transnational capital flows and urbanization in the Pearl River Delta, China," *Southeast Asian Journal of Social Science*, 19(1–2): 154–79.

Steinle, W. J. (1988) "Telework: opening remarks and opening debate," in W. B. Korte, S. Robinson and W. K. Steinle (eds), *Telework: Present Situation and Future Development of a New Form of Work Organization*, Amsterdam: North-Holland.

Tafuri, Manfredo (1971) *L'urbanistica del riformismo.* Milan: Franco Angeli.

Tarr, J. and Dupuy, G. (eds) (1988) *Technology and the Rise of the Networked City in Europe and North America.* Philadelphia, PA: Temple University Press.

Thrift, Nigel J. (1986) *The "Fixers": the Urban Geography of International Financial Capital.* Lampeter: University of Wales Department of Geography.

Thrift, Nigel J. and Leyshon, A. (1992) "In the wake of money: the City of London and the accumulation of value," in L. Budd and S. Whimster (eds), *Global Finance and Urban Living: A Study of Metropolitan Change*, pp. 282–311. London: Routledge.

Time (1993) Special issue on mega-cities, January 11.

Venturi, Robert et al. (1977) *Learning from Las Vegas: The Forgotten Symbolism of Architectural Form.* Cambridge, MA: MIT Press.

Vessali, Kaveh V. (1995) "Transportation, urban form, and information technology," Berkeley, CA: University of California, unpublished seminar paper for CP 298 I.

Wellman, Barry (ed.) (1999) *Networks in the Global Village.* Boulder, CO: Westview Press.

Wheeler, James O. and Aoyama, Yuko (eds) (2000) *Cities in the Telecommunications Age.* London: Routledge.

Woo, Edward S. W. (1994) "Urban development," in Y. M. Yeung and David K. Y. Chu (eds), *Guandong: Survey of a Province Undergoing Rapid Change.* Hong Kong: Chinese University Press.

Zukin, Sharon (1992) *Landscapes of Power.* Berkeley, CA: University of California Press.

CHAPTER
NINE

The Culture of Cities in the Information Age

(1999)

The Great Twenty-first Century Paradox: An Urban World without Cities?

The intellectual debate on cities at the turn of the millennium is a debate on the state and prospects of human civilization. Cities have been throughout history, and in our time, the sources of cultural creativity, technological innovation, material progress, and political democratization. By bringing together people from multicultural origins, and establishing communication channels and systems of cooperation, cities have induced synergy from diversity, dynamic stability from competition, order from chaos. However, with the coming of the Information Age, cities as specific social systems seem to be challenged by the related processes of globalization and informationalization. New communication technologies appear to supersede the functional need for spatial proximity as the basis of economic efficiency and personal interaction. The emergence of a global economy and of global communication systems subdue the local into the global, blurring social meaning and hampering political control, traditionally exercised from localities. Flows seem to overwhelm places, as human interaction increasingly relies on electronic communication networks.

Thus, cities, as specific forms of social organization and cultural expression, materially rooted in spatially concentrated human settlements, could be made obsolete in the new technological environment. Yet, the paradox is that, with the coming of a new techno-economic system, urbanization, understood as spatial concentration, is in fact accelerating. We are reaching a predominantly urban world, which, by 2005, may include at least 50 percent of the planet's population. Core activities and a growing proportion of people are, and will be, concentrated in multi-million metropolitan regions. This pattern of socio-spatial evolution could lead to urbanization without cities, as urban/ suburban sprawl diffuses people and activities in a very wide metropolitan span, in which local societies may become socially atomized and culturally meaningless.

Are we heading toward the disappearance of cities as a cultural form at the very moment we enter a predominantly urban/metropolitan world? Is the culture of cities coming to an end precisely because of the pervasiveness of metropolitan settlements? Are virtual communities and electronically based communication networks (including fast transportation systems) substituting for the urban community? What are the differential patterns of spatial concentration and dispersion? And how do spatial locality and transterritorial virtuality interact in the shaping of function, form, and meaning? The tentative answer to these fundamental questions requires a long and complex intellectual detour which constitutes the subject matter of this chapter.

A Metropolitan Planet: Spatial Concentration in the Network Society

While our economy and society are built around decentralized networks of interaction, the spatial pattern of human settlements is characterized by unprecedented territorial concentration of population and activities (Satterthwaite, 1995; Castells, 1996). At the turn of the millennium we are experiencing the largest wave of urbanization in human history. According to World Bank data, in 1970 urban population accounted for 37 percent of the total population of the planet. In 1996, the corresponding figure was 46 percent, and current projections indicate that, around 2005, the majority of people will live in cities. Sub-Saharan Africa, the least urbanized region in the world, is the one with the fastest rate of urban growth (an annual rate of 5.2 percent in 1975–95), so that, by 2020, 63 percent of the population will likely live in cities. In 1998–9 South America was 78 percent urban, Western Europe 82 percent, Russia 75 percent, and the US 77 percent. In 1996, Japan and the Korean peninsula were 78 percent urban, South-east Asia 37 percent, Pakistan, 35 percent. China, with 30 percent in 1996, and India with 28 percent in 1998, were still, by and large, rural countries, and they account for over one-third of humankind. Yet the projections are for India's urban population to almost double between 1996 and 2020, jumping from 256 million to 499 million. China's urban population is expected to increase even faster, from 377 million in 1996 to 712 million in 2020, thus representing more than half of the projected total population of China.

A growing share of this urban population is concentrated in very large areas, which I call metropolitan regions because they are not necessarily cities (or mega-cities) in sociocultural terms. They are large settlements whose cultural meaning is open to question and observation. The proportion of the population living in agglomerations of more than one million people in Latin America reaches about one-third now; in South Asia it doubled between 1980 and 1996, reaching 14 percent, approximately the same level as that in Sub-Saharan Africa. South-east Asia concentrates about 11 percent of the population in these areas. The rich countries, in 1996, had about 30 percent of their population in metropolitan regions, with the US figure standing at 26.5 percent in 1990. Projections are for an increasing concentration of the population in these large metropolitan areas. Thus, when we take a century-long perspective on urbanization patterns, there is a secular trend toward urbanization and metropolitanization of human settlements, which is accelerating over time, leading to an overwhelmingly urban and metropolitan world in the twenty-first century. The largest metropolitan settlements in the world are already in the so-called developing world, and this will increasingly be the case (Cohen et al., 1996).

Why so? Why do urban and metropolitan areas continue to grow in size and complexity, in spite of increasing technological ability to work, and interact, at a distance? The fundamental reason is the spatial concentration of jobs, income-generating activities, services, and human-development opportunities in cities, and particularly in the largest metropolitan areas (Sassen, 1991; Daniels, 1993; Graham, 1999). On the one hand, increasing productivity in the advanced sector of the economy, and the crisis of agricultural and extractive activities, eliminate jobs in the rural areas and laggard regions, inducing new rural–urban migrations. On the other hand, metropolitan areas concentrate the higher value-generating activities, both in manufacturing and services (Hall, 1998). As they are the sources of wealth, they provide jobs, both directly and indirectly. And because there is a high level of income in these areas, they offer greater opportunities for the provision of essential services, such as education and health. Furthermore, even for those migrants at the bottom of urban society, the spillover of opportunities provides better chances for survival, first, and for the promotion of future generations later, than those that could be found in increasingly marginalized rural areas and depressed regions (Massey et al., 1999). Besides, as long as metropolitan areas continue to be cultural centers of innovation, their residents have access to unparalleled chances for cultural enhancement and personal enjoyment, thus improving the quality and diversity of their consumption. Yet, why do the new production and management systems of the Information Age favor metropolitan concentration? This question is examined next.

The Informational City: Metropolitan Areas as Milieux of Innovation

Knowledge generation and information-processing are the sources of value and power in the Information Age. Both depend on innovation, and on the capacity to diffuse innovation in networks that induce synergy by sharing this information and knowledge (Castells, 1989, 1996). Twenty years of urban and regional research have shown the importance of territorial complexes of innovation in facilitating synergy (Hall, 1998). What Philippe Aydalot, Peter Hall, and myself named some time ago "milieux of innovation" seems to be at the heart of the ability of cities, and particularly large cities, to become the sources of wealth in the Information Age. This is certainly the case for Silicon Valley (and the San Francisco Bay area as a whole), the acknowledged birthplace of the information-technology revolution (Saxenian, 1994). But, as shown by Peter Hall and myself in our world survey of technopoles, the argument extends to all societies (Castells and Hall, 1994). All major centers of technological innovation have appeared in and from large metropolitan areas: Tokyo–Yokohama, London, Paris, Munich (succeeding Berlin after the war), Milan, Moscow, Beijing, Shanghai, Seoul–Inchon, Taipei–Hsinchu, Bangalore, Bombay, São Paulo–Campinas, and, in the US, the San Francisco Bay area, Los Angeles/Southern California technopole, Greater Boston, and, lately, Seattle, although there are secondary milieux of innovation in such areas as Austin, Dallas, North Carolina's research triangle, Minneapolis–St Paul, Princeton's corridor, Portland, and Denver. New York is a major exception (which has an historical explanation), largely compensated for by its innovative role in finance, business services, media, and cultural industries. Moreover, Peter Hall, in his latest book, extended the argument of the relationship between cities and innovation to the entire Western history of cultural creativity and entrepreneurial innovation (Hall, 1998). If so, it seems logical that when we reach the Information Age cultural creativity becomes a productive force, thus reinforcing the competitive advantage of cities as sources of wealth.

But the innovation potential of cities is not restricted to information-technology industries. It is even more apparent in advanced business services, which are the leading money-making sector in our economy. Services such as finance, insurance consulting, legal services, accounting, and marketing are the nerve centers of the twenty-first century economy. And they are concentrated in large metropolitan areas, with New York/New Jersey being the prominent area in the United States (Moss, 1987; Sassen, 1991; Daniels, 1993; Michelson and Wheeler, 1994; Graham, 1999). Advanced services are unevenly distributed between the central business district and the new suburban centers, depending on the history and spatial dynamics of each area. What is critical is that these advanced services centers are territorially concentrated, built on interpersonal networks of decision-making processes, and organized around a territorial web of suppliers and customers (Thrift, 1996; Graham, 1997).

A third set of value-generating activities concentrated in metropolitan areas comprises the cultural industries: media, in all their forms; entertainment; art; fashion; publishing; museums; cultural creation industries, at large. These industries are amongst the fastest growing, and the highest value-generating activities in all advanced societies (Hall, 1998; Scott, 1998; Muschamp, 1999). They also rely on the spatial logic of territorially concentrated milieux of innovation, with a multiplicity of interactions, and face-to-face exchanges at the core of the innovation process, to be complemented, not contradicted, by on-line interaction.

Moreover, the development of the Internet, the ultimate placeless technology, has led to an increasing concentration of Internet domains in the largest metropolitan areas in the world (in the US predominantly in New York and San Francisco), as demonstrated in the pioneering doctoral dissertation by Matthew Zook (Zook, 1999). The reason is simple: since the Internet processes information, Internet hubs are located in the main information systems which are the basis of the economy and institutions of metropolitan regions. However, this does not mean that the Internet is a metropolitan phenomenon. Instead, it is a network of metropolitan nodes. There is no centrality, but nodality, based on a networking geometry.

It is precisely because of the existence of advanced telecommunication networks that these milieux of innovation, and these high-level networks of decision-making, can exist in a few nodes in the country, or in the planet, reaching out to the whole world from a few blocks in Manhattan, in Wilshire Boulevard in Santa Clara County, in the City of London, in the Quartier de l'Opera in Paris, in Tokyo's Ginza, or in São Paulo's Nova Faria Lima. While concentrating much of the production and consumption capacity of a vast hinterland, these territorial complexes of knowledge generation and information-processing link up with each other, ushering in a new global geography made up of nodes and networks (Graham, 1999).

The New Global Geography: Networks of Metropolitan Nodes

Globalization is a major feature of the Information Age. It is the process by which core activities in the economy, in media communication, in science and technology, and in strategic decision-making are linked worldwide in real time, thus having the potential of daily working as a unit on a planetary scale (Castells, 1996; Held et al., 1999). In fact, most activities are not global. Indeed, they take place in a local or regional setting. But the jobs these activities create locally, and the livelihood of people involved in these activities, are largely dependent on a globalized core, whose performance is organized in networks of global interaction via telecommunications, information systems, and electronically based, fast transportation systems. As these core activities are based in major metropolitan areas there is a concomitant process of global interaction between these metropolitan nodes (Castells, 1989). This process has often been described under the misleading concept of global city. In this view, some cities are global, others are not. In fact, this is a new version of an old urban paradigm which, twenty years ago, proposed the notion of world cities, referring to the largest, dominant urban centers.

In fact, both concepts are prisoner to a nineteenth-century, hierarchical conception of our society and space. What characterizes our society is its structure in networks and nodes, not in hierarchies of centrality and periphery. So, no city is entirely global. Queens in New York and Kunitachi in Tokyo are very local, as is Hampstead in London. Yes, Wall Street and the City of London and Palo Alto work/interact in a global network. But so do many smaller metropolitan areas at various degrees. In fact, hundreds and thousands of localities are connected in global networks of information-processing and decision-making. All large metropolitan areas in the developed world, and all of the largest in the developing world, are thus global to some extent, with their relative nodal weight in the network varying depending upon time and issues. And yet most people in these same cities live local lives. So, there are not a few global cities (although some cities are very important in the global networks), but one global city. This global city is not New York or London. It is a transterritorial city, a space built by the linkage of many different spaces in one network of quasi-simultaneous interaction that brings together processes, people, buildings, and bits and pieces of local areas, in a global space of interaction. The global city is not a city, it is a new spatial form, the space of flows, characterizing the Information Age (Sassen, 1991; Mitchell, 1995; Castells, 1996; Scott, 1998; Graham and Marvin, 1999).

These global networks of metropolitan regions are extremely versatile, as is the global economy they process. Flows of capital, production, and information go in and out of these nodes, increasing or reversing their amount and speed of circulation, depending on the value they can generate, or the losses they can avoid. Thus, global competitiveness, and inter-regional competitiveness, condition the fate of cities and metropolitan areas, as they are connected or disconnected from strategic global networks, depending on their valuation or devaluation in these networks. Old industrial cities, such as Buffalo or Cleveland, are increasingly bypassed by global networks, thus being largely excluded from the global city. High-technology centers (such as the San Francisco Bay area), or leading business, and information centers (such as Boston), old or new, reinforce their nodal position in the global city. Yet, the instability of the system, and the velocity of its transactions, imply that this transterritorial, global city is a space of variable geometry and changing components. At any rate, wherever and whenever a major node of this global network is formed, and expands, it generates a new spatial form: the metropolitan region.

A New Spatial Form: The Metropolitan Region

The concentration of population and activities in a large-scale territorial unit is ushering in a new spatial form. I call it "metropolitan" (rather than "mega-city") to reserve the use of the notion of cities for a specific cultural form, in the long-standing tradition of Max Weber's theory of cities as cultural and political constructions. And I call it "region" to indicate that there is a functional connection between activities scattered in a very vast territory, usually defined in terms of a specific labor market, consumer market, and media market (for example, television). The metropolitan region is not just a very large urban area. It is also a distinctive spatial form, close to what a brilliant journalist, Joel Garreau, labeled as "Edge City," after reporting on new spatial developments in some of the largest American metropolitan areas (Garreau, 1991). In most cases, the metropolitan region does not even have a name, let alone a political unity or institutional agency. When we speak of the "Bay area" (in my case meaning the San Francisco Bay area), we are referring to a large constellation of cities and counties, extending at least from Santa Rosa in the North Bay to Santa Cruz in the south of the South Bay, and from the western cliffs of San Francisco to the outer suburbs of the East Bay, all the way to Livermore; which is almost 7 million people living in an expanse that is about 60 miles long and 40 miles wide. Indeed, the largest city in the San Francisco Bay area is not San Francisco, but San Jose, with a population of about 907,000 in 1999. The real settlement pattern is already reaching far beyond this area, linking up with Sacramento and the Central Valley, and absorbing, across the Nevada border, Lake Tahoe, and toward the south, Monterey and Carmel, as secondary residences for Bay area dwellers.

An even more striking case is the Southern California metropolitan region, which merges in one largely integrated space the area extending from Ventura in the north to the southern tip of Orange County, with about 17 million people living, working, consuming, and traveling in this territory without boundaries, name, or identity other than as a market (Scott, 1992). Furthermore, the freeway links up Orange County with San Diego, and, beyond the border, with Tijuana, making this area a binational, multicultural, nameless, mega-urban constellation. Outside California, the New Jersey–New York–Long Island–Rhode Island–Connecticut or the New England mega-region are similar examples of new spatial agglomerations.

In Asia, some of the largest metropolitan regions in the world are being formed, such as the region in process of articulation between Hong Kong–Shenzhen–Canton–Macau–Zuhai, and the Pearl River delta, with a population of about 60 million. Or the Tokyo–Yokohama–Nagoya region, extending, via Shinkansen, to Osaka–Kobe and Kyoto, within a 3–4-hour transportation time framework (Lo and Yeung, 1996). Seoul–Inchon, Shanghai–Pudon, Bangkok metropolitan region, Jakarta megapolis, Calcutta, Bombay (Mumbai), Greater Mexico City, Greater São Paulo, Greater Buenos Aires, Greater Rio de Janeiro, Paris–Ile de France, Greater London, and Greater Moscow are all major areas, most of which have no clear boundaries, or defined identity, beyond the vague images of what used to be their central city. And I am not even mentioning areas of 7 million plus, such as Lima, Bogota, or Manila, which continue to grow both as magnets *vis-à-vis* their hinterlands in crisis, and as sources of growth and survival through their connections to global networks.

In Western Europe, the building of a dense, high-speed train network is integrating London with Paris, Paris with Lyon and Marseille, and with northern Italy; Paris–Lille–Brussels with the Netherlands; and Frankfurt and Cologne with the French network; in the south, Lisbon–Seville–Madrid–Barcelona–Bilbao are scheduled to link up with the European network in 2002–4. Overall, in Central/Western Europe an extraordinary concentration of population, production, management, markets, and urban amenities is being connected within a 3-hour transportation time-frame (it is currently less than 3 hours between central London and central Paris), not including air shuttles with flights between 30 minutes and 2 hours connecting most of Western Europe. Thus, the new spatial structure emerging at the heart of Western Europe is that of a series of interconnected metropolitan regions, each one connecting several conurbations, each one with millions of people, and jointly harnessing a significant share of the world's wealth and information (Hall, 1998).

These settlements blur the traditional distinctions between cities and countryside, and between cities and suburbs (Kuntsler, 1993). They include, in spatial discontinuity, built-up areas of various density, open space, agricultural activities, natural areas, residential expanses, and concentrations of services and manufacturing activities, scattered along transportation axes, made up of freeways and mass transit systems (Brotchie et al., 1995). There is no real zoning, as workplaces, residential and commercial areas are dispersed in various directions. Moreover, while these regions are usually centered around a major central city, smaller urban centers gradually become absorbed in intra-metropolitan networks. New nodes constantly emerge, as areas concentrate decentralized business/industrial activities. Other localities grow in their role of providers of services for the metropolitan population at large. This regional metropolitan structure is entirely dependent upon transportation and communications. Work at a distance, from home or between spatially disjointed locations increases considerably (Cervero, 1989; Brotchie et al., 1995; Graham and Marvin, 1996; Hall, 1998).

But we do not see, and we will not see, the disappearance of the workplace. Telecommuting as the prevaling working mode of a large segment of the population is not happening on a large scale, at least not yet (Graham and Marvin, 1996; Smart Valley Inc., 1997). However, many people work, and will work, from home, on-line, in addition to (not instead of) traveling to their work places, in their area, or in a networked node that they will reach by fast transportation, including air transportation and high-speed trains (Graham, 1999). It is, in fact, a world of stepped-up mobility, and multi-location pattern of activities, rather than the futuristic image of people working on-line from their computers at home (indeed, there will be no self-contained personal computers very soon, as we move to on-line, network technologies, with information retrieved and exchanged from devices either portable or multi-located – the ubiquituous office). So, metropolitan regions are characterized, simultaneously, by spatial sprawl and spatial concentration, by the mixing of land-use patterns, by extreme mobility, and dependence on communications and transportation, both intra-metropolitan and inter-nodal (Castells, 1992; Scott, 1992; Office of Technology Assessment, 1995; Hall, 1998). They are also characterized by extreme spatial fragmentation, and social segregation, and, in most of the world, by staggering environmental problems on an unprecedented scale.

The Unsustainable City: The Ecological Crisis of Twenty-first Century Metropolitan Regions

The rise of ecological consciousness is one of the major cultural and political transformations of the past three decades (Capra, 1995). When looked upon from an ecological perspective, the process of urbanization, in its current form, presents a daunting challenge. These large urban constellations, which increasingly concentrate people and activities, grow by destroying their natural environment (Wheeler, 1999). Mobility is essential in the new metropolitan and inter-metropolitan structures, and mobility means cars, planes, and environmentally damaging high-speed trains. Endless metropolitan expansion means the conversion of agricultural land to built environment, and the reduction of open space to densely used urban public areas, the protection of which is often overwhelmed by the pressures of a growing metropolitan population. In developing countries, the large numbers of people who start their settlements as informal housing and uncontrolled land use create huge habitats in the most appalling environmental conditions, thus inducing epidemics and irreversible environmental damage (World Health Organization, 1996). Many areas on the outskirts of some of the largest metropolitan regions in the world are on the verge of ecological catastrophe, as water and sanitation become the most poignant urban issues, and the building of urban infrastructure runs way behind the pace of urban growth (Cohen et al., 1996).

While poverty plays a role in this crisis, the pattern of wild urbanization and environmental irresponsibility accounts in large part for the deterioration of urban liveability (Borja and Castells, 1997). The environmental problematic in the twenty-first century will increasingly be a metropolitan issue (Stren et al., 1992; Wheeler, 1999). It is essential to acknowledge that growing urban environmental problems are not a necessary consequence of development. They mainly result from a mixture of the unrestrained logic of short-term profit-seeking and ecological ignorance. We have the knowledge, and the technology, to pattern economic growth in ways compatible with environmental sustainability. That we do not do so is simply a matter of priorities. We do not include future generations in the developmental equation; that is, the grandchildren of our grandchildren. The issue is cultural and political. It is made more acute by the fact that, with the enclosure of humans in a metropolitan world, we accentuate the distance between our social system and our ecosystem. The artificial preservation of nature in *ad hoc* reservations, such as national parks and planned open space, does not avoid the fundamental undermining of our overall ecological balance. This leads, for instance, to global warming as a result of the greenhouse effect, directly linked to current patterns of metropolitan concentration and highly polluting transportation systems. In the last two decades of the twentieth century, an ecological consciousness indeed emerged and permeated the minds of millions of citizens around the world. Yet, at the same time, the process of destruction of our global ecosystem accelerated overall. This is occurring to such an extent that we can say that, for the time being, the main practical effect of our newly acquired consciousness is to be aware of the process by which our species is committing environmental suicide. This debate is just starting, and it will be at the forefront of the culture of cities in the new century.

The Fragmented Metropolis: Spatial Segregation and the Breakdown of the Urban Contract

Spatial segregation is an old feature of the industrial city. However, as Douglas Massey (1996) has shown in his review of empirical evidence, in the past two decades there has been an unprecedented spatial concentration of wealth and poverty in distinctive spaces. The trend is observed between countries, between regions, within regions, and within metropolitan areas. The spatial segregation proceeds along the lines of income and ethnicity. It does not limit itself to the traditional split between cities and suburbs. Residential areas are increasingly specified in their social characteristics, within cities, within suburbs, and within the vast span of metropolitan exurbia (Goldsmith and Blakely, 1992). The newest, and most significant, trend is that the upper and upper-middle income groups have separated themselves from the city, and built increasingly distinct communities, so that the spatial index of residential concentration of the wealthy is currently higher than the index of concentration of poverty and ethnic minority populations (Massey, 1996). The extreme manifestation of this trend is the construction boom in gated communities, in the United States and around the world, particularly in the developing world. In the US, Blakely and Snyder (1997) have documented the rise of what they label "Fortress America," the fastest growing segment of new residential construction in some areas, such as Southern California. The main explicit motivation for the separatism of affluent households is fear of crime. Yet urban crime significantly declined in the US in the 1990s. It seems that broader sources of fear spread in the metropolitan region, as its growing multiculturalism and social diversity, traditionally a feature of the urban world, are resisted and rejected by those groups who have the means to do so: by exiting the city and retrenching in their communities.

New communication technologies, and a metropolitan transportation system, allow people to stay selectively in touch with those individuals/groups they want to, while disconnecting from the city at large. The development of this increasingly individualized world, atomized in individual homes, and/or grouped in segregated, homogeneous communities, both at the top and bottom of the social ladder, is tantamount to the breaking of the urban contract: an urban contract by which citizens from different cultures, and with different resources, agreed to be citizens; that is part of a shared culture, and institutions, where conflicts were part of life, but where a common ground could be found. By fragmenting the city, the accelerating process of spatial segregation may be undermining our capacity to live together. The end of the urban contract may signal the end of the social contract.

Reconstructing the City (I): The City and the Grassroots

Local societies are not the mere byproduct of structural forces. People act, and react. Thus, while there are powerful trends pushing toward the fragmentation of the city and the individualization of social relationships, people, from all social classes, ethnic groups, and cultures, build up communities, establish networks of interaction, and recreate urban society from the grassroots. Claude Fischer (1982) demonstrated almost twenty years ago that there are new forms of sociability in the metropolis that do not necessarily relate to residential vicinity, but are built around selective networks. Barry Wellman (1999) has shown how these networks may in fact be expanded and reinforced in the Information Age by the emergence of virtual communities around the Internet. Empirical studies document the fact that some of these virtual communities are relatively stable networks of social interaction, and many of them do relate to face-to-face interaction, thus bridging the virtual city with urban networks based on personal affinity (Wellman and Gulia, 1999). In my own research I have shown the essential role played by community organizations and urban social movements in shaping the city, and in aggregating citizens, at the grassroots level, around interests, identity, and projects (Castells, 1983). Thus, there are forms of social aggregation, both in urban communities and around networks of personal communication, including electronic communication. The issue remains, however, whether this elective aggregation in social sub-sets, combined with the structural trends toward metropolitan fragmentation, will not in fact accelerate the breaking up of the city as a meaningful social unity. Or, in other words, the reconstruction of social meaning in elective networks and defensive communities is not equivalent to the communication of these various sources of meaning in a shared culture of the city. Growing urban diversity requires the building of cultural and institutional bridges, if metropolitan regions are to be cities rather than mere habitats populated by self-defined networks of individualized interaction.

Reconstructing the City (II): The City of Women

The city, as society, has throughout history been based on the work of women, subordinated to men in the patriarchal family structure. Current processes of social transformation are altering the relationship between cities and women, raising a new set of urban issues. The massive entry of women into the paid labor force in the past thirty years has created new needs in urban services, and child care, while increasing the bargaining power of women within the family and in society at large. Dual wage earning families, and new residential and job location patterns, have impacted upon the dynamics of metropolitan structure. The problems created by wild urbanization processes around the world are being managed by an immense effort on the part of women, from securing water and sanitation and maintaining a liveable level of household hygiene in poor countries to managing multiple service bureaucracies and the diverse transportation needs of family members in the metropolises of advanced countries. Women manage the daily urban system by their work. And they change it, by their mobilizations, as women are the predominant actors in community organizations and urban social movements (Borja and Castells, 1997).

Furthermore, the emergence of a feminist consciousness (ideologically articulated or spontaneously practiced) has impacted upon the way in which cities are organized and managed. Not only have women exerted pressure for the delivery of urban social services, but they have also argued for a new kind of urban design, in which personal safety issues are included, and where the concerns and values of women and children are taken into account (Hayden, 1981; Sandercock and Forsyth, 1992). By emphasizing the use value of public spaces, by networking around schools, and children's activities, and by claiming a safe, friendly environment, as a fundamental dimension of the quality of life, women are reconstructing the city – not only by making it more liveable, but by enhancing sociability at large. The catch is that most men are not responding to the call for an egalitarian family, as the crisis of the patriarchal family deepens, and the family as we used to know it becomes a minority phenomenon in economically advanced countries. Furthermore, public institutions often reinforce the split beween genders through discriminatory policies, as documented by Ida Susser (1995). Thus, the city of women might then proceed on the basis of networks of women and their children, increasingly distinct from rather isolated men. (A reminder: in the US the proportion of households made up of a heterosexual couple with children, including children from different marriages, stands currently at less than a quarter of all households.) Can the city of women be also the city of men? Or are we witnessing another fundamental crack in the social fabric of the city?

Reconstructing the City (III): Metropolitan Governance and the Evolution of Planning

The size and complexity of metropolitan regions, and their unstable relationship to global networks, require, more than ever, regulatory and management mechanisms that can only be exercised by active forms of metropolitan governance, using new planning tools. The diversity of local and regional situations makes it literally impossible for national governments to respond in a flexible manner to a changing global environment. Hence the growing importance of local and regional governments around the world. The global age is the age of local management, albeit in a network of interactions with national and supranational governmental institutions. Yet, local governments *stricto sensu* cannot manage the metropolitan region. Metropolitan governance becomes a critical issue.

However, the justified attachment of societies (for example, the United States) to local democracy, and local governance, makes implausible, and probably damaging, the shift of power from the local level to a metropolitan government. Cities around the world are experimenting with associations of local governments, delegating some of their powers, to govern together on a metropolitan scale. In the United States, the most successful experience of metropolitan planning, that of Portland, Oregon, is usually credited to the dynamism and innovativeness of its metropolitan government, as documented in Wheeler's (1999) doctoral dissertation. In Europe, the success of Barcelona is partly based on the association between the city government and the government of its large metropolitan environs in providing solutions to largely shared economic, social, environmental, and transportation problems (Borja and Castells, 1997). However, local governments acting in a global environment, and under the pressures of local change, cannot expect to be effective without extending their cooperation to other local governments, and without calling upon citizen participation.

Thus, on the one hand, networks of local governments have spread in some areas of the world, particularly in Europe, sharing information, devising common negotiating strategies, and adopting the culture of simultaneous competition and cooperation which has become the feature of the most successful private firms in the networked economy. On the other hand, citizen participation has become essential so that local governments have a political margin of maneuver in a constantly changing environment. This margin of maneuver can only be provided by fully informed citizens, who know the whys and hows of government policy because of their regular involvement in the decision-making process. While this kind of citizen participation is the exception rather than the rule, wherever it exists (Barcelona, Amsterdam, Portland, Curitiba), it considerably enhances the effectiveness of governance. On both grounds (networking of local governments, citizen participation) the uses of electronic communication greatly facilitate the sharing of information and interactive decision-making, as exemplified by Amsterdam's Digital City or Seattle's Community Network.

Planning remains a crucial tool for managing the relationship between society, economy, space, and political institutions, along the lines debated and decided by people's representatives. However, planning has substantially changed, from a rigid land-use document to a flexible negotiating tool, under the guidance of a strategic plan, which provides a blueprint for the various cities and communities in the metropolitan area (Teitz, 1996, 1997). Environmental planning and strategic planning are the key devices in the age of flexibility, both based on real-time information systems and hands-on management of planning by goals rather than by rules. This is why citizen participation and open information systems are essential, so that citizens can judge the substance of each decision, rather than its formal compliance to standard rules. Planning as negotiation and planning as strategic guidance substitute for planning as the rule of preconceived rationality in allocating the uses of space and dictating spatial forms. Thus, planning as an instrument of metropolitan governance may reconstruct the city, not only by optimizing the allocation of resources, but by providing a ground for people to negotiate their interests and values, so finding a common denominator on which to build a metropolitan community. On the other hand, the capture of planning by specific interests on behalf of unidimensional visions of the city (for example, real estate development, freeway builders and transportation engineers or an all-out search for economic competitiveness) will increase the distance between a technocratic bureaucracy and the irreducible, segmented interests of individuals and local communities (Benveniste, 1989).

Rethinking Cities in the Information Age: Space of Flows, Space of Places, and the Production of Urban Meaning

The extraordinary transformation of technology, society, and space characterizing the Information Age demands new developments in urban theory (Mitchell, 1995; Boyer, 1996). Cities are made of spatial processes, as well as of cultural forms. And space and time are contingent categories, in society as in nature, relative to their context and practice. Thus, it seems appropriate to hypothesize, on the basis of empirical evidence, the emergence of a new form of space in the Information Age. I call it the space of flows because it works across distance through communication flows, processed and transmitted by telecommunications, electronic networks of information systems, and transportation networks. The space of flows includes locales, but these do not exist in such space by themselves: they are nodes of a network. Most dominant activities in our societies, such as financial markets, high-level management, multi-regional and multinational production of goods and services, media communication, and science and technology, work in/by the space of flows. But it is also increasingly the case in commerce, education, miscellaneous information, interpersonal communication, virtual communities, public debate/political activity, and so on, operating in the Internet. In other words, the space of flows, which started as the space of power and dominant functions, is extending its realm to the whole diversity of human activity.

Why call it space? Because space, in theoretical terms, is not a territory, but the material support of simultaneity or chosen time (Innis, 1952). Until the advent of the telephone and radio communication simultaneity was associated with spatial contiguity. Electronic communication, and the fast transportation systems made possible by new technologies, have expanded non-contiguous shared practices to an increasing domain of social organization and human interaction. The space of flows becomes now a pervasive, dominant form of organizing this interaction, with very different attributes from those characterizing place-based interaction. Rather than claiming the end of the spatial dimension in our practices, it is analytically more fruitful to distinguish between the space of flows, and the space of places, to consider their interaction, as a fundamental feature of urban life, and of society at large, in the new technological paradigm, characteristic of the network society.

The space of places, based on territorial contiguity, continues to exist. Indeed, it constitutes the prevailing space of personal experience and cultural identity for most people in the world (Jacobs, 1993). It does not follow that the space of flows is meaningless. In fact, its meaning is precisely the transcultural, transhistorical affirmation of placelessness, as in the mosaic of Internet-based hypertexts, or in the random formal mixture of corporate, postmodern architecture. The critical matter is not the lack of meaning, but the problematic communicability of various codes of meaning. If people's experience is fragmented in culturally specific places, and the functions of power, production, wealth, innovation, and communication escape into a different code, formed around the real virtuality of the space of flows, there are no longer symbolic transmitters in the urban experience. Without meaningful centralities, cities cease to function as cultural integrators of diverse meanings. Without cathedrals, no transcendent meaning, and without transcendence, segmented cultural identities become urban tribes. In the absence of symbolic bridges between non-communicable spaces of places, and the global, a-historical, primarily instrumental space of flows, we may assist in creating the crisis of urban civilization.

The New Culture of Cities

The new culture of cities is the culture of meaningful, interactive communication enacted by a multimodal interface between the space of flows and the space of places. Its relevance is highlighted by the fact that communication in our societies is breaking down between their components, through a juxtaposition between an electronic hypertext and the fragmented existence of secluded communes and self-centered individuals (Kraut et al., 1998). In the vast expanse of metropolitan sprawl, cities, and their culture, constitute the fundamental mediation between home and global communication networks. Cities have always been communication systems, based on the interface between individual and communal identities and shared, social representations (Meier, 1962). It is their ability to organize this interface materially in forms, in rhythms, in collective experience, and communicable perception, that makes cities producers of sociability, and integrators of otherwise destructive creativity (Zukin, 1992). The challenge is greater than ever in the Information Age because of the power of communication flows, and their ability to separate function from meaning (Dutton, 1999). Even milieux of innovation, anchored in the metropolis, could become specialized and reduced to an instrumental function, while abstracting themselves from the communicative quality of cities' culture. On the other hand, the opportunities are extraordinary, as the extension of the human mind by electronic networks can link up historical, geographical, and cultural diversity, and induce an unprecedented interface between our physical experience and our virtual experience, both equally real (Wheeler and Aoyama, 1999).

This interface between electronic communication and the space of places may occur in all kinds of spatial forms. The old debate in terms of density versus sprawl as the basic divide in inducing urban meaning or meaningless-ness seems to be obsolete, and confined to the dwindling stream of belief in spatial determinism. Depending on history, culture, and technology, cities can be characterized by high density or high sprawl, or both at the same time (Hall, 1998). Los Angeles is not less of a city than Rome, it is just a different kind of city – at least for the time being. Rome can be as isolating as Los Angeles, and indeed it is, when we move away from the Trastevere. However, if the spatial manifestations can be diverse, there are a number of features, spatial, technological, and institutional, that are positively associated with the development of a new culture of cities, extending its traditional communica-tive function into the technological paradigm of the twenty-first century. The main features seem to be the following:

- The reconstruction of urban centrality, on the basis of a new, multi-nuclear structure. This structure does not necessarily imply a hierarchy between centers, but it requires a combination of functional and sym-bolic centrality related to a specific sub-set of the metropolitan region or to the metropolitan region as a whole.
- The decisive role of public space as a bridge between communities and individuals. The privatization of public space (for example, enclosed in private shopping malls) reinforces socio-spatial separatism. The foster-ing of space, and its openness to spontaneous use (including redefini-tion of use), is the most important physical bridge between various sources of meaning, bringing them together in the urban experience.
- A new monumentality, able to provide symbolic meaning to spatial forms, marking in terms of meaning the metropolitan sprawl. Public art, singular architecture, urban design oriented to the metropolitan infrastructure (freeways, bridges, telecommunications towers, and so on), and public/private support for urban design of neighborhoods, and of metropolitan sub-centers, are critical devices to restore meaning in the new city form.
- Schools as community-building devices, linking up what is left of the family with its surrounding community through their last common interest: children (Carnoy, 2000), which, by the way, includes the socialization of the new urbanite generation in a less individualized mode, attenuating the effects of atomized individuation induced by predominant exposure to the multimedia world.
- Not-for-profit, local computer/media networks, connecting the local experience to the electronic hypertext, thus providing a material

bridge for interaction between the two sources of information and meaning.

The explicit interface between spatial symbolism, centrality, cultural identity, and the space of flows can be articulated around major cultural institutions, which become the nodes of this physical–virtual interface. Museums, redefined in the Information Age, are becoming key sources of urban revitalization, urban design, and communicative bridges between art, electronic networks, and the city, from Bilbao's Guggenheim to the Massachusetts Museum of Contemporary Art (Muschamp, 1999). Furthermore, new metropolitan cultural centers, such as the Cité des Sciences et de l'Industrie in Paris, the Casa de la Caritat in Barcelona, or the Tate Modern gallery in London, are explicitly targeting the interface between multimedia, the Internet, and urban culture, in its diversity, as their new role of cultural senders/symbolic exchangers which will be at the source of a new culture of cities.

So, ultimately, if the city as a source of cultural specificity is to survive in the new technological paradigm it must become a hypercommunicated city, communicated locally and globally, through a variety of communication channels (symbolic, virtual, physical), then building bridges between these channels. The culture of cities in the Information Age brings together local identity and global networks to restore the interaction between power and experience, function and meaning, technology and culture.

Urban Studies at the Turn of the Millennium: Back to the Future?

During the twentieth century the field of urban studies was intellectually marked by two major debates that originated from research and thinking in the early years of the century. The first arose from the utopian, yet pragmatic views of British urbanists, such as Ebenezer Howard, and, in a different, but related approach, from American social critics such as Lewis Mumford. They sought to affirm cities as cultural centers and neighborhoods as liveable, sustainable places, in the face of unbalanced, market-driven urbanization and industrialization. Or, in other words, cities and neighborhoods should be built for their use value, and not be reduced to their market value. The second theme was articulated, in the 1920s, around the venerable tradition of the Chicago School of urban sociology (Park, Burgess, McKenzie, Wirth), focusing on social integration in the urban society. Both traditions were submitted to stern criticism throughout the second half of the century. Believers in the economic and social virtues of metropolitan growth assailed the view of traditional urbanism, hoping, instead, to solve urban problems by a combination of technology and social engineering. Critics of the integrationist approach of the Chicago School emphasized the role of urban social movements and competitive politics as underlying forces in shaping the city. The subsequent interaction between these influential and opposite trends yielded a wealth of urban research, which grounded these fundamental debates in observation and reasoning, thus helping to put ideological statements into perspective. Urban studies became, probably second only to economics among the social sciences, a research field which was actually able to influence public and private decision-making, in ways that affected, for good or bad, the lives of millions of citizens, and of future generations, around the world.

Now that the twenty-first century is under way, it is safe to predict what will be the main axes of the next phase of urban research, stemming both from the intellectual debates of the last century, and from the new urban problems, as identified in this chapter. These revolve, essentially, around four major questions. The first is the transformation of cities, and of urban space by information and communication technologies. The second is the place of the local in a world of global networks. Both are, already at this point, well established fields of research, with a steady stream of scholarly contributions, including a growing number of doctoral dissertations around the world.

But there are two other themes which link directly to policy debates and bring back, under new terms, the century-old debates about urbanization and society. One of these is the issue of environmental sustainability. The other is the survival of cities as specific societies, which is tantamount to considering the conditions for urban social integration in the age of globalization, fragmentation, and individualization. In other words: can we live in a fully urbanized world in harmony with nature? And can we live with each other, in differentiated, yet communicated local societies, in these giant, nameless, territorial constellations which are, and will be, the forms of human habitat in the twenty-first century? On both grounds, the lessons from the debates of the early twentieth century are invaluable: the notion of garden cities, the urban version of humanistic environmentalism, represented by Lewis Mumford and, later, by Kevin Lynch and Jane Jacobs, and the Chicago School's concern for a balanced urban ecology, and for social integration among a disparity of cultures and social groups. Naturally, the fruitful development of these intellectual traditions requires us to adapt their teachings to the new technological and cultural context of the twenty-first century.

I see as the cutting edge of urban research the convergence of the technology-led school, which focuses on the globalization and telecommunication of urban spaces, with a renewed concern for social integration, environmental sustainability, and local democracy. There are already significant developments in this direction, as exemplified in the work of a new generation of urban researchers, such as Stephen Graham, François Ascher, Anna Lee Saxenian, Lisa Servon, and Eric Klineberg. I believe the conditions are in place for a holistic approach to the study of cities, able to renew the historical link with the Chicago School, but without its functionalist bias, and with the help of new methods of social research, integrating ethnographic studies with computer-based models of analysis, such as geographic information systems and iterative simulation.

The new breakthrough in urban studies in the coming years will be based on the integration of an eco-social approach with a techno-economic study of cities, and with an urban design perspective, within the context of a cross-cultural, comparative framework. This is not too different, intellectually speaking, from what took place in the formative period of the field. But we now have the accumulated knowledge, the methodology, and the interdisciplinary, insti-tutional basis, from which we can accomplish the intellectual promise of the founding fathers of the field. So doing, we may be on the way to understand-ing how cities and nature can be preserved, and their quality enhanced, in the Information Age. Considering that we are entering a predominantly urban world, this accomplishment would be no small feat. It would constitute a meaningful connection between scholarly research and peoples' well-being in the frontiers of the mind in the twenty-first century.

Acknowledgments

This chapter was prepared for the conference "Frontiers of the Mind in the Twenty-first Century," Library of Congress, Washington DC, June 14–18, 1999. I would like to acknowledge the research assistance of Malo Hutson, formerly a graduate student at the Department of City and Regional Planning, University of California, Berkeley.

REFERENCES

Benveniste, Guy (1989) *Mastering the Politics of Planning*. San Francisco: Jossey Bass.
Blakely, Edward J. and Snyder, Mary Gail (1997) *Fortress America: Gated Communities in the United States*. Washington, DC: Brookings Institution Press.
Borja, Jordi and Castells, Manuel (1997) *Local and Global: Management of Cities in the Information Age*. London: Earthscan.
Boyer, Christine (1996) *Cybercities*. New York: Princeton University Press.
Brotchie, J. F. et al. (eds) (1995) *Cities in Competition: Productive and Sustainable Cities for the Twenty-first Century*. Melbourne: Longman.
Calthorpe, Peter (1993) *The Next American Metropolis: Ecology, Community and the American Dream*. Princeton, NJ: Princeton Architectual Press.
Capra, Fritjof (1995) *The Web of Life*. New York: Anchor Books.
Carnoy, Martin (2000) *Sustaining the New Economy: Work, Family, and Community in the Information Age*. Cambridge, MA: Harvard University Press.
Castells, Manuel (1983) *The City and the Grassroots: A Cross-cultural Theory of Urban Social Movements*. Berkeley, CA: University of California Press.

Castells, Manuel (1989) *The Informational City: Information Technology, Economic Restructuring and the Urban Regional Process*. Oxford: Blackwell.

Castells, Manuel (1992) *European Cities, the Informational City, and the Global Economy*. Amsterdam: University of Amsterdam, Center for Metropolitan Studies.

Castells, Manuel (1996) *The Rise of the Network Society*. Oxford: Blackwell.

Castells, Manuel and Hall, Peter (1994) *Technopoles of the World: The Making of Twenty-first century Industrial Complexes*. London: Routledge.

Cervero, Robert (1989) *America's Suburban Centers: The Land Use–Transportation Link*. Boston: Unwin Hyman.

Cohen, Michael et al. (1996) *Preparing for the Urban Future*. Washington, DC: Smithsonian Institute.

Daniels, P. W. (1993) *Service Industries in the World Economy*. Oxford: Blackwell.

Dutton, William H. (1999) *Society on the Line*. Oxford: Oxford University Press.

Fischer, Claude (1982) *To Dwell among Friends: Personal Networks in Town and City*. Berkeley CA: University of California Press.

Garreau, Joel (1991) *Edge City: Life on the New Urban Frontier*. New York: Doubleday.

Goldsmith, William W. and Blakely, Edward J. (1992) *Separate Societies: Poverty and Inequality in US Cities*. Philadelphia, PA: Temple University Press.

Graham, Stephen (1997) "Telecommunications and the future of cities: debunking the myths," *Cities*, 14 (1): 21–9.

Graham, Stephen (1999) "Global grids of glass: on global cities, telecommunications, and planetary urban networks," *Urban Studies*, May.

Graham, Stephen and Marvin, Simon (1996) *Telecommunications and the City: Electronic Spaces, Urban Places*. London: Routledge.

Graham, Stephen and Marvin, Simon (1999) *Splintering Networks, Fragmenting Cities: Urban Infrastructure in a Global–Local Age*. London: Routledge.

Hall, Peter (1998) *Cities in Civilization*. New York: Pantheon.

Hall, Peter (2000) *Megacities, World Cities and Global Cities*. Amsterdam: Megacities Foundation 2000, Megacities Lecture.

Harvey, David (1973) *Social Justice and the City*. London: Edward Arnold.

Harvey, David (1990) *The Condition of Postmodernity*. Oxford: Blackwell.

Hayden, Dolores (1981) *The Grand Domestic Revolution*. Cambridge, MA: MIT Press.

Held, David et al. (1999) *Global Transformations: Politics, Economics, and Culture*. Stanford: Stanford University Press.

Innis, Harold (1952) *Changing Concepts of Time*. Toronto: Toronto University Press.

Jacobs, Allan B. (1993) *Great Streets*. Cambridge, MA: MIT Press.

Kraut, Robert et al. (1998) "Internet paradox: a social technology that reduces social involvement and psychological well-being?," *American Psychologist*, September: 1017–31.

Kunstler, James Howard (1993) *The Geography of Nowhere*. New York: Touchstone.

Lo, Fu-Chen and Yeung, Yue-Man (eds) (1996) *Emerging World Cities in Pacific Asia*. Tokyo: United Nations University Press.

Lynch, Kevin (1981) *A Theory of the Good City Form*. Cambridge, MA: MIT Press.

Massey, Douglas S. (1996) "The age of extremes: concentrated affluence and poverty in the twenty-first century," *Demography*, 33 (4): 395–41.

Massey, Douglas S. et al. (1999) *Worlds in Motion: Understanding International Migration at the End of the Millennium*. Oxford: Oxford University Press.

Meier, Richard (1962) *A Communication Theory of Urban Growth*. Cambridge, MA: MIT Press.

Michelson, R. and Wheeler, J. (1994) "The flow of information in a global economy: the role of the American urban system in the 1990s," *Annals of the American Association of Geographers*, 84 (1): 87–107.

Mitchell, William J. (1995) *City of Bits: Space, Place, and the Infobahn*. Cambridge, MA: MIT Press.

Moss, Mitchell (1987) "Telecommunications, world cities and urban policy," *Urban Studies*, 24: 534–46.

Muschamp, Herbert (1999) "Culture's power houses: the museum becomes an engine of urban redesign," *The New York Times*, April 21: D1–D6.

Office of Technology Assessment (1995) *The Technological Reshaping of Metropolitan America*. Washington, DC: US Congress.

Sandercock, Leonie and Forsyth, Ann (1992) "A gender-agenda: new directions for planning theory," *Journal of the American Planning Association*, 58 (1): 49–59.

Sassen, Saskia (1991) *The Global City: New York, London, Tokyo*. Princeton, NJ: Princeton University Press.

Satterthwaite, David (1995) "Global report on human settlements," report to the Habitat II Conference. Nairobi: Habitat/United Nations.

Saxenian, Anna L. (1994) *Regional Advantage*. Cambridge, MA: Harvard University Press.

Scott, Allen (1992) *Metropolis*. Berkeley, CA: University of California Press.

Scott, Allen (1998) *Regions in the World Economy*. Oxford: Oxford University Press.

Smart Valley Inc. (1997) *Telecommute America, California Style*. Survey Report, December.

Stren, Richard, White, Rodney, and Whitney, Joseph (eds) (1992) *Sustainable Cities: Urbanization and the Environment in International Perspective*. Boulder, CO: Westview Press.

Susser, Ida (1995) "Creating family forms: the exclusion of men and teenage boys from families in the New York City shelter system, 1987–1991," *Critique of Anthropology*, 13 (3): 267–85.

Teitz, Michael B. (1996) "American planning in the 1990s: evolution, debate, and challenge," *Urban Studies*, 33 (4–5): 649–71.

Teitz, Michael B. (1997) "American planning in the 1990s. Part II: The dilemma of the cities," *Urban Studies*, 34 (5–6): 775–95.

Thrift, Nigel (1996) "New eras and old technological fears: reconfiguring the goodwill of electronic things," *Urban Studies*, 33 (8): 1463–93.

Wellman, Barry (ed.) (1999) *Networks in the Global Village*. Boulder, CO: Westview Press.

Wellman, Barry and Gulia, Milena (1999) "Net-surfers don't ride alone: virtual communities as communities," in B. Wellman (ed.), *Networks in the Global Village*. Boulder, CO: Westview Press, pp. 331–66.

Wheeler, Stephen (1999) "The institutions of metropolitan planning: a comparison between Portland Oregon, and Toronto, Ontario," unpublished PhD thesis, University of California, Department of City and Regional Planning, Berkeley, California.

Wheeler, James O., Aoyama, Yuko, and Warf, Barney (eds) (2000) *Cities in the Telecommunications Age: The Fracturing of Geographies*. London: Routledge.

World Health Organization, Centre for Health Development (1996) *Urbanization: A*

Global Health Challenge. Washington, DC: World Health Organization.

Zook, Matthew (2001) "The geography of the Internet industry: venture capital, Internet start-ups, and regional development," unpublished PhD thesis, University of California, Department of City and Regional Planning, Berkeley, California.

Zukin, Sharon (1992) *Landscapes of Power*. Berkeley, CA: University of California Press.

Conclusion: Urban Sociology in the Twenty-first Century

(2000)

A Retrospective Perspective

In 1968 I published my first academic article, under the title "Is there an urban sociology?" (Castells, 1968). Thirty-two years later, with the hindsight of historical perspective and a life of practicing social research on cities, the answer is: yes, there was; no, there is currently not; but perhaps, with luck, it will resurge in the twenty-first century, with new concepts, new methods, and new themes, because it is more necessary than ever to make sense of our lives – which will be lived, for the large majority of people, in urban areas of some sort.

Urban sociology was one of the founding fields of modern social science. It originated from the issues raised by fast urbanization as a consequence of industrialization, breaking down the patterns of rural life that had characterized the livelihood of humankind for millenniums. It was built around the central theme of social integration in a new, urban society made up of recent rural immigrants, and where the traditional institutions of social integration were crumbling under the weight of population growth, economic development, social mobility, and social struggles. Because American metropolitan areas were the epitome of growth, immigration, and change, they provided the social laboratory in which social scientists could explore the conditions of integration into the urban society of the masses of uprooted immigrants, flocking to the new Babylon from both the countryside and overseas. Chicago was simultaneously the center of social struggles (May 1 commemorates the killing of striking workers in Chicago), of Bertolt Brecht's theater ("St Jeanne of the Slaughterhouses"), and of some of the most innovative sociologists of the time (Park et al., 1925; Zorbaugh, 1929; Wirth 1938), who created the Chicago School of urban sociology, the founding act of urban sociology as a scholarly discipline.

The Chicago School was ideologically biased around the notion of urban culture – a unified culture that would characterize city dwellers regardless of their class, gender, or ethnicity. Yet, by emphasizing the conditions and contradictions of social integration for an extraordinarily diverse local society, the Chicago sociologists were dealing with the central problem of American society at the time: how to make a society out of a collection of disparate communities and competitive individuals fighting for survival. While the conditions in European cities were not so extreme, the issue of the reconstruction of patterns of social interaction for former peasants and transients in an urban–industrial context was equally poignant, even though a lack of interest among socialist ideologies in the urban question led to the reduction of urban contradictions to the secondary dimension of broader class conflict.

Alongside the study of social integration, urban sociology focused on the study of spatial patterning, also formalized by another stream of Chicago School sociologists, linked to social Darwinism in the development of what came to be known as human ecology (Hawley, 1956; Schnore, 1965). Thus, the study of forms and processes of human settlements under the notion of competition and social selection, and the analysis of the social conditions for cultural integration, were the founding themes of an urban sociology that, while ideologically biased, responded to the historical issues raised by industrialization and urbanization in the first half of the twentieth century. Regardless of the theoretical and political divergences I have with the Chicago School, urban sociology blossomed under its influence because the Chicago sociologists were dealing, with as much rigor and imagination as early sociologists could do, with the key issues of their time – with the process of formation of a new society, spatially organized in large urban centers. Because of the strength of this scholarly tradition, its themes, methods, and theoretical framework greatly outlasted the relevance of the approach – although history has its surprises, as I will elaborate later.

In the 1960s and 1970s, social problems in general, and urban issues in particular, were very different from those that gave birth to the Chicago School. Social/cultural integration was not the issue any longer. The struggle over the control and orientations of an urban–industrial society was now at the forefront of urban problems. Furthermore, new social movements were arising, challenging the very notion of development and industrialization, calling for the pre-eminence of human experience over economic growth and for new forms of relationship between society and nature. Gender issues were raised as fundamental. The diversity of the urban experience throughout a multicultural world was finally acknowledged by social science, disqualifying the ethnocentric theory of modernization as Westernization. Widespread state intervention in people's lives by means of its control of social services and public amenities became the key element in the organization of both everyday life and urban processes. When everything was contested, debated, fought over, and negotiated between social groups with conflicting interests and alternative projects, the very notion of integration in a shared culture appeared utterly obsolete. Thus, a new urban sociology emerged from a new urban reality. It took different orientations in America and in Europe. In America, pluralist political science placed political conflict and bargaining at the center of urban social analysis (Banfield and Wilson, 1963; Mollenkopf, 1983). While I disagree with its consideration of social actors and interest groups outside the constraints of their class interests and cultural frameworks, the approach of urban political science, philosophically rooted in the tradition of liberalism, represented a major break with the theme of social integration, putting conflict and its negotiation at center-stage of urban social science. However, for reasons that historians of knowledge will explore some day, during the 1970s, the field of urban sociology was strongly revitalized by the so-called "new urban sociology" school, which originated in France, essentially around the work of two individuals who were in sharp intellectual disagreement: the great Marxist philosopher Henri Lefebvre (1968), and myself. The new urban sociology, which was never a unified school of thought, was built around four major themes, two introduced by the first theorist, the other two by the second. The first two themes, later elaborated by David Harvey and Edward Soja, were the production of space and the right to the city. Space was to be considered as a process of production (e.g. capitalist production), whose outcome would ultimately frame people's lives in spatially constrained patterns. As a corollary, when capital did not consider it profitable or useful to keep people in the city, but could not send them back to the countryside because they were needed as urban workers, a new, intermediate space was built: the suburb – high rise and working class in the European version; single family dwelling and middle class in the American version, but equally anti-urban. Thus, after being expelled from their rural communities, people were now expelled, or induced to move out, from the city they had made into a liveable place. Now they were losing their right to the city.

The two other critical themes of the new urban sociology were built on the notions of collective consumption and urban social movements. The city was considered as a system organized around the provision of services necessary for everyday life, under the direct or indirect guidance/control of the state. Housing, transportation, schools, health care, social services, cultural facilities, and urban amenities were part of the elements necessary to the economy and to daily life that could not be produced or delivered without some kind of state intervention (e.g. public housing and public transportation in Europe, federally backed housing mortgages and subsidized highway systems in the United States). Collective consumption (that is, state-mediated consumption processes) became at the same time the basis of urban infrastructure, and the key relationship between people and the state. Cities became redefined as the points of contradiction and conflict between capital accumulation and social redistribution, between state control and people's autonomy. Around these issues, new urban social movements – that is, movements centered both on the control of community life and on the demands of collective consumption – emerged as new actors of social conflict and political power. Urban sociology was turned upside-down, from the discipline studying social integration to the discipline specializing in the new social conflicts of postindustrialism.

Then, suddenly, in the last years of the twentieth century, a deep silence. Urban sociology receded into obscurity, in spite of the orderly pursuit of academic careers and the regular publication of scholarly journals that dutifully printed thousands of papers re-stating, re-elaborating, and refining the issues, themes, and concepts produced in the two big waves of urban sociology, in the 1920–30s and in the 1960–70s. Yet, by and large, urban sociology ceased to connect with the new issues arising in cities, space, and in society at large. The "new urban sociology" became obsolete *vis-à-vis* its new urban context, marked by the early stages of the Information Age, just as the Chicago School had become obsolete in relation to the mature industrial society. The lack of excitement of both students and intellectuals *vis-à-vis* urban sociology reflects an understanding of the exhaustion of its sources of inspiration from the challenges happening in the real world.

In order to understand the crisis of urban sociology at the turn of the millennium, and the avenues for its intellectual reconstruction, we have to recast the transformation of cities and urban issues in the new historical period, which I conceptualized as the Information Age. This could be a long and complicated detour, but I will build on the analysis of this matter presented in chapter 9 of this volume, "The Culture of Cities in the Information Age." Thus, here I will simply underline the key trends of urban transformation at the turn of the century to link them to the theoretical challenges to be answered by urban sociology in the twenty-first century.

A New Urban World

Spatial transformation must be understood in the broader context of social transformation: space does not reflect society, it expresses it, it is a fundamental dimension of society, inseparable from the overall process of social organization and social change. Thus, the new urban world arises from the formation of what I have analyzed as the emergence of a new society, the network society, characteristic of the Information Age, as a result of the interaction between the information-technology revolution, socio-economic restructuring, and cultural social movements. The key developments in spatial patterns and urban processes associated with these macro-structural changes, can be summarized under the following headings:

- Because commercial agriculture has been, by and large, automated, and a global economy has integrated productive networks throughout the planet, the majority of the world's population is already living in urban areas, and this will be increasingly the case: we are heading toward a largely urbanized world which will comprise between two-thirds and three-quarters of the total population by the middle of the century.

- This process of urbanization is concentrated disproportionately in metropolitan areas of a new kind: urban constellations scattered throughout huge territorial expanses, functionally integrated and socially differentiated, around a multi-centered structure.

- Advanced telecommunications, the Internet, and fast, computerized transportation systems allow for simultaneous spatial concentration and decentralization, ushering in a new geography of networks and urban nodes throughout the world, throughout countries, between metropolitan areas, and within metropolitan areas.

- Social relationships are characterized simultaneously by individuation and communalism, both processes using, at the same time, spatial patterning and on-line communication. Virtual communities and physical communities develop in close interaction, and both processes of aggregation are challenged by increasing individualization of work, social relationships, and residential habits.

- The crisis of the patriarchal family, with different manifestations depending on cultures and levels of economic development, shifts sociability from family units to networks of individualized units (often women and their children, but also individualized co-habiting partnerships), with considerable consequences in the uses and forms of housing, neighborhoods, public space, and transportation systems.

- The emergence of the network enterprise as a new form of economic activity, with its highly decentralized, yet coordinated, form of work and management, tends to blur the functional distinction between spaces of work and spaces of residence. The work–living arrangements characteristic of the early periods of industrial craft work are back, often taking over the old industrial spaces, and transforming them into informational production spaces. This is not just New York's Silicon Alley or San Francisco's Multimedia Gulch, but a phenomenon that also characterizes London, Barcelona, Tokyo, Taipei and Buenos Aires, among many other cities. Transformation of productive uses becomes more important than residential succession to explain the new dynamics of urban space.

- Urban areas around the world, but particularly in the developed world, are increasingly multi-ethnic and multicultural; an old theme of the Chicago School, now amplified in terms of its extremely diverse racial composition.

- The global criminal economy is solidly rooted in the urban fabric, providing jobs, income, and social organization to a criminal culture, which deeply affects the lives of low-income communities and of the city at large. This gives rise to increasing violence and/or widespread paranoia of urban violence, with the corollary of defensive residential patterns.
- The breakdown of communication patterns between individuals and between cultures, and the emergence of defensive spaces, lead to the formation of sharply segregated areas: gated communities for the rich, territorial turfs for the poor.
- In a reaction against trends of suburban sprawl and individualization of residential patterns, urban centers and public space become critical expressions of local life, measuring the vitality of a given city. Yet, commercial pressures and artificial attempts at mimicking urban life often transform public spaces into theme parks where symbols rather than experience create a life-size, urban virtual reality, ultimately destined to the real virtuality projected in the media. This gives rise to increasing individualization, as urban places become consumption items to be individually appropriated.
- Overall, the new urban world seems to be dominated by the dual movement of inclusion into transterritorial networks and exclusion by the spatial separation of places. The higher the value of people and places, the more they are connected into interactive networks. The lower their value, the lower their connection. At the extreme, some places are switched off and bypassed by the new geography of networks, as in the case of depressed rural areas and urban shanty towns around the world.
- The constitution of mega-metropolitan regions, without a name, without a culture, and without institutions, weakens the mechanism of political accountability, of citizen participation, and of effective administration. On the other hand, in the age of globalization, local governments emerge as flexible institutional actors, able to relate at the same time to local citizens and to global flows of power and money; not because they are powerful, but because most levels of government, including the nation-state, are equally weakened in their capacity of command and control if they operate in isolation. Thus, a new form of state emerges, the network state, integrating supranational institutions made up of national governments, nation-states, regional governments, local governments, and even non-governmental organizations. Local governments become a node in the chain of institutional representation and management, able to input the overall process, yet with added value in terms of their capacity to represent citizens at a closer range. Indeed, in most countries, opinion polls show that people have a higher

degree of trust in their local governments, relative to other levels of government. However, institutions of metropolitan governance are rare (and when they exist they are highly centralized, with little citizen participation), and there is an increasing gap between the actual unit of work and living (the metropolitan region) and the mechanisms of political representation and public administration. Local governments compensate for this by cooperating and competing, yet, by defining their interests as specific sub-sets of the metropolitan region, they (often unwillingly) contribute to further fragmentation of the spatial framing of social life.

- Urban social movements have not disappeared, by any means. But they have mutated. In an extremely schematic representation, they develop along two main lines. The first is the defense of the local community, affirming the right to live in a particular place, and to benefit from adequate housing and urban services in that place. The second is the environmental movement, acting on the quality of cities within the broader goal of achieving a better quality of life: not only a better life but a different life. Often, the broader goals of environmental mobilizations become translated into defensive reactions to protect one specific community, thus merging the two trends. Yet, it is only by reaching out to the cultural transformation of urban life as proposed by ecological thinkers and activists that urban social movements can transcend their limits of localism. Indeed, enclosing themselves in their communities, urban social movements may contribute to further spatial fragmentation, ultimately leading to the breakdown of society.

It is against the background of these major trends of urban social change that we can re-think the issues, themes, and prospects of urban sociology in the coming years.

The Newest Urban Sociology

To make the transition from the observation of urban trends to the new theorization of urban sociology, we need to grasp, at a more analytical level, the key elements of socio-spatial change. I think the transformation of cities in the Information Age can be organized around three axes: the first relates to function, the second to meaning, the third to form.

Functionally speaking, the network society is organized around the opposition between the global and the local. Dominant processes in the economy, technology, media, and institutionalized authority are organized in global networks. But day-to-day work, private life, cultural identity, and political participation are essentially local. Cities are supposed to link up the local and the global, but this is exactly where the problems start since these are two conflicting logics that tear cities from the inside when they try to respond to both, simultaneously.

In terms of meaning, our society is characterized by the opposing development of individuation and communalism. By individuation, I understand the enclosure of meaning in the projects, interests, and representations of the individual; that is, a biologically embodied personality system (or, if you want, translating from French structuralism, a person). By communalism, I refer to the enclosure of meaning in a shared identity, based on a system of values and beliefs to which all other sources of identity are subordinated. Society, of course, exists only in-between, in the interface between individuals and identities mediated by institutions, at the source of the constitution of "civil society" – which, as Gramsci argued, does not exist against the state but in articulation with the state, forming a shared public sphere, *à la* Habermas. Trends I observe in the formative stage of the network society indicate the increasing tension and distance between personality and culture, between individuals and communes. Because cities are large aggregates of individuals, forced to coexist, and the settlement for most communes, the split between personality and commonality brings extraordinary stress upon the social system of cities as communicative and institutionalizing devices. The problematic of social integration again becomes paramount, albeit under new circumstances and in terms radically different from those of early industrial cities.

This is mainly because of the role played in urban transformation by a third, major axis of opposing trends, this one concerning *spatial forms. This is the tension and articulation between the space of flows and the space of places*, as defined in chapter 8. The space of flows links up electronically separate locations in an interactive network that connects activities and people in distinct geographical composites. The space of places organizes experience and activity around the confines of locality. Cities are structured and destructured simultaneously by the competing logics of the space of flows and the space of places. Cities do not disappear in the virtual networks. But they are transformed by the interface between electronic communication and physical interaction, by the combination of networks and places. As William Mitchell (1999), from an urbanist perspective, and Barry Wellman (1998), from a sociologist perspective, have argued, the informational city is built around this dual system of communication. *Our cities are made up at the same time of flows and places, and of their relationships.* Two examples will help to make sense of this statement, one from the point of view of urban structure, another in terms of the urban experience. Structurally speaking, the notion of "global cities" was popularized in the 1990s. Although most people assimilate the term to some dominant urban centers, such as London, New York, and Tokyo, the concept of global city (Castells, 1989; Sassen, 1991) does not refer to any particular city, but to the global articulation of segments of many cities into an electronically linked network of functional domination throughout the planet. The global city is a spatial form rather than a title of distinction for certain cities, although some cities have a greater share of these global networks than others. In a sense, most areas in all cities, including New York and London, are local, not global. And many cities are sites of areas, small and large, which are included in these global networks, at different levels. This conception of global city as a spatial form resulting from the process of globalization is in fact closer to the original analysis by Saskia Sassen than to its popularized version by city marketing agencies. Thus, from the structural point of view, the role of cities in the global economy depends on their connectivity in transportation and telecommunication networks, and of the ability of cities to mobilize human resources effectively in this process of global competition. As a consequence of this trend, nodal areas of the city, connecting to the global economy, will receive the highest priority in terms of investment and management, as they are the sources of value creation from which an urban node and its surrounding area will make their livelihood. Thus, the fate of metropolitan economies depends on their ability to subordinate all other urban functions and forms to the dynamic of certain places that ensure their competitive articulation in the global space of flows.

From the point of view of the urban experience, we are entering a built environment that is increasingly incorporating electronic communication devices everywhere. Our urban life fabric, as Mitchell (1999) has pointed out, becomes an e-topia, a new urban form in which we constantly interact, deliberately or automatically, with on-line information systems, increasingly in the wireless mode. Materially speaking, the space of flows is folded into the space of places. Yet their logics are distinct: on-line experience and face-to-face experience remain specific, and the key question then is to assure their articulation in compatible terms.

These remarks may help the theoretical reconfiguration of urban sociology in response to the challenges of the network society, and in accordance with the emergence of new spatial forms and processes.

The Themes of Twenty-first Century Urban Sociology

It should now be clear why the issue of *social integration* comes again at the forefront of urban sociology. Indeed, it is the very existence of cities as communication artifacts that is called into question, in spite of living in an urban world. But what is at stake is a very different kind of integration. In the early twentieth century the quest was for assimilation of urban subcultures into the urban culture. In the early twenty-first century the challenge is the sharing of the city by irreversibly distinct cultures and identities. No more dominant culture because only global media have the power to send dominant messages, and the media have, in fact, adapted to their market, constructing a kaleidoscope of variable content depending on demand, thus reproducing cultural and personal diversity rather than superimposing a common set of values. The spread of horizontal communication via the Internet accelerates the process of fragmentation and individualization of symbolic interaction. Thus, the fragmented metropolis and the individualization of communication reinforce each other to produce an endless constellation of cultural sub-sets. The nostalgia of the public domain will not be able to countervail the structural trends toward diversity, specification, and individualization of life, work, space, and communication, both face to face and electronic. On the other hand, communalism adds collective fragmentation to individual segmentation. Thus, in the absence of a unifying culture, and therefore of a unifying code, the key question is not the sharing of a dominant culture but the communicability of multiple codes. Since this is not a policy paper but theoretical text, the matter to be considered is not what to do to restore communication (thus city life), but how to research the processes underlying it. *The notion of symbolic communication protocols is central here*, protocols that may be physical, social, and electronic, with additional protocols being necessary to relate these three different planes of our multidimensional experience.

Physically, the establishment of meaning in these nameless urban constellations relates to the emergence of a new monumentality and new forms of symbolic centrality which will identify places, even through conflictive appropriation of their meaning by different groups and individuals. Urban semiotics appears, surprisingly, at the forefront of new urban research, enabling us to understand the processes by which new cathedrals and new agoras are created, whatever their surprising forms may be in the Information Age. However, the methodological prerequisite for urban semiotics to fulfill its promise is to return to its origins in formal linguistics, using the new tools of survey research and computerized modeling, instead of escaping into the much easier path of metaphoric commentary and interpretative narration.

The second level of symbolic analysis refers to social communication patterns. Here, the diversity of expressions of local life, and their relationship to media culture, must be integrated into the theory of communication by doing rather than by saying. In other words, how messages are transmitted from one social group to another, from one meaning to another in the metropolitan region, requires a redefinition of the notion of public sphere – moving from institutions to the public place. Public places, as sites of spontaneous social interaction, are the communicative devices of our society, while formal, political institutions have become a specialized domain that hardly affects the private lives of people; that is, what most people value most. Thus, it is not that politics, or local politics, does not matter. It is that its relevance is confined to the world of instrumentality, while expressiveness, and thus communication, refers to social practice, outside institutional boundaries. Therefore, in the practice of the city, its public spaces, including its transportation networks and their social exchangers (or communication nodes), become the communicative devices of city life. How people are, or are not, able to express themselves, and communicate with each other, outside their homes and off their electronic circuits – that is, in public places – is an essential area of study for urban sociology. I call it the sociability of public places in the individualized metropolis.

The third level of communication refers to the prevalence of electronic communication as a new form of sociability. Studies by Wellman (1999) and by Jones (1998), and by a growing legion of social researchers, have shown the density and intensity of electronic networks of communication, providing evidence to sustain the notion that virtual communities are often communities, albeit of a different kind than face-to-face communities. Here again, the critical matter is the understanding of the communication codes between various electronic networks, built around specific interests or values, and between these networks and physical interaction. There is no established theory yet on these communication processes as the Internet is still in its infancy. But we do know that on-line sociability is specified, not downgraded, and that physical location does contribute, often in unsuspected ways, to the configuration of electronic communication networks. The sociology of virtual communities is the third axis of the newest urban sociology.

Furthermore, *the analysis of code-sharing in the new urban world also requires the study of the interface between physical layouts, social organization, and electronic networks.* It is this interface that Mitchell (1999) considers to be at the heart of the new urban form, what he calls e-topia. His intuition is most insightful. We now have to transform it into research. In a similar vein, but from a different perspective, Graham and Marvin's (2001) analysis of urban infrastructure as splintered networks, reconfigurated by the new electronic pipes of urban civilization, opens up the perspective of understanding cities not only as communication systems, but as machines of deliberate segmentation. In other words, we must understand at the same time the process of communication and that of incommunication. The contradictory and/or complementary relationships between new metropolitan centrality, the practice of public space, and new communication patterns emerging from virtual communities, could lay the foundations for a new variety of urban sociology, the sociology of "cyborg cities" or hybrid cities made up of the intertwining of flows and places.

Let us go farther in this exploration of the new themes for urban sociology. We know that telecommuting – meaning people working full-time on-line from their home – is another myth of futurology. Many people, including you and me, work on-line from home part of the time, but we continue to go to workplaces, as well as moving around (the city or the world) while we keep working, with mobile connectivity to our network of professional partners, suppliers, and clients. The latter is the truly new spatial dimension of work. This is a new work experience, and indeed a new life experience. Moving physically, while keeping the networking connection to everything we do, is a new realm of human adventure of which we know little. *The sociology of networked spatial mobility is another frontier.* To explore it in terms that would not be solely descriptive we need new concepts. The connection between networks and places has to be understood in a variable geometry of these connections. The places of the space of flows – that is, the corridors and halls that connect places around the world – will have to be understood as exchangers and social refuges, as homes on the run, as much as offices on the run. The personal and cultural identification with these places, their functionality, their symbolism, are essential matters that do not concern only the cosmopolitan elite. Worldwide mass tourism, international migration, and transient work are experiences that relate to the new huddled masses of the world. How we relate to airports, to train and bus stations, to freeways, to customs are part of the new urban experience of hundreds of millions. We can build on an ethnographic tradition that addressed these issues in the mature industrial society. But here, again, the speed, complexity, and planetary reach of the transportation system have changed the scale and meaning of the issues. Furthermore, the key reminder is that we move physically while staying put in our electronic connection. We carry flows and move across places.

Urban life in the twenty-first century is also being transformed by the crisis of patriarchalism. This is not a consequence of technological change, but I have argued in my book *The Power of Identity* (Castells, 1997) that it is an essential feature of the Information Age. To be sure, patriarchalism is not historically dead. Yet it is contested enough, and overcome enough, so that everyday life for a large segment of city-dwellers has already been redefined *vis-à-vis* the traditional pattern of an industrial society based on a relatively stable patriarchal nuclear family. Under conditions of gender equality, and under the stress suffered by traditional arrangements of household formation, the forms and rhythms of urban life are dramatically altered. Patterns of residence, transportation, shopping, education, and recreation evolve to adjust to the multidirectionality of individual needs that have to share household needs. This transformation is mediated by variable configurations of state policies. For instance, how child care is handled – by government, by firms, by the market, or by individual networking – largely conditions the time and space of daily lives, particularly for children. We have fully documented how women are discriminated against in the patriarchal city. We can even empirically argue (see chapter 9) that women's work makes the functioning of cities possible, while rarely being acknowledged in the urban studies literature. Yet we need to move forward, from denunciation to the analysis of specific urban contradictions resulting from the growing dissonance between the de-gendering of society and the historical crystallization of patriarchalism in the patterns of home and urban structure. How do these contradictions manifest themselves? What are people's strategies to overcome the constraints of a gendered built environment?

How do women in particular reinvent urban life, and contribute to re-designing the city of women, in contrast to the millennial heritage of the city of men? These are the questions to be researched, rather than stated, by a truly *post-patriarchal urban sociology*.

Grassroots movements will continue to shape cities, as well as societies at large. They will come in all kind of formats and ideologies, and we should keep an open mind on this matter, not deciding in advance which ones are progressive, and which ones are regressive, but taking all of them as symptoms of society in the making. We should also keep in mind the most fundamental rule in the study of social movements. They are what they say they are. They are their own consciousness. We can study their origins, establish their rules of engagement, explore the reasons for their victories and defeats, link their outcomes to overall social transformation, but not interpret them, not explain to them what they really mean by what they say. Because, after all, social movements are nothing else than their own symbols and stated goals, which ultimately means their words. Based on the observation of social movements in the early stages of the network society, two kinds of issues appear to require privileged attention from urban social scientists. The first one is what I called "the grassrooting of the space of flows," that is, the use of the Internet for networking in social mobilization and social challenges. This is not simply a technological issue because it concerns the organization, reach, and process of formation of social movements. Most often these "on-line" social movements connect to locally based movements, and they converge, physically, in a given place at a given time. A good example was the mobilization against the World Trade Organization meeting in Seattle in December 1999, which, arguably, set a new trend of grassroots opposition to uncontrolled globalization, and redefined the terms of the debate on the goals and procedures of the new economy. The sociology of social movements on-line, and their interaction with their place-based frame of reference (which can be multiple), assigns new tasks to the study of urban social movements, renewing the tradition of urban researchers in the 1960–70s.

The other major issue in the area of social movements is the exploration of the environmental movement, and of an ecological view of social organization, as urban areas become the connecting points between the global issues posed by environmentalism and the local experience through which people at large assess their quality of life. To redefine cities as ecosystems, and to explore the connection between local ecosystems and the global ecosystem, lays the ground for the overcoming of localism by grassroots movements. On the other hand, the connection cannot be operated only in terms of ecological knowledge. Implicit in the environmental movement, and clearly articulated in the "deep ecology" theory, as reformulated by Fritjof Capra (1996), is the notion of cultural transformation. A new civilization, and not simply a new technological paradigm, requires a new culture. This culture in the making is being fought over by various sets of interests and cultural projects. Environmentalism is the code word for this cultural battle, and ecological issues in the urban areas constitute the critical battleground for such struggle.

Besides tackling new issues, urban sociology will still have to reckon in the twenty-first century with *the lingering questions of urban poverty, racial and social discrimination, and social exclusion.* In fact, recent studies show an increase in urban marginality and inequality in the network society. Furthermore, old issues in a new context become, in fact, new. Thus, Ida Susser (1997) has shown the networking logic underlying the spread of AIDS among New York's poor along networks of destitution, stigma, and discrimination. Eric Klinenberg (2000), in his social anatomy of the devastating effects of the 1995 heat wave in Chicago, shows why dying alone in the city, the fate of hundreds of seniors in a few days, was rooted in the new forms of social isolation emerging from people's exclusion from networks of work, family, information, and sociability. The dialectics between inclusion and exclusion in the network society redefines the field of study of urban poverty, and forces us to consider alternative forms of inclusion (e.g. social solidarity or, otherwise, the criminal economy), as well as new mechanisms of exclusion – technological apartheid in the era of the Internet.

The final frontier for urban sociology, indeed for social science in general, is *the study of new relationships between time and space in the Information Age.* I have proposed the notion of the emergence of timeless time as characteristic of our society, in parallel with the formation of a space of flows. By timeless time, I mean the destruction of the sequence, at the source of chronological time, either by time compression (as in instant financial transactions in the electronic markets) or by the blurring of the sequence (as in the discontinuous pattern of working time in the week or throughout life). In the same way that the space of flows coexists with, and contradicts, the space of places, timeless time coexists with chronological time, and is opposed by "glacial time," that is, by the time of very slow motion, as in the ecological processes that characterize the planet's ecosystem. Each form of time and space is embodied in the projects of social actors, and formalized in the organization of society, always in flux, as the actual spatio-temporal processes depend on the overall process of social change. In my analysis of the new relationships of time and space I went further, proposing the hypothesis that, in the network society, space structures time, in contrast to the time-dominated constitution of industrial society, in which urbanization and industrialization were considered to be part of the march of universal progress, erasing place-rooted traditions and cultures. In our society, the network society, where you live determines your time-frame of reference. If you are an inhabitant of the space of flows, or if you live in a locality that is in the dominant networks, timeless time (epitomized by the frantic race to beat the clock) will be your time – as in Wall Street or Silicon Valley. If you are in a Pearl River delta factory town, chronological time will be imposed upon you as in the best days of Taylorism in Detroit. And if you live in a poor village in the Atitlan lake in Guatemala biological time, usually a much shorter life-span, will still rule your life. Against this spatial determination of time, environmental movements assert the notion of slow-motion time, the "clock of the long now" in the words of Stewart Brand (1999), by broadening the spatial dimension to its planetary scale in the whole complexity of its interactions – thus including our great-grandchildren in our temporal frame of reference. Thus, the newest urban sociology has a great deal to accomplish in the twenty-first century – a task that can only be undertaken with the help of new concepts and new methods.

Urban Sociologists in the Trenches of Research

For urban sociology to renew itself by confronting the extraordinary range of issues that I have outlined, it must create new tools, both theoretical and methodological. It must also abandon futile exercises of deconstruction and reconstruction enclosed in the verbal games of most postmodernist theorizing, and go back to its origins, in fieldwork research, in the generation of new information, in the discovery of the hidden realms of society, and in the fascination for urban life with all its glamour and miseries. We do not need new urban ideologies or well-meaning utopias – we should let people imagine their own myths. What urban sociologists of the twenty-first century really need are new tool boxes (including conceptual tools) to take on the hard work necessary to research and understand the new relationships between space and society.

Concepts: networks, space of flows, space of places, local, global, communities (physical, virtual, face-to-face), urban social exchangers, mobile places, de-gendered homes and cities, switched-off locales, links of inclusion, glocal social movements, shared time/spaces, time–space regimes, individuation, communalism, urban constellations, metropolitan regions, urban monumentality, multi-nodal centrality, meaning, function, form. I deliberately provide a list that reads like Borges's Chinese encyclopedia because to structure and assemble this collection of concepts, or even to define them, would constitute a theoretical framework, and this is not my purpose in this text, although it must be done sometime, somewhere, through collective, interactive theorizing. I simply want to indicate a style of inquiry, and to evoke the kind of concepts that could fit into a research design able to address the questions that I consider critical for twenty-first century cities. For readers irritated by the allegorical character of this elaboration I can refer to work I have already initiated toward a systematic theorization of the network society (Castells, 2000), a perspective that needs, however, to be specifically focused on the study of cities and spatial processes.

Urban sociologists also need new methods. The Internet is not only an object of research, but a research tool. It allows access to a wide variety of sources. And helped by automated translation programs, the Internet will enable true multiculturalism in the sources and issues of urban research. A global system will be tackled from a global perspective, even if the entry points of the analysis will continue to be culturally and institutionally singular. New computing power, and its ubiquitous distribution, will allow, at last, the use of simulation modeling as a tool of formalization and verification of hypotheses on the basis of qualitative material. The new mathematics of complexity, powered by fast computer processing, will free statistical analysis from the constraints of linearity, in a giant leap toward understanding a social reality that, by definition, is non-linear. Hard-to-do ethnographic fieldwork will continue to be the essential, distinctive tool of urban social scientists, but here, also, new technological tools will enable researchers to record, check, and analyze their observations against their database in real time. Mobile computing capacity, on-line connection to modeled systems of analysis, and interactivity will allow urban social scientists to systematize qualitative observations, to build their database as they go on their fieldwork, and to feed back into their observation and interviewing the meaning of these observations for their overall analytical framework.

Yet, with all these new tools, urban sociology will only be up to the task if urban sociologists in the twenty-first century continue to have the same passion for cities, and the same empathy for their fellow citizens, that most of us, earlier urban sociologists, felt in the twentieth century.

REFERENCES

Banfield, E. and Wilson, J. Q. (1963) *City Politics*. Cambridge, MA: Harvard University Press.

Brand, Stewart (1999) *The Clock of the Long Now*. New York: Basic Books.

Capra, Fritjof (1996) *The Web of Life*. New York: Doubleday.

Castells, Manuel (1968) "Y a-t-il une sociologie urbaine?," *Sociologie du Travail*, 1: 72–90.

Castells, Manuel (1989) *The Informational City*. Oxford: Blackwell.

Castells, Manuel (1995) "L'ecole française de sociologie urbaine vingt ans apres," *Les Annales de la Recherche Urbaine*, 64: 58–60.

Castells, Manuel (1996) *The Rise of the Network Society*, 2nd edn 2000. Oxford: Blackwell.

Castells, Manuel (1997) *The Power of Identity*. Oxford: Blackwell.

Castells, Manuel (2000) "Materials for an exploratory theory of the network society," *British Journal of Sociology*, 51 (1): 5–24.

Graham, Stephen and Marvin, Simon (2001) *Splintering Urbanism*. London: Routledge.

Harvey, David (1973) *Social Justice and the City*. London: Edward Arnold.

Hawley, Amos (1956) *Human Ecology*. New York: Free Press.

Jones, Stephen (ed.) (1998) *Cybersociety 2.0*. London: Sage.

Klinenberg, Eric (2000) "The social anatomy of a natural disaster: the Chicago heat wave of 1995," unpublished PhD thesis, University of California, Department of Sociology, Berkeley, California.

Lefebvre, Henri (1968) *Le droit à la ville*. Paris: Anthropos.

Mitchell, William J. (1999) *E-topia*. Cambridge, MA: MIT Press.

Mollenkopf, John (1983) *The Contested City*. Princeton, NJ: Princeton University Press.

Park, R. E., Burgess, E. W., and McKenzie, R. D. (1925) *The City*. Chicago: University of Chicago Press.

Schnore, Leo F. (1965) *The Urban Scene*. Glencoe, Ill.: The Free Press.

Sassen, Saskia (1991) *The Global City: New York, London, Tokyo*. Princeton, NJ: Princeton University Press.

Susser, Ida (1997) "Inequality, violence and gender relations in a global city: New York, 1986–96," *Identities: Global Studies in Culture and Power*, 5 (2).

Wellman, Barry (ed.) (1999) *Networks in the Global Village: Life in Contemporary Communities*. Boulder, CO: Westview Press.

Wirth, L. (1938) "Urbanism as a way of life," *American Journal of Sociology*, 44: 1–24.

Zorbaugh, W. (1929) *The Gold Coast and the Slum*. Chicago: University of Chicago Press.

Bibliography of Urban and Regional Studies by Manuel Castells, 1967–2000

This is a select bibliography of urban and regional studies and does not include other works by Manuel Castells. The works are cited in the language of original publication with translations as appropriate.

Books

Author or main author

Problemas de investigación en sociologia urbana (Madrid–Mexico: Siglo XXI, 1971) (translated into Portuguese).

La question urbaine (Paris: Maspero, 1972; rev. edn, Paris: La Decouverte, 1980) (translated into English as *The Urban Question*; London: Edward Arnold, 1977; also translated into Spanish, Italian, German, Portuguese, Greek, Polish, and Japanese).

Luttes urbaines (Paris: Maspero, 1973) (translated into Spanish, Italian, German, Portuguese, and Greek).

Monopolville: l'entreprise, l'état, l'urbain (Paris: Mouton, 1974).

Sociologie de l'espace industriel (Paris: Anthropos, 1975) (translated into Spanish).

City, Class, and Power (London: Macmillan; New York: St Martin's Press, 1978) (translated into Japanese).

Crise du logement et mouvements sociaux urbains: enquête sur la région parisienne (Paris: Mouton, 1978) (part translated into Portuguese).

Crisis urbana y cambio social (Madrid–Mexico: Siglo XXI, 1981).

Capital multinacional, estados nacionales y comunidades locales (Madrid–Mexico: Siglo XXI, 1982).

The City and the Grassroots: A Cross-cultural Theory of Urban Social Movements (Berkeley, CA: University of California Press, 1983) (translated into Spanish, Japanese, and part translated into Korean).

The Informational City: Information Technology, Economic Restructuring and the Urban–Regional Process (Oxford: Blackwell, 1989) (translated into Spanish and Chinese).

The Shek Kip Mei Syndrome: Economic Development and Public Housing in Hong Kong and Singapore (London: Pion, 1990).

Global Economy, Information Society, Cities, and Regions (Tokyo: Aoki Shoten, 1999, published only in Japanese).

Co-authored books

La rénovation urbaine à Paris (Paris: Mouton, 1973).

Technopoles of the World: The Making of Twenty-first Century Industrial Complexes, with Peter Hall (London and New York: Routledge, 1994).

Local and Global: The Managements of Cities in the Information Age, with Jordi Borja (London: Earthscan, 1997) (translated into Spanish).

Edited or co-edited books

Estructura de clase y politica urbana en America Latina (Buenos Aires: Sociedad Interamericana de Planificacion, 1974).

High Technology, Space, and Society (Beverly Hills, CA: Sage, 1985).

Territorial Development and Global Restructuring (London: Sage, 1986).

Dual City: Restructuring New York, with J. Mollenkopf (New York: Russell Sage Foundation, 1991).

Las grandes ciudades en la decada de los noventa (Madrid: Sistema, 1991).

Andalucía: innovación tecnológica y desarrollo económico (Madrid: Espasa-Calpe, 1992).

Estrategias para la reindustrialización de Asturias (Madrid: Editorial Civitas, 1994).

Articles

"Mobilité des entreprises et structure urbaine," *Sociologie du travail*, 4 (1967), pp. 369–405 (co-author).

"La mobilité des entreprises industrielles dans la région parisienne," *Cahiers de l'Institut d'Amenagement et d'Urbanisme de la Région Parisienne*, 11 (1968) (co-author).

"Y a-t-il une sociologie urbaine?", *Sociologie du travail*, 1 (1968), pp. 72–90 (translated into English, 1976).

"Entreprise industrielle et développement urbain," *Synopsis* (September 1969), pp. 69–79.

"Le centre urbain," *Cahiers internationaux de sociologie* (May 1969), pp. 83–106.

"Théorie et ideologie en sociologie urbaine," *Sociologie et sociétés*, 2 (1969), pp. 171–91 (translated into English, 1976).

"Vers une théorie sociologique de la planification urbaine," *Sociologie du travail*, 4 (1969), pp. 130–43 (translated into Spanish, 1974, and English, 1981).

"La rénovation urbaine aux Etats-Unis," *Espaces et sociétés*, 1 (1970), pp. 107–37.

"Reconquête urbaine et rénovation-déportation à Paris," *Sociologie du travail*, 4 (1970), pp. 488–514 (co-author).

"Structures sociales et processus d'urbanisation," *Annales* (August 1970), pp. 1155–99.

"El mito de la cultura urbana," *Revista latinoamericana de estudios urbanos*, 3 (1971), pp. 27–42.

"La sociologie et la question urbaine," *L'architecture d'aujourd'hui* (September 1971), pp. 91–100.

"L'urbanisation dependante en Amerique Latine," *Espaces et sociétés*, 3 (1971), pp. 5–23 (translated into Spanish and Italian).

"Luttes de classes et contradictions urbaines," *Espaces et sociétés*, 6–7 (October 1972).

"Symbolique urbaine et mouvements sociaux," *Versus: studi semiotici* (1972).

"Il rinova urbano di Parigi: aspetti economici e politici," *Archivio di studi urbani e regionali*, 2 (1973).

"Movimiento de pobladores y lucha de clases en Chile," *Revista latinoamericana de estudios urbanos*, 3 (1973).

"Tesi sulla questione urbana," *Archivio di studi urbani e regionali*, 1 (1973).

"Contradizione e desiguaglianza nella citta," *Il mulino*, 1 (1974).

"Remarques sur le pouvoir local," *Revue française de sociologie* (June 1974).

"Advanced capitalism, collective consumption and urban contradictions," in Leo Lindberg et al. (eds), *Stress and Contradiction in Modern Capitalism* (Lexington, MA: Heath, 1975), pp. 175–98.

"Immigrant workers and class struggles: the Western European experience," *Politics and Society*, 5 (1) (1975), pp. 33–66 (translated into French).

"La fonction sociale de la planification urbaine: le cas de la région de Dunkerque," *Recherches sociologiques*, 3 (1975).

"Urban sociology and urban politics: from a critique to new trends of research," *Comparative Urban Research*, 3 (1) (1975); reprinted in John Walton (ed.), *The City in Comparative Perspective* (Beverly Hills, CA: Sage, 1976).

"Crise de l'état, consommation collective et contradictions urbaines," in Nicos Poulantzas (ed.), *La crise de l'état*, pp. 179–208 (Paris: Presses Universitaire de France, 1976) (translated into Spanish and Danish).

"La crise urbaine aux Etats-Unis: vers la barbarie?," *Les temps modernes* (February 1976), pp. 1178–240 (translated into Dutch in book form, Amsterdam: EU, 1978).

"Theoretical proposition for an experimental study of urban social movements," in G. C. Pickvance (ed.), *Urban Sociology: Critical Essays*, pp. 147–73 (London: Tavistock, 1976).

"The wild city," *Kapital–State*, 4–5 (Summer 1976), pp. 1–30; reprinted in Joe R. Feagin (ed.), *The Urban Scene* (New York: Random House, 1979).

"Apuntes para un analisis de clase de la politica urbana del Estado mexicano," *Revista mexicana de sociologia*, 4 (1977).

"Les conditions sociales d'émergence des mouvements sociaux urbains," *International Journal of Urban and Regional Research*, 1 (1) (1977).

"Marginalité urbaine et mouvements sociaux au Mexique: le mouvement des posesionarios dans la ville de Monterrey," *International Journal of Urban and Regional Research*, 1 (2) (1977), pp. 145–50.

"Towards a political urban sociology," in Michael Harloe (ed.), *Captive Cities*, pp. 61–78 (London: John Wiley, 1977).

"Mouvements sociaux urbains et changement politique," in Alain Touraine (ed.), *Mouvements sociaux d'aujourd'hui* (Paris: Les Editions Ouvrières, 1978).

"Urban social movements and the struggle for democracy: the citizen movement in Madrid," *International Journal of Urban and Regional Research*, 2 (1) (1978), pp. 133–46.

"La intervención administrative en los centros urbanos de las grandes ciudades," *Papers: revista de sociologia*, 11 (1979), pp. 227–50.

"Revisar a Engels," *Argumentos* (July 1979).

"Local government, urban crisis, and political change," *Political Power and Social Theory: A Research Annual*, vol. 2, pp. 1–20 (Greenwich, CT, 1981).

"Cultural identity and urban structure: the spatial organization of San Francisco's gay community," with Karen Murphy, *Urban Affairs Annual Reviews*, vol. 22, pp. 237–60 (Beverly Hills, CA: Sage, 1982).

"Squatters and politics in Latin America," in Helen J. Safa (ed.), *Towards a Political Economy of Urbanization in Third World Countries*, pp. 242–62 (New Delhi: Oxford University Press, 1982); reprinted in Josef Gugler (ed.), *The Urbanization of the Third World* (Oxford: Oxford University Press, 1988).

"Crisis, planning, and the quality of life," *Environment and Planning D*, 1 (1) (1983), pp. 3–21 (translated into Portuguese and Spanish).

"Class and power in American cities," *Contemporary Sociology*, 13 (3) (1984), pp. 270–73 (review essay).

"Madrid: planeamiento urbano y gestión municipal," *Ciudad y territorio* (January–June, 1984), pp. 13–40.

"Participation, politics, and spatial innovation: commentary on Bologna, Orcasitas, and SAAL," in Richard Hatch (ed.), *The Scope of Social Architecture: Columns*, vol. 1 (New Jersey Institute of Technology and Van Nostrand, 1984).

"El impacto de las nuevas tecnologías sobre los cambios urbanos y regionales," in Peter Hall et al. (eds), *Metropolis: territorio y crisis*, pp. 37–62. (Madrid: H. Blume, 1985).

"Urbanization and social change: the new frontier," in Orlando Fals Borda (ed.), *The Challenge of Social Change*, pp. 93–106 (London: Sage Studies in International Sociology, 1985).

"High technology and urban dynamics in the United States," in Mattei Dogan and John D. Kosarda (eds), *The Metropolis Era*, vol. 1 (Beverly Hills, CA: Sage, 1986).

"The new urban crisis," in Dieter Friek (ed.), *The Quality of Urban Life* (Berlin: Walter de Gruyter, 1986).

"Technological change, economic restructuring and the spatial division of labor," in Walter Stohr (ed.), *International Economic Restructuring and the Territorial Community* (Vienna: United Nations Industrial Development Organization, 1986).

"Crisis urbana, estado y participación popular," lectures to the Colegio de Arquitectos, Cochabamba, Bolivia (1988).

"Innovation technologique et centralité urbaine," *Cahiers de la recherche sociologique*, 6 (2) (1988), pp. 27–36.

"The new industrial space: information technology manufacturing and spatial structure in the United States," in George Sternlieb and James W. Hughes (eds), *America's Market Geography* (New Brunswick, NJ: Center for Urban Policy Research, Rutgers University, 1988).

"Nuevas tecnologías y desarrollo regional," *Economia y sociedad*, 2 (1989), pp. 23–40.

"Social movements and the informational city," *Hitotsubashi Journal of Social Studies*, 21 (1989), pp. 197–206 (translated into Japanese, 1989, and German, 1991).

"Die zweigeteilte Stadt – Arm un Reich in den Stadten Lateinamerikas, der USA un Europas," in Tilo Schabert (ed.), *Die Welt der Stadt* (Munich–Zurich: Piper, 1991), pp. 199–216.

"Estrategías de desarrollo metropolitano: la articulación entre crecimiento económico y calidad de vida," in Jordi Borja et al. (eds), *Las grandes ciudades en la decada de los noventa* (Madrid: Sistema, 1991).

"Informatisierte Stadt und Soziale Bewegungen," in Martin Wentz (ed.), *Stadt–Raume*, pp. 137–48 (Frankfurt: Campus Verlag, 1991).

"European cities, the informational society, and the global economy," *Journal of Economic and Social Geography*, 84 (4) (1993), pp. 247–57.

"L'école française de sociologie urbaine vingt ans après: retour au futur?," *Les annales de la recherche urbaine*, special issue (October, 1994).

"Globalization, flows and identity: the new challenges of design," in William Saunders (ed.), *Architectural Practices in the Nineties* (Princeton, NJ: Princeton Architectural Press in New York City, 1997).

"The informational city is a dual city: can it be reversed?", in Don Schor et al. (eds), *Information Technology and Low-income Communities*, pp. 25–42 (Cambridge, MA: MIT Press, 1998).

"The real crisis in Silicon Valley: a retrospective perspective," in *Competition and Change*, 2 (1998).

"The culture of cities in the Information Age" (1999), included in Ida Susser (ed.), *Frontiers of the Mind in the Twenty-first Century* (Washington, DC: The Library of Congress, 2001).

"Grassrooting the space of flows," *Urban Geography*, 20 (4) (May–June, 1999), pp. 294–302.

"Russian federalism and Siberian regionalism, 1999–2000," with E. Kiselyova, in *City* (June 2000).

Index

Action for Accountable Government 213
advanced capitalism: anti-imperialism 15, 402; class struggles 73–4; consumption 108–9; development 75; immigration 75, 78, 85; space 117–18; transport 121; urban social movements 124
advanced services: concentration 316; decentralization 321–2; educational requirements 286; employment 288, 316; global economy 316–17; regional centers 321–2; spatial organization 370–1
The Advocate 186, 209
AFL-CIO 143, 165, 169, 177
Africa, urbanization 27, 30, 368
agrarianism 27, 46, 258, 394
AIDS 403
air traffic controllers' strike 273
Algeria 104
Alianza Caucus 152, 166
Alice B. Toklas Democratic Club 211–12
alienation 49, 51, 122
Alinsky, Saul 146
Alinskyites: community action 139, 142, 145–6; and Latinos 165–6; Mission Coalition Organization 139, 152, 169, 177–8, 232–3; Model Cities Programme 160, 167–8
Alioto, Joseph 136, 144–5, 149, 151, 157

Allende, Salvador 2, 5
Althusser, Louis 2
America, North: urban phenomenon 26; urbanization 30; *see also* United States of America
Amin, Ash 327
Amsterdam's Digital City 380
anarchism 47
Anderson, N. 21, 39–40
anti-imperialism 15, 402
Aoyama, Yuko 324
archaeology 23
architecture: de-localization 353; postmodern 350–4, 361n19, 361n20; space of flows 349, 351
arson 187
artificial intelligence 262
arts, gay community 208, 215
Asia: metropolitan regions 373–4; urban phenomenon 26; urbanization 30, 368
AVE station, Madrid 352–3
Axelrod, M. 55
Aydalot, Philippe 324, 360n9

Bailey, Thomas 297
Balibar, E. 2
banking industry 331
Barcelona: airport 352; governance 380; Paseo de Gracia 357; Las Ramblas 356
BART, San Francisco 131, 135, 136, 143, 172, 173